VOICES IN STONE

PAUL BRUMMELL

Voices in Stone

The Lives of Public Statues

HURST & COMPANY, LONDON

First published in the United Kingdom in 2026 by
C. Hurst & Co. (Publishers) Ltd.,
New Wing, Somerset House, Strand, London WC2R 1LA
Copyright © Paul Brummell, 2026
All rights reserved.

The right Paul Brummell to be identified as the author of this publication is asserted by him in accordance with the Copyright, Designs and Patents Act, 1988.

Distributed in the United States, Canada and Latin America by Oxford University Press, 546 Fifth Avenue, New York, NY 10036, United States of America.

A Cataloguing-in-Publication data record for this book is available from the British Library.

ISBN: 9781805265245

EU GPSR Authorised Representative
Easy Access System Europe Oü, 16879218
Address: Mustamäe tee 50, 10621, Tallinn, Estonia
Contact Details: gpsr.requests@easproject.com, +358 40 500 3575

This book is printed using paper from registered sustainable and managed sources.

www.hurstpublishers.com

Printed and bound in Great Britain by Bell and Bain Ltd, Glasgow

To Adriana and George

CONTENTS

Introduction	1

PART ONE
BIRTH

1.	Patrons and Promoters	17
2.	Sculptors	29
3.	Physical Characteristics	49
4.	Proprietary Statues	81
5.	Statues and National Identity	93
6.	Memorialising Loss, Tragedy and Evil	113
7.	Exporting Statues	135
8.	Statues of Women	151
9.	Location	167

PART TWO
LIFE

10.	Commemoration	181
11.	Moving, Talking, Living Statues	195
12.	Interfering with Statues	215
13.	Relocation	233
14.	Recontextualisation	245

PART THREE
DEATH

15.	Toppling Statues	263
16.	Rebirth and Revenge	291
Conclusion		297

CONTENTS

Acknowledgements 301
List of Illustrations 303
Notes 307
Bibliography 329
Index 354

INTRODUCTION

Iconoclasm is in the air. One generation's heroes are another's villains. The removal of a seated statue of mining magnate Cecil Rhodes from the University of Cape Town in 2015, the dunking into the harbour of the statue of Bristol merchant and slave trader Edward Colston during a Black Lives Matter protest in June 2020, and the taking down since 2015 of statues in the United States of figures linked to the Confederacy all reflect actions by groups that saw nothing to celebrate and much to despise in the subjects of commemoration. Yet as statues come down, so they go up. Campaign groups lobby for representations of new heroes, football stadia are adorned with bronze portrayals of club legends, and there are calls for more statues of women and other groups historically underrepresented in metal or stone.

A bitter debate has been raging. In one camp sit those calling for the removal of statues of those now cast as foul people responsible for foul deeds. In the other, those calling to keep them, on the grounds that history should be remembered in all its complexity, and that obliterating memorials to all historical figures whose views are problematic from a modern perspective risks sweeping up almost everyone, hero and villain alike, in its unforgiving wake. This is an important debate, and one to which we will return. Yet it is an unsatisfactory starting point for a discussion of the role of statues. It calls to mind the cautionary words of author and literary critic G. K. Chesterton that, before deciding to take down a fence, you should ensure you understand why it was put up in the first place.[1] Starting with that question prompts various considerations: why erect figurative representations of human subjects? What is the significance of their location? What changes do they experience? Understanding why a statue is there informs the debate on whether it should fall.

VOICES IN STONE

The following account focuses on public statues, drawing on a wide range of disciplines, and encompassing broader studies of monuments and memorials. I should start with some definitions. 'Statue' derives from the Latin noun *statua*, and in turn from the verb *stāre*, 'to stand', or 'to remain'. It refers to a portrayal of a human or animal in durable material, typically at, close to or larger than life size. The term excludes small portrayals of humans or animals, which would characteristically be described as a figurine or statuette.

The origins of the word 'monument' lie in the Latin noun *monumentum*, which is itself derived from the verb *moneō*, meaning 'to bring to the notice of', 'to remind', or, more ominously, 'to warn'. The role of a monument then is to facilitate remembrance—of someone or something. Monuments are about memory. For ethics researcher Benjamin Rossi, 'a monument is a type of public, honorific art',[2] public, in that it is intended to be on view in a public space, and honorific in that it seeks to express admiration or esteem, whether for a person, place or concept. A monument might itself be or incorporate a statue, or indeed many statues, but not all statues are monuments. A statue may simply be intended as an artistic representation of a human or animal without any pretence to facilitate remembrance. As historian Christopher Dickenson notes, however, when a statue is placed in a public setting, particularly when put on a plinth and accompanied by an explanatory inscription, our expectations of its purpose change. 'Surely one of the most common expectations we have of statues encountered on street corners or public squares is that they are not simply works of art but they have been erected to commemorate someone or something.'[3] It is such public statues that are also monuments, seeking to facilitate remembrance of their subject, that form the focus of this book.

These public statues aim to inspire, provoke reflection, generate awe. They typically seek to convey a positive view of their subject,[4] as someone whose life and achievements are viewed as worthy both of celebration and emulation: both honouring their achievements and making a statement that those erecting the statue share the values and ideals the subject is considered to represent.[5] To be immortalised in bronze or marble is thus a great honour, albeit one that in many cultural contexts is achievable only posthumously. But before we look at what makes a monument, let's pause briefly to observe

INTRODUCTION

that the receipt of such a glorious honour has not always guaranteed a happy ending for its subject.

The Tricky Business of Statues

In ancient Rome, the well-to-do toiled and conspired in equal measure to secure the prestige that came with the granting of an honorific statue. Getting one did not however always bring what they had expected. On the route of the Roman road between Feltria and Tridentum (modern Trento), to the south of the Tridentine Alps, a block of red limestone bearing an inscription was unearthed in the mid-eighteenth century. The inscription reads, in part,

> They make [me] a gilded [statue] with money produced from all sides. Great envy grew from the honour; the citizens, as if they were masters, attempt to drive [their] patron into exile.[6]

Rather than glory and acclaim, banishment then was nearly the outcome. The remains of a large podium have also been unearthed, and historian Freya Martin has speculated that this may have supported a funerary monument. The inscription is incomplete, and the name and profession of the subject of the statue unknown, though Martin thinks he may have been a junior magistrate. The surviving part of the inscription describes the largesse that gave rise to the award of a statue: a wonderful gladiatorial show and subsidising the grain price three times in a year. The provision of bread and circuses indeed, suggesting a strategy of benefactions aiming to bolster his voting base. But it all turned sour. Other nobles would have borne most of the expense of constructing the statue, and both statue and expense would have exacerbated natural rivalries. It seems they sought to remove the benefactor by the route through which he secured the honorific statue in the first place: the manipulation of public opinion, resulting in his almost being driven out. Statues are not straightforward.

What Makes a Monument?

In a 2003 article, art scholar Andrew Butterfield describes four constitutive elements of a monument.[7] First, its marker: a durable

3

physical object. At its simplest this might be a large stone, unadorned and unembellished. Whether menhir or dolmen, rocks served from prehistoric times as markers of remembrance. Megalithic complexes like Stonehenge are an obvious example. For the Romanian historian of religion, Mircea Eliade, there was for the ancients 'nothing nobler, more frightening than the glorious rock, the granite block that rises boldly.'[8] The rocks might represent the deities or ancestors of the community.

The construction of stone altars might be undertaken through divine guidance. Moses is told by God that 'if thou wilt make me an altar of stone, thou shalt not build it of hewn stone: for if thou lift up thy tool upon it, thou hast polluted it'.[9] Stone was associated not just with religious worship but also the drawing up of legal codes. The Ten Commandments, inscribed by the finger of God on two stone tablets, are an obvious example. The stone served as a witness. Consider the story of Jacob and Laban in the Book of Genesis. After Laban had caught up with his fleeing nephew Jacob, they agreed to a covenant. As witness to their arrangement 'Jacob took a stone, and set it up for a pillar. And Jacob said unto his brethren, Gather stones; and they took stones, and made an heap.'[10]

Rocks became a place for meditation. Albrecht Dürer's 1514 engraving *Melencolia I* involves a figure seated reflectively on a stone. A similar pose was used by Rodin in his famous statue of *The Thinker*. Scholar of comparative literature Theodore Ziolkowski suggests that the identification of stone with religion, law and meditative thinking explains why stone, rather than say wood or bone, was the preferred material for crafting some of the earliest statues of humans—such as the limestone Palaeolithic 'Venuses' of Willendorf in Austria and Laussel in the Dordogne.[11]

The second element of the monument is the memoranda, the biographical information contained within the marker. Monuments often don't record a great deal of information, though the name of the person or event commemorated is usually featured. The monument may or may not include imagery. Wording is often formulaic. For Butterfield, this standardisation limits 'the commemoration of an individual to a single aspect: how the dead personified a social ideal that is regarded as a central and permanent value.'[12] The objective is

INTRODUCTION

less a balanced assessment of the subject than to emphasise exemplary qualities. The monument is used by those in power to present the specific narrative about the past they want to emphasise, for example to justify the present authority of that power. As historian Brian Ladd puts it, monuments are 'selective aids to memory; they encourage us to remember some things and to forget others.'[13]

Our focus is on a specific type of monument, the public statue, its purpose, in a sense, to keep the dead alive.[14] The statue embodies their essential qualities and memorialises them, projecting the values and ideals with which they are associated. Statues are bad at telling complex stories. They evoke narratives known in more detail elsewhere, perhaps in works of biography or accounts of the historical events depicted on the statue. What you get on the statue is shorthand. Historian Simon Schama has argued that 'statues are not history; rather, its opposite. History is argument: statues brook none.'[15] In stifling historical debate, they can end up rather dull. As Schama puts it, 'aspiring to convey immortality, it ends up delivering stony lifelessness.'[16]

The third element is the precinct, or the specific location of the monument. This is not a matter of chance: the location is typically chosen to ensure either that the monument is seen by many people, or that it is set in a specific meaningful space for the community, where individuals can reassert their identity as part of that community. These places often hold a sanctified dimension. Because a statue takes up space in the urban fabric, it not only expresses certain values, but also imposes those values on that place.[17]

The fourth and final element is the act of commemoration. Butterfield criticises the tendency among some scholars to treat monuments purely as objects, such as a category of sculpture. Monuments, he argues, can only be properly understood in terms of the uses to which they are put.[18]

Statues Across Time and Place

While monuments are used for remembrance across human societies, the figurative statue is not characteristic of all times and cultures. It has however appeared in many places at many times, with earlier usages influencing later cultures. There were figurative sculptures in early urban cultures in Mesopotamia in the third millennium BCE, influencing the development of statuary in ancient Egypt, which in turn influenced Greece, where, by the fifth century BCE, statues had become increasingly lifelike in form. By the fourth century BCE, a tradition had become established of erecting honorific statues of notable individuals. Rome proved an enthusiastic adopter of the Greek statuary tradition, and the proliferation of figurative statues reached remarkable proportions, especially in parts of the Roman empire, such as Greece, still peppered with statues from earlier times.[19] In his *Natural History*, Pliny, quoting Mucianus, refers to 3,000 statues in Rhodes alone, surmising that there were a similar number in Athens, Olympia and Delphi.[20]

The tide, however, turned. Economic headwinds and early Christian iconoclasm discouraged figurative statuary. Across the Islamic world, figurative representation was largely avoided for religious reasons, given the condemnation of idolatry in the Quran, in favour of a focus on geometric forms. In some other cultures, in contrast, statues were largely confined to religious images, from images of saints in Medieval Europe to statues of Buddha across parts of Asia. In some societies, figurative sculptures were linked to ancestor worship, such as the Māori art forms currently enjoying renewed popularity in New Zealand.[21]

Public figurative statues experienced a renaissance in, well, the Renaissance, when the city states of Italy rediscovered the classical tradition and deployed it for their political purposes. The practice spread across Europe, centred on statues of rulers. The nationalism of nineteenth-century Europe generated a demand for figurative statues of heroes to support the building and cementing of national identity, unleashing a period of 'statuemania' in many European countries. Imperialism generated a demand for statues as markers of imperial power, and so did the process of decolonisation, as newly independent states embarked on the process of building their own national identities.

Monuments and Fashion

On 9 July 1776, amid the fervour of the American Revolution, a crowd pulled down the equestrian statue of King George III in New

INTRODUCTION

York, decapitated it, and broke it up into chunks to be melted down and made into musket balls.[22] Art historian Kirk Savage notes that the aftermath of the removal of statuary of the colonising power offered an opportunity for the new United States to consider whether figurative statuary, with its implicit messages about the inevitability of rulership, was appropriate for a country of progressive ideals. North Carolina Congressman Nathaniel Macon suggested not, in declaring in 1800 that 'monuments are good for nothing.'[23] But the moment passed, statues of new heroes appeared, and by 1816 Macon himself was calling for a statue of George Washington for the North Carolina State Capitol, a request which would lead to the procuring of a particularly beautiful work from renowned Italian sculptor Antonio Canova.

The point here is that figurative public statues have been promoted or discouraged not just according to religious teachings, but also through considerations of politics and fashion. One hundred and fifty years later, the mood had changed again. The modernist thinking of the 1930s was not enamoured with monuments. Theorists agonised over whether monuments had any place in progressive, modern cityscapes. For US historian Lewis Mumford, 'the very notion of a modern monument is a contradiction in terms: if it is a monument, it cannot be modern, and if it is modern, it cannot be a monument.'[24] In Europe, Nazi Germany and the Communist USSR had embraced monumentalism to promote their regimes, serving further to discredit monuments and statues in the eyes of many architects and planners in the United States and democratic societies in Europe.

A short manifesto developed in 1943 by US-based Catalan artist Josep Lluís Sert, French painter Fernand Léger and Swiss architectural historian Sigfried Giedion sought to reconcile the monumental with the modern, arguing that monumental buildings had an important role to play in modern cities, but that to fulfil this role they must be conceived in a different way. Entitled *Nine Points on Monumentality*, the authors first set out the role of monuments. They were intended to outlive the period of their creation, linking past and future. They expressed the feelings of the people, and thus required a unifying popular consciousness, a unifying culture. The authors decided that most monuments of the last hundred years had failed to do any of this: 'The so-called monuments of recent date have, with rare exceptions, become empty shells. They in no way represent the spirit or the collective feeling of modern times.'[25] Modern architects had disregarded the monument precisely because of this failure.

It did not need to be this way. For Sert, Léger and Giedion, the monument had its place. People wanted their aspiration for monumentality to be satisfied. This would not be achieved by those still imbued with nineteenth-century ideals. It required a harnessing of modern creative forces, integrating monuments into new urban centres. Monumental buildings needed planned sites, with plenty of space, making use of modern materials and technologies. Referencing developments in advertising, they noted that 'during night hours, colour and forms can be projected on vast surfaces. Such displays could be projected upon buildings for purposes of publicity or propaganda.'[26] For many proponents of this 'new monumentality', however, like Swiss architect and critic Peter Meyer, the role of monuments was less to do with commemoration than standing out and structuring their environment.[27] Given our starting point that monuments are about remembering, the question arises as to whether the new monumentality is addressing monuments at all.

The modernist critique has failed to dampen enthusiasm for figurative statues in many modern societies. Compared with earlier periods, what impresses most strongly is the diversity of subjects. Today's public statues are as likely to be of sports personalities, or generic monuments celebrating a deep-rooted local industry, as saints or kings.[28]

The Myth of the Timeless Statue

Most public statues are crafted from materials, principally marble and bronze, which are intended to be durable. Patrons and sculptors create a statue in the hope and expectation that it will stand for generations, telling the story of its subject far into the future. Kirk Savage draws attention to an incongruity here around render-

INTRODUCTION

ing 'the fashion of the moment in the eternity of marble'.[29] There is a hubris in envisaging that statues will serve as timeless monuments, 'endlessly relevant across generational shifts and other social transformations.'[30]

That hubris has never been described better than in Percy Bysshe Shelley's sonnet *Ozymandias*. In 1817, the head and torso of an ancient, colossal statue of Ramesses II began its long journey from Thebes in Egypt to London, where it was to be displayed in the British Museum. The statue would not arrive in the UK until the following year—but that only increased the excitement among London's Egyptophiles. The young poet Shelley and his friend Horace Smith agreed a friendly competition to write a poem about the pharaoh, also known by his Greek name Ozymandias, taking its cue from a reference in the *Bibliotheca historica* of first century BCE Greek historian Diodorus Siculus to an Egyptian statue with an inscription reading: 'King of Kings am I, Ozymandyas. If any would know how great I am and where I lie, let him surpass my works.'[31]

Prepare to feel sorry for Horace Smith, for his contribution to the competition is routinely ignored. Shelley's sonnet however stands as a masterpiece. It records the poet's meeting with 'a traveller from an antique land' who describes a wrecked statue, two 'trunkless legs of stone' standing in the desert, with a half-sunk head nearby. Its features, 'frown, and wrinkled lip, and sneer of cold command', speak of the sculptor's skill in perceptively rendering his subject. The inscription described by Diodorus is recorded in the sonnet, its hubris and ultimate failure accentuated by the poet's closing comment, that around the wrecked statue 'boundless and bare / the lone and level sands stretch far away.'

Although just fourteen lines long, Shelley's poem offers the perspectives of no fewer than four interpreters of the events.[32] At the centre of events, but foiled by them, is Ozymandias himself, and his boastful assessment. Then comes the sculptor, who counters Ozymandias' self-assessment with a rendering suggesting a cruel, unpleasant leader. Then the traveller, who appears to endorse the sculptor's judgement of the ruler: 'well those passions read.' Finally, the poet, who accepts the traveller's verdict about Ozymandias but turns this into a larger point about the transience of power and the oblivion awaiting even the grandest and proudest of rulers,[33] an oblivion that no statues can forestall.

Robert Musil and the Invisibility of Monuments

In a 1936 essay, the Austrian writer Robert Musil identified a curious feature of monuments. They were, he concluded 'conspicuously inconspicuous. There is nothing in this world as invisible as a monument.'[34] While the purpose of monuments was to attract attention, they had the opposite effect, the viewer's glance tending to slide off them like water droplets on an oilcloth. Statues served well and good as points of orientation in the urban landscape, but 'you never look at them, and do not generally have the slightest notion whom they are supposed to represent, except that perhaps you know if it's a man or a woman.'[35]

For Musil, this invisibility is bound up in the failure of monuments to achieve the timelessness to which they aspire. He argued that the expectation that monuments would endure eventually rendered them invisible, rather like the way that an initially annoying buzzing sound gradually becomes unnoticed. Monuments needed to try harder to attract attention, and could usefully draw lessons from the advertising industry. Movement might help—the statues could at least blink—or perhaps a well-chosen logo, like 'Goethe's Faust is the best!'[36] But sculptors preferred the motionless and monochrome, and the result was that, for the great figures selected as subjects for immortalisation, all of this seemed 'a carefully calculated insult.'[37]

Cultural geographer Tim Edensor similarly argues that commemorative statues have become part of the mundane fabric of the city. Statues were erected to commemorate values and achievements of their era: forgotten or incomprehensible to modern audiences. They serve today as ghosts in stone or bronze, haunting the spaces they occupy.[38] The statues remain in situ, except in rare examples where the person or event depicted is so jarring to modern sensibilities that removal is deemed necessary. They are sustained by city planners and conservationists who award them institutional forms of protection based on the historical or artistic value

INTRODUCTION

ascribed to them. It is then the durability of statues, the product of a hubristic desire for their messages to live on into perpetuity, that means they frequently outlast the rationale for which they were built. Commemoration stops. They become a vague reminder of an outdated set of memories.[39]

If many statues then convey messages largely irrelevant to modern audiences, Edensor argues this does not mean that the statues themselves are irrelevant. Their haunting presence has an impact. They form part of a lingering backdrop of everyday expressions of nationhood described by social psychologist Michael Billig as 'banal nationalism',[40] often ignored because of their quotidian nature. They are like unwaved flags, no longer objects of commemoration or even of particular interest, but still hanging around. Their persistence across the urban landscape seeps at the collective subconscious, tending to reinforce old power structures.[41]

Edensor argues that the ubiquity of such statues means they continue to influence how an esteemed hero should be commemorated. He looks at Albert Square in central Manchester, an important civic space in front of the town hall. It is home to five statues: a mix of national and local figures. The best known are Prince Albert, consort of Queen Victoria, and prime minister William Gladstone. The statue least likely to generate a flicker of recognition from passers-by today is James Fraser, Bishop of Manchester from 1870 to 1885, a work speaking to the centrality of religion in late nineteenth-century public life. Even if Fraser is forgotten, and its message about religion outmoded, the statue still commands authority, as the bishop stares down from his tall plinth with a patrician gaze, his left arm forward, giving him the air of one smoothing out a petty quarrel. For Edensor, the statue continues to convey an authority and power that discourages any suggestion of removal.[42]

Alois Riegl and the Value of Monuments

The early twentieth-century work of an Austrian art historian provides a helpful framework for our study. In 1903, Alois Riegl wrote *The Modern Cult of Monuments: its Character and Origin*, an essay intended to inform legislation to protect cultural heritage in the

Austro-Hungarian Empire, in which Riegl worked as a General Conservator.[43] Riegl's starting point is what he describes as an 'intentional' (sometimes translated as 'willed') monument: created with commemoration in mind, to keep an individual or event alive in the minds of its audience, now and through future generations. Such 'intentional' monuments form the focus of this book. Riegl argued that these are not the only form of monuments. He suggested that a modern cult of monuments emerged from the Renaissance, built around not such 'intentional' monuments, but 'unintentional' (or 'unwilled' ones). These were not built with commemorative intent but may acquire a value as a monument through age and decay—for example, a castle built for military purposes that crumbles into a romantic ruin.

Riegl associated different kinds of value with different monuments. Intentional commemorative value requires the monument to be maintained in immaculate condition. Any decay suggests that its subject is being treated with less than reverence. The monument has started the process of being forgotten or, in Musil's terms, becoming invisible. Age value is in many ways the reverse: acquired by the passage of time, it is inimical to the commemorative value of monuments. Age instils an atmosphere Riegl thought central to the modern cult of monuments. He thought that monuments might also hold historical value. Use value related to the functional use of the monument, while art value referred to its aesthetic appeal. Some of these various forms of value are natural bedfellows, while others clash. Thus, use value tends to conflict with both commemorative and age value.

What this means for our statues is that while intentional commemorative value is likely to decline over time with the passing of generations and emergence of new heroes, the statue may gradually acquire historical value. As the years smooth its edges and mute its colours, it may acquire progressively more age value. And it may appeal for its art value, as an artwork separate from its commemorative meaning. All of this suggests that the value of a statue is a complicated question not solely answered by the matter of whether we wish to continue to commemorate the life and deeds of its subject.[44]

In studying the removal of monuments during the collapse of the Soviet Union, philosopher Mikhail Yampolsky focuses on the close

INTRODUCTION

relationship between these different forms of value and the effects of time. Monuments centred on age value are imbued with the imprint of time. Ruins are visual reminders of the power of time over the creations of human hands.[45] Intentional commemorative monuments have the opposite effect. Such monuments aim to preserve the memory of an event or person. For Yampolsky, this means they endeavour to negate the passage of time. They must be constantly renovated and restored, or they will be ravaged by the effects of time. A large statue of Lenin in October Square in Moscow was intended to be the most important Lenin monument in the entire Soviet Union. Its construction was not just a matter of putting up a statue but necessitated the reconstruction of the square. Had the statue been left among gradually ageing neighbouring buildings, the monument itself would have been unable to check the passage of time. The only solution was to place the ahistorical monument within equally ahistorical surroundings.[46] This created a kind of protective zone around the monument within which time was static. Yampolsky argues that such time-negating monuments were ideally suited to the Soviet regime, whose aim was to build a permanent, ahistorical, state of Communism.

The destruction of monuments breaks the time negation created by their intentional commemorative value. Dismantled statues placed in museums are subject to historical rather than intentional commemorative value and start to age.[47] The break-up of the Soviet Union, argues Yampolsky, had the effect of suddenly starting time as the monuments, symbols of Soviet atemporality, came down. This was felt as rapid, disorienting change, with those who switched on the clock by destroying the monuments of the old regime immediately condemning themselves to be left behind.[48]

The Lives of Statues

The consideration that statues may be characterised by different kinds of value at different stages of their existence underlines the importance of what historian Angelos Chaniotis terms the 'life of statues'. Statues have biographies. He notes that the statues of ancient Greece served as the centrepieces of rituals, as part of which they might be washed, offered food, perfumed or touched, and that they might be moved or stolen, damaged and repaired, and eventually destroyed or forgotten.[49]

The lives of statues structure this book. We explore first their births, investigating the motives of their patrons and sculptors in creating the statues, and the significance of their form, material, subject matter and location. We then turn to their daily lives, defined in relation to their interactions with humans. And finally, and inevitably, to their deaths, whether as the unnoticed last act in the life of a monument that has become progressively more invisible through its lifetime, or in a dramatic final scene of destruction of a statue turned toxic through the association of the subject with events and behaviours unacceptable to new generations. The lives of statues are complex and subject to frequent contestation.

PART ONE

BIRTH

1

PATRONS AND PROMOTERS

At Waterloo station in London, a family group stands on seven plump suitcases, one for each day of the week. They are dressed in their Sunday best, a sign that their arrival at the station was a special occasion. They hold hands in a demonstration of love and mutual protection, and as a symbol of the strength of the family. They look out onto an uncertain world, facing different directions. Father, mother and daughter, the latter holding her left hand to her chest, a symbol of pride. The mother, her hands holding the other two, is the fulcrum of the family group. This is the National Windrush Monument (see fig. 1).

The monument's journey kicked off with a request in 2018 from then UK Prime Minister Theresa May to Liberal Democrat peer Baroness Floella Benjamin to chair a Windrush Commemoration Committee to create a permanent tribute to the Windrush Generation. It was to be funded by the UK Government through the Department of Levelling Up, Housing and Communities.

The question of who funds a statue is an important one. As historian Simon Schama puts it, 'statues are revelations—not about the historical figures they represent, but about the mindset of those who commissioned them.'[1] The fee for the sculptor and costs of materials, installation, landscaping and maintenance all mean that putting up a statue requires significant resources or the means of raising them. It is not just about money, though. As we will see in a later chapter, the impact of a statue depends on its location in a prominent spot. Access to prestigious spaces tends to require political as well as economic power. The patronage of statues is often then in the hands of elites.

VOICES IN STONE

The form of government is significant in determining *which* elites are involved. In autocratic regimes, decisions over who to commemorate may be in the hands of the ruler; such was the case in Turkmenistan under late president Saparmurat Niyazov, whose choice of subject was frequently himself, albeit smothered in language suggesting that the president was simply bowing reluctantly to popular acclaim. In other contexts, a wider range of actors may be involved. Art historian Kirk Savage, examining the construction of monuments in the nineteenth-century United States, argues that while 'in an earlier century, public monuments had been part of a cult of rulership; now they claimed to be revelations of the popular will.'[2] Savage argues that the impetus for such monuments lay with local elites, but that these groups needed to legitimise their projects in the democratic context of the United States by demonstrating that they enjoyed widespread popular enthusiasm. Statue-building projects were frequently the work of elite-led voluntary associations, which took pains to emphasise that the monuments were realised through 'popular subscription', even if in practice most of the money came from a few wealthy donors. For Savage, the process of soliciting popular sentiment meant however that the resulting project was not simply a reflection of a state-sponsored narrative, since the wider public, once consulted, 'had opinions about what constituted proper commemoration.'[3]

We will explore in later chapters some of the motivations for erecting a statue, from a marker of possession to an attempt to build a national identity in the manner desired by the statue's commissioners. More basic motivations may also be at play. In some cases, this is mostly self-promotion. The seventeenth-century poet and writer John Milton secured a memorial in Poets' Corner in Westminster Abbey only in 1737. A bust of the poet by sculptor John Michael Rysbrack sits on a large inscription, reading, in its entirety:

> In the year of Our Lord Christ one thousand seven hundred thirty and seven this bust of the author of PARADISE LOST was placed here by William Benson Esquire one of the two Auditors of the Imprests to his Majesty King George the second, formerly Surveyor General of the Works to his Majesty King George the first. Rysbrack was the statuary who cut it.

The inscription tells you more about the benefactor than the subject of the sculpture, and it is hard to escape the conclusion that William Benson, who purchased the bust from its previous owner, was mostly interested in getting a reference to himself and his most prestigious roles into the abbey. Ironically, he had little to crow about. His appointment as Surveyor of the King's Works, replacing Sir Christopher Wren, ended acrimoniously when he falsely insisted that the chamber of the House of Lords was in imminent danger of collapse, his structural investigations damaging a previously safe space. Receiving only four votes when seeking to be member of parliament for Shaftesbury in the 1727 general election, he cut off the town's water supply in a fit of pique.[4]

However powerful the promoters of statues, the realisation of their monument is typically a complex business requiring the surmounting of opposing voices, negotiation and compromise. Let us consider three case studies, before looking at the creation of monuments by those seeking to challenge the narratives of those in power. We will return to the Windrush memorial for the first, in which the promoter is the government itself. The second involves a private citizen seeking a monument to her hero. A private citizen is also the patron in our third story, but here his plans clash with government priorities.

The National Windrush Monument

The term 'Windrush Generation' typically refers to migrants arriving in the United Kingdom from the then British colonies of the Caribbean from 22 June 1948, the date of arrival of the *Empire Windrush* at Tilbury port on the Thames estuary, until the 1971 Immigration Act. The migration flow was facilitated by the British Nationality Act of 1948, giving people from British colonies the right to live and work in Britain. The Act responded to a labour shortage in the war-weary Britain of the late 1940s.

Pathé newsreel footage in 1948 reported the arrival of the *Empire Windrush*, capturing passenger Aldwyn Roberts, better remembered as calypsonian Lord Kitchener, cheerfully singing 'London is the place for me.' A jaunty expression of optimism about the journey, and destination. But the reality of life in Britain often failed to live up to that optimism, as newcomers arrived in a city battered from the long years of World War II, with continued food rationing, and faced racist discrimination and harassment.

The story of the Windrush Generation is one of the perseverance of Caribbean arrivals who helped forge a modern Britain despite hardships, prejudices and mistreatments. The National Windrush Monument was to celebrate their resilience and all they had achieved. Floella Benjamin, as chair of the Commemoration Committee, embodied this journey. Born in Trinidad, she arrived in Britain at the age of ten, becoming a household name as presenter of children's television series *Playschool* and *Play Away*. The rest of the committee similarly comprised former Caribbean migrants or their descendants who had forged impressive careers. Descriptive panels behind the monument include a poem by Professor Laura Serrant, entitled *You Called…And We Came*. It offers a refrain of 'remember…you called', a reminder that Windrush Generation migrants were specifically requested by the homeland. They came in response to that call. And they shaped British society for the better, as with the melting of 'the "snow" at the peaks of our profession', as Serrant's poem puts it.

The choice of Waterloo station marked the fact that thousands of migrants arriving from the Caribbean reached London by train from Southampton to Waterloo before heading out across Britain. For Baroness Benjamin: 'I remember vividly my own moment of arrival as a ten-year-old—stepping off the train and standing on Platform 19 at Waterloo Station.'[5] Four sculptors, all of Caribbean heritage, were shortlisted, and feedback on their proposals was encouraged via public consultation, particularly targeted at people with a British Caribbean background. US-based Jamaican artist Basil Watson was awarded the commission in September 2021. Statues of Jamaican sprinting stars Usain Bolt and Merlene Ottey had featured in his, er, track record, as had a large statue of Martin Luther King Jr in Atlanta. Basil Watson's own parents were part of the Windrush Generation, arriving in England in 1952.[6] A text on the panels sets out its purpose as 'a permanent place of reflection, fostering greater understanding of the Windrush Generation's talent.' The font used is itself called Empire Windrush, inspired by the lettering of the ship.

All this might suggest that the monument ought to be relatively uncontroversial, a celebration of achievement through adversity. There was however a complicating political context. Those who came from the Caribbean between 1948 and the early 1970s received no documents on arrival in the UK—they had no need of any, having the right to settle in Britain by virtue of birth in a British colony. By 2012, there was growing concern about a different kind of migrant: those arriving in the UK illegally. The government announced a 'hostile environment' policy. New requirements were introduced for landlords, employers and others to refuse services to anyone unable to prove legal residence in the UK. Concerns soon emerged that Windrush Generation migrants were falling foul of this policy if they were unable to prove their right to remain. There were reports of people losing their jobs and access to services while cases were investigated, and of unreasonable demands for documentation from often elderly people. The UK's National Audit Office found in December 2018 that the Home Office had 'failed to protect their rights to live, work and access services in the UK.'[7]

This backdrop led some to argue that a government-sponsored monument to the Windrush Generation felt inappropriate while there remained contested issues around the Windrush scandal, including compensation arrangements. Campaign group Windrush Lives, seeking an independent Windrush Compensation Scheme and a statutory inquiry into both the causes of the scandal and the 'hostile environment' policy, concluded: 'until that's done, stuff your statues and memorials.'[8]

In 2022 Professor Gus John penned an open letter to Floella Benjamin and Michael Gove, then Secretary of State for Levelling Up, Housing and Communities, turning down his invitation to the opening ceremony. He criticised the statue as embodying a narrative under which the Windrush Generation were portrayed as 'pioneers who clocked up notable accomplishments in a free and open society in which they enjoyed equal opportunities for their considerable talents to flourish', underplaying what he characterised as 'a perennial struggle against systemic racism, neo-fascism and English nationalism.'[9] John concludes that 'while acknowledging Basil Watson's remarkable work, this is a monument to unforgivable political illiteracy and an entrenched colonial mindset. What's more, it is a monument to state racism, hypocrisy and hubris.'[10]

Amongst those supportive of commemorating the achievements of the Windrush Generation with a monument, not all were convinced by the Windrush Commemoration Committee proposal. Most prominent among these opponents was the Windrush Foundation, a charity established in 1996, which highlights the contribution of African and Caribbean peoples to economic and cultural life in Britain. On its website, the foundation's director, Arthur Torrington CBE, implored people to 'Say No to the Government's Windrush Monument at Waterloo Station'.[11]

There is a distinct flavour of concern around the loss of proprietorship of Windrush-related initiatives in the foundation's language. Torrington lamented that the Windrush Commemoration Committee had failed to speak with the Windrush Foundation, even though the latter had organised 'yearly Windrush commemorative events in the UK from 1997.'[12] While many later arrivals had passed through Waterloo station, this had not been true of those arriving at Tilbury Dock on the emblematic first voyage in June 1948. Those without places to go had been accommodated overnight at Clapham South Deep Shelter in Brixton. Many secured jobs at the local labour exchange and set up home in Brixton, a district of London still strongly associated with the Caribbean community, with Windrush Square at its centre. Torrington argued that Brixton was therefore the proper location for a Windrush monument.

The debate was about different visions, with the question of location central to both issues of who the statue was celebrating and its intended audience. If the statue was meant as a celebration of Caribbean migrants to the UK throughout 1948 to 1971, a location in Waterloo Station made sense. If it was about those arriving on 22 June 1948 aboard the *Empire Windrush*, it did not. And should the statue be in a part of London with a large and vibrant Caribbean community, where that community could best admire it, or should it be placed in a location where it would be seen by a larger and more disparate audience? For the British government as sponsors of the memorial, their objective of a monument that would both honour the contribution of the Windrush generation to the development of modern Britain and celebrate a multicultural society was best served by a location that was both highly visible and relevant to as many as possible of the Caribbean migrants to the United Kingdom.

The Windrush Foundation took a legal route, filing trademark applications for the terms 'Windrush Monument', 'Windrush Memorial', 'Windrush 75', 'Windrush' and 'Windrush Day'. The applications were opposed by the UK government Department for Levelling Up, Housing and Communities, funders of the monument, in part on grounds of bad faith, arguing that the Windrush Foundation was aware of the government's scheme to build a Windrush Monument when filing the applications. At the hearing, Arthur Torrington conceded that the charity's action was in opposition to the government's approach, which he considered that of 'Windrush revisionists, who are those who would change the original Windrush narrative to that which is more suited to their objectives.'[13] The Hearing Officer found in favour of the government on this score, and the foundation was ordered to pay £3,800 in costs.[14]

The controversies around the statue notwithstanding, and equally not to underplay the challenges both confronted and still to come, the journey of the Windrush Generation is surely worth celebrating.

Marc Bolan's Rock Shrine

On 16 September 1977 a Mini driven by Gloria Jones, girlfriend of Marc Bolan, glam-rock icon and frontman of the band T. Rex, crashed into a fencepost and then tree after crossing a bridge on Queens Ride close to Barnes Common in southwest London. Marc, who had not been wearing a seatbelt, was killed. Gloria survived. The story of the erection of a commemorative statue to Marc Bolan at the place of his death is the story of persistence by dedicated fans, above all by Fee Warner, a follower of the group since 1970. Fee, like other T. Rex fans, visited the crash site many times following Marc's death. In April 1999, she formed the T. Rex Action Group (TAG), with the goal of long-term care and improvement of what was now billed as 'Marc Bolan's Rock Shrine' (see fig. 2). The following year, TAG took on the leasehold of the site and became legal owners of 'the Bolan Tree.'

One might question why fans of Marc Bolan should feel a protective attachment to the tree. It was, after all, the object that caused their idol's death. The TAG website explains that, while some fans do indeed blame the tree, others find the place a spiritual one. 'Many prefer the relaxed nature of this "Woodland Retreat" to the ordered neatness of Golders Green Crematorium.'[15]

Visiting the site in autumn 2024, I found it less bucolic than I had imagined from that description. The crash site comes as Queens Ride descends from a bridge over the railway. The incline has generated a low bank, with a private road, Gipsy Lane, at the bottom, flanked by smart houses. At the foot of the bank stands the first permanent memorial on the site, a headstone installed by the Performing Right Society in 1997, marking the twentieth anniversary of Bolan's death. This is sober in tone, recognising Bolan's 'outstanding contribution to British music.' Just to the left are five wooden steps, fashioned from railway sleepers, installed by TAG in 2000 as their first main undertaking in beautification of the site.

At the top of the steps is a bronze bust of Bolan, the work of Canadian sculptor Jean Robillard, donated by Fee Warner. This was installed in 2002 on the twenty-fifth anniversary of Bolan's death. The size and position of the bust reflect negotiations with local homeowners, who were clearly not as enthused by the music of T. Rex as were members of the Action Group. They disagreed with TAG's original proposed location for the bust at the base of the bank, mirroring the Performing Right Society stone, not wanting commemorative congestion to spill onto their private road. And they stipulated a maximum height for the bust. Not wanting their planning application rejected, TAG complied. The bust, portraying Marc, his hair a mass of curls, in a loose shirt, is a poignant memorial, its tone one of loss and sorrow. Around the bases of both statue and Performing Right Society stone are ceramic white swans, referencing one of T. Rex's hits. There are plastic model Tyrannosaurus Rex dinosaurs, and several frogs. The bust faces away from the road, from which it is hidden by a barrel festooned with photographs and garlands of plastic flowers. Greater visibility would be secured by facing the statue directly onto the road, but this evidently was not what was desired. In part perhaps it reflects a deliberate turning away from the road, and the reminder of the accursed car, and towards the nurturing woodland. And in part it reflects an evident desire for a private shrine; a place for deliberate pilgrimage and contemplation rather than a site to be stumbled upon by chance.

A noticeboard is covered with photos and poetry from fans. 'Keep a little Marc in your heart', we are urged. A letter of 16 September 2022, respectfully penned to 'Dearest Marc', from Jen Guzman of New York, records her pilgrimage to 'this sacred space'. It ends: 'Boogie on, Cosmic Dancer.' Who could disagree with that? On the corner of the board is pinned a fifteen-point 'conditions for entry' to the rock shrine, put up by TAG. Graffiti, annoyingly loud music, and introducing or removing anything to or from the site that should not be introduced or removed are banned, basically. Infringement may lead to removal 'by any officer of TAG, or by any constable', which has the effect of making TAG sound like a paramilitary organisation. Since another group of T. Rex fans was known as the Marc Bolan Liberation Front, perhaps it goes with the territory.

On the steps have been placed memorial plaques to other members of T. Rex who died young, as well as one to Marc's widow, June Bolan. The plaques are a reminder of the extraordinary degree of premature death associated with the band. Bass player Steve Currie, 'died in a car crash in Portugal.' Of percussionist Steve Peregrin Took, we are told: 'Tookie remained a stalwart of the Ladbroke Grove Underground Community until he choked on a cocktail cherry and died aged 31.' At least Took's successor Mickey Finn lasted long enough to attend the unveiling of the bronze bust in 2002, though he only made it to the following year.[16]

Marc Bolan's Rock Shrine has emerged as the vision of dedicated fans, though a vision tempered not only by funding constraints but also by the need to negotiate compromises with homeowners and other stakeholders less persuaded that the memorialisation of a glam rock singer should be a prominent feature of the local landscape.

The Enthusiasm of Jevgeņijs Gombergs

In a well-heeled residential area in the Latvian seaside resort of Jūrmala, an equestrian statue of Peter the Great unexpectedly stands in the garden of a private house. The story of how it got there involves businessman and statues enthusiast Jevgeņijs Gombergs, whose house this is. The statue was first installed in 1910, marking the 200th anniversary of the Russian conquest of Rīga, in the heart of the Latvian capital, on the site of the current Freedom Monument, which we will meet in a later chapter. Tsar Nicholas II and his family visited Rīga for the unveiling. In 1915, when bronze statues across the empire were being melted down to support the war effort, the statue was loaded onto a ship bound for St Petersburg. It never made it, torpedoed by a German submarine off Estonia. It was recovered, in pieces, by Estonian divers in the 1930s, who sold the statue back to Latvia—minus the horse's ears, presumably still at the bottom of the sea.

The Latvians had other priorities. They were building a grand new monument to Latvian identity and had no interest in restoring one to a former occupying leader, so the fragments of Peter the Great languished in a warehouse. By 1991, the pieces risked ending their days as scrap metal. An engineer named Stanislav Razumovsky managed to track down most of the statue but lacked the funds to reconstruct it. He persuaded a Russian military unit to store the pieces, other than Peter's head, which he took home. When the Russian unit withdrew from Latvia, Razumovsky fretted about the statue's fate, delivering the head to the Russian embassy in Rīga to focus attention on its plight. Jevgeņijs Gombergs then entered the picture, offering to pay for the monument's restoration in time for the city's 800th birthday celebrations in 2001.[17] A wealthy businessman who had once worked as a part-time tour guide in Rīga,[18] he was enthused by the city and its statuary.

Gombergs' offer met with less than resounding approval from Latvian authorities, who saw little to commemorate in Russian imperial occupation of Latvia, and a rival plan was hatched to offer the disassembled statue to St Petersburg, which lacked a decent equestrian statue of Peter the Great, for their 300th anniversary celebrations in 2003. Gombergs encouraged the Russian ambassador to persuade St Petersburg to refuse the gift, and the Russian authorities eventually responded that they would be happy to accept a copy of the statue but had no wish to deprive Latvia of the original. Underpinning this dispute was a difference in perspective between the Latvian-speaking majority in the Baltic republic, who saw no place in their independent state for a statue reminding them of the earlier Russian occupation, and the Russian-speaking minority, who argued that all periods of the city's history were deserving of remembrance. In 2001, the restored statue was briefly installed in a city park. Opponents then forced its removal, initially to a parking lot behind Gombergs' offices in Rīga. There it rested for twenty years, until Gombergs retired and sold his office in 2021. The statue followed him to his Jūrmala home.

History repeated itself. Prince Michael Andreas Barclay de Tolly was a member of a Baltic German family serving as a Russian field marshal in the Napoleonic Wars, whose contribution to defeating Napoleon's invasion made him a hero, even if the scorched earth policy he adopted was controversial. A standing statue of the field marshal, holding his baton of command in a relaxed and confident pose, was unveiled in central Rīga in 1913, part of commemorations of the centenary of Napoleon's defeat. The statue was taken down, its bronze destined for military repurposing, in World War I, though the stone pedestal remained. Gombergs, ever the enthusiast of the statuary history of the Latvian capital, financed a replica, installed in 2002.

Following the Russian invasion of Ukraine in 2022, all statues in Latvia appearing to celebrate Russia as an occupying power came under scrutiny. As we shall see in a later chapter, attention first fell on statues dating from the Soviet occupation, but calls also came for the removal of those linked to the earlier period of Tsarist rule. In October 2024, following a Rīga City Council vote, the statue was taken down, to be returned to Gombergs. The pedestal was also removed and the site levelled, leaving no trace of the field marshal. The then mayor of Rīga, Vilnis Ķirsis, announced on social media 'Esplanade Square is free from the symbol of Russian imperialism.'[19] As a sponsor of statuary, Jevgeņijs Gombergs combines passion with the financial means to realise his dream: the examples of Peter the Great and Barclay de Tolly demonstrate however that money alone may not be enough where the project conflicts with the political imperatives of the authorities.

VOICES IN STONE

The Creation of Monuments from Minority Perspectives

As we have outlined, monuments are typically commissioned by, and serve the purposes of, those with power, both political and economic. The examples of the T. Rex Action Group and the statuary passions of Jevgeņijs Gombergs show however that private citizens with no particularly privileged access to the corridors of power can and do deliver statues. In some cases, the sponsors of monuments seek to counter the core narratives of those in power. We will examine later the case of dialogic monuments, constructed deliberately to oppose the narratives of existing monuments. But others are independent of any earlier monument. Their construction is often fraught and challenging, because the groups concerned lack access to the political and economic power that would make their task more straightforward.

Sociologist Adrienne Burk has studied two monuments in Vancouver, Canada, addressing violence against women. The first commemorated fourteen women murdered in 1989 at a university building in Montreal, where a gunman separated women from men and shot only the former. The choice of location of the monument, *Marker for Change*, in a city far from the massacre, aimed to generalise the monument, so it was not about the actions of one man, but part of the larger issue of violence against women. Some residents of the neighbourhood selected to host the monument, Downtown Eastside of Vancouver, felt however that attention might be better focused on a specific concern of the neighbourhood itself around disappearances of poor, often Indigenous, women, which had generated little public attention. A second monument was conceived, highlighting the disappearance of local women.[20]

Even for monuments whose purpose is to challenge dominant viewpoints, the influence of those in power can be crucial. Geographer Owen Dwyer has looked at monuments and markers to the civil rights movement in the American South. While the number of these has increased rapidly, and the civil rights movement now has an important place in the public memorial space,[21] a reliance on public or corporate funding makes them susceptible to the goals of those holding power, such as catering to the heritage tourism market[22] rather than changing society going forward.

2

SCULPTORS

Paris in the springtime. A passionate love affair beckoned, and sculptor Alice Nordin's was with a fellow Swede, composer Hugo Alfvén. It was intense but did not last. The affair did however produce a patinated plaster bust: a female figure in a moment of rapture; eyes closed, head back, hands under her cheek (see fig. 3). The expression is suggestive of listening to something powerful, moving and important to the subject. Nordin, who had arrived in Paris in 1898 through a prize from the Stockholm Academy of Fine Arts, called it *Andante Patetico*, its name taken from the slow third movement of Alfvén's violin sonata Op. 1. The Nationalmuseum in Stockholm displays a slightly later variant, created in 1904 and entitled *A Memory*, influenced by the Art Nouveau style in vogue at the time.[1] The bust then is a deeply personal memory of a passion extinguished.

The sculptor takes centre stage in the production of a statue, but the sculptor generally works to a commission by the organisation or individual providing the funding. The brief may be tightly drawn or may allow the sculptor considerable leeway. While some statues, like *Andante Patetico*, are suffused with the intense emotions and desires of their sculptor, others are an exercise in delivering a brief in a swift and effective fashion. There can be a tension between sculptor as auteur and sculptor as service provider, which we will explore through examination of the careers of three Scandinavian sculptors, each honoured with a museum by their grateful homelands, but who navigated that tension in different ways, as well as the work of a sculptor operating in the very different environment of the Soviet Union.

VOICES IN STONE

Bertel Thorvaldsen

Bertel Thorvaldsen is Denmark's most famous sculptor, but spent most of his career in Rome, where he lived from 1797 to 1838, making only one trip to Denmark during that time. He had arrived in the Eternal City thanks to a scholarship from the Copenhagen Academy of Art, and it was the classical sculptures of Rome that inspired him as he developed into one of the great Neoclassical sculptors of the nineteenth century.

With his scholarship money almost exhausted, he faced a return to Copenhagen when English art collector Thomas Hope came to his rescue, commissioning in 1803 a marble statue of his plaster work *Jason with the Golden Fleece*. The work depicts the naked Jason stepping towards the viewer and the future. He holds the Golden Fleece over his left arm, gripping its hoof tightly, as well he might, given its value in guaranteeing his right to his kingdom and promise of fertility to boot. Characteristically for a Thorvaldsen sculpture, the scene depicts not the moment of greatest drama in the story, the killing by Jason of the dragon guarding the fleece, but a more introspective moment, as the victorious Jason contemplates his golden future. The Jason depicted by Thorvaldsen is the 'new man' of the nineteenth century, ready to assert his rights at the dawn of a new age.[2]

In Rome, Thorvaldsen amassed collections of classical objects, which infused and inspired his work. He moved in circles of archaeologists, and restored ancient sculptures, including pediment sculptures from the temple of Aphaia on the Greek island of Aegina for Ludwig of Bavaria. He was, in short, steeped in the classical world.

As one of the most famous sculptors of his day, Thorvaldsen made his fortune from commissions from the rich and powerful from many countries. His efforts to meet the requirements of his clients often resulted in departures from his preferred style, a point demonstrated by examination of his two equestrian statues, plaster casts of which stand obligingly at each end of the Grand Hall of the Thorvaldsen Museum in Copenhagen. Józef Poniatowski, whose sculpture was undertaken in 1826–7 and now stands in Warsaw, was a champion of Polish liberty, a hero wounded at the Battle of Leipzig in 1813

SCULPTORS

when fighting on the side of Napoleon. It is said that he rode out to his death in the White Elster River rather than be taken prisoner by the Coalition armies. Others offer a more downbeat account, suggesting that his injuries arose from friendly fire and that he was simply trying to escape when he drowned, but let us stick with the romantic version, as more congruent with the statue. This has strong classical antecedents, taking its cue from the statue of Marcus Aurelius on the Capitoline Hill in Rome. The classical theme is reinforced by Poniatowski's attire—that of a Roman general, a Neoclassical device intended to signify that the subject and their achievements are raised above the constraints of time and space.

In 1814, a few months after Poniatowski's death, a campaign was launched to raise funds for a commemorative monument. Permission having been secured from Tsar Alexander I, the project began in earnest. Stanisław Mokronowski, a former Polish Army general who was coordinating the project, wrote to Thorvaldsen in 1817 asking him to make a statue of the Polish hero. Mokronowski suggested that Poniatowski be depicted in modern dress, though the intention was always that the horse should be modelled on the Marcus Aurelius statue. But Thorvaldsen preferred classical attire. He also emphasised his wish to make the model in Rome, where he would be surrounded by classical inspiration.[3] While Thorvaldsen did experiment with sketches including Polish dress, as well as a different composition involving the horse at half-halt, about to jump into the river, the final version corresponded with Thorvaldsen's classical preferences.

The monument was ready to be installed in Warsaw by 1832, but following the failed November 1830 uprising against Tsarist rule, permission to erect it had been withdrawn, and following various adventures it was only unveiled in its rightful place in 1923, only to be blown up on German orders in 1944 after the Warsaw Uprising, and replaced in 1952 by a new cast taken from the model at the Thorvaldsen Museum in Copenhagen.[4] Poniatowski is a picture of calm control, even if his brow is furrowed, reflecting the seriousness of his situation. He looks to the left, surveying his unseen troops, while his sword points forward and rightwards, towards the enemy. There is no saddle, and his horse is skittish, adding to the sense of a military leader calmly able to control a clearly alarming situation.

The plaster cast at the other end of the hall, that of the equestrian statue of Maximilian I of Bavaria, who ruled in the early seventeenth century, contains some echoes of the Poniatowski statue, notably Maximilian's gaze to one side while pointing towards the other, an attempt to demonstrate calm control of his environment. But there are important differences. Maximilian sports not classical Roman dress but the attire of his own time. His horse has none of the nervous skittishness of that of Poniatowski. The choices adopted by the sculptor owe much to the objectives of the commissioner of the statue, which stands in the Wittelsbacherplatz in Munich. King Ludwig I of Bavaria wanted a statue of Maximilian, like him a member of the noble Wittelsbach family, to legitimise his right to rule by highlighting his distinguished ancestor. This necessitated the use of dress appropriate to Maximilian's time. It also required a portrayal embodying calmness and stability, to emphasise the strength and continuity of rule. A nervous, skittish horse, as in the Poniatowski statue, would not do at all, and hence Maximilian's steed is a model of calm solidity.

Notwithstanding Thorvaldsen's fame, commissions could be highly specific. In 1833, Princess Helena Poninska ordered a grave relief for her eldest son for the family chapel at Chervonohorod in Ukraine. Tragically, the princess's eldest daughter also died before the monument had taken shape, and its format was adjusted to make it a memorial to both children. Preserved correspondence makes clear that the princess had definite views about the form of the relief. She was the source of the central idea of the two youths floating through space from the world of life to that of death. They are guided to their destination by the winged Angel of Death, while a distraught mother, kneeling on the world of life, tries to cling on to her daughter, floating away from her. The princess commented frequently and often as the sketches for the relief took shape.[5] There is no evidence of the sculptor objecting to this: meeting the requirements of his clients was clearly important to him. The timeliness of his completion of work was another matter: Thomas Hope waited years for his Jason.

SCULPTORS

Although Thorvaldsen had left Denmark, he retained contacts with the country, including with both King Frederik VI and Christian VIII. He made a portrait of the former, as well as one of his wife and daughters, and the latter visited his atelier in Rome in 1820, commissioning a statue of his wife. A request from Christian VIII resulted in a statue of King Christian IV in Roskilde Cathedral. The most famous Danish commission produced by Thorvaldsen was however the sculptural decoration of the Lutheran Church of our Lady, the Cathedral of Copenhagen, rebuilt by C. F. Hansen in a Neoclassical style following a 1795 fire and the bombardment of the city in 1807. Thorvaldsen's contribution was a focus of his return visit to Copenhagen in 1819, that single return of his Rome sojourn.[6] It centres on the statue of Christ above the altar, bathed in a golden light reflected from the wall behind. This is a compassionate, forgiving Christ, opening his arms to us as children, a bearded, long-haired figure, his gaze downwards. The statue has helped shape the Protestant view of what Christ looked like. Running along the nave, statues of the Apostles flank Christ, Judas Iscariot replaced by St Paul. They are portrayed together with the implements of their martyrdom, or other accoutrements associated with them. As a symbol of nonchalance, it is hard to beat the figure of Bartholomew gazing intently at the knife that would be used to skin him.

It was Copenhagen that showcased the legacy of the great Dane. Buoyed by the king's promise that a museum would be built to house his work, he donated all he possessed to the city of Copenhagen on his return home in 1838 after more than forty years in Rome. This was a cunning move on Thorvaldsen's part: Denmark was at the time, though not for many years longer, an absolute monarchy, so had he donated the works to country rather than city they would have become the king's private property.[7] The 67-year-old sculptor returned in triumph, arriving on a royal frigate. The museum built in his honour, in a prime site close to Christiansborg Palace, is a temple to the man, to his works, and to classical antiquity. It was the work of architect Michael Gottlieb Bindesbøll, who had travelled through the Mediterranean and visited Thorvaldsen's workshop in Rome. Its vaulted ceilings resemble sites of antiquity such as those of Pompeii. Thorvaldsen's foliage-covered grave stands in the central courtyard, whose pavement is inspired by an ancient racecourse and whose walls are decorated with palm trees. 'I'm ready to die now that Bindesbøll has finished my grave',[8] Thorvaldsen reportedly declared at a dinner party on the eve of his death in 1844.

Around the museum, excepting only the columned façade topped by a winged Nike controlling a four-horse chariot, runs a frieze, the work of artist Jørgen Sonne, under Bindesbøll's direction. This tells three stories, one on each side. Along the canal side on the north of the building is painted the triumphal return of the ageing sculptor to his home city. He is helped ashore by deferential local worthies. The straw-hatted oarsmen who conveyed him to the quayside raise their oars in salute. Hats and scarves are waved aloft. There is a band. City notables are pictured, including Hans Christian Andersen clinging to a mast.[9] The social status of the greeting party descends with increasing distance from the object of their attention. A youth is being fished out of the water in the final scene, a little local drama unrelated to the main event.

Along the shorter end wall, wrapped Thorvaldsen treasures are being offloaded from a ship. A supervisor carefully notes down the consignments. On the south side of the building, closest to the palace, the treasures have been unwrapped. They are conveyed in a perspiring procession towards the museum, aping portrayals of captured foreign loot in classical friezes. This scene serves as a portrayal of the museum's greatest hits, the highlights of the selection within. Here comes the equestrian statue of Józef Poniatowski. Now the seated Pope Pius VII, the commission for which made him the only non-Catholic to deliver a sculpture for St Peter's Basilica. The solidity of that statue provides a natural focus for the viewer's gaze. The reaction to the statues of the figures displayed on the frieze is very different. For sweating hauliers, the statues are simply heavy weights to be moved. A couple of youths seem over-awed at the sight of the pope.[10] Art lovers stop a workman in his tracks for a better look at a relief.

Thorvaldsen was conscious of his legacy. One of the museum's treasures is an 1859 marble version by his associate H. W. Bissen of his self-portrait, *Bertel Thorvaldsen with the Statue of Hope*. Thorvaldsen portrays himself as confident and determined, staring towards the viewer. He is in his working clothes, holding a hammer and chisel. He leans on an unfinished statue of the Goddess of Hope he has evidently been working on. He has increased his own height and reduced that of the statue. Behind him is an uncarved block of marble. The composition takes us then from unworked stone to partially worked classical sculpture to a finished depiction of the sculptor himself in his working attire.[11] He is literally a self-made man.

Thorvaldsen then was an outstanding Neoclassical sculptor; his style steeped in the classical Greek art he identified as the mark of great sculpture. And yet, ever professional, he was also responsive to the requirements and demands of those commissioning works from him.

Einar Jónsson

On the Skólavörduholt hilltop in central Reykjavik stands a distinctive building offering some parallels to the Thorvaldsen Museum in Copenhagen. This pebbledash creation has an appearance somewhere between a castle and a public library. It honours the first Icelander to make his career as a sculptor—Einar Jónsson.

Born in 1874, Einar studied at the Royal Danish Academy of Fine Arts. He was drawn to subjects evoking Icelandic folklore and Norse mythology, though would gradually turn to more allegorical works, underpinned by a complex symbolism. He returned to Iceland in 1920, living in the country until his death in 1954. Einar wrote to the Icelandic parliament as early as 1909, offering his oeuvre as a gift to Iceland, provided they stump up a building to house it. The pebbledash castle on the hill is the result: secured by a mix of government funding and private donations. When it opened in 1923, it was Iceland's first public art museum in dedicated premises. Designed by Einar himself, it was dubbed Hnitbjörg, the place of storage of poetic mead in Norse mythology. Einar and his wife Anna lived in the building, in a charming but small penthouse apartment. Anna remained director of the museum until well into her eighties.

There are plaster casts of Einar's work on display, and bronzes in a sculpture garden outside. Their titles underline his fascination with allegorical pieces: *Sleep, Earth, Fate, Grief*. Certain shapes and features recur. Einar was it seems a fan of sculpting lithe barebreasted female figures with arms outstretched. Processions of tightly packed figures receding into the horizon are another favourite. Icelandic mythology provides frequent inspiration. *Dawn* for example involves a bare-breasted female figure, arms outstretched, escaping the clutches of a fearsome-looking creature. This 1906 work was inspired by the tale of the night troll. Our heroine is alone in the farm on Christmas Eve, her relatives having headed off to church. She must watch over the farm. Unfortunately, a troll appears outside, seeking to lure her into the darkness. Girl and troll embark on a night-long battle of wits, but just as the troll succeeds in taking the girl into his clutches the dawn arrives, turning the troll to stone. The girl is depicted escaping his stony grasp as she reaches out to the sun, her saviour.

Einar Jónsson's statues stand across Reykjavik: a collection of public statuary speaking to Icelandic identity and its heroes. The works represent a series of tussles between sculptor and the organisations commissioning them. While the latter tended to want statues offering realistic, naturalistic representations of their subject, Einar wanted to craft symbolic pieces that illustrated their characters through allegorical scenes.

Take Jónas Hallgrimsson. A poet active in the early nineteenth century, known for his writing on Icelandic nature, Hallgrimsson tragically passed away aged 37 when a slip down the stairs of his Copenhagen home resulted in a broken leg, then blood poisoning. His statue by Jónsson was the first by an Icelandic artist installed in a public place. Erected in 1907, it originally stood in the centre of Reykjavik, before being relegated in 1947 to Hljómskálagardur Park. The youthful-faced writer sports a coat with large buttons, clasping flowers in his left hand. Einar was unhappy with the commission. He found the task of having to make a lifelike representation of Hallgrimsson unsatisfactory in all senses except financial. He chafed that he might just as well have been asked to make the guy a pair of shoes. He would eventually make another statue of Hallgrimsson, decades later, a work entitled *In the Memory of the Poet*. An allegorical piece, it sought to symbolise what the poet had been trying to achieve. A plaster cast rests in the museum.

SCULPTORS

With Jón Sigurðsson, a central figure in Icelandic efforts to secure independence, Einar was more successful in getting some leeway to interpret the subject's character and importance. Not through the statue itself, where the commission again insisted on a lifelike representation, but by means of a relief on the plinth. Sigurðsson is portrayed grandly, holding the lapels of his coat and staring haughtily towards the parliament building across the square. The plinth tapers rather like a mountain, and on it is placed Einar's relief. The latter is entitled *The Pioneer*, portraying Sigurðsson as a pathfinder for the Icelandic people, a great man struggling through a landscape of tall basalt columns, shifting them out of the way so a tightly packed group of people, in a procession stretching to the horizon, can follow him.

The story of the statue's location is a demonstration of national-identity building. It was unveiled in 1911 in front of the government offices, a prominent spot in central Reykjavik. But there was a better one. Austurvöllur, the square in front of parliament. It was occupied by a gift made by Copenhagen City Council to the people of Reykjavik to mark the thousandth anniversary in 1874 of the settlement of Iceland by Norwegian chieftain Ingólfur Arnarson.[12] The chosen gift was the self-portrait by sculptor Bertel Thorvaldsen, another copy of which we have encountered at the Thorvaldsen Museum. The gift was intended to emphasise the connections between Iceland and Denmark through the personality of the sculptor, who had an Icelandic father, and in Iceland is sometimes described as a Danish-Icelandic sculptor. Since it appears he never set foot in the place, this might be stretching it.

The statue was installed in 1875 on Thorvaldsen's birthday, the first public sculpture in the city. However, as Iceland pushed for full independence from Denmark, the presence in this prime location right in front of parliament of a statue emphasising links with Denmark looked increasingly awkward, and in 1931 Thorvaldsen was demoted to an inferior location in the Hljómskálagardur Park. He stands there today, close to Jónas Hallgrimsson. The Jón Sigurðsson statue was moved to the prime spot in Austurvöllur, a true Icelandic patriot for such a politically infused spot. For the square is a place for both celebration and confrontation. Icelanders gather here on 17 June to mark the country's national day. It was also the venue for protests during the economic crisis of 2008, when angry citizens banged together pots and pans in what became known as the Kitchenware Revolution.

The conflict between Einar's allegorical ambitions and commissions calling for a realistic depiction of the subject came to a head over a statue of that first settler, Ingólfur Arnarson. The idea of a monument to Arnarson had been discussed by Icelandic intellectuals ahead of the thousandth anniversary of settlement, but this had come to nothing, and Icelanders had been required to make do, as we have seen, with the self-portrait by Thorvaldsen.[13] Jónsson had been experimenting with a statue to Arnarson as early as 1902, while in Rome. He continued working on it back in Copenhagen, exhibiting a maquette in 1906. At the end of a visit that year of a delegation of Icelandic parliamentarians to Denmark, the suggestion was made that the Icelanders might be gifted Bertel Thorvaldsen's statue of *Jason*, but Danish press reaction was negative, and the proposal surfaced that Jónsson's model of Iceland's first settler might be a better gift. This was welcomed back in Iceland, where a statue of a Viking hero was a more enticing prospect than a character from Greek mythology.[14]

The Danes eventually decided against a gift, but an idea had been born, and the Icelandic Craftsmen's Association launched a fund to purchase the statue and erect it on Arnarhóll, a mound in central Reykjavik said to have been where Arnarson's ship washed ashore. The Ingólfur Committee set up to mastermind the project was happy with Einar's statue of Arnarson himself. This depicts the first settler in the style typically used for Viking subjects: portraying Arnarson as a bold and prodigiously well-armed warrior. He stands by the high-seat pillar of his ship, decorated with a dragon's head. He wears chain mail, holds a tall halberd, has a sword in its scabbard and a shield resting by his side. On the reverse of the pillar a frieze focuses on the god Odin, with his ravens Hugin and Munin on his shoulders.

This was all fine with the committee. But they were not enthused with Einar's plan for the pedestal. He wanted to place bas reliefs on all four sides, to present a wider narrative about settlement in Iceland,

SCULPTORS

expressed in an allegorical way. The reliefs employed familiar Jónsson imagery. One, entitled *Twilight of the Gods*, featured a procession of tightly packed people tapering to the horizon. When photographs of the planned monument were placed on public exhibition in Reykjavik, there was general appreciation for the statue, but the reliefs left viewers confused. The committee felt the scenes detracted from the message they wanted about Ingólfur as a strong and resolute Viking. They suggested that Jónsson furnish different reliefs, adopting a narrative account from the *Book of Settlements*. He refused.

The committee also fretted about the motto, 'lead thyself', which Jónsson wanted to carve onto the high-seat pillar. It underlined the autonomy of action of the settlers. This didn't suit the committee's narrative. They pointed to historical sources suggesting that the settlers' choice of Reykjavik followed the guiding hand of the gods and thought a better motto might be 'the oracle points to Iceland.' Again, Jónsson was not prepared to accept this.[15] The project was delayed, with fund-raising attention increasingly moving to the planned Sigurðsson monument. The statue was finally unveiled in 1924, minus reliefs and motto. Einar did not show up to the ceremony. The absence of the reliefs is still felt, as the statue today stands on a boring concrete plinth.

The depiction of Viking leaders as heavily armed resolute warriors has had some unforeseen outcomes, as shown by the contrasting fates of two bronze statues by Einar Jónsson of Norse explorer Thorfinn Karlsefni. Karlsefni followed the better-known Leif Erikson in reaching Vinland, on the coast of North America, where he made an ultimately unsuccessful attempt to establish a permanent settlement. His wife bore him a son, Snorri, who earned the probable distinction of becoming the first child of European descent born in the New World. But his group comprised far more men than women, the cause of dissent which led them to abandon the settlement after a few years.

Einar received a commission from Joseph Bunford Samuel to create a statue of Karlsefni, part of a bequest from his wife to the Fairmount Park Art Association in Philadelphia; a series of sculptures illustrating the history of America. The statue was unveiled in 1920. It depicts a martial Karlsefni, in defiant pose, leaning against a battle-axe. A shield is slung across his shoulder, his sword resting in a decorated scabbard. This is all rather fantastical, since there are no accounts suggesting that Karlsefni ever fought in a battle. Another casting was made and erected in Reykjavik, initially placed close to Reykjavik Pond in the city centre. Einar reportedly never liked the chosen site, and when in 1962 plans were drawn up to expand the pond to support Reykjavik's water birds, it was removed and placed in storage. It was eventually given a new location, though one suspects Einar would have liked this one even less: a peripheral spot close to a retirement home for former fishermen and a suburban cinema.[16]

If the Reykjavik statue has had an uncontroversial but undistinguished later life, becoming almost invisible, its counterpart in the United States became a focus of considerable interest, albeit not in a welcome way. From at least 2007, a white supremacist group known as the Keystone State Skinheads, attracted by all that Viking weaponry and defiance, held annual rallies on Leif Erikson Day, meeting at the statue. This prompted counter-protests from anti-racist groups, with activities extending to spray painting the statue. In October 2018, Karlsefni was found at the bottom of the adjacent Schuylkill River.[17] At the time of writing, it was reportedly being kept in safe keeping, although the head was broken off when the statue was dragged out of the water. Given its history of appropriation by hate groups, the Philadelphia authorities seem in no rush to return it to its previous site.

The career of Einar Jónsson then involved a series of tussles with the organisations commissioning his sculptures: with the sculptor seeking to offer allegorical interpretations of his subjects while sponsors frequently sought more straightforwardly realistic representations.

Gustav Vigeland

Norwegian sculptor Gustav Vigeland also made an agreement with the authorities, in this case the local municipality of Oslo, under which they would construct him a studio and apartment in return for his entire artistic output, the studio transforming into a museum in his honour after his death. In Vigeland's case, this arrangement between sculptor and authorities provided him with the headquarters from which he would transform the adjacent parkland into the manifestation of his artistic vision. Vigeland Park in Oslo contains more than two hundred of his sculptures, most clustered in an axis comprising large sculptural groups centred around the compositions *Monolith* and *Fountain* and along the walls of a bridge.

Gustav Vigeland was born in 1869 in the southern Norwegian town of Mandal, the son of a cabinetmaker. Determined to forge a career as a sculptor, he made study tours abroad. While in Paris in 1893, he visited Auguste Rodin's studio several times, becoming influenced by Rodin's depictions of love and sexuality and by his realism. Early Vigeland sculptures, such as *A Worker* from 1900, show human figures in weary poses. A naked man powers forward, his hands clenched in determination to keep going. In common with Rodin's *Burghers of Calais*, Vigeland drew inspiration from medieval sculpture, a choice of source material reinforced by his work on the restoration of Nidaros Cathedral from 1897 to 1902, where he created forty-four figures, part of a programme influenced by the burgeoning Norwegian independence movement, looking back to a medieval golden age.[18] The medieval influence is also seen in Vigeland's enduring fascination with dragons and other mythical creatures.

Vigeland was fortunate in his timing. His emergence as a clearly talented sculptor coincided with the securing of Norwegian independence from Sweden in 1905. The Norwegian government changed the name of its capital, hitherto Kristiania, to the more Norse Oslo, and embarked on a programme of public works, including art, to deliver a suitably grand capital for the newly independent state. Vigeland worked hard to develop his name. He produced busts of influential Norwegians, often, as with that of Henrik Ibsen, on his own initiative rather than through a commission. The bust of Ibsen was modelled when the playwright was 72 years old and in poor health. He agreed reluctantly to Vigeland's request to model his features, and accepted only three sittings of ten minutes each, grumbling vigorously when Vigeland exceeded the agreed time. No wonder the final bust looks surly. Art historian Marthje

Sagewitz argues that Vigeland was deliberately seeking to set himself up as a national artist by linking his work to important Norwegians.[19]

Vigeland made his name with his monument to mathematician Niels Henrik Abel, unveiled in the Palace Park in Oslo in 1908. It marked his determination that his sculptures would not be the typical idealised representations of their subjects but would seek to capture something greater. This is surely the most dramatic statue of a mathematician ever created. The young Abel is portrayed as an Adonis-like figure, standing on the backs of two naked men who appear to be falling, arms outstretched, through the air. Abel's expression is one of quiet determination. Theirs, understandably, is one of blind panic. This is mathematician as celestial surfer, a superhero who knows his equations.

There are other Vigeland sculptures in and around the Palace Park. His bronze statue of Norwegian writer Camilla Collett was produced for a commission organised by the Norwegian Association for Women's Rights, for which Vigeland submitted the winning design. Unveiled in 1911, it was titled *I Storm* (In the Storm), depicting the writer in advanced age, pulling her shawl around her against a clearly fierce wind, which is causing her skirt to flutter. The statue is protected behind wrought iron railings portraying stylised leafless trees, battered by the wind: a nice example of Vigeland's attention to ironwork. The effect is to show Collett, widowed early and beset by financial problems for much of her life, resisting bravely and alone the trials besetting her.

Just outside the park stands Vigeland's 1911 statue of Rikard Nordraak, composer of the Norwegian national anthem, who died of tuberculosis at the age of just 23. An idealistic youth, staring forward with determination, he stands on a ledge incised in a rough-hewn stone plinth. Attention here is focused on the wrought iron railings, a riot of curious spiky forms. Two chained iron dragons guard the steps in front of the statue, baring fearsome teeth to all who approach. The dragon on the right, when looking towards the statue, has a bird-like countenance, with a pointed nose and swept-back head. Its partner has horns and a beard, giving it the appearance of an evil dragon goat.

Critics and the press lapped all this up, hailing Vigeland as a major artist; an accolade he took advantage of in securing funding for the projects he wanted to pursue, transforming himself into a true auteur. The sculptural composition *The Fountain*, centred on a large basin held up by six naked men, was modelled by Vigeland at his initiative. The model attracted admiring attention when exhibited in 1906 in the Museum of Applied Art. He sought to persuade the authorities to fund its installation in Oslo, but disagreed with the location they chose, Eidsvoll Square, in front of the parliament building. The proposed location was moved to the Palace Park in 1915, and then again at the beginning of the 1920s outside the studio building in the Frogner suburb that the city had by then agreed to build for him in return for his oeuvre. Vigeland moved into an apartment on the second floor of the building in 1924 and would live there until his death in 1943 when the place was transformed into a museum and memorial to the man. Also in 1924, the final location for *The Fountain* was agreed: the Frogner Fields close to the studio. This would form the nucleus of Vigeland Park, and the sculptor would devote the rest of his life to populating the park with his work. The park and its statuary represent Vigeland's single-minded vision.

The statuary reflects a change of style in Vigeland's work which had taken place around 1909. Influenced by French contemporaries Aristide Maillol and Antoine Bourdelle, his figures became fuller and less detailed, carved in a simplified, monumental fashion. The sculptures of Vigeland Park display his preoccupation with the relationships between men and women: whether tender and intimate or unforgiving and hostile. The men in Vigeland's work are often the more vulnerable.

Passing through the extravagant wrought iron gate, the visitor encounters stone columns topped with statues featuring interactions between humans and lizards. The creature takes a protective approach to the woman, wrapped in its scaly arms. The lizard's interaction with the male figure is in contrast distinctly martial. The influence of his spell creating gargoyles for Nidaros Cathedral is palpable.[20] Beyond is *The Bridge*, festooned with sculptures. Visitors make a beeline for a muscular man in the process of kicking and thumping angry babies. The head and arms of a baby boy being propelled by the man's foot have been rubbed shiny. There is a balancing statue of a man protectively cradling a baby in his arms, but few visitors show any interest in this one.

The most famous statue here is *The Angry Boy*, reportedly sketched by Vigeland during an excursion to London in 1901, and he is absolutely furious (see fig. 4). Captured in mid-scream, he stamps his foot and clenches his fists. Angry Boy has a female counterpart, who I am calling Mildly Distressed Girl, and who appears to be just about holding back the tears.

Continuing along the main axis of the park, you reach *The Fountain*. Its central feature of a large basin from which water flows into the surrounding pool is restrained by a wall punctuated by sculptures of people, either alone or in groups, doing things under or in a tree. An annoyed man tries to pluck wailing babies from the canopy. A couple are entwined upside down in the imprisoning branches. A worried child, alone on a branch, nervously sucks his thumb.

The main axis continues to *The Monolith*, a seventeen-metre column into which are carved 121 figures. Work began on it in 1929, and it would take three stonemasons thirteen years to finish the job. Are the packed naked bodies rising to the top, only to be deposited on by bird gloop when they get there, or are they gradually falling? Or simply squeezed together, going nowhere? The steps up to the monolith are separated by twelve lines, each of three granite compositions. These display groups of naked people in various, often disconcerting, relationships. Particularly alarming are the children riding their mother like a horse, a rope in her mouth serving as a bridle. A man holds a woman, curled in a foetal style, on his back, holding her painfully by her hair. There is a group of young mothers huddled together, their backs to us. In their conversation they have forgotten about their children. A toddler picks up a snake. The axis ends at the *Wheel of Life*, a ring formed by entwined naked figures.

Work on Vigeland Park continued during the Nazi occupation after 1940, and a criticism sometimes levelled at the sculptor is that his work has a fascist aesthetic about it. Certainly, the muscular naked bodies of Vigeland's sculptures fitted Nazi perceptions of the idealised Aryan form. It is true too that Vigeland welcomed occupying forces into the park,[21] though probably mostly out of a concern that the work on it be allowed to continue. But in other respects, the imperfections in human relationships laid bare by Vigeland are far from the ideals propagated by fascism. One of the few sculptures standing aside from the main axis is a piece entitled *Surprised*. A girl is caught naked, covering her breasts with her arms and raising her right leg to preserve remaining modesty. It was installed in the park only in 2002, from a plaster model completed by Vigeland in 1942. Ruth Maier, a Jewish refugee and one of the two models for the statue, was sent to Auschwitz a few months later.[22]

Vigeland died shortly before the completion of *The Monolith* in 1943, hailed as a genius and engulfed in posthumous glory. The Vigeland Park serves as a monument to a single-minded artist creating something distinctive and not a little disturbing, combining modernism with Norwegian medieval influences. In the tension between sculptor as auteur and sculptor as service provider, Vigeland was accorded a freer rein to pursue his vision than either of the earlier two Scandinavian sculptors whose work we have examined.

The Motherland Calls

The emblematic Soviet victory of the Great Patriotic War, as Russians term World War II, was the Battle of Stalingrad, the bloody encounter that turned the tide of war on the eastern front from German to Soviet advantage. The grand monument celebrating that victory is *The Motherland Calls*. This 52-metre statue of a female figure, the Motherland, brandishing not a telephone but a sword, stands on top of the hill known as Mamaev Kurgan in the city of Volgograd, formerly Stalingrad. While the centralising and standardising context of the command economy of the Soviet Union might appear a challenging environment for the individuality of a sculptor's vision to shine through, the ambitions and objectives of the sculptor were highly relevant here too, as our last sculptor story demonstrates.

The Motherland Calls stands at the centre of a monument complex incorporating various sculptures and a cylindrical Pantheon of Glory to the Soviet People. The complex was structured to immerse the visitor within the kind of large monuments more usually viewed at a distance.[23] Historian Scott Palmer has demonstrated that the final form of the memorial complex, and with it the way the Battle of Stalingrad is commemorated, owes much to the machinations of sculptor Yevgeny Vuchetich, depicted by Palmer as a thoroughly unsympathetic figure.[24]

Vuchetich was a sculptor in the Socialist Realist style, whose career was a matter of increasingly grandiose examples of the genre. A Communist Party member, with a distinguished military record, Vuchetich was already by 1951 lobbying Politburo members for a memorial in the city of Stalingrad to the great battle fought there, offering his services to build it. Stalin had been lukewarm over grand monuments to the Great Patriotic War, but his death in 1953 opened the way for the proposal. An official competition was announced in 1954, and the entry of Vuchetich and architect Yakov Belopolsky was selected. A 1958 decree entrusted implementation of the project to an 'authors' collective' headed by Vuchetich.

The elaborate design centred on a large statue of The Motherland, though in the original plan she held aloft not a sword but a furled banner, with a Red Army soldier in front of her on bended knee, placing the sword of victory at her feet. The statue would be 30 metres tall. Beneath it would be a subterranean circular room, a Panorama, decorated with a 360-degree mural depicting the Red Army victory over German forces. It was to be completed for the twentieth-anniversary celebrations of the victory on 2 February 1963. Not only was this deadline wholly unrealistic, but the project was troubled from the outset by cost overruns, difficulties in procuring materials, and design challenges. Cost-cutting measures were introduced, including a decision to construct the sculptures of concrete rather than granite. Yet, just as officials were frantically trying to cut costs, new requirements were added, including a demand from Khrushchev that the height of the main monument be increased from 30 to 52 metres, an order that had its roots in Cold War rivalries and Khrushchev's desire that the statue's height should exceed that of the Statue of Liberty.

Palmer shows how Vuchetich took advantage of these delays and difficulties to refashion the project to suit his objectives. The Panorama, the painting of which was entrusted to an artists' brigade headed by Anatoly Gorpenko, was the one part of the project over which Vuchetich had no direct control. The original plan to locate it within the hillside immediately below the main monument proved too difficult, and the Panorama was instead to be placed in a separate circular building. This became problematic when Vuchetich discovered in 1963, the original project deadline already passed, that the Panorama building would obscure sight lines for the main monument. During a tour of the construction site in autumn 1963, guided by Vuchetich, Khrushchev was persuaded to agree to a major design change. In place of the Panorama, a less ambitious and lower cylindrical structure would house a 'Pantheon of Glory of the Soviet People', covered in mosaics and centred on an eternal flame held aloft by a torch-bearing hand emerging from the floor. That sculpture would of course be designed by Vuchetich, thereby stamping his imprint on that part of the memorial too.

Vuchetich also revised the main statue, dropping the kneeling Red Army soldier and replacing the figure holding the banner with one wielding a sword. The iconography was now one of the Soviet Motherland calling the people forward to battle. Palmer argues that Vuchetich's motivation here was about securing future commissions, especially the design for a victory monument in Moscow, for which the new *Motherland Calls* statue would provide an ideal precursor for the monument he envisaged there.[25]

This remodelling changed the meaning of the complex. What had initially been envisaged as a memorial to Red Army successes at Stalingrad was now a broader statement about the role of the Soviet people. Understandably, some military leaders of the Stalingrad battles were not pleased. Marshal Andrey Yeryomenko, an early campaigner for a monument to the Battle of Stalingrad, was vocal in lamenting that it no longer acknowledged the central role of the Red Army. He received support from Col. Gen. Mikhail Shumilov. Vuchetich was adroit in playing military leaders off against each other. The principal military consultant to the project was Marshal Vasily Chuikov, who had commanded the 62nd Army. Vuchetich helped keep him on side by using Chuikov's face as the model for a sculptural composition at the site, *Stand to the Death*, a flattering work in which a muscular bare-chested hero emerges from the rock, brandishing a machine gun and anti-tank grenade. Vuchetich had already developed a personal link to Chuikov, whose statue he had sculpted earlier in his career.

The monument was inaugurated on 15 October 1967, more than four years after the original deadline, the occasion marking the fiftieth anniversary of Soviet power. It was pronounced a great success.[26] While the Soviet Union was supposedly about collective rather than individual vision, the sculptor Vuchetich was able to play off different parts of the system against each other in making the project his own.

3

PHYSICAL CHARACTERISTICS

Above a small island in the Narmada River in the Indian state of Gujarat rises a statue of politician Sardar Vallabhbhai Patel, an independence activist who served as India's first Deputy Prime Minister (see fig. 5). A statue to a leader of the independence movement is hardly unusual in India, but Patel stands 182 metres tall, a bronze-clad Gulliver in a Lilliputian world: the tallest statue on the planet at the time of writing.

The empty plinth on Cavendish Square in London once home to a statue of the Duke of Cumberland, third son of King George II, an unpopular figure noted for his brutality following the Battle of Culloden in 1746, was briefly reacquainted with the duke in 2012. The new statue of the 'butcher of Culloden' by Korean sculptor Meekyoung Shin was crafted in soap around a metal armature. The soap gradually eroded, exposing the metal beneath, until four years later all remnants of the duke were cleared away. This was all a statement about the mutability of history, or possibly about the deficiencies of soap as a construction material.

The honorary grave of legendarily beautiful Hollywood actress Hedy Lamarr in Vienna is marked not by a realistic sculpture of her features but by a series of vertical stainless-steel rods within which are placed eighty-eight balls. The monument, by designer Christian Thomas, highlights a less known aspect of Lamarr's life, as the developer of a 'frequency hopping' technology intended for use in torpedo guidance systems in World War II that would be a forerunner of modern wireless communications like Bluetooth.

VOICES IN STONE

The use of unexpected size, material and form in crafting monuments pursues specific objectives. In the three examples above these might be, respectively, as a mark of praise for the subject, as a mark of contempt, and to highlight achievements involving intellect rather than beauty. But most monuments and statues conform to a more expected view as to their physical characteristics. We have noted that two necessary features of a monument are a marker, a durable physical presence, and memoranda, the provision of information on that marker. Public statues have a further defining feature: the memoranda must include a visual representation of a subject, either a real person, or possibly an animal, or a representation in human or animal form of an event, virtue or quality that the sponsors of the monument wish to portray. It is time now to look at why statues have expected physical characteristics, and what it means when the statue does not conform to those expectations.

Size

Since statues are figurative representations, they have an expected size—that of the human they represent. A statue larger than human size suggests special praise and honour towards its subject. It states that this is someone who *really* deserves to be remembered.

We will explore later the role of royal statues in ancient Egypt in housing the *ka*, the 'life force' of the pharaoh's soul. The audience of these statues included the gods themselves. For the pharaoh, there was everything to be gained by making the statue colossal, visible to the gods as a mark of a strong, capable, enduring reign.[1] Egyptologist Campbell Price notes that colossal statues of the pharaoh were distinguished from other statuary by their individualised names, incorporating both name and attributes of the pharaoh. Because of their size, they could not generally be positioned within the enclosed (and restricted) space in the temple, tending to sit in open forecourts or on the boundary of the temple area, providing a visibility and accessibility which promoted popular worship. Their scale, while mostly intended at a divine audience, fostered a cult among the living one. This was attested by the discovery of steatite scarabs, bearing the names of cult colossi of Ramesses II, and steatite statuettes which seem to have been models of the colossi.[2]

PHYSICAL CHARACTERISTICS

For Jacques Derrida, colossal proportions reflect incongruity with whatever the object is supposed to represent.[3] Mikhail Yampolsky similarly suggests that immense size promotes unrepresentability, giving the colossal monument an elemental quality. While such monuments claim to be figurative representations, this correspondence is weak: 'it is simply a colossus, a huge magic mound, existing in complete contrast to the laws of mimesis, similitude and imitation.'[4]

The Soviet Union is known for its predilection for big statues, though it did not start out that way. Initial Bolshevik government efforts, in economically straitened times during and after the Civil War of 1917–22, were modest affairs: small busts generally cast in cheap materials like plaster. But large monuments suited the spacious public areas generated by Soviet urban planning, forming ideal venues for ostentatious ceremonies promoting the regime. Industrial plants were developed to facilitate casting of larger bronzes, and gigantism suited regime efforts to demonstrate superiority over the West. A 1931 tender for a Lenin monument in Leningrad seaport specified that it had to become the highest monument in the world.[5]

Of all subjects of giant statues, Buddhas stand out for the frequency of portrayal in particularly large forms and the historical longevity of the practice. There are giant Buddha statues across Central and Eastern Asia dating from the first millennium CE, and giant Buddhas continue to be erected today, in what sometimes feels a frenzied competition for record-breaking height. Art historian Dorothy Wong notes that the giant statues of the first millennium CE were focused on certain specific depictions of Buddha, including Maitreya, the Future Buddha. Wong links this to the belief that Maitreya will be reborn into the utopian kingdom of Ketumatī, during a morally healthy era, when humans will live to be 84,000 years old and grow to great height, albeit eclipsed by Maitreya, who will reach 106.5 metres. Huge statues of Maitreya depicted a realisation of this utopian kingdom.[6] Also frequently depicted of great size is Vairocana, the Transcendent Buddha, supreme and omniscient, who towered over other buddhas.

To these devotional considerations is added a political one. Wong argues that construction of large statues of Buddha was also linked with notions of Buddhist kingship: that a king should rule with devotion and righteousness, supporting organised Buddhism. Large Buddha statues served a dual purpose, emphasising both the universality of Buddha and the status of the ruler supporting the project. Wu Zhao, who founded the Wu Zhou dynasty in 690 as a Buddhist state, was to date the only female ruler in Chinese history. Her reign was linked to large Buddha statues, in part fuelled by Wu Zhao's self-proclamation in 694 as the Maitreya Incarnate.

Projects for large Buddha statues were often initiated by Buddhist monks, who sought the support of rulers or local officials to marshal the funding. The largest first millennium Buddha statue was carved from sandstone on Mount Lingyun in Leshan, Sichuan (see fig. 6). A 75-metre seated Maitreya image, the project, initiated in 713 by a monk named Haitong, was only completed in 803. The inscription expresses Haitong's hope that the Buddha would help calm the treacherous waters of the river below.[7]

The modern-day revival of construction of giant Buddhas began in 1993 with a 26.4-metre bronze seated Buddha on Lantau Island in Hong Kong. Like several later modern Buddhas, it is placed on a hill reached by a long stairway, a visual image Wong interprets as combining traditional images of Chinese kingship and the representation of Buddha as a cosmic ruler commanding a beautiful vista.[8]

Some modern-day Buddhas are enormous. The standing Vairocana in Pingdingshan City, Lushan County, Henan, known as the Great Buddha of the Central Plain, reaches a height of 108 metres, with the total complex, including stairway below, rising 208 metres. Construction was supported by the central and local government, and while there was a religious intent at play, tourism development was also a significant consideration.[9] The standing image of the bodhisattva Avalokiteśvara, known as the Guanyin of Nanshan, on the south coast of the island of Hainan, also reaches 108m. It is a public-funded steel and concrete affair. Avalokiteśvara is often depicted in coastal locations and at colossal scale, because of the bodhisattva's perceived ability to protect believers from shipwrecks.

The motivation behind colossal modern images of Buddha has some commonalities with those constructed in the first millennium CE, but there are differences too. In Communist China, arguments about 'Buddhist kingship' are perhaps less relevant. But there is a

PHYSICAL CHARACTERISTICS

touristic and commercial motivation behind some modern projects, alongside one of religious devotion.

Some statues owe their impact not to particularly large size but to a particularly small one. We will encounter later the diminutive bird of St Petersburg known as Chizhik-Pyzhik. In Stockholm, tour guides in the old town like to offer a 'secret sight' in the walled cobbled courtyard behind the Finnish Church. Here, on a low square metal base, is a little metal table. On it sits a stylised statuette of a boy, his arms protectively around his knees. Just 15 centimetres tall, he is known as *Järnpojke* ('Iron Boy'), the 1954 work of Swedish sculptor Liss Eriksson, installed here in 1967 (see fig. 7).

Järnpojke may be tiny, but he is the object of more commemorative attention than any of the grand statues of Swedish kings around the nearby Royal Palace. Swedes look after him, dressing him up in a warming bobble hat and scarf in the winter, and perhaps toy sunglasses in warm weather. The table is festooned with coins, and maybe a sweet or two. When I visited, he had been joined by a little plastic duck. His head has been rubbed shiny by visitors in search of good fortune. A little good fortune, anyway.

Plinths and Elevation

If the size of a statue can elevate the status of its subject, then so, quite literally, can its placement on a pedestal or plinth. If a statue as a figurative representation has an expected size, then equally there is an expected height: eye level in relation to the viewer. Elevation above this suggests respect: the statue looks down on the viewer. A plinth has practical advantages too. It creates a space on which can be written an inscription, setting out who is being commemorated, and why. The plinth allows for further exultation of the subject beyond the statue itself. It offers space for reliefs depicting the subject's achievements, or perhaps a list of their military honours. There is space too to acknowledge sculptor, donors and benefactors, and, to beef up the adulation further, the plinth can be embellished with more statuary: perhaps some scantily clad female representations of virtues embodied by the distinguished subject.

Statues of heroic figures erected during the nineteenth-century western European 'statuemania' rarely however include much biographical information: perhaps due to wariness of the implication that loads of detail suggests that the viewer may not already be entirely familiar with the subject. A one-word inscription, such as 'Wellington', shows that the subject is so important they need no further introduction. A plinth also reduces risks around vandalism and inappropriate conduct: the statue is literally rendered inaccessible.

A plinth makes a statue seem more inaccessible the closer you get to it. Typically placed in open areas such as public squares, statues on plinths are viewed comfortably from afar, but close to they violate the principle of urban architecture that objects intended to be seen should be placed at eye level. Those seeking to commemorate the subject of the statue are kept at a distance.[10] To the modern mind, this role of plinths in elevating their subject above ordinary mortals may seem less a mark of respect and more a suggestion of aloofness. Superiority in a bad way rather than good. In pedestrianised streets in almost every European or North American capital these days, there are statues to be encountered at eye level, their feet on the ground like the rest of us, not on a plinth. The plaque may be set into the ground beside the statue. The axing of the plinth is a democratising move: the subject of the statue is one of us, with no pretensions to lord it over the crowd. This has important consequences. Plinths are protective, making it harder to interact with the statue. At ground level, statues invite interaction. Take a selfie with your hero. As we shall see, bronze statues at ground level are particularly prone to rubbing. And should the subject of the statue be unpopular in certain quarters, there is little to protect them from vandalism.

An invitation to interact is taken a step further in that subset of plinthless statues that place the seated subject at one end of a bench, with plenty of space next to them for the viewer to pose for that all-important selfie. In 1995, a statue was unveiled in London's Bond Street, marking the fiftieth anniversary of the end of World War II. Entitled *Allies*, it depicts Winston Churchill and Franklin D. Roosevelt sitting on a wooden bench. Roosevelt looks relaxed, smiling, his arm stretching out in a friendly manner. Churchill, cigar in hand, strains towards the American president to catch the conversation. And well he might, for they are seated at opposite ends

PHYSICAL CHARACTERISTICS

of the bench, perfectly allowing the visitor to interpose themselves between the wartime leaders. The plaque tells you the name of the piece, its sculptor, Lawrence Holofcener, and the fact of its inauguration by HRH The Princess Margaret. It gives a long list of sponsoring businesses but doesn't mention the names of the subjects. The patrons of the statue clearly concluded that some peoples' renown transcends the need for such niceties.

The bench is not always a bench. In Armação dos Búzios, it is a suitcase. The former fishing village on the Brazilian coast was made famous in 1964 when Brigitte Bardot turned up with her then Brazilian boyfriend Bob Zagury, launching a transformation of the place into the Brazilian St Tropez, attracting celebrities from Jagger to Madonna.[11] Búzios returned the favour, erecting a statue to Bardot on the waterfront in 1999. She is in holiday mode, relaxed in sleeveless T-shirt and jeans, seated on a suitcase, large enough to accommodate a holiday-snap seeking visitor next to her. Or, if you would like to get more personal with Brigitte's statue, and many visitors would, you can sit on her conveniently extended leg and have your photo taken while embracing the bronze film star.

Triumphal Columns

If a plinth elevates the status of its occupant, a statue adorning a tall column takes this principle to extremes. Pliny the Elder, writing in the early years of the Roman Empire, was clear that the 'purport of placing statues of men on columns was to elevate them above all other mortals'.[12] Writing in 1911, English architect Stanley Adshead, in a brisk survey of monumental columns from Roman times to the then present day, concludes that 'the column used as the pedestal of a statue should be reserved for rare occasions, and to honour men whose distinction is exceptional.'[13]

Monumental columns provide so much in the way of pedestal that they offer more than just height. The column provides a considerable canvas on which much may be written. A curious answer to the question of what to do with all that column is provided by the rostral column. It is decorated with depictions of the prows of ships, jutting out laterally in Christmas-tree fashion, typically symbolising enemy ships captured or destroyed in a great naval victory. This form appears to have originated in ancient Rome with the exploits of Gaius Duilius, who secured in 260 BCE Rome's first victory in a notable battle at sea against the Carthaginians. He was honoured with a column topped with his bronze statue and decorated with bronze *rostra* or ramming beaks from captured ships.[14]

The height of monumental columns offers another potential use. They might serve as a belvedere: offering an impressive view of the cityscape below. Let us take the example of the Mirador de Colón, the monument to navigator Christopher Columbus in Barcelona, completed for the Universal Exhibition in that city in 1888. Historian Stephen Jacobson argues that the exhibition, whose backers were mainly local, aimed to position Barcelona as a driving force and industrial heartland of a confident and unified Spain.[15] Standing 60 metres in height, the column is topped by a bronze statue of Columbus, pointing energetically seawards, although the direction of his outstretched fingers is apparently towards Algeria rather than the New World. Inside the iron column, an elevator takes visitors to a poky viewing gallery below the statue.

The column's height, taller than Nelson's Column in London, speaks to the magnitude of Spain's achievement in reaching the New World, albeit secured by a navigator from Genoa in present-day Italy. The column was part of a larger port redevelopment project that included a new Columbus Boulevard, helpful additions in this context to an urban landscape in Barcelona that otherwise included few street names honouring Imperial Spain and its successes.[16] The importance of Catalonia to Spanish achievement is emphasised by the sculptures of Catalans involved in Columbus's voyages among those around the base of the column. Lions flank the staircases at the base. Hardly a New World animal, but then statues of llamas wouldn't have had the desired effect. The elevator added a flavour of Barcelona's modernity and technological achievement. If the purpose of the exhibition, and the column, was to promote a triumphant liberal Spanish nationalism, any success in that direction was, concludes Jacobson, short-lived, with the nascent political movement of 'Catalanism' making great strides over the next few years.[17]

The various uses to which a monumental column may be put mean that interpreting the intent behind ancient examples is not

PHYSICAL CHARACTERISTICS

always straightforward. Take Trajan's Column. This triumphal column, located in Trajan's Forum in Rome, was completed in 113 CE, and is noted for its continuous helical frieze, commemorating Roman emperor Trajan's military victory in the Dacian Wars (see fig. 8). A statue of Trajan topped the column, though Saint Peter the Apostle, a sixteenth-century addition, now occupies the place instead. The inscription at the base of the column, in describing its purpose, refers not to the Dacian Wars but suggests that the column aimed 'to show how high was the mountain—the site for great works, after all—that was cleared away.'[18] Archaeological work revealed earlier structures below the column itself, so this appears not to be a literal reference to removal of earth to the height of the column on its precise site, but rather to the requirement to remove part of the Quirinal Hill to build the adjacent Trajan's Forum.[19]

Historian Penelope Davies believes the explanation for the inscription lies in the column's role as a belvedere. A narrow spiral staircase leads up to a viewpoint. From here, the viewer could appreciate Trajan's Forum below: to see, as suggested by the inscription, how much of the hillside had been cleared away, and to take in the forum, designed to resemble a military camp to hint at Trajan's exploits as a successful general. The whole served to proclaim the success of Trajan's ventures, and drum up support in an empire beset by financial challenges for his next proposed military campaign, against the Parthians.[20] The reliefs on the frieze reinforce this purpose: there is relatively little focus on battles, and much on the lands conquered and images of Trajan and his forces in complete control throughout.

The column serves another purpose: as a funerary monument. Following Trajan's death in 117 CE, his ashes were brought to Rome and deposited at the base of the column in a golden urn, though were stolen in the Middle Ages. Academics have long debated whether the column was designed as an imperial tomb in the first place, or whether it took on that function after the emperor's death. Davies believes it was always intended as a tomb. There is a chamber, albeit very small, in the base, which would have added to the technical challenges in its construction and hints therefore that a tomb may have been intended from the outset. She argues too that the column base, decorated with depictions of captured Dacian weaponry, recalls a typical Roman funerary altar, and that the viewing of the helical frieze aped Roman funerary rituals, which involved for mourners a circumambulatory walk around the pyre.[21]

The Romans paid much attention to remembrance after death: a means of obtaining immortality through being remembered by others. The helical frieze and belvedere together perpetuated the remembrance of Trajan and his illustrious deeds. Trajan was required though to tread carefully, as it should not be too obvious that the monument was intended as a tomb. To select a site in the centre of the imperial city would have been regarded as presumptuous: this was an honour to be bestowed only on the most virtuous. Hence, believes Davies, the place was masked as a triumphal victory column, which could later take up its planned role at the appointed time.[22]

The inscription on Trajan's Column also tells us that it was erected not by Trajan but for Trajan—a gift from the senate and the Roman people. Historian Marcel Danner suggests it should be understood as the product of negotiation between senate and emperor in which both contributed ideas.[23] It reflects not only the emperor's goals, but also those of the senate. Danner notes that the form chosen—a triumphal column—recalls models from the Roman Republic such as, as we have seen, the rostral column of Duilius. The frieze incorporates scenes emphasising Trajan's qualities as a leader: for example, depicting him in evidently open consultation with his generals. The senate's objective here was perhaps to present Trajan as a leader committed to restoration of senatorial liberty and certain republican values, counterposing him with arrogant and autocratic emperors such as Domitian. His respectful treatment of the senate, in combination with his military triumphs, made him an exemplar, and the column was an embodiment of that.[24]

Form

As a statue is a figurative representation of a human or animal, its expected form might be as realistic a portrayal of its subject as the sculptor can manage. Sure enough, ancient Greece of the Archaic period from the eighth to early fifth centuries BCE was characterised by human sculptures portrayed with gradually increasing realism. In the early Archaic period, statues of *kouroi* represented male youths in portrayals of idealised beauty. The youths were depicted naked; shown off in public places for the edification of all. The equivalent female version was the *korai*, depicted more chastely clothed, but similarly as images of ageless perfection. These sculptures initially provided a formulaic interpretation of idealised youth, with a relative lack of detail, the weight placed equally on both legs, arms by the side.[25] But change was in the air. Later *kouroi* and *korai* showed a gradual development towards realism. Thus, the Anavysos Kouros, taking its name from the Greek town where it was unearthed, displays more naturalistic features than earlier examples.[26] With the move into the early Classical period in the fifth century BCE, this process accelerated. The Parian marble statue known as the *Kritian Boy*, dating from around 480 BCE, and excavated on the Acropolis of Athens, marks the first known use of *contrapposto* in statuary, with most of the weight of the figure placed on one foot, producing a more naturalistic style.

Notwithstanding this progression towards realism, not all thinkers and artists in the Classical period were ready to abandon the search for the ideal. It finds expression in the writings of Classical-period philosopher Plato, whose Theory of Forms suggests that the physical world lacks the truth of timeless ideals. The sculptor's task was not to replicate the physical appearance of the subject in a realistic way, but to transcend the physical, and instead capture the ideal. The human body should not be portrayed as it was, but in its ideal state, revealing physical perfection and bodily symmetry.

Greek sculptor Polykleitos, active in the fifth century BCE, adopted a mathematical approach to determining the ideal proportions of the human body, setting this out in the *Canon of Polykleitos*. The Canon no longer survives, but scholars have attempted to recreate it from references to the work by other ancient writers, together with a bronze statue, *Doryphoros*, the Spear Bearer, sculpted by Polykleitos in conformity with the Canon. It features an idealised naked male figure which some scholars have suggested may represent Achilles, the heroic Greek combatant of the Trojan War.[27] The proportions are perfectly balanced, the weight focused on one leg, the left arm holding a spear while the right hangs down empty. The task of recreating the Canon from this statue is made none the easier by the fact that it has not survived either. What have survived are Roman marble copies. Among noble attempts to recreate the Canon, art historian Richard Tobin proposed in 1975 that it had a somewhat obsessively geometric character, with the determination of all proportions of the human figure deriving from the length and width of the distal phalange of the little finger.[28]

Another lost Greek bronze sculpture of the fifth century BCE demonstrates the representation of idealised beauty through the depiction of a male athlete at the peak of his performance. The *Discobolus*, portraying a naked male youth in the act of propelling a discus, was the work of the sculptor Myron. The style is naturalistic, with the weight borne by one leg. One arm is stretched back, holding the discus, while the other hangs free. The trunk is twisted to face the viewer. The result intensifies the illusion of a living being, captured while carrying out an action. Again though, idealism triumphs over realism. The sculpture captures a moment of intense physical effort, as the discus is about to be launched, yet the athlete is calm and composed. No grunt is about to emerge from those lips. The statue captures an idealised perfection, not the real tensions and emotions of an actual discus thrower.[29] The sculpture again survives today through the Roman habit of making marble copies of admired Greek statuary.

The focus of Polykleitos and Myron on proportion and symmetry then moves away from natural towards idealistic representation. Charles Stocking, a US academic specialising in the history of physical culture, has observed that Greco-Roman sculpture of idealised male bodies incorporates physical features beyond the bounds of anatomical possibility even for the fittest of humans. A notable example is the degree of development in many sculptures of the feature known as 'Apollo's belt', the shallow grooves running from hip bone to pubis. The pronouncement of this feature, the extent of its curvature, and its continuation around the back of the body frequently exceed the humanly possible. Reality is exceeded, Stocking concludes, because an unnatural curvature and definition of the Apollo's belt provides a pleasing symmetry of form with the projection and curvature of the chest, and thus between upper and lower parts of the torso.[30]

The *Riace bronzes* are rare examples of surviving ancient Greek bronzes. Dating from the fifth century BCE, they were found off Calabria in 1972, forming the star attraction at the Museo Nazionale della Magna Grecia in Reggio Calabria. The figures, depicting two naked bearded warriors, are *contrapposto*, their subjects exhibiting what seems at first sight to be physical perfection. Classicist Nigel Spivey, in the 2005 BBC documentary series *How Art Made the World*, describes them as 'absolutely the best statues ever made.'[31] Yet, they are anatomically impossible. The figures lack a coccyx bone at the base of the spine; an omission intended it seems to 'improve' the curve of the back. The groove running up the centre of the torso is too deep. Their legs are relatively too long. In the cause of proportion and symmetry, of idealised perfection, the statues have become 'more human than human'.[32]

The appeal of these idealised or hyperreal figures to both ancient and modern audiences hints that we may be seeking more from statues than realistic portrayals of their subjects. Neuroscientist V. S. Ramachandran and philosopher William Hirstein have attempted an explanation as to why this might be. They draw on 1950s research by Dutch biologist Nikolaas Tinbergen developing the concept of the supernormal stimulus. Tinbergen looked at the behaviour of herring gull chicks, who peck at the red stripe on their parent's bill to secure food through regurgitation. The chick will peck just as vigorously at a brown stick with a red stripe at the end. What brings the chick into a pecking frenzy though is a stick with three red stripes at the end. It provides a 'super stimulus' of greater intensity than that provided by the actual beak.[33] Interviewed on the BBC series *How Art Made the World*, Ramachandran argues that statues which are simply realistic, like *Kritian Boy*, are boring. We are driven by an instinct to exaggerate.[34] For Ramachandran and Hirstein 'all art is caricature.'[35] Effective statues provide an exaggerated, amplified version of the original. This is not just true of ancient Greece, but a universal imperative.

In *How Art Made the World*, Nigel Spivey takes us back to the Palaeolithic, and to the Venus of Willendorf, an 11-centimetre figurine found during an archaeological dig in 1908 near the village of Willendorf in Austria. This naked female figure is one of many Palaeolithic 'Venus figurines' unearthed across Eurasia. It is anything but realistic. Some body parts, notably the breasts, stomach and thighs, have been enlarged to enormous proportions, while others, including face and arms, are ignored. For Spivey, the figure illustrates Ramachandran and Hirstein's thesis around the imperative of exaggeration. What was exaggerated was culturally specific. In ancient Greece, with its obsession with human bodily perfection, exaggeration surrounded the idealised male form. For Prehistoric hunter-gatherers, eking out a harsh existence and reliant on uncertain sources of food, the physical traits emphasised were around fatness and fertility.[36]

This friction between imitation, the realistic portrayal of the human form, and idealism, exaggerating the qualities important to the time, has recurred throughout the long history of statuary. Accentuation of the positive has usually prevailed. Sculptor Gian Lorenzo Bernini, when discussing his bust of Louis XIV with diarist and art collector Paul Fréart de Chantelou, stressed his emphasis on the beautiful and grand to underscore the nobility of the project. What was to be avoided was 'servitude of imitation'.[37] Bernini, working in the seventeenth century, was the leading sculptor of his age. He sought not realistic portrayal of his subjects but to turn them into gods. According to German art historian Damian Dombrowski, if the central challenge of a bust is that the figure is artificially cut off below the neck, Bernini exploits this to exalt and isolate the head. A curved lower edge of the bust gave the portrait a sway, while in representations such as that of Francesco Barberini the Elder, the breadth of the shoulders is accentuated, giving the body almost the appearance of wings.[38] Most striking is the use of drapery, employed by Bernini in an exaggerated way, creating swirling folds of no evident practical purpose. Rather, in Bernini's 1665 *Portrait of Louis XIV* the folds remove any sense that the body has been artificially cut off. The subject's head is elevated above the mundane concerns of the mortal world.

The bust might also literally be elevated. Chantelou tells us that the bust of Louis XIV was intended to be mounted on a globe raised by representations of virtues and military spoils. Bernini's last work, a *Bust of Christ* sculpted in 1679, was planned on a pedestal held up by two kneeling angels. The ensemble reached a height of three metres, accentuating the immortal status of Christ, elevated above humanity.[39] All these substructures further separated the bust from the realm of ordinary life.

We have noted that what represents ideal sculpture is culturally specific. It follows that the choices of earlier cultures may fail to resonate today. Art critic Jonathan Jones makes this point in relation to the *Apollo Belvedere*, a Roman marble copy of a bronze statue created around 330 BCE by Greek sculptor Leochares. Now in the Vatican Museums, it is a nude statue of the Greek god Apollo, depicted as an archer who has just shot his arrow. The statue, depicting its subject in *contrapposto*, was long admired, including by eighteenth-century champion of neoclassicism Johann Joachim Winckelmann, as a crowning statement of the Greek aesthetic ideal. For Jones, this perfection represents the problem for a modern audience. He writes: 'it was admired two hundred years ago as an image of the absolute rational clarity of Greek civilisation and the perfect harmony of divine beauty. All that bores us stiff nowadays. Who wants perfection?'[40] Ramachandran suggests that realistic statues are similarly boring. But Jones is championing another form of idealistic caricature. He contrasts the modern-day lack of interest in the *Apollo Belvedere* with the popularity of the *Venus de Milo*, another statue famed for its portrayal of classic beauty, this one a Greek marble sculpture probably from the second century BCE, depicting a Greek goddess with a bare torso and drapery covering her lower body. The reason for her continued success, believes Jones, is that the statue has lost its arms. This has rendered it 'an accidental surrealist masterpiece', a statue that is at once 'perfect but imperfect, beautiful but broken.'[41]

Art historian Kirk Savage goes further, arguing that figurative sculpture is obsolete and has been for some time. A statue that is simply realistic offers no more than the 'mere likeness' of a waxwork representation, while a more idealistic approach, such as dressing up modern heroes in the style of sculptures of Greco-Roman antiquity, was never likely to succeed in giving such statues a timeless quality. He concedes that there have been interesting experiments along the way, such as an attempt to combine realism and idealism by pairing realistic portraits of their subject with allegorical sculptures, depicting their qualities or virtues. The results of such endeavours were though by no means to everyone's taste, as demonstrated by the *Boy Scout Commemorative Tribute*, a 1964 artwork in Washington DC by Donald De Lue. It depicts an eager young scout, striding forward with his walking stick. He is dwarfed by two large scantily dressed allegorical figures, representations of American Manhood and Womanhood, or, for Savage, 'a fresh-faced scout leading two Marvel-comic super-allegories.'[42]

Savage laments that, despite the obsolescence of public sculpture, it continues to colonise public spaces, grudgingly accepting that it will live on: 'even if it could never achieve timelessness, traditional sculpture has maintained a niche for itself in a world that feeds on the timely.'[43]

Bulk

Monuments occupy space. They possess mass, a function of their volume and density. Sergei Kruk, exploring monuments built in Latvia during the Soviet occupation, argues that their mass offers additional meanings beyond the actual person or event depicted, for example in depicting stability or movement, change or stasis, speed or slowness. He distinguishes between static and dynamic statues.[44]

Static sculptures have a heavy, solid appearance, standing firmly on a pedestal, conveying stability and certitude. A monument to Lenin in the town of Balvi, the 1973 work of sculptor Juris Mauriņš, depicted a monolithic figure, sculpted from the waist up, the legs lost in a pedestal serving like a podium from which Lenin delivered his powerful oratory. This kind of static sculpture suited the stagnation of the 1970s USSR under Leonid Brezhnev, supporting the discourse of the victory of socialism.

Dynamic sculptures were generated by such devices as maintaining a disproportionately small contact area between sculpture and pedestal, the use of casings of metal plates concealing a hollow carcass, or the employment of cantilever technology. The World War II monument in the town of Valmiera involves two walls faced

PHYSICAL CHARACTERISTICS

with travertine limestone, linked by the bronze figure of a fallen soldier placed as a horizontally attached cantilever, looking for all the world like a football goalkeeper attempting a save. The material used could be relevant here too. A spherical bust in the port town of Ventspils depicted cosmonaut Yuri Gagarin, his face encased by his helmet, its form also intended to suggest the descent vehicle of the spacecraft *Vostok*. The original plan had been to craft the bust in granite, but this was changed to bronze, offering a lighter appearance, a more plausible candidate for space flight. The narrow area of contact between statue and pedestal, the round plinth resembling a launch pad, and two clusters of tall poles behind the helmet/space vessel reinforced the impression of imminent vertical ascent into the cosmos.[45]

Material

A large range of materials has been, and is, used for the crafting of statues: clay, wood, stone, metal, concrete, Lego bricks. Whether in ancient Greece and Rome, Renaissance Italy or during the 'statuemania' of nineteenth-century Europe, two materials however stand out as the choice of patrons and sculptors of outdoor public statues: marble and bronze.

Marble, a metamorphic rock derived from limestone, offers a fine grain, allowing the rendering of intricate detail. It has a slight translucency, deriving from light absorbing a short way beneath the surface until it is refracted in subsurface scattering. This is the quality that can make marble sculptures almost come to life in the hands of the finest sculptors. After initial resistance, the Romans embraced with enthusiasm the Greek tradition of carving in marble. Livy reports a complaint by Cato the Elder about 'far too many people praising and marvelling at the ornaments of Corinth and Athens, and laughing at our terracotta antefixes of the Roman gods.'[46] When Augustus took up the material, 'Greek' marble became mainstream in Rome, such that a statue that would have looked Greek to Cato would have seemed entirely Roman to later generations.[47]

There is, however, a downside to marble. It possesses great compressive but poor tensile strength.[48] It is vulnerable to fracturing. In a standing figure, the ankles are among the danger points for the sculptor. Various strategies have been adopted to provide stabilisation and support for the most vulnerable areas. One is the use of clothing. Long overcoats and flowing dresses descending to the base of the statue increase the amount of marble in contact with the base, strengthening the composition. Consider Thomas Ridgeway Gould's *The West Wind* from the 1870s. It features a young woman, naked from the waist up, turning away from the fierce wind. The sculptor, desiring to portray her as lithe and graceful, has put her on tiptoes, creating minimal contact between the body of the sculpture and the base, greatly increasing its vulnerability. That is mitigated by her skirt. It has a compositional role, billowing out in the wind, but also a structural one. While the skirt is finely sculpted to appear delicate, it is a solid block of marble. The skirt flaps against a tree stump, providing the all-important connection to the base.

That reference to tree stumps brings us to the second strategy to support vulnerable areas of the statue: the deployment of attributes and other ancillary objects, combining compositional and supportive roles. All those tree stumps in marble sculptures may convey symbolic meanings, of a life cut short, or spiritual renewal, but mostly they are there to support the human figure. Weapons and staffs reaching down to the base are another common ruse, as are columns, vases and even dolphins.

Sometimes the sculptor's task is particularly challenging. A standing nude presents a daunting prospect, with no clothing available to support the statue. In the most difficult cases, the sculptor may resort to the deployment of struts, non-compositional masses of marble typically bridging two parts of the statue to stabilise it. The struts tend to be polygonal solids, such as quadrilateral bars with flat surfaces. Importantly, no attempt is made to blend them into the statue: they are clearly alien to the composition. Struts are found in both ancient Greek and especially Roman marble statues. Their unsightly appearance to the modern eye has led some to suggest that struts were used to stabilise a statue during transportation from workshop to destination and were intended to be removed following installation. Art historian Mary Hollinshead disagrees, arguing that removal would have involved a high risk of fracturing, as well as losing the long-term stabilising benefits provided by the struts. She goes further, proposing that admiration for the ingenious sculptor who disguises structural supports through clothing or attributes may just be modern taste. For Roman audiences, the presence of struts might suggest the sculptor's daring and talent in tackling challenging pieces, taking on sculptural forms at the limits of the technical possibilities of the material.[49]

Let us consider one of the most famous nudes of the ancient world: the Aphrodite of Knidos, created by virtuoso sculptor Praxiteles in the fourth century BCE. We know from Pliny that the original was made of marble, but is now lost, so we only have Roman copies to go on. The sculpture featured much daring on the part of the sculptor, and not just in relation to its portrayal of naked female flesh in an era when audiences were more accustomed to statues of naked men than women. Thus, the right arm hangs freely in front of the body. But Praxiteles' daring is mitigated by the use both of embellishing objects and struts. With her left hand, Aphrodite drops her drapery onto an adjacent jug. This has a compositional role, explaining the nudity of the figure by demonstrating that she is preparing to bathe, but also provides a solid pillar of marble, a vertical mass adjacent to the main figure and supporting it. Its solidity is disguised by the appearance of softness of the cloth and the apparent instability of the jug.[50] Additionally, Roman copies of the original generally have either one or two struts connecting Aphrodite's body to the adjacent drapery and jug, further reducing the strain on the marble.[51]

Struts could be tiny. A statue of Dionysus accompanied by a panther found in the submerged nymphaeum of Claudius off Punta Epitaffio has a little strut connecting penis to scrotum; the sculptor evidently concerned about the risks of a severed member.[52]

Marble, while overall durable, as the high quality of antique marble statues demonstrates, is vulnerable to the degrading effects of the acid rain of industrialised countries. As early as 1860, Julia H. Layton was complaining that American marble sculptures were already showing signs of wear not apparent in their ancient counterparts. This observation was a starting point for her call for the use of bronze statuary in preference to marble, for bronze 'apparently embodies the quintessence of immortality, and boldly defies the canker tooth of decay.'[53]

Her championship of bronze would have resonated in ancient Rome, where marble statues, for all their popularity, were less prestigious than bronze, with gilded or silvered bronze the most prized statues of all.[54] Bronze offers strength and ductility, allowing a bronze statue to be fastened to its base with just a small common surface. A bronze dancing satyr found at Pompeii and now in the Naples Museum stands on tiptoes, arms raised aloft.[55] No supporting clothing or tree stumps are necessary.

Bronze has historically however suffered from one major problem. The desirability of the metal. We will encounter examples of bronze statues of the heroes of great victories cast from captured enemy weaponry as a means of underlining the extent of humiliation of the defeated enemy. The reverse is historically also common: at times of crisis, triumphant bronze statues of past leaders can feel an extravagance, finding themselves melted down in favour of weapons and ammunition. Equally, bronze statues can be recast in the image of the leaders of today, rather than those of yesterday. Many bronze originals of famous statues have been lost.

In the case of numerous celebrated Greek bronzes, we have only Roman marble copies to console us. The extent of the struts required to reproduce the more ambitious of these statues is further evidence for many commentators of the superiority of bronze over marble. Take the bronze *Apoxyomenos* sculpted by Lysippos, court sculptor of Alexander the Great, in around 330 BCE. It depicts a naked athlete scraping sweat from his body. According to Pliny the Elder, the statue, which had been installed in Rome around 20 BCE, so entranced the emperor Tiberius that he had it removed from the Baths of Agrippa and placed in his bedroom, until he was shamed into replacing it following heckling in the theatre. A marble copy discovered in Rome in 1849, the *Vatican Apoxyomenos*, required a long strut, now broken off save for two stumps, between the athlete's right thigh and right wrist. Another surviving strut links his torso and left wrist.[56]

Lest all this suggest a subordinate role for marble, struggling to copy innovations in bronze, let us consider a statue found in a ship-

PHYSICAL CHARACTERISTICS

wreck discovered in 1907 off Tunisia. The ship was full of Greek works of art intended for Roman buyers, and some believe might have been part of the spoils of war brought back by Roman general Sulla during his campaigns against King Mithridates between 88 and 84 BCE. The statues include a bronze work bearing the signature of Boethus of Chalcedon, depicting a winged youth supported by a herm, the latter a stylised sculpture involving a head atop a square-based column, left largely unadorned other than the sculpting of the subject's genitalia. Archaeologist Brunilde Ridgway asks why a bronze work requires a herm for support? It has no technical need for it. Here, she concludes, is a likely example of a bronze statue imitating a marble original.[57]

Materials used in the construction of statues might have specific meanings. In ancient Egypt, turquoise was associated with fertility and was sacred to the goddess Hathor. Granodiorite had associations with the god Osiris, with the underworld and with the fertile black lands of the Nile plain.[58] The use of concrete as the construction material for Berlin's Memorial to the Murdered Jews of Europe suggests alienation and impersonality.[59]

Individual statues might incorporate different materials. In Archaic Greece, many female *korai* statues were once adorned with diadems or earrings of a different material to the statue, revealed by the presence of attachment holes. There was a Greek preference for rendering in bronze details on marble statues that in real life would have been made of metal, such as weapons. And some Hellenistic and Roman marble sculptures were enlivened in a rather startling way with the addition of bronze eyelashes.[60]

Colour

When we think of statues in marble or bronze, we tend to think of them as monochrome. This is how they are usually presented in museum galleries and city squares. There is much evidence however that statues across the ancient world were more typically painted colourfully. The use of colour also characterised religious sculptures of the medieval world. The loss of colour from our statues is linked to the priorities and attitudes of the two great Classical revivals:

Renaissance and Neoclassical. It draws from the fact that painted surfaces tend to be less durable than the statue itself, thereby colouring (or more accurately, uncolouring) views around what ancient statuary looked like. In Renaissance Europe, the excavation of ancient sculptures such as the *Apollo Belvedere* and *Laocoön and His Sons* appeared to endorse the opinion that the ancients sculpted in monochrome,[61] reinforcing a focus on form rather than colour. But even those Renaissance sculptors most strongly identified with the crafting of sculptures in single colour were not averse to the production of polychrome figures. The *Santo Spirito Crucifix*, a polychrome wooden sculpture dated to around 1492, has been attributed to Michelangelo, and Donatello employed both painted features and gilding to add realism to his statues.[62]

Neoclassical opinion was more doctrinaire. Sculpture was perceived to be about form. Colour was felt to demean this. It was however during this period that archaeological excavations such as those at Herculaneum and Pompeii were confirming that ancient Greek and Roman sculpture was largely polychrome, challenging an earlier view that while colouring of statues was commonplace in primitive art, it largely ceased during the classical period. The influential German art historian Johann Joachim Winckelmann revised his 1764 *Geschichte der Kunst des Alterthums* for a second edition, published posthumously in 1776, with a new section on 'painted statues.'[63] This did little however to bolster enthusiasm for colour. German philosopher Georg Hegel's *Lectures on Aesthetics* insisted that sculpture 'avails itself not of a painter's colours but only of the spatial forms of the human body'.[64] His compatriot Arthur Schopenhauer too argued that sculpture was form: the addition of colour, as in wax models, produced not an aesthetic experience but simply 'deceptive imitation.'[65]

Research into the colouring of ancient statues has made major advances through scientific techniques such as ultraviolet fluorescence, infrared reflection and raking light, allowing the detection of traces of paint unseen by the naked eye.[66] Coloured plaster casts and other reconstructions have been attempted since the nineteenth century to give modern publics a feel for what ancient statues would have looked like. But extrapolating from fragmentary traces is challenging, and while the monochrome ancient statues seen today are not an accurate representation of how they would once have looked, the suggested reconstructions are so heavily based on conjecture that they cannot be said to be much more 'accurate'.[67]

Complicating matters further, many statues were undoubtedly subject to touching-up or repainting, not necessarily faithful to the original colour scheme. One of the most heavily analysed ancient sculptures showing traces of colour is the statue of Emperor Augustus, crafted from expensive Parian marble, discovered in 1863 in the villa of Livia at Prima Porta, a few kilometres outside Rome. The statue, probably the marble replica of a bronze original, depicts Augustus as a victorious general, his breastplate decorated with deities and the personifications of conquered territories. Gathered around his waist is the cloak or *paludamentum* denoting his rank as emperor. His bare feet and the larger-than-lifesize statue suggest his divine qualities.[68] There are indications on the breastplate of the replacement of a blue colour by a golden one, a retouching probably dating from late Antiquity, corresponding to the changing tastes of the times.[69]

The preciousness of materials like the Parian marble from which the Prima Porta Augustus was cut, prized for its translucence and fine grain, causes continued puzzlement in modern reassessments: why use such fine material only to cover it in paint? Part of the answer is probably that some pigments would have penetrated the marble, not simply sitting on it, producing subtle effects in combination with the material. Such would have been the case for the organic red pigment chosen to colour the *paludamentum* of the Prima Porta Augustus.[70] The pigments chosen for prestige projects such as the statue of Augustus, like red cinnabar and Egyptian blue, were themselves expensive and highly prized.[71] And not all the surface of ancient statues may typically have been painted. In the case of the Prima Porta Augustus, research led by Paolo Liverani at the Vatican Museums identified traces of colour on the cloak, details on the breastplate, hair and eyes, but not on the skin or the background of the breastplate.[72] Classical historian Mark Bradley argues that the application of colour to a sculpture is best considered as one of a range of surface treatments, all part of the process of 'finishing' the statue. These also included *ganosis*, the application of a mix of melted wax and olive oil, with the aim both of protecting the marble and bringing out the colours of painted surfaces.[73]

Recognition of the importance of polychromy in ancient sculptures underscores the role of artistic collaboration between sculptor and painter. There is a reference in Pliny the Elder's *Natural History* to a question posed to Praxiteles as to which of his marble works he most valued, to which he replied: '"the ones to which Nikias has set his hand"—so much value did he assign to his colouring of surfaces (*circumlitio*)'.[74]

Bradley has analysed the role of colour in ancient marble sculpture, identifying four central functions. The first was visibility. Complicated reliefs of Imperial Rome, such as the frieze spiralling around Trajan's Column, would have been difficult for the viewer to read. Colour would have brought out key features, such as the purple garments of the emperor. The reliefs told a political message: colour would have spelled this out clearly for the viewer.[75] The second function was 'finish'. For Bradley, 'an ancient statue without colour...is like a mannequin without clothes.'[76] To ancient sensibilities, colour would have completed the work. The third was realism. Our grounding in Neoclassical aesthetics leads us to accept monochrome white marble figures: yet this fails to square with a search for realism; an attempt to produce 'living' images. This was an important consideration in Qin dynasty China as well as ancient Greece and Rome: the famous terracotta army buried with emperor Qin Shi Huang was originally painted in a lifelike way and carried real weapons.[77] The reality sought in the ancient world was admittedly sometimes a stereotyped rather than naturalistic one: a world of suntanned warriors, pale ladies and red-headed barbarians from the north.[78] Bradley describes the fourth function as '*trompe l'oeil*', an attempt to disguise the artificial quality of the statue and bring it into the world of the viewer. We will look later at how statues might be brought to life: an important consideration in the case of cult statues, a home for the gods they represented. In the ancient world, gods and heroes both resembled mortal humans and were different from them. Their statues were accordingly both lifelike and unnaturalistic. They might be larger-than-life, standing out further through particularly bold colours.[79]

PHYSICAL CHARACTERISTICS

Colour was not only achieved through artificial polychromy, applying pigment to a diverse range of materials. Natural polychromy was also adopted, utilising the chromatic properties of the materials themselves, including through inlays.[80] In early Imperial Rome, polychrome marbles were used to produce different colours: whiter marbles for the skin, darker ones for the hair.[81] Fine variations in material could be significant. Anna Garnett of the British Museum, discussing the colossal statue of Ramesses II brought to the museum in 1818, notes that the block from which the statue was cut incorporates an area of fine pink granite with a larger area of darker granodiorite. This bichrome structure was exploited, with the head cut from the pinker granite and the rest of the body from the granodiorite, offering a pleasing distinction. Since the statue would have been painted in whole or in part, it is not clear however the extent to which this distinction would have been perceptible in the finished product.[82]

Gilding

Gilding was also frequently used in the ancient world to highlight specific features of marble sculptures such as metal accoutrements, and to focus the eye on heroic figures in complex compositions.[83] What though of statues gilded in their entirety?

Let us consider the tradition of golden statues of Buddha, a practice that has much to do with the value placed on that metal in Buddhism. The ancient Dirgha Agama text describes the Buddha physically as 'golden shining like pure gold'.[84] Through its purity and rarity, gilding with gold adds to the status of a Buddha statue. Scholars Xiangyu Liu and Xinyi Huang trace the birth of gilded statues of Buddha to first-century Gandhara.[85] The tradition spread eastwards to China. Here, it influenced the development of Chinese gold craft. Liu and Huang note that two methods of gilding Buddha statues were practiced in China. Both used existing technologies, used to provide items for wealthier noble families, often utensils and other small artefacts. Buddhist temples rapidly took over as the chief customer.

The first method was mercury gilding. Gold leaf was mixed at high temperatures with molten mercury, producing gold amalgam.

This was coated on metal objects. When heated further, the mercury evaporated, leaving the gold on the surface. The second was gold leaf gilding. This required the boiling of adhesive materials, which were spread over the surface of the statue, to which pieces of gold leaf were then added. Overall, the method of gold leaf gilding was more satisfactory, but given the enormous demand for gilded statues, it required the mass production of gold leaf. This in turn stimulated technological advances such as the invention of Wujin paper as the liner material, allowing the simultaneous hammering of numerous layers of gold leaf. Buddha statues gilded with gold were often very large. Built in 1152, the Tongnan Buddha in Chongqing is for example 18.43 metres high, gilded with 369,000 pieces of gold leaf.[86]

The enormous demand for gold leaf from the temples could feel extravagant during straitened economic times. Following the An Lushan Rebellion between 755 and 763, the victorious Tang dynasty was weakened by conflict, and the imperial court ordered that gilded Buddha statues be stripped of their gold, to be handed over to the State Treasury. Similarly, in 1040, at the beginning of the Song dynasty, a prohibition was placed on Buddha statues decorated with gold leaf.

Accoutrements

We have explored the use of accoutrements such as tree stumps and trailing items of clothing as strengthening devices to counter the vulnerabilities of marble statues. But the addition of objects and other accoutrements to statues is often less to do with helping physically to stabilise the composition than to enliven it, enabling the viewer correctly to identify its subject through the depiction of items with which they are associated, and in a more symbolic way hinting at qualities associated with the subject. The incorporation of an owl into the composition, for example, might suggest the subject's wisdom, a device with its roots in portrayals of Athena, Greek goddess of wisdom, with her sacred owl.

In some cases, features that might typically be expected to be depicted as part of a realistic portrayal of the subject served a more symbolic role. Thus, classical art expert Peter Stewart notes that the head and body of Roman portrait statues typically performed different functions. The head represented the person being commemorated, would be modelled to reflect their features, and was the most important element of the statue. The body on the other hand was typically standardised, serving to provide an indication of the subject's social role.[87]

The Equestrian Statue

In the world of statuary, one accoutrement stands out: a horse. Equestrian statues have been built since ancient times. The eccentric British sixties band the Bonzo Dog Doo-Dah Band, whose oeuvre fell somewhere between pop, jazz and music hall, wrote a song about them. *The Equestrian Statue* comes across as an upbeat rejoinder to Robert Musil: not for them an invisible future for the monument, but a sight guaranteed to brighten up the day of all who pass by, causing little old ladies to exclaim 'well, I declare!' Which is optimistic as regards the enduring impact of equestrian statues but doesn't dent the immediate point that there are a goodly number of the things. An energetic Dutchman named Kees van Tilburg set up an online inventory of equestrian statues, identifying 1,257 originals and another 159 copies around the world by May 2021.[88]

Placing the subject of the statue on a horse emphasised their status. In ancient Rome, a seated statue tended to suggest a higher rank than a standing one, with an equestrian statue more prestigious still. Top of the monumental pecking order was a victorious leader portrayed in a triumphal chariot.[89] Roman equestrian statues were usually of emperors. The one Roman bronze equestrian statue to have survived largely intact to the present day, serving as an inspiration for the genre in later times, is the statue of Marcus Aurelius in Rome, erected around 175 CE, probably owing its survival to a misidentification with Constantine the Great.[90] The statue oozes power. The emperor is depicted larger than life-sized, his right arm raised as he prepares calmly to address his troops. It portrays a leader who is victorious, conquering, in control and athletic. No wonder that such depiction appealed to rulers.

Renaissance sculptor Donatello drew extensively from classical sculpture, and in 1453 completed the equestrian statue of *condottiero*

Erasmo da Narni, better known as 'Gattamelata' (honeyed-cat), that today stands in the Piazza del Santo in Padua. The statue draws inspiration from that of Marcus Aurelius, like the earlier statue portraying a rider in control and in triumph. Unlike Marcus Aurelius, who rather dominates his horse, Gattemelata is depicted life-sized in relation to the horse, Donatello giving him control and power by the attention to detail on the rider's features while the horse is more generalised.[91] Gattemelata was not a head of state, but a military leader. He carries a baton in his left hand, a statuary attribute depicting military command, and has a sword of considerable length at his side. Equestrian statues have continued to be largely reserved for heads of state or military commanders.

One oft-repeated story has it that an equestrian statue whose horse has both front legs raised suggests that the rider died heroically in battle; one leg raised is suggestive of serious battle wounds, while all four legs on the ground characterises a rider dying of natural causes. This appears to be an urban myth. It is though supported to a certain degree by the inclination of sculptors to depict military leaders known for their exploits in battle in more active poses, redolent of the dangers of conflict, while equestrian statues of rulers and other subjects less familiar with the battlefield might better portray stable and secure leadership, for which all four legs of the horse firmly planted on the ground serves nicely.

Saints and Their Symbols

Statues of saints to be found in Roman Catholic and certain other churches are awash with accoutrements, some decidedly unusual. They follow an iconographic tradition that developed when congregations were largely illiterate. The common characteristics and background of many saints raised the challenge of distinguishing one from another, particularly where statues were placed high up, far from the viewer's gaze. Saints must be depicted positively, underscoring their goodness. Martyrs have an idealised youthful beauty, adopt an upright posture, and hold the palm frond of victory over evil.[92] The many saints who were bishops generally sport the robe, mitre, staff and book of their calling. They all therefore tended towards a similar appearance. The solution lay in the deployment of

PHYSICAL CHARACTERISTICS

symbols illustrating their lives, and commonly the manner of their deaths, serving both an identification function and a storytelling one. Symbols underlining a saint's qualities, or the tribulations they endured, also served a devotional role, focusing attention on the example provided by their lives. Thus, to take our bishops, St Ambrose is commonly depicted with a beehive, referencing a story that, as an infant, a swarm of bees entered and then left his mouth, foretelling his eloquence, while St Blaise is identified by steel combs, recalling the manner of his martyrdom.[93]

Statues of St Agatha customarily portray the saint holding a plate on which sit what look like two round puddings. They are breasts. Agatha lived in Catania in Roman Sicily, in the third century. A chaste and pious girl of a noble family, she had consecrated herself to God, taking the ritual of velatio, the red veil worn by consecrated virgins. Alas, in stories of virginal martyrdom, a villain inevitably appears. In this case it takes the form of Quintianus, the Roman Proconsul. He lusted after Agatha, but she summarily rejected his advances. The new Roman emperor Decius ordered his subjects to perform a sacrifice to the gods in honour of the emperor's well-being. The emperor was not big on trust, and for this test of loyalty sacrifices had to be confirmed by a signed and witnessed certificate from a magistrate. Quintianus, knowing Agatha was a Christian, shopped her and brought her before the judge. The outcome of proceedings was never in doubt, since Quintianus was himself the judge. She was duly found guilty.

Her first punishment was to be imprisoned in a brothel run by the brazen Aphrodisia, entrusted with educating Agatha in the art of love. She refused to succumb, and Aphrodisia disgustedly sent her back. Quintianus subjected her to trial, and Agatha bettered him in all reasoned arguments. This did her no good, and she was subjected to some particularly brutal torture involving the removal of her breasts with pliers. Through it all, she retained her faith. She was released to prison, where St Peter came to her in a vision and healed her breasts. Quintianus, becoming both ever more desperate and vindictive, ordered a further torture involving burning over hot coals, clad only in her red veil. Still, she refused to abandon her faith. Back in prison, she died on her own terms, asking the Lord to accept her spirit.

The depictions of St Agatha holding her severed breasts on a plate explain her patronage of breast cancer sufferers and her status as patron saint of wet nurses. This imagery has also resulted in some unexpected patronages. The breasts having a somewhat bell-like appearance, she has become the patron saint of bell founders. Their resemblance to puddings explains why she is also patron saint of bakers. Close to her feast day on 5 February, you can buy in pastry shops around Catania a variant of the Sicilian cassata, known as a Cassatella di Sant'Agata. This is a domed pastry covered in white icing with a cherry on top. A sweet representation of the severed breast of a saint.

St Agatha is also patron saint of Catania, credited with preventing numerous lava flows on the erupting Mount Etna from reaching the city over the centuries, most recently in 1886, stopping the oncoming lava in its tracks when her veil was placed in its path. Almost every place in the city linked to the trials and tortures of St Agatha is marked with a church. You will find Sant'Agata la Veteri, where she was put on trial, Sant'Agata al Carcere, where she was held prisoner, and Sant'Agata alla Fornace, where she was burnt over coals.

The importance of St Agatha to the people and city of Catania means that her representation by means of the standard attributes neither always suffices nor is always necessary. They know their saint. Her portrayal holding her severed breasts on a plate is a downbeat image, unsuitable for all occasions. The statue of St Agatha in the underground chapel of the church of Sant'Agata al Carcere, said to be the dungeon where she was kept, depicts a triumphant saint, no evidence of torture present. I stopped at G. La Rosa, purveyors of religious artefacts, conveniently close to the cathedral in Catania. The shop was stuffed with saints, crucified Christs, Virgins and nativities. Giuseppe didn't have a St Agatha statuette holding her breasts on a plate. The best-seller here, in the saint's hometown, was an entirely different representation. An opulent one. It showed the enthroned St Agatha, resplendent beneath a crown, wearing jewelled clothing and rings. Two angels sat on her shoulders. This was the processional Agatha, a miniature version of the model of the saint paraded around the city every February, but at other times of the year kept away from sight within the cathedral. The cathedral sou-

PHYSICAL CHARACTERISTICS

venir kiosk also offered only this upbeat image of the city's patron saint: dressed in the opulent garb gifted by a grateful city.

Gimmicks

Amidst a proliferation of public statuary across urban landscapes, there is a desire among sponsors of statues for that little something special to make theirs stand out. How about a statue that is warm to the touch? At the corner of the Royal Dramatic Theatre in Stockholm stands a statue of a lady wrapped up well against the Nordic chill in a puffed jacket. It is Margaretha Krook, a Swedish actress of film and theatre (see fig. 9). It is said that she turned down all offers for a statue in her honour, regarding statues as cold and uninviting things. So, in 2002, the year following her death, the theatre put one up which would be anything but cold. The statue stands at the spot where she would habitually smoke a pre-performance cigarette. She is placed at street level, accessible to the touch of visitors. Her nose and arms bear the golden patination suggestive of frequent rubbing, but the strongest golden hue comes from her jumper across her midriff. The attraction of Margaretha's stomach for passers-by is down to the fact that the statue is heated to 37 degrees year-round. In the depths of winter, a quick hug is a particularly attractive proposition.

Margaretha is not Sweden's only heated statue. Some 200 miles to the north, in the town of Hudiksvall, a life-sized bronze statue was erected in 2016 to honour Bosse Östlin, a stalwart of the Glada Hudik-Teatern, which encourages actors with educational impairments. Östlin was known in life for his love of hugs, and the statue encourages hugging by virtue of the internal heating coils maintaining a warm temperature through the year.

Or perhaps a statue that plays music: perfect to honour a musician or composer? In the Estonian seaside resort of Pärnu, in wooded parkland behind the beach, sits a statue of accordion-playing Raimond Valgre, a composer and musician responsible for some of the best-known popular Estonian songs, who played here in the 1930s. From a secreted speaker his music washes out across the statue, taking the viewer back to those far-off times.

4

PROPRIETARY STATUES

The piercing eyes strike you as you enter the gallery. The glass and calcite inserts placed in the bronze head make for an eerily realistic gaze, staring at the visitor across two millennia. The head is that of Roman emperor Augustus, part of a portrait statue intended as a statement of Roman control. The story of this statue speaks also of the fragility of that control. The head was hacked from its body by the Kushite enemies of Rome and taken to their capital of Meroë where it lay beneath the desert sand until its excavation in 1910. A long journey followed to its present home in the British Museum.

There are more preserved portrait statues of Augustus than any other Roman emperor. With more than two hundred known examples,[1] this owes something to the duration of his rule, and something to the fact that he was succeeded by members of his family, who continued to memorialise Augustus to emphasise the dynastic connection. But mostly, concludes Thorsten Opper, senior curator of the Greek and Roman collection at the British Museum, it was to do with Augustus's recognition of the value of portrait statues as propagandistic tools.

Public statues, like all monuments, are markers, containing information or memoranda. As markers, what they may mark is territory. They provide an indication of ownership, a statement that this is the place of whoever is represented by the marker. They are symbols of proprietorship.

Markers of Empire

The first known public statue of Augustus dates to 43 BCE: a gilded statue on horseback in the centre of Rome. It commemorated

Octavian's, as he was then known, settlement with the senate. Other early statues celebrated Octavian's naval victories over his rival Sextus Pompeius. One showed him standing on a rostral column; another had him in the pose of the sea god Neptune. Following Octavian's defeat of Mark Antony at the Battle of Actium in 31 BCE and consolidation of power, statues depicting Augustus as the victor of battles with political rivals became unnecessarily divisive. In his monumental first-person inscription, *Res Gestae Divi Augusti*, Augustus comments of Rome that 'about eighty silver statues of me on foot or on horse or in chariots had been set up in the city, which I myself removed.'[2]

In their place, new portraits of Augustus appeared, ones that stressed not a ruler defeating his enemies but the leader of the mighty and unified Roman empire. An emphatic turn of the head and furrowed brow stressed dynamism and serious-minded leadership.[3] These portrait statues of Augustus, such as that unfortunately ending its days bereft of a body beneath the sands of Meroë, were supplied to far-flung corners of the Roman empire: markers of the geographical reach of the emperor's power.[4]

Statues of emperors erected in territories under Rome's control were not however simply statements of imperial power: they also said much about local power relationships. Historian Christopher Dickenson has examined statues of Roman emperors in the Southern Peloponnesian city of Messene during the Imperial period. There was a clustering of statues of emperors in dynastic groups. Three bronze statues of Nero were erected in front of the Arsinoe Fountain outside the north-western entrance to the agora. Each was dedicated by a representative of a different prominent local family.[5] The benefactors tried to outdo each other in the strength of expression of their fealty to the emperor and to Rome. Thus, two dedications mention that the benefactors were priests of the cult of the emperor and of the goddess Roma. The Arsinoe Fountain was named after the mother of Asclepius, the ancient Greek god of medicine and a particularly important deity for Messene. The association of statues of Nero with this fountain thereby served to integrate the Roman emperor into the mythological history of the city.[6]

PROPRIETARY STATUES

Colonisation and Statues of Local Figures

First statues hold a particular interest. What inspires the erection of a statue in a place with no previous experience of such monuments? Occupation or colonisation often provide the answer, as a power with a statue-building tradition literally makes its mark on new territories. The British colonisation of India is an example. States such as Travancore in the south were ruled by maharajahs. As guardians of temples filled with representations of deities, the concept of a statue honouring a distinguished earthly personage seemed alien and unnecessary.[7] Lands governed by Muslim rulers had similarly no need of statues perceived as idolatrous. When the British arrived with their statue-building tradition, this spurred Western-minded Indian elites to follow suit, displaying their modernity as fellow members of the statue-building club.

The first statue to be built in Trivandrum, modern day Thiruvananthapuram, capital city of Travancore, and now Kerala, that was neither a statue of a deity nor placed in a temple was unveiled in 1893. The statue honours Sir T. Madhava Rao, a remarkable and modernising administrator. Born into a prominent family, but not a native of Travancore, he began his rise to power as tutor to the local princes. He was appointed Dewan, chief administrator of the state, with the role of supporting the Maharajah, at a challenging time. State coffers were bare and the administration chaotic. Rao set about putting the place in order, a task facilitated in 1860 when the new maharajah, Ayilyam Thirunal, came to the throne, for he had been Rao's pupil. Petty taxes were abolished, state debts cleared, and reforms introduced in education, public health and agriculture. Things went sour in 1872 over allegations of nepotism around Rao, and when the maharajah failed to give his former teacher his full support he left for Madras, to bring his able brain to the administration of other Indian states. But Ayilyam Thirunal did grant him a pension, land and a palace, and Rao retained both links with Travancore and relatives with prominent positions in the state.

As Rao's sixtieth birthday approached in 1887, an auspicious anniversary for Hindus, a committee was formed, in which one of his relatives played a leading part, to raise funds for a statue to the former dewan. The proposal was controversial. Some locals saw little to celebrate in an elite Brahmin administrator from outside the state. The project limped along, but in April 1891 something happened which reduced the controversies around it. This would have been happy news for Rao if it were not for the fact that the event in question was his own death. With the former dewan no longer alive, he was better able to serve as a unifying figure for the state, his statue a testimony to the modernity and vision of Travancore as a whole.

The statue was made in England, the work of Édouard Lantéri, a Frenchman resident in that country and professor of sculpture at the Royal College of Arts, with assistance from local artist Raja Ravi Varma, whose painting of Rao its pose evokes. It is a statue in the British tradition. As historian Robin Jeffrey puts it, the statue offered a message to the British that India too had its modernising statesmen.[8] It stands today in a prominent position opposite the Secretariat building in Trivandrum Rao helped to build. It gives the area its popular name of 'Statue Junction', a focal point within the city. But if the statue is well-known today as a landmark, it is not much noticed as a statue of a specific personage. Rao today does not seem a controversial figure, but nor is he an especially revered one. Musil's cloak of invisibility has descended upon the monument.

Lennart Meri Goes to the Toilet

Airports are functional places. They are weak on distinguishing features. A statue can help, providing both a marker of proprietorship and a means of associating the building with an icon of the host country, often the figure in whose honour the airport is named.

The check-in hall of the Lennart Meri airport in the Estonian capital of Tallinn is enlivened by a larger-than-life silver relief of the country's president through challenging times in the 1990s, as newly reindependent Estonia emerged from the shackles of the Soviet Union. Lennart Meri has a casual, slightly rumpled look, his left hand in his pocket. That's a detail rarely found on statues. The inscription is offered in Estonian and, curiously, though perhaps appropriately for a public figure known for his erudition,

PROPRIETARY STATUES

Latin. It tells us that the airport was renamed in Meri's honour on 29 March 2009.

The political career of Meri, who died in 2006, was entwined with the story of the airport. In March 1997, the president paid a visit to Japan with a business delegation in tow. He asked at a seminar whether his Japanese hosts had any suggestions as to what more Estonia might do to attract overseas investors. In a move that might be considered out of character in this most polite of countries, evidently fuelled by a still remembered horror over his experience of the place, one piped up that the airport toilets might be a good place to start.

Meri was stung into action, and on return held a press conference in the gents' loos in Tallinn airport to demonstrate what needed to change if Estonia was to become a more attractive, and indeed fragrant, country.[9] It is good to report that the press conference evidently had a positive effect. The airport today, though small, is full of good things like a ping-pong table, glass cabinets with a display about Estonian Olympic achievements and, best of all, the Rahva Raamat space. Put together by Estonia's largest booksellers, this has nothing for sale, but offers a haven of comfy chairs, board games and books to read on towering shelves. The latter are topped with cardboard heads of Estonian writers and public figures. These include the bespectacled Lennart Meri. A quotation scythes through the back of his head like an axe: 'The situation is shitty, but this is the fertilizer of our future.' A perfect statement as to how the deplorable state of the loos at Tallinn airport provided the motivation for change. The airport toilets today are fine.

Walt Disney's World

Walt Disney World in Orlando, Florida, is an institution whose founder remains so important to its identity that his name is in its title. It is built around the flamboyant spires of Cinderella's Castle. In front of this spot, the most identifiably Disney location in all of Disney World, is the statue that tells you whose place you are at. Entitled *Partners*, it is as schmaltzy as you knew it was going to be, portraying a beaming smartly-suited Walt Disney holding an equally beaming

Mickey Mouse by the hand (see fig. 10). It depicts Disney World as the joint achievement of one man and his mouse. Walt's right hand is outstretched, while Mickey has his left hand resting against his thigh. Their other hands are clasped in a fashion drawn by sculptor Blaine Gibson from footage of the Disney classic *Fantasia*, when Mickey shakes the hand of conductor Leopold Stokowski. Gibson apparently agonised for hours over how to get a natural-looking grasp between Walt's five-fingered hand and Mickey's four-fingered one.

The statue was installed in 1995, a replica of the first *Partners*, erected equally prominently at Disneyland in California in 1993. There are further copies at Tokyo Disneyland, Disneyland Paris and the Disney Studios in Burbank, each offering a story of partnership symbolising proprietorship. An early design apparently had Mickey holding an ice cream, but this was jettisoned as it gave the composition the air of an elderly man taking his grandson out for an afternoon treat. The design also owes something to a lithograph created by Disney illustrator Charles Boyer in 1981 in honour of Disneyland's 200 millionth guest, also entitled *Partners* and bringing together mouse and creator. There is a quote from Walt on the plinth: 'we believe in our idea: a family park where parents and children could have fun—together.'

During his lifetime, Walt was uninterested in becoming the subject of a commemorative statue. Blaine Gibson sculpted a bust of Walt in 1962 at the instigation of his manager, an initiative that did not however achieve the desired effect, as Walt disliked it. Walt died in 1966: his widow Lillian continued to reject proposals for statues. The pressing case for one came through the corporate history of Disney. When Michael Eisner became Chairman and CEO of the company in 1984, he wanted to increase attendance at the theme parks and, realising that permanent new crowd-pulling attractions would take time to be built, settled for short-term promotions, such as a Circus Fantasy at Disneyland California. These ruined the choreography of the park, blocking the view of Sleeping Beauty Castle from visitors as they walked down Main Street.

Designers Marty Sklar and John Hench felt their new boss was departing from Walt's vision, and alighted on the idea of a statue to occupy the crucial space in front of the castle, preventing the

PROPRIETARY STATUES

deployment of temporary installations and thereby preserving the iconic view. Eisner was persuaded by their pitch that Walt was gradually being forgotten. It was darkly suggested he might go the way of poor Milton Hershey, whose role in the creation of America's favourite chocolate bar is barely remembered. Disney family members were won over too, and the unveiling was set to commemorate Mickey's 65th birthday in 1993. The first *Partners* statue was duly inaugurated on 18 November in Disneyland California. It was all part of 'Mickey's Worldwide Kids' Party', involving 7,000 children from around the globe. A blue curtain surrounded the statue, and after official speeches and the appearance of Disney's Fab Five—Mickey, Minnie, Donald, Goofy and Pluto—the curtain dropped, and more characters appeared.[10]

There is another statue of Walt Disney at Walt Disney World. It was inaugurated in December 2023 at EPCOT, the place originally conceived by Walt as an experimental planned community, a centre for American enterprise and optimism—the Experimental Prototype Community of Tomorrow. After his death, this grand goal was quietly abandoned, replaced with a theme park combining a focus on innovation with a round-the-world exhibition. The statue *Walt the Dreamer* is again located at the iconic heart of the park, in this case in front of the giant golf ball known as Spaceship Earth. The statue depicts Walt at a later stage of his career, more relaxed in manner, with tie and mouse jettisoned. Walt sits, smiling and alone, on a concrete bench, his hands clasped in front of him. The Disney Photo Pass lady has set herself up here, giving you the chance to pose with Walt. We might, she suggests, want to scrumple our hands in an 'I'm so excited I'm getting to meet Walt Disney' pose.

Walt's brother Roy O. Disney also gets a statue at Walt Disney World. Following Walt's death in 1966, Roy postponed his retirement to oversee the completion of Disney World, inaugurating the Magic Kingdom Park in 1971. The Roy Disney statue, *Sharing the Magic*, is a sister piece to *Partners*. It has the same sculptor, Blaine Gibson, and similarly combines man and mouse, in this case Roy and Minnie. Roy sits cross-legged on a bench, with an adoring Minnie squeezed up next to him. They are holding hands, with Roy's underneath Minnie's, apparently in reference to Roy's role in supporting his brother. (Confession time. During my visit to the Magic Kingdom, I missed Roy completely. This was partly down to a ten-year old anxious to get to the Haunted Mansion, and partly because I think they had shifted the statue from Main Street to a side location to accommodate the Christmas tree. Such is the fate of sidekicks everywhere: not to receive quite the reverent treatment of the top stars.)

British Football Discovers Statues

Footballers would have been considered too plebeian a subject matter for statues during nineteenth-century statuemania, with its focus on royals, politicians and military heroes, and in the modernist climate of the early twentieth century there were few figurative statues being erected in Britain. The first British footballer commemorated with a statue was apparently the recently deceased Harold Fleming of Swindon Town FC in 1956. This hardly set a trend: the next football statue, that of Sir Stanley Matthews, did not appear until 1987.[11] Thereafter, the number of statues honouring footballers, managers and club owners has grown at pace. Researchers Christopher Stride, John P. Wilson and Ffion Thomas established the *From Pitch to Plinth* initiative to document them. By June 2011 their number had increased to fifty-two, fifty of these having been added in the previous twenty years.[12] Just over a year later, in August 2012, that figure was up to sixty.[13]

Around three-quarters of Britain's footballing statues are found in or around football stadia, with most of the remainder in the centre of the subject's hometown.[14] The mushrooming number of football statues around stadia is a product of two main factors. First, top-flight football provides an advantageous set of circumstances for the mobilisation and financing of statue projects. They may be funded by the club itself, offering a straightforward route to completion, with the club also the owner of the land. Or they may be fan led, generated by supporters' trusts viewing themselves as the true custodians of the club. These provide a ready organisational structure to take the project forward, and a defined body of potential sponsors, the fans, happy to contribute to fund-raising campaigns. Fan-led campaigns have sometimes engaged the wider group of supporters on key decisions, even including the preferred subject for the statue, as was the case at Bristol City, where the choice fell on striker John Atyeo.[15] Projects may also be instigated by local authorities and funded with public money, though for football-related statues the public sector is a less important source than in most other categories of statuary.[16]

The second factor promoting statues at stadia is to do with the stadia themselves. Large football grounds across the United Kingdom have become ever more homogeneous: 'identikit stadia evoking little memory or tradition.'[17] Arsenal Football Club in North London is a good example. It vacated its traditional home of Highbury in 2006 for a new state-of-the-art stadium, the break from the history and memories of the club accentuated by a sponsorship package that meant the ground would henceforth carry the title of 'Emirates Stadium' rather than a name rooted in the local area.

The fans liked the facilities offered by the new stadium but missed the tradition: they called for its 'Arsenalisation'. The club responded with the installation of a replica of the old stadium's iconic Church End clock on the new one. They also responded with statues. In December 2011, as part of the club's 125th anniversary celebrations, three were unveiled around the stadium. Herbert Chapman, manager of the club from 1925 to 1934, stands proprietorially, arms behind his back, gazing at the clock. Tony Adams, club captain through the 1990s, is depicted arms aloft, celebrating a goal. And striker Thierry Henry is also portrayed in celebration of a goal, but this a more defiant pose, on his knees, fists clenched.[18]

Christopher Stride and his colleagues argue that such statues perform three interrelated functions for the football clubs. The first is around branding through success. Statues serve as reminders of the club's achievements and stature. Success builds support, a fact documented by psychologist Robert Cialdini and his team in a study of student behaviour at (American) football-mad US colleges in the 1970s. They found that, following a victory of the school team, students were more likely to dress in school-identifying clothing and refer to the school's performance with a 'we', as against 'they', than following a defeat.[19] American students, like British football supporters, bask in the reflected glory of their team. The statue of Thierry Henry links Arsenal to an instantly recognisable footballer of global renown, providing a marker of the club's stature.[20]

For Christopher Stride and his colleagues, the Thierry Henry statue is however a 'hollow icon', able to perform multiple functions simultaneously. While to the casual supporter it speaks to the first function, branding through success, for the more ardent Arsenal fan it speaks to the second, an evocation of nostalgia. That diehard fan will recognise Henry's pose as his goal celebration in a 2002 match against London rivals Tottenham Hotspur. The ability of fans to understand the deeper meaning of the statue bolsters their self-image as dedicated Arsenal supporters. The third, related, function is that of building a distinctive visual identity for the club through its heritage.[21] The process of 'Arsenalisation' is delivered. The history of the club is trawled, its heroes standing proprietorially at the entrances to the stadia, welcoming the next generation of fans, and acclimatising them to the club's traditions. The statues are proprietary in the sense of serving as symbols of the greatness of the club, their presence emphasising that the stadium is not just a place to play football but a crucible in which the club's illustrious history is continually reforged.

Sir John Soane is Added to His Collection

Sir John Soane's Museum in London is the product of a juxtaposition of wealth and a quite magnificent battiness. Soane was a successful architect, the Bank of England his most celebrated achievement. His architectural practice was a money-spinner, and he used its proceeds to fund a private museum of considerable ambition. He and his family moved in 1792 to 12 Lincoln's Inn Fields, on the north side of that green rectangle in central London, later purchasing adjacent properties at numbers 13 and 14, demolishing and rebuilding all three to form a combination of family home, architectural practice and museum. The latter, comprising the miscellany of paintings, architectural drawings, sculptures and antiquities collected by Soane over many years, was already open to visitors in Soane's day, though he didn't allow visits when the weather was 'wet or dirty'.

PROPRIETARY STATUES

In 1833, Soane secured a private Act of Parliament to leave his home and collection to the nation, despite the protestations of his son George, who claimed that the Act would leave himself and his family destitute. The Act required a Board of Trustees to give free access to the house on at least two weekdays through April, May and June to 'Amateurs and Students in Painting, Sculpture and Architecture.' The Act requires the property to be kept as it was at the time of Soane's death in 1837, a provision that means the museum today lacks labelling, adding to the sense of a perambulation through a house packed from floor to rafters with assorted stuff.

Soane, the architect, was interested in the layout of artworks, and paid less heed to the showcasing only of items of value, with the result that the precious and the mundane are brought together. There is an eccentricity around the collection, which is shaped by the architect's interests and obsessions. This is nowhere clearer than in the Monk's Parlour, with its dark-panelled walls festooned with medieval sculpture. The room appears to have been designed to satirise the burgeoning public fascination with the Gothic, and employs Soane's alter ego, a fictional medieval monk named Padre Giovanni. Outside the window here is the Monk's Yard, with the fake ruins of the monastery of Padre Giovanni and the tomb of our pious monk. There is a burial here, though not of a monk, or indeed anyone human. Here lies Fanny, 'the faithful companion, the delight, the solace of his leisure hours', as Sir John wrote in his own description of the house.[22] Fanny was truly a Wonder Dog. 'Alas, poor Fanny!', laments Soane.

There are many statues in Sir John's collection. It is unsurprising that amongst them there should be a proprietorial bust of the master of the house. Soane's white marble bust depicts him in the garb of a Roman emperor. The sculptor was his friend Sir Francis Chantrey, and the bust appears to have been obtained in a barter arrangement in return for design work. The sculptor was pleased with the outcome, declaring according to Soane that it was among the finest work he had ever produced, it being impossible to determine whether the bust was that of John Soane or Julius Caesar. On reflection, that last point doesn't necessarily sound like praise.

What is interesting about the bust is its setting, arranged amongst other statuary on a balcony, above which is a domed sunlight, with a prized Egyptian sarcophagus below. Soane's statue is placed on a lion-headed pedestal, either side of which are statuettes of, respectively, Michelangelo and Raphael. These were models for figures made for the painter Sir Thomas Lawrence, gifted after Soane's death by the widow of the sculptor, John Flaxman. The composition associates the work of Flaxman and Chantrey, as well as Lawrence, whose bust sits on a shelf above this grouping. It also places together representatives of the three arts at the heart of the museum—architecture, sculpture and painting. Architecture, represented by Soane, is the most elevated of the three; but then you can't live in a painting or a statue.

Soane's bust then is a proprietary one, but unlike many examples of the genre, it is not placed at the entrance to the museum, welcoming in the visitor, or standing aloof in a prestigious but detached spot. It is right in the thick of things, part of the story. Soane gazes towards a familiar-looking statue of a naked youth with a quiver on his back, his modesty preserved by a leaf, a snake writhing up the tree trunk beside him. It is a cast of the *Apollo Belvedere* in the Vatican, made in 1718 for the earl of Burlington and placed in his villa at Chiswick. It was given to architect John White during later remodelling of the villa, and White passed it on to Soane, who was so pleased with the thing he took down a chunk of the wall to get it into place. Soane the collector has thus become part of his collection, his bust living on for the edification of students of painting, sculpture and architecture.

5

STATUES AND NATIONAL IDENTITY

The inauguration of the Voortrekker Monument near Pretoria in South Africa took place in December 1949, with the white supremacist Nationalist Party in power, as a physical embodiment of the Afrikaners' struggle for self-rule and independence.[1] The bulky granite monument celebrates the Great Trek from 1835, undertaken by Dutch-speaking settlers intent on moving north into the interior of modern-day South Africa beyond the reach of the British administrators of Cape Colony (see fig. 11). Its architect, Gerard Moerdijk, sited it on a small hill south of the capital, the mound serving as a kind of pedestal. The monument was generated by an emerging Afrikaner nationalism, itself serving to fuel that nationalism.[2]

We noted in our introduction that public statues are frequently also monuments, and that the task of a monument is to facilitate remembrance. What the proponents of a statue want us to remember tends to be linked to the achievements of its subject and the values they stand for. In some contexts, from late nineteenth-century statuemania in Europe and North America to statue building efforts of newly independent former colonies, national identity is at the heart of the matter.

In exploring the relationship between statues and the development of national identity it is useful to recall that a nation is, as Benedict Anderson puts it, an 'imagined community'.[3] Statues and monuments help to personify a concept which would otherwise be abstract. At the same time, the historical figure celebrated by the statue tends to become more abstract, a combination of myth and symbol, as history is mined to create illusions of unity.[4] Geographer

Andrew Crampton sees the construction of the Voortrekker Monument not just as part of building an 'imagined community' but more specifically as part of a process of binding memories of the Great Trek into a larger claim by Afrikaners to control of the government, a claim that would provide a source of legitimation for the segregations inflicted during the years of apartheid.[5] The monument's location, directly visible from the parliament, supported the goal of enshrining Afrikaner claims to the right to govern.

French historian Pierre Nora developed the concept of 'memory places', always rendered in the academic literature in the original French, as *'lieux de mémoire'*, presumably because this sounds posher. Nora's starting point is that memory and history are not synonymous, but concepts in opposition to each other. He draws on the principle elaborated by French philosopher Maurice Halbwachs that a society can have a collective memory, living beyond the individual. Memory is socially acquired, refashioned by each successive age for its own purposes.[6] Nora argues that, in the modern era, traditional societies of the sort that served as repositories of collective memory are on the retreat. Such collective memory has been replaced by history. Unlike memory, a living concept in permanent evolution, history is a reconstruction of the past. Nora argues that in the modern era, history has seized memory, creating a form of memory that is archival in nature, seeking to preserve everything, without any sense of what should be remembered. He cites the 300 kilometres of French Social Security archives and the proliferation of oral histories, each requiring an average of thirty-six hours of work for every hour of recording time.[7] The loss of real environments of memory, and let us follow the fashion and put this in French, *milieux de mémoire*, necessitates the generation of *lieux de mémoire*.

These are sites 'where memory crystallises and secretes itself.'[8] They can take many different forms: a commemorative date, a work of literature or, indeed, a figurative statue. They appear, according to Nora, when the great pool of collective memory disappears, as reconstituted objects created by the interplay between memory and history. They require a will to remember. This distinguishes them from simple historical sites. Their purpose is, essentially, 'to stop time, to block the work of forgetting.'[9] As another French historian,

François Hartog, puts it, they present the question as to how the past 'has been taken up again in the present, in order to create a significant past.'[10] *Lieux de mémoire* appear after the memory has already been lost.[11] Statues are not reflections of history; they are reflections of historical memory. And that is contested.[12] Because statues are expensive things to build, they tend to arrive late in the process of developing *lieux de mémoire*, consolidating work already carried out through other media. They are however, or at least are intended to be, highly durable. The ambition behind them is to fix memory long into the future.[13]

Eugenia Allier Montaño, analysing the recent past of Uruguay, argues that, alongside places of memory, we should acknowledge the existence of places of amnesia. These are places that seek to crystallise the forgetting of an unwanted historical event. She gives the example of the Punta Carretas shopping mall in Montevideo, located in the Punta Carretas Penitentiary building, the site of incarceration of political prisoners. While conserving the original prison façade, in transferring the place into a centre of consumerism it has become a place of forgetfulness.[14]

For Canadian historian Michael Ignatieff, statues are 'icons in a cunning, but also self-deceiving process of choosing the past one can bear to remember and consigning the rest—the undignified sorrow, the shameful suffering—to oblivion.'[15] Statues, then, select and deceive. Ignatieff gives the example of the monument to *Mother Motherland* in Kyiv, a 62-metre titanium statue inaugurated in 1981 in the presence of Soviet Communist Party General Secretary Leonid Brezhnev. Initiated by Soviet sculptor Yevgeny Vuchetich, who we met in Volgograd, but largely constructed after his death by Vasyl Borodai, the monumental female figure held aloft a sword and shield, the latter emblazoned with Soviet hammer and sickle, embodying a myth of Soviet identity in a part of the USSR where that unity was always a fiction.

This is but the largest of many deceptions surrounding the statue. A promenade at the monument's base was lined by marble blocks, each inscribed with the name of a major battle of the Great Patriotic War. Leningrad, Stalingrad, Kiev. In this company was placed Novorossiysk, which feels a decidedly junior member of the martial league. Ignatieff links its inclusion to the fact that the young Leonid Brezhnev, officiator at the monument's inauguration, played a minor but exaggerated role in the defence of that city.[16] Following the Russian invasion of Ukraine in 2022, the Soviet emblem was removed from the shield and replaced by the Ukrainian trident, though there was controversy about carrying out this work during wartime. The statue has been rebranded as *Mother Ukraine.*

The commemoration of the heroism of the dead through public memorials owes much to the formation of nation states in the nineteenth century, with the accompanying requirement for new narratives of loyalty and belonging at a national rather than community or regional scale.[17] As markers of national identity, monuments must be defended when the nation comes under threat. The sandbagged monuments of Ukraine became a defining image of Ukrainian resistance to the Russian invasion commenced on 24 February 2022. Their protection underlines the importance of the monuments in representing a Ukrainian national memory and identity, underlining too that it is these very elements that are under attack. The occupation of territories by Russian forces might be accompanied by a change of statues, providing new ideological markers. Or more typically, bringing back old ones. Thus, the occupying authorities in Melitopol in November 2022 reinstalled a statue of Lenin taken down by the municipal authorities in 2015.[18]

National Identity and Origin Myths

Origin myths are frequently a central component of nationalism, with origins viewed as golden ages.[19] Some nations look back to a pre-national ethnic group, and their statuary evokes these forebears. The *Hermannsdenkmal* stands on a hill in the Teutoburger Wald area of Germany. Built between 1838 and 1875 on the initiative of artist and sculptor Ernst von Bandel, it is a large statue, almost 25 metres in height, of a chieftain of the Cherusci people named Arminius, known in German as Hermann. It stands on a pedestal in the shape of a round Classical temple, giving the monument an overall height of more than 50 metres. Arminius led an alliance of Germanic tribes in an ambush of his former Roman allies in the Battle of the

STATUES AND NATIONAL IDENTITY

Teutoburg Forest in 9 CE. Their victory limited the Roman advance into modern-day Germany. For nineteenth-century nationalists calling for German rulers to unite, Arminius provided the perfect role model. However, construction of the monument proceeded sluggishly until the creation of the new German Empire following victory in the Franco-Prussian War of 1870–71, after which it captured the militaristic nationalistic spirit of the time. It was inaugurated in 1875 in the presence of the emperor, Wilhelm I.

Jean-Baptiste Jules Bernadotte was a military leader of the Napoleonic wars; a Marshal of the Empire who helped secure the French victory at Austerlitz. His wife, Désirée Clary, was a former fiancée of Napoleon. Jean-Baptiste's career changed dramatically in 1810 when he was elected heir-presumptive to the Swedish royal family, addressing the awkwardness that King Karl XIII lacked children. He owed his elevation to one Baron Carl Otto Mörner, a lieutenant in the Uppland Regiment, who simply offered Bernadotte the job, was promptly arrested by the Swedish government for his gall, but then, fortuitously for his own prospects, found his idea gaining favour. A successful military leader was exactly the ruler Sweden yearned for, reeling from the loss of Finland to the Russian Empire in 1809. And he delivered. Bernadotte gave himself the more regally Swedish-sounding name Karl Johan, and as regent and head of the Swedish armed forces busied himself countering an unprovoked French attack on Swedish Pomerania, following that up with the defeat of the Danish army and securing of Norway for Sweden. He ascended the throne in 1818 as Karl XIV Johan, presiding over a prosperous Sweden until his death in 1844 at the age of 81.

Karl turned to mythology to evoke a magnificent Swedish past as a means both of reinforcing military success in restoring the country's shattered self-image and cementing his place in that glorious story.[20] During his career as a Napoleonic general, Karl had been well aware of the way the French leader, like the revolutionary government before him, used the Louvre Museum as a means of legitimising the regime. He set about doing something similar in Sweden, establishing the world's first National Portrait Gallery at Gripsholm Castle and planning an art gallery in the grounds of his summer palace at Rosendal on the edge of Stockholm.

VOICES IN STONE

As the centrepiece of the art gallery, a rotunda was planned, which was to feature five larger-than-life marble sculptures commissioned from sculptors Niklas Byström and Bernt Fogelberg. Four of these depicted Karl's immediate predecessors, whose names followed the easy-to-remember sequence of Karl X, Karl XI, Karl XII and his adoptive father Karl XIII, the new king's choice of name placing him into this sequence. The statues of kings were to surround one of Norse god Odin, produced at the Rome studio of Bernt Fogelberg.

Odin fitted Karl's purposes perfectly. In the sagas, he had been a successful warrior, invited by the ailing and childless King Gylfe to Sweden to be king, all neatly matching Karl's career as a former military leader brought to Sweden to rule.[21] Fogelberg's statue of Odin arrived in Sweden in 1831. Fogelberg, steeped from his Rome studios in the classical tradition, based the head of the Norse king on the hirsute ancient Roman bust of Jupiter found in the eighteenth century at Otricoli, now in the Vatican Museum. This is supplemented by numerous references to Norse mythology, from the two ravens sitting on Odin's helmet to his peaked boots. He holds a spear and shield, his countenance calm.

Karl's plans for an art gallery at Rosendal never materialised, probably overtaken by the approval of a new Nationalmuseum, and it is there that the sculpture now stands. It has been joined by two later commissions delivered by Fogelberg, though these arrived from Rome only in 1845, a year after the king's death. The first depicts Thor, bare-chested, a fur around his waist, slinging a mighty hammer over his shoulders and clearly a fighter not to be trifled with, a sculpture that has echoes of classical portrayals of Roman demi-god Hercules. The second is different in character. It is Balder, the son of Odin and the wise god of light. He is depicted as a youth, holding no weapons, stretching his arms out in an open gesture of benediction, palms forward. His gown has slipped, exposing his bare chest. He need not fear attack: the natural world has sworn an oath to protect him. The broken arrows and sword at his feet are evidence of its effectiveness.

The invocation of Norse mythology allowed Karl to contrast his rule with the focus of the French Empire on ancient Greece and

STATUES AND NATIONAL IDENTITY

Rome. The Norse gods served well to bind the kingdoms of Sweden and Norway together,[22] and in Odin, Karl found the perfect means of weaving his own background as an outsider brought to Sweden to rule into the story of Swedish greatness.

National Identity and War

War provides another important source of nationalist heroes and imagery. Historian Helke Rausch has explored the deployment of statues in Germany to promote the concept of a nation emerging from war as a legitimising myth of late nineteenth-century nationalism.[23] Germany was the victor of the 1870–71 war with France, and the new memorial landscape of Berlin exploited the propagandistic idea of the emergence of the German nation from the glorious success of that war and the 'wars of unification' that had preceded it. The *Siegessäule*, a victory column erected in 1873, decorated with mosaic illustrations of these wars, expressed this explicitly. Relevant too was an outbreak of mostly equestrian statues of Prussian monarchs erected across Germany. The monarchs themselves attended some of the unveiling ceremonies, sporting full military uniform. The symbolism here was of great monarchs building national unity through war. For Rausch, this interpretation sidelined ordinary people, who were not perceived as participants in the project other than as members of the armed forces.

In 1880, the year following the death of its subject, a statue of Field Marshal Friedrich Graf von Wrangel was installed in Berlin. He was portrayed in uniform, wielding the baton of a marshal. Wrangel was known both for his successes in wars abroad and his role in defending the Prussian throne during the 1848 revolution, whose suppression, notes Rausch, was thereby defined as a necessary event in maintaining a path towards nation-building success. Alternative scenarios under which a successful revolution in 1848 might have built a more democratic and federal Germany, rather than a militaristic Prussian-dominated one, were not entertained.[24]

The conception of warfare underpinned by the late nineteenth-century monuments in Berlin was based around heroic figures. The emergence of total warfare with the Great War of 1914–18 would require a new symbolic language in the construction of monuments dedicated to the experience of war, one that focused on bereavement and on coming to terms with mass death, rather than simply celebrating the heroism of military leaders.[25] We will explore the implications of that development in the next chapter.

Heroic Defeat and the Construction of National Identity

Building national identity through statues and monuments is not just about commemoration of glorious victories. Defeats can work just as well; serving to emphasise the shared suffering of the community, and survival of the nation despite the humiliation endured.[26] Researcher in ideological conflict Steven Mock argues that symbols of defeat perform a particularly useful function in both serving to glorify the past and necessitating the destruction of that past in constructing an effective modern society.[27]

Glorious sacrifice is ideal here. For Mock, this typically involves an individual presented as a symbolic representative of the nation, who consciously chooses the path of martyrdom, but fights valiantly, is typically betrayed by a member of the community, to be killed by the enemy force comprising the community's age-old opponents. These traditional opponents are themselves subsequently killed or conquered, the story ending with an assertion of the spiritual indestructibility of the hero and nation.[28]

In the shadow of the Sugar Loaf in Rio de Janeiro, ignored by tourists making a beeline for the cable cars taking them up the iconic mountain, stands the *Monument to the Heroes of Laguna and Dourados*, centred on a column topped by an allegory of Glory, a series of statues and reliefs at its base (see fig. 12). The monument was first mooted in 1920, though inaugurated only in 1938. It describes two episodes of the 1864–70 war between Paraguay and the Triple Alliance of Argentina, Brazil and Uruguay. While the war was overall a resounding defeat for Paraguay, the episodes commemorated on the monument were not glorious Brazilian victories but glorious defeats.

They are linked to Paraguay's Mato Grosso campaign in the first part of the war, when Paraguay invaded that Brazilian province. Dourados was a frontier post guarded by Lieutenant Antônio João

Ribeiro with fifteen men. Facing a much larger Paraguayan force, Antônio João evacuated the civilians at the post, and with his men fought to the end, sacrificing themselves for their homeland. Brazil sent an expeditionary force to fight the Paraguayans in Mato Grosso. Under the command of Colonel Carlos de Morais Camisão, they reached Laguna, from where, faced by a larger Paraguayan force, they had to retreat. Assailed by Paraguayan bullets and riven by hunger and disease, many retreating Brazilian troops, including Camisão, did not survive.

A statue of Antônio João at the front of the monument depicts the lieutenant in the act of being shot, his arms stretched out to his sides in a pose evoking the crucifixion. The other two figures honoured with a statue are depicted in a calmer, seated pose. One is Colonel Camisão, in his uniform, the other the more rustic figure of José Francisco Lopes, known as Guia Lopes, or Lopes the Guide, who helped the Brazilian troops navigate their heroic retreat. The inclusion of Lopes, pictured wearing a hat marking him out as a peasant of the Brazilian outback, or *sertão*, has much to do with the political goals of Brazil's leaders at the time of the monument's finalisation. This was the period known as the Estado Novo, the new state, of President Getúlio Vargas, a project emphasising the creation of a distinctive Brazilian identity through racial miscegenation, engaging the humble rural dweller as much as urban elite. Lopes, with his loyalty, courage and humility, a simple man of the interior, perfectly symbolised that project.[29]

Another figure represented on the monument makes this point even more clearly. Between the three statues are reliefs depicting the harrowing retreat from Laguna. On one of these, a portrayal of the laborious transportation on stretchers of those sick with cholera, is a bare-breasted female figure. This is Ana Mamuda, the 'angel of charity', the black wife of one of the soldiers, who helped care for the sick. It is said she used her clothing to fashion bandages, providing the sculptor with the excuse to display a little nudity. The tale of Ana Mamuda suited the agenda of the Vargas government in highlighting racial integration in the new Brazil, offering a message that whatever your skin colour or social background, you can become a hero through bravery, self-sacrifice and commitment.[30]

Having languished for years, the project was completed with the support of the Minister of War, General Eurico Gaspar Dutra, whose father had fought in the Mato Grosso campaign. The monument played a role in constructing the identity of both the Brazilian armed forces and the nation itself. The retreat from Laguna and the heroic, doomed, defence of Dourados demonstrated the values of courage and self-sacrifice in the service of the nation looked for in an army, while highlighting failures such as a lack of adequate preparation that a modernising army must overcome. Beneath the monument is a crypt, containing the mortal remains of the heroes of the retreat, giving the monument a funerary character and allowing for a collective national mourning for the martyrdom willingly embraced in the cause of the nation.[31]

For France, the war of 1870–71 with Germany represented a traumatic defeat, resulting in the collapse of its Imperial government and the rise of republicanism. While the memorialisation of war took place therefore in an entirely different context to that in Germany, the experience of the 1870–71 conflict was also used in building national identity. In August 1883, the monument *Défense de Paris en 1870* was unveiled. It is based around three figures. In the centre stands an allegory of Paris, holding a sword. At her feet, a wounded soldier desperately defends the tricolour. Behind, an emaciated girl represents the privations endured by local people during the German siege. The monument presents a narrative of gallant French resistance, ended only by the material shortages suffered by the besieged people. Helke Rausch shows that this narrative, propounded by republican backers of the monument, was challenged both from the political left and right, the former favouring a revolutionary interpretation of events, the latter attached to a Bonapartist ideal of the French nation.[32]

Rausch's study of monuments constructed in late-nineteenth century Paris however suggests that narratives of heroic defeat were used only to a limited extent. The major example, the Défense monument, was put up in a peripheral location in the suburb of Courbevoie. A challenge for France in the exhortation of heroic defeat in the war of 1870–71 was that, unlike the case of Paraguay for the Brazilians, the Germans had not had their come-uppance.

They remained the victors. Other nation-building strategies around war were therefore deployed. One was the erection of statues to painters known for their military subjects. A bust of Denis-Auguste Raffet was put up in 1893 near the Pont des Arts. A tambour-major was depicted on the column supporting the bust, a reference to a Raffet painting with such a figure beating his drum across a battlefield to reawaken fallen soldiers to reap their revenge against French enemies.[33] While there is a whiff here of heroism in defeat, erecting statues of painters avoided any need to refer explicitly to that defeat, instead projecting a more generalised appreciation of France's military past.

Another strategy was to commemorate the successes of French colonial expansion, and it is to this theme we now turn.

National Identity and Colonialism

In 1898 a bust was erected to French expedition leader Francis Garnier, its plinth decorated with allegories representing the Asian rivers he had explored. A proposal more than twenty years earlier for a statue to Garnier had been rejected on the grounds that Garnier brought disaster upon himself by his unauthorised capture of Hanoi, leading to his murder by Chinese rebels in an act of revenge. By the 1890s, the assessment of French colonial policy in Indochina was more upbeat, and a statue was now possible, reflecting a republican view of the central importance of colonial policy, which could be invoked to gloss over the memories of military failure in 1870–71.[34]

The use of colonialism and imperialism in building national identity is also seen in late nineteenth-century Britain. Helke Rausch notes that there had been many statue-building projects in Britain following victory over France in 1815, for example Nelson's Column in Trafalgar Square and numerous statues of the Duke of Wellington. But these projects frequently proceeded slowly over a long time period, reflecting in Rausch's view the fact that the narrative of a Britain constructed as a Protestant, anti-French, anti-revolutionary nation had lost its power by mid-century.[35] Another narrative was needed, found in the proposal that British greatness rested no longer with wars and enemies in Europe but on its mighty colonial expansion. A new set of heroes was called for.

One was found in Sir Bartle Frere, commemorated in 1888 with a statue in Victoria Embankment Gardens in central London. The Prince of Wales himself headed the monument committee and spoke at the unveiling. Rausch argues that the monument reflects the aggressive imperial policy of the Conservative government of the Marquis of Salisbury.[36] This required some editing of Frere's career, which was far from uniformly glorious, particularly as the first High Commissioner of South Africa, when he was responsible for an assault on the Transvaal, prompting a war in which Britain failed to bring the Boer State under its control.

A nearby monument to Major General Sir Charles Gordon, also unveiled in 1888, has a different emphasis. The cult of Gordon was built around his heroic death at Khartoum, glossing over the fact that his attempt to recapture the city had involved his failure to stick to orders to coordinate troop withdrawals. Sculpted by Hamo Thornycroft, the statue depicts Gordon in uniform, but without a helmet and holding not weapons but a book, captured at a moment of contemplation. The statue is less about military aggression than a Christian morality, in which heroes such as Gordon were pursuing a civilising mission.[37]

The public reception of these monuments frequently ascribed different meanings to them than those intended by their champions. A case in point was the inauguration in 1895 in the borough of Knightsbridge (a place name managing the considerable feat of six consecutive consonants) of an equestrian statue of Field Marshal Lord Strathnairn. While speeches at its inauguration majored on Strathnairn's military and diplomatic triumphs in India, Syria and South Africa, the British press focused on his role in suppressing uprisings in Ireland to make contemporary political points.

New Heroes for a New State

The selection of suitable heroes to represent a newly ascendant order can prove a challenging and contested business, the subject of jostling between rival interest groups and political factions. The emergence of independent India from British colonialism provides a good example. Prime Minister Jawaharlal Nehru did not much care for the cult of personalities; British officials reported his concern that Indians might awake to find their 'address was now Gandhi Street, Gandhinagar.'[38] While other senior Indian politicians were keener on new statues to replace those of colonial rulers, there was little consensus around the most deserving subjects. Some made the case for B. R. Ambedkar, social reformer, chair of the committee drafting the Indian Constitution and campaigner against the discriminations of the caste system. But such campaigning did not endear him to others, and nor did his conversion to Buddhism. Others favoured more martial figures like Subhas Chandra Bose, leader of the Indian National Army during World War II, but his willingness to forge alliances with Nazi Germany and Imperial Japan was criticised by others. As we shall see later, a lack of consensus around the personalities to monumentalise to best reflect the values of independent India was one reason colonial-era statues lingered on for years after independence.[39]

Historian Robin Jeffrey has investigated a local-level example of the way jostling between political factions influenced the choice of subjects for new statues in the southern city of Trivandrum.[40] Opponents of the Chief Minister, Pattom Thanu Pillai, wanted to immortalise K. Ramakrishna Pillai, a journalist banished from the state in 1910 for his writings against the then dewan. Ramakrishna Pillai died young while in exile. He had published a biography of Marx, giving him impeccable credentials with the left and those opposed to retention of the remnants of the caste system. Ramakrishna Pillai's backers campaigned for his remains, or whatever could be found of them, to be brought from his place of exile to Trivandrum. The Pattom Thanu Pillai government refused to grant land for the statue, not wishing to provoke the ire of the palace. The affair was among the controversies leading to the Pillai government's fall in October 1948. Its departure paved the way for the construction of the statue, whose foundation stone was laid in September 1949 in front of an appreciable crowd. It took until 1957 and the election of a Communist government in the state to complete it. The result was a modest bust, portraying him as a besuited newspaper editor. Indeed, it is tempting to argue that the statue's promoters were more interested in using the business to bring down the Pattom Thanu Pillai government than in building the thing.

Non-Communist groups wanted a different hero, one who was not a symbol of desire to overthrow the social order. In 1956, under the lead of the then chief minister, from the Congress Party, they alighted on their hero, Velu Thampi, an aristocratic figure who served as dewan from 1804 to 1809, rebelled against British domination, and committed suicide when that rebellion failed. Thampi combined two essential qualities for his champions. He was patriotic—associated with resistance to foreign rule, thus suiting a nationalistic agenda. And as a former dewan, and a representative of a privileged Hindu caste, he represented the preservation of the established order. The Velu Thampi statue also took years to materialise, finally delivered in 1965 with a Congress government again at the helm. The statue, which stands within the Secretariat compound, wields a sword in patriotic rebellion.

Latvia's Freedom Monument

The role of statues in constructing and consolidating national identity can however change over time. A column rising 42 metres, topped with a female figure holding up three golden stars, Latvia's Freedom Monument occupies a central location in the capital city of Rīga. The monument, unveiled in 1935, had its origins in proposals for a war memorial to honour Latvians who died both during World War I and the war of independence that followed. Architect Eižens Laube was an early proponent, suggesting an obelisk on the site, once host to the equestrian statue of Peter the Great we met in an earlier chapter. Following criticism that Laube's proposed monument was rather dull, the government set up a contest. The jury failed to agree, but at a further attempt in 1929 the commission was awarded to sculptor Kārlis Zāle.

The imagery of Zāle's monument, centred on the statue of Freedom holding up stars representing Latvia's historic regions of Kurzeme, Vidzeme and Latgale, focuses less on those killed than what they had been fighting for: the creation of a free and indepen-

STATUES AND NATIONAL IDENTITY

dent Latvia. The inscription on the base, *Tēvzemei un Brīvībai* ('For Fatherland and Freedom'), is a quotation from Latvian writer Kārlis Skalbe. The sculptural compositions around the base seek to build a collective identity of the young nation, drawing on both origin myths and war. Red granite compositions at the corners of the monument highlight the family, labour, intellectual work and 'guarding the fatherland': the latter featuring two Latvian soldiers in the uniforms of the time flanking a soldier in medieval attire, his arms resting on a great sword. Travertine panels between these bear two reliefs; one depicting the 1905 uprising against the Tsarist authorities, the other the battle against the West Russian Volunteer Army of Pavel Bermondt-Avalov in the complicated events of 1919 through which Latvia established its independence.

Above these are four further sculptural groups in grey granite. Mother Latvia, in traditional dress and holding a sword, stands proud at the front of the monument. At the back, the 'chain-breakers' are casting off the shackles of subjugation. On the sides of the monument are two figures associated with Latvian folklore. Lācplēsis, the furry-eared heroic 'bear-slayer', wrestles a bear with his bare hands. And Vaidelotis, a pagan priest appearing in the *Lācplēsis* epic to offer a message of national awakening, holds the *kokle*, a traditional Latvian instrument. These iconic figures suggest, respectively, physical and spiritual strength.

One notable feature of the imagery on the statue is the recency of the events depicted. Given Latvia's long history of occupation by foreign powers, the events of emerging nationhood were recent ones: the 1905 revolution and the battle with Bermondt-Avalov in 1919. While Lācplēsis harked back to origin myths, the *Lācplēsis* epic that crystallised them was recent too, dating to 1888.[41] The monument assisted then in generating a collective Latvian memory. Its construction was itself a collective endeavour of the Latvian people, funded through donations secured through a nationwide fund-raising campaign that emphasised the duty of all to contribute what they could to honour those who died for Latvia's independence.

This begs a question. If the Freedom Monument was so clearly identified with Latvian national identity, why did the Soviets not tear it down during their long occupation? Historian Laura Ķeniņš notes, firstly, that Soviet policy towards the republics did involve some promotion of local cultures, for example cultural festivals underscoring the multi-ethnic character of the USSR.[42] Retention of the monument might have been seen in this perspective as a relatively minor concession to the Latvians. Second, many scenes and statues on the monument were relatively unproblematic, even positive, from the Soviet standpoint, or could be recast in an unproblematic way. The anti-Tsarist message of the relief depicting the 1905 uprising fitted the Soviet worldview. The *Lāčplēsis* epic, with its subtext the struggle between a Latvian peasantry and the Baltic German bourgeoisie, was also amenable to Soviet reinterpretation, and the epic was reworked along socialist lines by Jānis Sudrabkalns. Images of men breaking free from chains, and compositions highlighting family and labour, were straightforwardly positive from a Soviet perspective. There were also attempts, at least on the part of Intourist guides for foreign visitors, to falsify the meaning of some elements, notably in characterising the central female figure holding three stars as representing 'Mother Russia', the stars the three Baltic republics. Finally, celebrated Soviet sculptor Vera Mukhina, who was born in Rīga and knew Zāle, seems to have helped persuade the authorities that the monument was an important work and should not be destroyed.

Soviet attempts to co-opt or reinterpret the monument were however doomed to fail. Imbued with a Latvian national ideology, it symbolised the independence enjoyed by Latvia in the interwar years. Images of the monument were cherished by Latvian exiles. It provided a venue for protests against the Soviet regime. Until the 1980s these largely took the form of individual acts of resistance, notably the laying of flowers at the monument. In the second half of the 1980s, in the wake of Gorbachev's policy of *glasnost*, it accommodated larger scale protest activity, including around concerns over the environment and ongoing Russification. On 14 June 1987, human rights group Helsinki-86 organised a march to the monument in memory of victims of the deportations of 1941. As the focus of protests moved towards demands for independence, the monument became a symbol of that independence struggle.

The Freedom Monument today is thus a symbol both of independence won and independence regained. A monument built to hon-

STATUES AND NATIONAL IDENTITY

our Latvia's struggle for independence became itself an agent in Latvia's struggle for the restoration of that independence.

The Fourth Plinth and the Changing Identity of Trafalgar Square

London's Trafalgar Square stands at the heart of the capital of the United Kingdom, close to the institutions of political power, the site of festivals, protests and celebrations. Laid out in the 1840s, it is populated with statuary exemplifying the nineteenth-century national identity building project. It centres on the triumphal column to Admiral Nelson, hero of Trafalgar, flanked by statues to Charles Napier and Henry Havelock, celebrating their exploits in India. Behind sit an equestrian statue of George IV and, by a historical quirk, a vacant fourth plinth, originally intended for an equestrian statue to William IV as a pair to George, but which was never commissioned. Nelson's Column remains a celebrated landmark, but the rest of the statuary on the square has fulfilled Musil's observation on the invisibility of monuments. Journalist Gary Younge, who chaired meetings of the Fourth Plinth Commissioning Group, to which we will turn, recalled that with every request he received for a new permanent statue to fill the vacant plinth (candidates ranged from footballer David Beckham to comedian Benny Hill), he would 'make the petitioner an offer: if you can name those who occupy the other three plinths, then the fourth is yours.'[43] While this was never entirely in his gift, he had no need to test the deliverability of this promise, since no one ever did correctly identify the subjects.

The fourth plinth has in recent years provided the platform for a series of temporary statues and other artworks, an initiative kicked off in 1999 by the installation of works commissioned by the Royal Society of Arts as part of a discussion about an appropriate permanent work to occupy the plinth.[44] The municipal authorities concluded that temporary statues were better all round than a permanent addition to the square, and the new Mayor of London, Ken Livingstone, appointed a Fourth Plinth Commissioning Group to select works for the site. The programme was focused on the use of public space to engage with the arts, not about any deliberate attempt to craft national identity, but as sociologist Shanti Sumartojo argues, the location of the plinth in Trafalgar Square, such an important *lieu de mémoire* in the consolidation and remaking of British national identity, renders commentary on national identity unavoidable.

Several works chosen for the fourth plinth have addressed diversity, challenging the traditional predominance of 'triumphant male statuary' as artist Marc Quinn, sculptor of the first installation chosen by the Fourth Plinth Commissioning Group, put it.[45] That statue, *Alison Lapper Pregnant*, depicted disabled artist Alison Lapper eight months pregnant. The statue seemed to challenge the male, imperial, monarchical and military power represented by the other statues on the square.

Promotion of diversity of subjects was taken to its extreme by an installation curated by artist Antony Gormley entitled *One and Other*. People across Britain could apply to stand on the fourth plinth for an hour; the scheme running for 100 days in 2009. They were lifted by cherry-picker and, once on the plinth, were free to express themselves however they wanted, though were encouraged not to break the law or to get too close to the edge. Gormley's intention was to create 'a picture of Britain',[46] providing a democratic response to the historical narratives of the square. What picture of Britain emerged from the project? Given that the attire sported by participants ranged from town crier to giant pigeon, it is difficult to say. Someone dressed as Godzilla and proceeded to destroy a cardboard model of London landmarks. It all provided a contrast to the nineteenth-century nation-building narrative of the rest of the square, and this was perhaps the intent, although the alternative it offered was no coherent modern narrative but a dizzying series of individual voices, giving the impression of a view of Britain as curated from the Big Brother house.

The occupant of the fourth plinth succeeding *One and Other* could not have been more different. Air Chief Marshal Sir Keith Park was the Royal Air Force commander during the Battle of Britain, that 'finest hour' when German plans to invade Britain were thwarted by British aerial tenacity. The temporary presence of a statue of Park on the plinth was an uneasy compromise between the Sir Keith Park Memorial Campaign, which felt Park was the ideal candidate for permanent memorialisation on the vacant plinth, and those who wished the plinth to remain as the venue for temporary artworks. The then Mayor of London, Boris Johnson, while ultimately siding with the latter, at least offered the Sir Keith Park Memorial Campaign the promise that 'some day your plinth will come.'[47]

For the Sir Keith Park Memorial Campaign, the case for a permanent statue to Park was that it would fit perfectly the historical narrative established by the rest of the square, providing continuity with Nelson's Column in paying tribute to great British military commanders. The fact that this reasoning secured Park only a temporary place on the plinth suggested that the commissioning authorities felt such a perspective no longer adequately presented contemporary national identity. The Westminster Council planning report rejecting the proposal that Park occupy the place permanently concluded that this would be 'too representational and traditional', denying the square 'a site ideally suited for the display of provocative contemporary art.'[48]

While it is tempting to contrast the 'democratic' variety of installations inhabiting the fourth plinth with the 'official' space of the rest of the square, with its memorials to nineteenth-century military leaders and monarchs, this neglects the fact that the works on the fourth plinth have been carefully selected by a commissioning group reporting to the municipal authorities. And that, as Shanti Sumartojo has pointed out, the London authorities have focused Trafalgar Square as a venue for multicultural festivals,[49] developing a new narrative for the square based on multiculturalism and social cohesion that is supported by the temporary works on the plinth, many of which address diversity. The fourth plinth project is in this sense an attempt to refashion and reorient what Trafalgar Square stands for as a *lieu de mémoire*. The initiative which best fits the description of a bottom-up campaign, challenging the official vision for the square, was that of the Sir Keith Park Memorial Campaign. For those who like a happy ending, it is good to report that Sir Keith's plinth did indeed come. The temporary statue in Trafalgar Square was moved after six months to a new home at the Royal Air Force Museum in north London. A permanent statue to Park was unveiled by the Memorial Campaign in Waterloo Place in central London on 15 September 2010, marking the seventieth anniversary of the Battle of Britain.

6

MEMORIALISING LOSS, TRAGEDY AND EVIL

How does one memorialise an event so unfathomably terrible as the Holocaust? German philosopher Theodor W. Adorno famously commented that 'to write lyric poetry after Auschwitz is barbaric'.[1] As with the poetry, so is the erection of statues surrounded by risk in the face of the overwhelming evil of the events. They might serve to console the viewer or redeem the events when neither consolation nor redemption is appropriate.[2]

If monuments are traditionally affirmative in character, praising, lauding and glorifying,[3] to what extent do they need a different form if the purpose of the monument is to record a darker event: a manifestation of evil or tragedy? And when its focus is not a single heroic figure, but many victims? There was a change in both the form and focus of public monuments during the twentieth century, stemming at least in part from the major traumas of the time, from World War I to the Holocaust. It involved a shift of focus from celebration of heroes to mourning of victims. A shift of perspective, from designs forcing the viewer to look up to monuments to those addressed at eye level. And a shift from figurative sculptures to modernist minimalism. 'Monuments' gave way to 'memorials', reflecting a switch from celebration of heroism and achievement to reflection on loss and victimhood.[4]

But is there no place for the figurative statue in the memorialisation of loss, tragedy and evil? To explore this question, we should start in the darkest of places, the memorialisation of the Holocaust.

VOICES IN STONE

Memorialising the Holocaust

Historian Harold Marcuse has chronicled the emergence of a new memorial tradition in commemorating the horrors of the Holocaust. This took years, and only in the 1960s had the new genre really gained currency.[5] Many early memorials were derived from the models of traditional war memorials or took classical forms such as obelisks.

Marcuse notes that memorials in western Europe mostly adopted an abstract rather than figurative style given the sensitivities around the depiction of people in monuments dedicated to such horror. This was not however the case in the Communist eastern bloc, where there was more use of figurative representation, typically in the prevailing style of socialist realism. Rather than individual figures, it was common to see grouped displays, emphasising solidarity and collective resistance. The elaborate memorial at the Buchenwald concentration camp in the then East Germany centres on a bronze sculpture of eleven figures entitled *Revolt of the Prisoners* by sculptor Fritz Cremer (see fig. 13). Dedicated in 1958, and standing in front of a 55-metre bell tower, it is a picture of defiance, its focus not on the murder of Jews but on resistance to Nazism.

This reluctance to focus specifically on Jews as targets of the Holocaust is a common feature of memorials in the Communist bloc, where the monuments served to reinforce a narrative of collective struggle of a united Communist world against the fascist enemy. The Holocaust memorials of Latvia serve as a good example. A memorial erected in 1967 on the site of the Salaspils concentration camp features a long concrete wall, physically separating the territory of the camp, and death, from the outside world, and life. An inscription reads, in Latvian, 'the ground groans beneath these gates.'[6] Concrete sculptures in the ceremonial square behind the wall reflect the ideology of Soviet resistance to Nazi cruelty, ignoring the different backgrounds of those incarcerated. This original memorial contains no reference to Jews or to members of the Polish or Latvian resistance movements.

The 1955 Soviet memorial at the Šķēde Dunes near the coastal city of Liepāja, where 3,000 Jews, mainly women and children, were shot between 15 and 17 December 1941, is an obelisk. Its inscription, beneath a red Soviet star, talks about the 19,000 'Soviet patriots' of Liepāja killed by the Nazis. Its twin features of overstating the number of victims and anonymising them under the generic description of 'patriots' are typical. At Rumbula, outside the Latvian capital Rīga, 25,000 prisoners brought from the Rīga ghetto were shot during two actions at the end of 1941. A memorial stone erected in 1964 simply read 'to the victims of fascism', albeit written in Yiddish alongside Latvian and Russian.

This concealing of Jewish victims was not true of monuments in Israel or the United States, where the reverse was more likely to be true, with a focus solely on Jewish victims of the Holocaust.[7] The differing goals of those initiating the monuments are important here: those of socialist governments emphasising anti-fascist resistance were a mile away from those of Jewish groups highlighting the systematic persecution of their people. With the reestablishment of Latvian independence in 1991 and the end of Soviet occupation, a new style of memorial emerged, emphasising Jewish symbols and traditions, in part reflecting funding from Jewish organisations and individuals based overseas and from governments and public bodies in Germany, Israel and the USA. At Rumbula, a new memorial designed by architect Sergey Rizh was unveiled in 2002. Centred on a menorah, it is surrounded by uncut stones, recollecting a traditional Jewish burial ground, engraved with the names of some of those executed here (see fig. 14).[8] At Šķēde, a memorial built in 2005 features a giant stone menorah laid on the ground, its flames symbolised by large rough-cut stone slabs inscribed in Hebrew with quotations from the Lamentations of Jeremiah. These Latvian memorials are part of the wider tradition identified by Marcuse of a new genre of Holocaust memorial: complex, abstract, experiential spaces full of symbolic elements.[9] Figurative statues have struggled to find a place in such memorials. Let us though consider in more detail an early Holocaust memorial that features much figurative sculpture.

The Warsaw Ghetto Monument

The Warsaw Ghetto Monument was unveiled on 19 April 1948 to mark the fifth anniversary of the uprising. It was the work of Jewish sculptor Nathan Rapoport, born in Warsaw in 1911. Rapoport was also a socialist, and developed his technique outside the Jewish tradition, with its grounding in the Second Commandment prohibition against making graven images.[10] Following the German invasion of Poland he fled to the USSR, where he refined his figurative sculpture in the socialist realist manner, turning out busts of heroic figures of the Great Patriotic War. Rapoport was determined to produce a monumental commemoration of the Warsaw Ghetto insurrection as soon as he learned of the events, which he perceived as both a Jewish and socialist revolution.[11] Back in Warsaw in 1946, he secured support from the Warsaw Jewish Committee for his proposed monument; an idea eventually endorsed by the Warsaw City Arts Committee.

For Rapoport, the monument had to be figurative not abstract in form. 'Could I have made a stone with a hole in it and said, "Voila! The Greatness of the Jewish People"? No, I needed to show the heroism, to illustrate it literally in figures everyone, not just artists, would respond to.'[12]

The monument was a free-standing wall of rough stone, recalling a great tombstone, the Ghetto walls, and indeed the Western Wall in Jerusalem. The wall supports two bronze relief groups, offering very different representations of the Warsaw Uprising. On the western wall, facing the open square, is a grouping of heroically sculpted figures centred on Mordechai Anielewicz, leader of the revolt, a resolute, proletarian figure, bare-chested and clutching a home-made grenade. Around him, similarly determined figures hold improvised weaponry, while behind him a mother engulfed by flames raises her right arm, clutching her baby in her other hand. Bare-breasted, she recalls Delacroix's symbol of Liberty, and through this reference, revolutionary insurrection in general.

The monument is dedicated to 'the Jewish People—its Heroes and its Martyrs'. The martyrs are on the other side of the wall: twelve huddled figures walking slowly from right to left, the bayonets and helmets of their otherwise invisible Nazi tormentors just perceptible behind them. A rabbi, holding a Torah scroll, looks to the heavens, the rest dejectedly at the ground. The outcome then is what US academic James E. Young describes as a deliberately 'two-sided monument'.[13]

MEMORIALISING LOSS, TRAGEDY AND EVIL

The monument was built literally on the ruins of the Warsaw Ghetto. The architect commissioned to build the base, finding it impossible to clear the rubble from the site with the equipment to hand, simply poured the concrete of the base over it. This would occasion later cracks. In an even starker symbolic note, while searching for granite blocks for the retaining wall, Rapoport found perfectly cut blocks in Sweden ready for the job—they had originally been intended for a planned monument in Berlin to celebrate Hitler's victory.[14]

The monument's subsequent life in Communist Poland placed it amongst an overwhelmingly non-Jewish population, for many of whom the German Occupation had been replaced by another unwanted external domination: that of Soviet influence. James E. Young notes that this made it an ambivalent monument for Poles, recalling less the Jewish Warsaw Ghetto Uprising than the fact there was no equivalent memorial to the 1944 Polish Uprising against Nazi Occupation.[15] The leaders of the Solidarity movement in the 1980s, while continuing to demand a monument to the 1944 uprising, also identified opportunities presented by the existing Ghetto Monument to further their cause: using a monument commemorating the righteousness of past resistance to make the case for contemporary resistance.[16] Young argues that one curious consequence of this was that the authorities doubled down on perpetuation of the memory of the Jewish uprising, for example through wreath-laying ceremonies at the memorial, in an apparent effort to limit commemorations to the purposes originally intended, blocking space for symbolic references to contemporary resistance movements.[17] This effort was largely unsuccessful.

The Warsaw Ghetto Monument has been reproduced, in whole or in part, in both Israel and the United States, but the meaning drawn from it in these countries has been different to that in Poland. In Israel, a reproduction was commissioned by Leon Jolson, philanthropist and Ghetto survivor, for the Yad Vashem memorial in Jerusalem. In the Israeli context, the monument links past Jewish heroism and resistance with that of present-day Israeli resistance against external opponents.

Representations in the United States have more frequently been restricted to the relief on the eastern wall of the Warsaw monument featuring the procession of martyrs. This can be encountered, notes Young, at synagogues and seminaries in Dallas, Syracuse and New York City. The focus on the Jews who perished in the Holocaust, without highlighting heroes of the resistance to the Nazis, is consonant with an American memory of the Holocaust that focuses on martyrdom, unlike that in Israel, where martyrdom and heroism are twinned.[18]

Counter-Monuments

If memorialisation of the Holocaust is difficult in any context, how does one do it in Germany? Here, this is not memorialisation created from the perspective of a victim of the events, but from that of a state which had, under an earlier and disgraced regime, been the perpetrator. And all this in a country in which the use of grand monumental forms had been a device of that very perpetrator to build its legitimacy and power. In West Germany in the 1980s, when the country was grappling with the challenge of how to represent its troubled past, a group of young artists adopted an approach unlike, indeed a reaction against, that of traditional monuments and statues.

The approach they devised has been described by James E. Young as the 'counter-monument'.[19] For Young, traditional monuments, in wrapping up the ideals they represent into a fixed and immutable form, divest the viewer of the obligation to remember. While traditional monuments seek permanence, counter-monuments may be designed to be ephemeral. They depend on the audience, and it is the interaction between counter-monument and viewer that forms the essence of the monument. The Diana, Princess of Wales Memorial Fountain in London's Hyde Park, the work of Kathryn Gustafson and Neil Porter, is a ring-shaped watercourse. Sit on the grass, jump across the stream, even wade in. With a counter-monument, the burden of remembering is passed from monument to viewer. Minimalist or abstract forms are frequently employed, all the better to resist fixed interpretation.[20] They frequently lack explicit visual symbols or explanatory text.

Counter-monuments, in contrast to the solid, figurative character of the traditional statue to a hero, can take the form of emptiness—a void representing the loss of the victims commemorated by the memorial. We will examine the Vietnam Veterans Memorial in Washington, which serves as a good example. So too does the *Reflecting Absence* memorial, tracing the bases of the lost World Trade Centre buildings in New York. The Peacekeeping Monument in Ottawa depicts three soldiers standing above a landscape symbolising the destruction of war. Such representations may seek to generate a therapeutic space where visitors can come to terms with loss.[21]

The extensive literature on counter-monuments usually starts with the *Harburg Monument against Fascism, War and Violence—and for Peace and Human Rights* designed by Jochen Gerz and Esther Shalev-Gerz, unveiled in 1986 in Harburg, a suburb of Hamburg. The designers took the commission from the local council for a monument to recall the terror of fascism and become a beacon for peace as the opportunity to propose a counter-monument. Their monument was twelve metres high, with a square base, constructed of hollow aluminium and plated with soft lead. At each corner, a steel-pointed stylus attached by a cable could be used to etch into the lead. Instructions next to the monument invited visitors to inscribe their names, signing up against the injustice of fascism. When that segment of lead was covered with names the monument would be lowered into the ground, where a chamber had been constructed as deep as the monument was high. The more active the participation of visitors, the faster the monument would be lowered, until it disappeared altogether. All that would be left of the monument would be its memory. The monument was lowered by 140 centimetres eight times until by November 1993 it was gone. All that remains is an observation window along the side of the underground shaft in which it is enclosed, and a plaque.[22]

Gerz and Shalev-Gerz had envisaged that audience interaction would take the form of neat rows of names, as passers-by signed up to confirm their opposition to fascism, but this only happened in part. Scribbles and scrawls took over. We discovered that Jürgen loves Kirsten. Swastikas appeared. Since counter-monuments are designed to be shaped by audience interaction, it is to be expected that they may take directions not anticipated by their creators. This brings a risk that they become the memorial equivalent of

Frankenstein's monster. All that graffiti added to the unpopularity of the monument among local people, such that its disappearance in 1993 became a cause for celebration in a sense that its authors may not have intended.

If the agency of counter-monuments is claimed to have been passed to the viewer, the experience of the *Harburg Monument against Fascism, War and Violence—and for Peace and Human Rights* does not wholly feel like that. Numerous instructions were given on how to interact with the monument—on the accompanying plaque, in newspaper articles and by the presence of the artists at events, even if the responses etched into the monument were often at variance with them.[23] Each lowering of the monument involved a ceremonial event, with the participation of public officials, and since an observation window and plaque were left as reminders of the monument, its planned ephemerality should not be overemphasised. Its authors took care to ensure it would not be forgotten. Some Harburg citizens, far from empowered participants in a collaborative project, felt they were the victims of an ugly and unwanted monument imposed upon them.[24]

At their most extreme, counter-monuments can involve the creation of a monument of which there is no visible evidence, not only of its lasting presence but even of its original construction. Jochen Gerz was later appointed visiting professor at the Saarbrücken School of Fine Arts. There, he developed an initially clandestine project with his students. In front of the Saarbrücker Schloss stands a large cobblestoned space. This held strong links to the evils of the Nazi regime. The building housed a Gestapo unit, and local Jews were brought to and humiliated at this square during *Kristallnacht* in 1938. It was from here that the remaining Jews of the city were deported in October 1940, to meet their terrible fates.

Starting in 1990, Gerz's students surreptitiously prised cobblestones from the square, replacing them with similarly sized stones they had brought with them, embedded with a nail to allow for future location by a metal detector. The removed stones were inscribed with the names of one of the 2,146 Jewish cemeteries existing in Germany before the outbreak of World War II, which were vandalised or destroyed during the Nazi regime. These

1. The National Windrush Monument, London. A celebration of the role of migrants from the Caribbean in forging a modern Britain (see p. 17).

2. Keeping a little Marc in our hearts. Marc Bolan's Rock Shrine, Barnes Common, London (see p. 23).

3. In memory of a love affair. Variant of Alice Nordin's *Andante Patetico*, Nationalmuseum Stockholm (see p. 29).

4. Norwegian auteur Gustav Vigeland turns his attention to a furious child. *The Angry Boy*, Vigeland Park, Oslo (see p. 44).

5. At the time of writing, the tallest statue on the planet. Sardar Vallabhbhai Patel, Gujarat (see p. 49).

6. The Leshan Giant Buddha, Sichuan, built to calm the treacherous waters of the river below (see p. 52).

7. A tiny figure, but a big attraction. *Järnpojke*, the Iron Boy of Stockholm (see p. 53).

8. Trajan's Column, Rome, a belvedere, funerary monument and canvas for an intricate frieze, all perpetuating the remembrance of Trajan and his illustrious deeds (see p. 57).

9. The heated statue of Margaretha Krook, providing welcome warmth in the Stockholm winter (see p. 79).

10. *Partners*, Walt Disney World, Florida, commemorating the achievement of one man and his mouse (see p. 86).

11. The Voortrekker Monument, Pretoria, an embodiment of Afrikaner claims to the right to govern (see p. 93).

12. Celebrating heroic defeat. The *Monument to the Heroes of Laguna and Dourados*, Rio de Janeiro (see p. 100).

13. A memorial focusing not on the murder of Jews but on resistance to Nazism. *Revolt of the Prisoners*, Buchenwald (see p. 114).

14. Following the end of Soviet occupation in Latvia, a new style of Holocaust memorial emphasised Jewish symbols and traditions. The Memorial to the 1941 Massacre of Jews at Rumbula (see p. 115).

15. Bust of Ronald Reagan, Skulte, Latvia, erected in gratitude to the US president for helping to secure the restoration of Latvia's independence (see p. 136).

16. Poet and ploughshare: statue of Robert Burns, Sydney (see p. 138).

engraved stones were returned by the students to their original places, but face down, so no evidence of the activity remained. What counter-monuments do require is publicity, and Gerz wrote to Oskar Lafontaine, then Minister-President of Saarland and a future leader of the Social Democratic Party, asking for support. This was secured in 1991, and in 1993 a plaque was unveiled naming the place as the Platz des Unsichtbaren Mahnmals, the Square of the Invisible Monument.[25]

Those sceptics who identify a student proclivity to take any short cut that presents itself might question whether every one of these *2,146 Stones Against Racism* really were painstakingly removed, inscribed and replaced, only for all that effort to be unseen, and proponents of counter-monuments would argue that this is not the key issue anyway, rather that the site invites reflection on the dreadful events to which the stones were witness. There are challenges in doing so. The curious name of the square is the only visual clue to the monument, so prior knowledge about the project is required of the visitor. The cobblestones are witnesses to the events, but because inscriptions have been hidden from view, they are silent witnesses. For Gerz, the visitor, as the only standing form in the square, became the memorial.[26] But to take on this role, they needed to know the back-story to the project. All this points to an underpinning risk of counter-monuments: that they become illegible or invisible, their purpose unclear.[27]

A further risk around counter-monuments, as often ephemeral, mutable forms deriving their essence from audience interaction, was that their architects became caught in a spiral of ever more provocative proposals to generate the continued publicity upon which audience interaction depended. James E. Young recalled that in the 1994 competition for a Berlin memorial to the murdered Jews of Europe, Horst Hoheisel's proposal involved detonating the Brandenburg Gate, which would be ground into dust, sprinkled across the site and covered in granite plates. For Hoheisel, a people whom the Nazis had sought to destroy would be better commemorated by destroying a monument, and what better than one celebrating Prussian glories, rather than constructing one.[28] Since the Brandenburg Gate is still with us, Hoheisel's non-monument was clearly never realised. Let us look in more detail though at the monument that was chosen.

Memorial to the Murdered Jews of Europe

The idea of a monument in Germany to the memory of Jews murdered in the Holocaust emerged in the late 1980s, promoted by German television journalist Lea Rosh and historian Eberhard Jäckel through an initiative known as *Perspektive Berlin*, which later morphed into the Society for the Promotion of a Memorial for the Murdered Jews of Europe. German reunification, and the intensified focus on national identity this engendered, contributed to sentiment in favour of a monument to face up to the horrors of the Holocaust.

A competition for a memorial was announced in 1994. Some 528 proposals were submitted, among them Hoheisel's detonation of the Brandenburg Gate, and even a proposal to construct a large Ferris wheel whose carriages would be substituted by cattle trucks.[29] There was reportedly little meeting of minds among the jury, with lay jurors favouring what the specialists decried as kitsch figurative works, while the latter favoured what the former perceived as elitist minimalist designs.[30] The proposal eventually emerging, Christine Jackob-Marks' tilted concrete plate, to be engraved with the recoverable names of 4.5 million murdered Jews, failed to secure approval in all quarters, including from German Chancellor Helmut Kohl, and the organisers went back to the drawing board.

An accompanying memorial exhibition of all 528 designs impressed counter-monuments champion James E. Young, who wrote: 'better a thousand years of Holocaust memorial competitions than any single "final solution" to Germany's memorial problem.'[31] Young's concern was that a completed monument might attempt to bury German guilt for the Holocaust: finishing the monument risked finishing the memory.[32] In a similar vein, professor of German and comparative literature Andreas Huyssen worried that the proposed Holocaust memorial was part of a wider memorial craze throughout Germany: with every new monument completed, the easier it was to forget the past: 'redemption, thus, through forgetting.'[33]

MEMORIALISING LOSS, TRAGEDY AND EVIL

A *Findungskommission* was appointed to make an authoritative recommendation on the memorial. Notwithstanding his scepticism to date about the project, Young agreed to join that body, with the proviso that the memorial must reflect the concern of many artists over the appropriateness of traditional memorials, which so often served as redemptory sites of mourning and places of self-aggrandisement.[34] The champion of counter-monuments was thus now championing a monument: provided, that is, it retained something of the ethos of the counter-monument.

The design alighted on was a collaboration between architect Peter Eisenman and artist Richard Serra, and took the form of numerous concrete stelae of varying heights, arranged in a large grid. The design intended to instil a sense of dislocation in the visitor, taking a grid, a form usually associated with order, but introducing a disorienting quality through the different heights of the stelae,[35] sometimes so low as to be barely present, in other places standing far above head height, creating concrete canyons. The monument has no obvious focal point, and indeed no defined boundary or single entrance.[36] The visitor simply enters it from any of the surrounding streets.

The chosen site was central, close to the Brandenburg Gate, underscoring the project's importance, and taking advantage of an empty plot of land, but it was not a site specifically linked to Holocaust atrocities. For Young, this was a strength: the lack of pre-connections to the Holocaust meant this would not be a site of preservation and passive reception of the past but required a deliberate act of remembrance.[37] Others were less convinced, perceiving a risk that building the memorial obscured the complex history of the German capital. The filling of a void, even with a memorial, might have the effect of tidying up, or 'forgetting', a difficult past.[38]

The choice of design was far from the end of the monument's long journey. Changes were insisted upon, including to reduce the number of concrete pillars from some 4,000 to 2,711, better to fit the site. The architect, Eisenman, was willing to accommodate these, but the artist, Serra, was not, and quit the project.[39] There were numerous controversies along the way, such as concerns unearthed by journalists that the company contracted to provide anti-graffiti coating for the stelae had links with the Holocaust.[40] There was protracted debate about the monument's scope, with some criticising its exclusive focus on murdered Jews. This has been assuaged by the decision to construct further monuments nearby to honour the memories, respectively, of Sinti and Roma and homosexual victims of National Socialism and of victims of National Socialist 'euthanasia' killings. By December 2004, construction was complete, and the memorial was inaugurated the following year.

While far from a counter-monument as originally envisaged by Young, the memorial shares important qualities with that form, notably in placing responsibility to remember on the viewer, by offering nothing, at least above ground, in the way of representational imagery or text. Anthropologist Damani Partridge writes of his experience accompanying a group of German youths of Palestinian and Turkish heritage to the memorial; part of a programme motivated by what had been perceived as a latent anti-Semitism of members of the group. They were enveloped by the grey pillars of the monument, an experience they struggled to interpret in the absence of an awareness of the Holocaust. For Partridge, the problem is that the monument 'cannot reach beyond those who already remember, or at least partially know.'[41] The monument failed to speak to the contemporary racism experienced by members of the group, in its focus on atonement for the evils of the Holocaust.

The monument's accessibility and lack of signage raise the question of rules of behaviour. The ethos of the counter-monument, in which the visitor is an active participant in the act of remembrance, would suggest that there are none. The essence of the monument is created through interactions. The monument's structure seems to encourage running between pillars, the picnicking of weary tourists on the stelae, and other behaviours that others perceiving the monument as a site for respectful contemplation will find jarring, just as the etching of graffiti on the Harburg monument provoked disquiet.

Selfies proved a particular point of controversy. In 2017, satirist Shahak Shapira responded to the proliferation of selfies taken at the monument and posted on social media with the 'Yolocaust' project, superimposing these selfies onto pictures of concentration camp life. It was a deliberate act of shaming, requiring the original posters to write to Shapira with a request to be 'undouched' to secure removal of the pictures. While Shapira's initiative received support from those concerned that selfie culture trivialised engagement with sensitive sites, others questioned whether it was always fair. For some, taking a selfie may have been a serious act in the process of figuring out their relationship with the events commemorated.[42]

As if in response to these concerns, the memorial does have a more didactic side, but you must hunt it out in the subterranean information centre, also designed by Eisenman. Above ground, there are now plaques setting out 'regulations for visitors'. Cigarettes and alcohol are not permitted, nor is jumping between stelae, bicycles and pets are out and, intriguingly, 'the Field of Stelae can only be entered slowly.' The agency of the viewer is therefore a constrained one. The addition of these plaques, setting out appropriate rules of conduct, suggests a desire for monuments to be recognised as such to generate respect.[43] The figurative representations and tall pedestals of traditional monuments mark them out straightforwardly for what they are. With more abstract memorials, there is a decision to be made about whether to accept the lack of respect that accompanies a vague monument with ill-defined boundaries, or to seek to generate that respect by signposting what exactly is being commemorated. The latter action, of course, demolishes an underlying principle of the counter-monument.

The Vietnam Veterans Memorial

Let us turn from the Holocaust to other examples of loss, to explore whether similar considerations apply in relation to their memorialisation. The Vietnam War, a humiliating military defeat for the United States in a war many Americans had opposed, does not provide straightforward subject matter for a memorial. Yet the Vietnam Veterans Memorial in Washington DC is the most visited memorial on the National Mall, attracting more than five million people yearly.[44] It is a monument whose birth was controversial yet is now regarded with respect and affection.

The story of the memorial is helpfully told in a 1988 made-for-television movie, *To Heal a Nation*, starring Eric Roberts as the hero of the tale, Vietnam War veteran Jan Scruggs. He meets a fellow veteran by chance at a fast-food joint. They discover they had an acquaintance in common, killed in the war. Neither could quite remember the guy's name. Jan's wife Becky tells him that for most people this isn't a war worth remembering. He resolves to build a memorial. Fellow veterans poo-pooh the idea, arguing that the priority lies in more practical matters, like ensuring veterans receive benefits due to them. But Jan is, of course, tenacious. He incorporates the Vietnam Veterans Memorial Fund in April 1979, as a non-profit organisation to finance construction of the memorial. He gains supporters and sets an impossible-sounding deadline: to inaugurate the memorial on Veterans Day 1982.

Of course, there are setbacks. Any movie charting a hero's journey requires them. Roger Mudd on *CBS Evening News* jokes about the Fund, noting it had raised a princely $144.50 over its first month of operation.[45] But Jan and his friends persevere. US Senators Charles Mathias and John Warner support the plan, helping steer through legislation authorising a site close to the Lincoln Memorial.

To Heal a Nation contains a scene in which Jan receives a letter from a girl, enclosing the five dollars her late father gave her for a hamburger before setting out for war. This provokes his realisation that the memorial had to include her father's name, and those of all US service personnel killed in the war. The objective is to create a symbol of national reconciliation through honouring those who died. In October 1980, Jan and the team announce a national design competition, open to all adult US residents. The competition rules booklet insists that the memorial's tone must be conciliatory; honouring the dead, but not the war itself.[46] 1,421 entries are submitted in the largest such competition ever launched in the USA, and, crucially, they are judged anonymously. The winning design proves not to have come from a professional architect or sculptor but a 21-year-old undergraduate student at Yale, Maya Ying Lin.

Maya Lin's design took the route of the counter-monument: two walls of black granite set into the earth in an extended V-shape. The walls are inscribed with the names of 58,000 dead, listed not alphabetically but chronologically. This chronological listing starts on the right-hand side of the 'hinge' of the V-shape, beginning again on the far left of the monument and continuing back towards the centre. The name of the first US soldier killed in Vietnam in 1959 abuts the last soldier killed in 1975.[47] The names are listed without further elaboration. This chronological listing of names was initially opposed by many veterans on the practical grounds that this would hinder the ability of relatives to locate their loved-one's name. But it was central to Maya Lin's vision of a journey through the war, a journey that is ultimately a circular one. Scruggs and members of the Fund were puzzled by Maya Lin's attitude of deliberate detachment towards the veterans, including in opting not to read their accounts of the war.[48]

Mild misunderstandings between the Fund and Maya Lin paled against the strongly negative reception that greeted Maya Lin's proposed monument from those veterans' groups for whom the modernist design resembled a 'black gash of shame and sorrow', as one put it.[49] It was seen as a monument to national guilt over the war. Marita Sturken, a professor of media, culture and communication, argues that for many of its critics, the monument wasn't phallic enough. In failing to stand proud above the landscape, skulking instead below the ground, 'to its critics this antiphallus symbolises the open, castrated wound of this country's venture into an unsuccessful war.'[50]

Criticism of Maya Lin's design threatened to derail the project. James G. Watt, the Secretary of the Interior, declined to sign off the building permit in the face of the controversy. *To Heal a Nation* depicts a tense make-or-break meeting involving the various factions. Would the opponents of the winning design torpedo the whole project? In the end, a compromise saved the day. Much to Maya Lin's disgust, the Fund agreed to add a realist statue and flagpole to respond to concerns that the design was too shame-faced in relation to the veterans. A counter-monument was saved by a statue.

The choice of sculptor was pragmatic. Lacking the time or energy to set up another competition, the Vietnam Veterans Memorial Fund gave the job to Frederick Hart, who together with architect Sheila Brady had produced a design placing third in the main competition, making Hart the highest-placed sculptor. His bronze statue, *Three Soldiers*, was unveiled on Veterans Day 1984, two years after the main monument. The statue depicts three standing battle-weary soldiers, reflective of the ethnic diversity of US service personnel in Vietnam, looking towards the monument. Hart's approach to the commission was the reverse of Maya Lin's detachment. 'I researched for three years—read everything. I became close friends with many vets, drank with them in bars.'[51] The statue is a product of those boozy conversations, filled with the detail of the veterans' stories: like the towel hung over the shoulders and dog tag strung through an eyelet of a boot.[52]

Those who criticised Maya Lin's design as cold and shame-faced had forgotten one important point. The point that was so essential to Jan Scruggs. The names. This was no blank surface of black granite, but a chronicle of 58,000 service personnel, their names making up the story of the war. From the moment of inauguration of the memorial, friends and relatives came not only to find the names of their departed loved ones but to leave personal artefacts: photographs, letters, teddy bears, medals. The monument became a shrine. The National Park Service decided to store all these items, except for unaltered US flags and perishables like flowers, at its Museum and Archaeological Regional Storage facility[53]—MARS. Yes, really. Controversies around the design evaporated in the face of the emotional response of those who came to mourn. The personal artefacts they left at the monument in turn proved moving to those who had not themselves lost a loved one in the war, but who sought to understand.

Which is not to say that no controversies remained. In 1993, a Vietnam Women's Memorial was dedicated nearby. To a design by Glenna Goodacre, it depicts three uniformed women, one tending a wounded male soldier, symbolising the role of nurses and other female specialists in the war. The impetus behind this statue appears to have been provided by Hart's representation of three men, a portrayal that, to the Women's Memorial founders, highlighted the neglect of the women who fought in the war.[54] There was though criticism of the new monument too, some pointing out that of the 58,000 US service personnel killed during the Vietnam War, only eight were women. Maya Lin was upset at this further tampering with her original design. There is no place on the wall for those who

MEMORIALISING LOSS, TRAGEDY AND EVIL

died after the conflict but from causes linked to it, whether suicide or exposure to Agent Orange.

The memorial has long provided a place for the veterans. It commemorates those who survived as well as those who died,[55] and in many ways has lived up to the lofty ideal that Jan Scruggs set out for it: *To Heal a Nation*.

Memorial to the Kent State University Shootings

The chugging, dirge-like refrain of the Crosby, Stills, Nash and Young protest song *Ohio* refers to 'four dead in Ohio'. Those four dead were Jeffrey Miller, Allison Krause, William Schroeder and Sandra Scheuer, shot by members of the Ohio National Guard attempting to quell a 1970 student protest against President Nixon's 'Cambodian Incursion' on the campus of Kent State University in Ohio. Schroeder and Scheuer had not even been participating in the protest—they were shot while walking between classes. The shootings marked the culmination of four days of unrest: vandalism in the town; the burning of the Reserve Officers' Training Corps building; protests and tear gas. They sparked protests on campuses throughout the country, further polarising an already divided public opinion. The university established the following year a Center for Peaceful Change, teaching courses in conflict resolution, as a living memorial to those who died.

There was thus a challenging and contested backdrop to the memorialisation of the victims of the shootings of 4 May 1970. When in 1982 the Kent State University administration launched a competition for an official memorial to the tragedy, they wanted to ensure that it was neither accusatory or laudatory, but emphasised reflection, inquiry and learning. Given the injunction not to take a stance one way or another in relation to the events of 4 May 1970, it is unsurprising that the resulting memorial, dedicated in 1990, avoids figurative statuary. Nor is there much written description. Chicago-based architect Bruno Ast produced a counter-monument involving a plaza, with a jagged border, whose 'fractured edge suggests the tearing of the fabric of society'.[56] The words 'inquire, learn, reflect' are engraved on the stone threshold of the plaza, suggesting Ast had taken the competition brief particularly literally. Four polished black granite disks take the visitor from the plaza to four granite-tiled pylons. There is a fifth disk nearby. The ensemble sits on a wooded site overlooking the university Commons, the focal area of the 1970 protests.

In ensuring that it avoids the twin traps set out in the brief of being either accusatory or laudatory, Ast's monument ends up saying little at all. Is the casual visitor likely to guess that the jagged border of the plaza offers a message about the tearing of the fabric of society? And while a visitor with some knowledge of the events commemorated may work out that the four disks and pylons refer to the four students killed in the shootings, not many are likely to divine Ast's intent that the fifth disk represents the wider impacts of the events.

The 1990 memorial is not the one envisaged by either the university administration or the architect. It was not even the winning design. That honour went to a Canadian named Ian Taberner, whose entry was disqualified because of competition rules restricting eligibility to US citizens. Through a mix of cost overruns and underwhelming fund-raising, Ast was forced to scale down his design.[57] The memorial does offer a place for contemplation, and the hill on which it is placed was further enlivened by more than 58,000 daffodils, one representing each of the US service personnel killed in the Vietnam conflict. This planting of spring bulbs came at the initiative of a professor of sculpture named Brinsley Tyrrell. He had been another entrant to the memorial competition excluded because of Canadian citizenship, but his spring bulb proposal nonetheless caught the attention of the university administration. Tyrrell thought the flowers would help bring a divided community together. Vietnam veterans had criticised the idea of a monument to those protesting the war: Tyrrell's flowers brought the troops in Vietnam into the picture. The downside is that it muddied the question of who exactly is being commemorated.

The unclear messaging of the 4 May Memorial, and its peripheral location, set apart from both the centre of gravity of the protests on the university Commons and the site of the killings, meant this official memorial never properly encapsulated commemoration of the events of 1970. Alternative places of commemoration are provided by a series of sites and objects not intended as monuments but linked to the shootings, like a hole from a National Guardsman's bullet that pierced an abstract sculpture by Don Drumm entitled *Solar Totem #1*.[58] They form what Alois Riegl would term 'unwilled monuments'. The lack of any named reference in Ast's memorial to the students killed in 1970, other than on a later plaque, is remedied by newer memorials at the places where they fell. Where they fell was a car park: the Prentice Hall parking lot, and the memorials reclaim the parking spaces where each student was shot through six illuminated bollards placed around each space. Granite markers bear the name of the students. The slight awkwardness around this is that the car park is still in use. When it fills up, the risk is that drivers tut at the memorials, for blocking up a space. The dead are 'in the way'.[59]

A commemorative landscape to the killings of 4 May 1970 at Kent State University thus developed in a cautious and haphazard way, with both official and informal memorials. A counter-monumental approach to the official memorial based on a brief that urged a focus on inquiry and reflection rather than a particular stance towards the events resulted, perhaps inevitably, in a memorial that is difficult to understand. As the decades have passed, more interpretive material has been made available at the site. A walking tour was added in 2010 and a Visitors Centre in 2012, serving to link together the various memorials.[60] As statements on the events of 1970, none of the physical memorials has approached the power of Crosby, Stills, Nash and Young's song.

The Death of Romas Kalanta

On 14 May 1972, in a wooded park in front of the State Musical Theatre in Kaunas, Lithuania's second city, 19-year-old student Romas Kalanta set himself on fire. He was protesting the Soviet regime: his last words 'freedom for Lithuania!' The location for his action was chosen carefully: it was in the Musical Theatre building in 1940 that a puppet legislature asked the USSR to admit Lithuania as one of its constituent republics. Riots followed his funeral. In 2002, a commemoration monument entitled *Field of Sacrifice*, the work of sculptor Robertas Antinis, was unveiled in the park. It is literally a field. Hollow metal stones stud the grass, there is a low retaining wall inscribed with the names of the sculptor and architects, and a slab on the pavement bears the inscription 'Romas Kalanta 1972'. There is otherwise little to distinguish the memorial from the rest of the park, and it is used by visitors as an amenity space.

Like the Memorial to the Murdered Jews of Europe, the *Field of Sacrifice* is an indeterminate monument, its form blurred and imprecise. Urban design lecturer Quentin Stevens suggests that such monuments seek simultaneously to induce reflection on their subject matter and maintain the space as a wider amenity for the city, open for a full range of potential uses.[61] The subtle blending of memorials with the ordinary life of cities gives them the potential to disturb meanings. The design of monuments without clear boundaries around them blurs the traditional divide between monuments as representing commemorative space and the everyday space of the city.[62]

Figurative Statues versus Abstract Monuments in the Memorialisation of Loss

Does our survey of the memorialisation of loss, tragedy and evil suggest that such appalling events have pushed sculptors inexorably towards abstract and counter-monuments, or is there still space for figurative statues? In the wake of mass tragedies of the twentieth century, particularly World War I and the Holocaust, sculptors recoiled from traditional heroic interpretations of the events. They had no interest in crafting figurative sculptures which risked the glorification of horror. Where figurative sculpture was employed at all, it often took the form of downtrodden, antiheroic depictions, such as the *Fallen Man* and *Seated Youth*, two 1917 works by Wilhelm Lehmbruck.[63] And some circumstances call for abstraction. As we have seen, the Vietnam Veterans Memorial acknowledges US ambivalence towards the Vietnam War in ways that figurative monuments could not.[64] This was a central reason a figurative sculpture was later added to the memorial complex, providing a clearer interpretation for veterans of the value of their service.

But this is not the whole story. The government organisations and private donors responsible for commissioning monuments needed to provide justification for the appalling suffering, to offer the message that those who died did not do so in vain, and for these purposes abstract memorials worked poorly. Such aims continued best to be served by figurative imagery. And they wanted to create a collective, shared remembrance of events. Abstract monuments are more suited to the encouragement of personal, private, interpretations.[65] The call of figurative statues remains strong.

7

EXPORTING STATUES

In the Lithuanian capital Vilnius, a bust was erected in 1995 of US musician Frank Zappa, who had died two years earlier. Zappa never visited Lithuania, but he did have a fan club in the country, run by photographer Saulius Paukštys, which developed the statue project. The bust, which stands on a metal pole, was the work of Konstantinas Bogdanas, an elderly sculptor who had spent much of his career crafting likenesses of Lenin. The bust is part of one of those municipal 'talking statues' projects in which you give it a call via a QR code. Zappa the statue tells you that the explanation for his presence in the Lithuanian capital can be found on a track on his 1966 album *Freak Out!* Evoking one of those quests forming the plot of a Dan Brown novel, I discover that the track is entitled 'You're Probably Wondering Why I'm Here.' The answer, it transpires, is 'so am I'. In truth, the bust is less about Zappa specifically than about the way his authority-defying underground music symbolised the freedoms and possibilities offered by the release from communism.

The bust of Zappa was one of several statues appearing following the collapse of the Soviet Union and the restoration of independence of the Baltic States that embodied the Western values and lifestyles to which their populations aspired. Unlike proprietary statues, statues of heroes and icons of one polity placed on the territory of another may have no accompanying claim to that territory. The motivation may instead be to serve as a stimulus to the local country to adopt the values represented by the subject, values that appeal to local promoters of the project like Paukštys.

The 'exportation' of statues may also be a form of acknowledgment and thanks, either to the specific individual portrayed on the statue or the polity they represent, perhaps for wartime alliance or economic support in times of hardship. To give another example from the Baltic States, the visitor to the Latvian village of Skulte may be surprised to see on the front lawn of a private house a bust of former US president Ronald Reagan, or 'Ronalds Reigans', as he is rendered in Latvian (see fig. 15). Erected in 2013, it was the initiative of the house owner in recognition of Reagan's role in securing the restoration of Latvian independence and its anchoring to the west.[1]

The statue may also arise as an initiative not of patrons and promoters in the territory it stands but from those in the country of origin of the subject. It may be offered as a diplomatic gift: a statue of a widely admired individual serving as a calling card for the gifting polity and a demonstration of their soft power. The statue might also reference a specific positive event in the historical relationship between the two countries, in a manner intended to suggest a long-standing partnership and friendship.

Global Burns

Scottish poet Robert Burns is the subject of more than fifty life-sized or larger-than-life statues worldwide.[2] The first notable monument to the poet was his mausoleum, erected in Dumfries in 1819, featuring a marble mural by Peter Turnerelli depicting Burns at the plough while Coila, the muse Burns created for his poem *The Vision*, shelters him with her cloak. In the first sign of the competition between Scottish towns for a share of the Burns legacy that would intensify over the coming decades, the mausoleum campaign in Dumfries sparked calls for a monument opposite the church in Alloway, close to his birthplace, for which Edinburgh architect Thomas Hamilton offered his services free of charge.[3]

A particularly vigorous period of erection of statues to Burns accompanied the wider 'statuemania' of late Victorian Britain. The numbers of people involved both in fund-raising for statues and attendance at inauguration ceremonies marks the extent to which Burns had reached the hearts of the Scottish people. Some 40,000 one-shilling subscriptions were contributed for a statue to Burns in Glasgow, unveiled in 1877 at a ceremony attended by perhaps 100,000 people.[4]

EXPORTING STATUES

Statues to the Scottish bard were not confined to Scotland. Many were erected across North America in the late nineteenth and early twentieth centuries. New Zealand academic Paul Millar identified eight statues of Burns in Australia and four in New Zealand, outpacing the popularity of Shakespeare, for whom he found two and one, respectively.[5] This global Burns statuary in part reflects Burns' role as a unifying force for Scottish diasporas across the British Empire and English-speaking world, part of a process reflected today in the convening of Burns Suppers among Scottish communities worldwide. Looking at Australia and New Zealand, Millar argues that Burns' poetry, and its wistful depictions of rural Scottish life, resonated with settlers forging new lives in distant lands.[6] The network of Burns Clubs worldwide, consolidated in 1885 into the global Burns Federation, provided a natural focus of both effort and fundraising in the realisation of Burns statues.

The international appeal of Burns is not just a matter of a glue for Scottish diasporas. Burns resonated to audiences worldwide, though in different ways, a reflection of the notoriously difficult challenges in placing Burns within any single clear political ideology, though many have tried.[7] Scottish historian Christopher Whatley has demonstrated that the initial impulse within Scotland to commemorate and memorialise Burns came largely from the elite.[8] They looked to rural paternalism as a more comforting social model than ideals emerging from rapid industrialisation and urbanisation, and found supportive sentiments in Burns' writing, such as the close-knit humble peasant household described in *The Cotter's Saturday Night*. Yet Radicals also found much in Burns to sustain their cause. *A Man's a Man for A'That* is a statement of egalitarianism, drawing from Paine's *Rights of Man*, much sung by Radicals alongside the patriotic *Scots Wha Hae*, later used as a party song of the Scottish National Party. Burns sided with the American Revolution, and with the Jacobins in the French Revolution, but as the prospect of a French invasion grew, joined the Dumfries Volunteers and penned *Does Haughty Gaul Invasion Threat?*, a clarion call for British unity against the foreign foe.

Burns has been treated in different ways by different international audiences, with a broadly conservative usage in England, North

America, Australia and New Zealand, but more frequently as a radical in Scotland, mainland Europe and some non-white former British colonies.[9] For Scottish historian Murray Pittock, Burns' ability to convey complex ideas in simple and accessible imagery, and his refusal to tie himself to any clearly articulated political standpoint, facilitated his simultaneous adoption by both radical politicians around the world and those wedded to cautious advancement of progressive universal aspirations.[10] Translated into Russian in 1947 by Soviet writer Samuil Marshak, who oriented the language more squarely towards themes of class conflict, and omitted some of the religious, royalist and Jacobite material,[11] Burns proved enormously popular in the USSR, selling more than 600,000 copies. For the Soviet regime, the useful message conveyed by Burns was that peasants might have advanced radical ideas and need not be dismissed as reactionaries. Similarly, in Cultural Revolution China, Burns served to demonstrate the values of the peasantry.[12]

Since Burns was appreciated in different ways by different viewers, the way the poet was memorialised might not correspond to what was valued. Paul Millar explores the reaction in 1905 of Australian bush poet Henry Lawson, for whom the Scottish poet was a great influence, to the unveiling of a statue in Sydney, depicting Burns leaning against a ploughshare (see fig. 16). The unveiling was performed by State Governor Sir Harry Rawson in the presence of several thousand people, though the weather was lousy, and proceedings were rushed through. In his poem, *Bobbie's Statue*, Lawson complains that the fearsome crowd at the unveiling knew nothing more of Burns than the first verse of *Auld Lang Syne* and the chorus, a knowledge that enabled them to talk glibly of 'Rabby'. If the real Burns turned up at their home, they would turf him out.

Statues as Diplomatic Gifts

Gifts have been central to diplomacy since ancient times. The Amarna Letters, a series of clay tablets dating from the Egypt of Pharaoh Akhenaten, were the diplomatic correspondence of their day. They are full of references to gifts sent or desired. While today's diplomatic gifts are mostly distinctly more modest than the copious quantities of gold dripping from the text of the Amarna Letters, the practice has proved remarkably durable. The work of French sociologist Marcel Mauss suggests an explanation for the importance of gifts in diplomacy: that gifts have a social function, creating and nurturing social relationships.[13] A single purchase creates no enduring link between buyer and seller. In gift exchange, in contrast, the act of giving establishes a social relationship, binding giver and receiver. That relationship depends, according to Mauss, on three obligations: that to give presents, that to receive them, and that to repay gifts received.[14] It is the third obligation, reciprocation, that ensures a continuing social relationship. Diplomacy is about the conduct of business between geographically distinct polities. A continuing social relationship is vital; and here diplomatic gifts play an important role in establishing and nurturing these relationships.[15]

The choice of gift serves the interests of the giver, a consideration the Trojans would have done well to remember when presented with that lovely wooden horse by the Greeks. Gifting strategies include highlighting the achievements or culture of the gifting country, as a form of soft power; focusing on a specific event or person embodying friendship between the two countries; praising the culture and values of the receiving country; or a more personal gift seeking to appeal specifically to the passions of the individual recipient.[16] While many diplomatic gifts these days are quotidian affairs, chosen in haste by hardworking teams putting together senior visits, for the more important diplomatic gifts throughout history effort has been made to ensure they are special. The gifting strategy of the Mamluks embodied the concept of *tuhaf*, or 'marvels': gifts should have the ability to generate wonder.[17] Marcel Mauss, in his exploration of gift exchange in Melanesia, found that specific items were gifted, different in character to the useful goods involved in other forms of exchange in the same societies.[18]

The gift from Felipe IV, King of Spain, to Charles, Prince of Wales, in 1623 of Giambologna's *Samson Slaying a Philistine* was firmly based around its appeal to the recipient. Charles, the son of King James I, was enthusiastic about marriage to the Infanta Maria Anna in Spain but frustrated at the slow pace of negotiations over the match. He decided to speed matters up, turning up unannounced in March 1623 at the residence of the British ambassador in Madrid in the company of the Duke of Buckingham. They had been travelling as John and Tom Smith,[19] sporting false beards. Negotiations over the marriage would come to nothing, but Charles had more success in the secondary objective of his Spanish sojourn: the acquisition of art. He and Buckingham spent substantial sums on purchases, and Charles hinted heavily to his Spanish hosts at his desire for diplomatic gifts of artworks, securing a couple of Titians from King Felipe IV.

In September, Charles and his party left Madrid, negotiations still ongoing and destined to fail. En route for his rendezvous with the English fleet, which was to pick up his party in Santander, Charles stopped off at the royal residence in Valladolid, where he saw one final opportunity to secure more artistic diplomatic gifts. He was greatly taken with a fountain centred on a statue depicting Samson about to thwack a fallen Philistine with the jawbone of an ass, the work of Florence-based Flemish sculptor Giambologna, who had made it around 1560 for the House of Medici. It had already served as a diplomatic gift, from the Grand Duke of Tuscany to the Duke of Lerma, who had built the palace in Valladolid. Charles, pushing the limits of etiquette around diplomatic gifts, convinced his Spanish hosts in the absence of the king, who had remained in Madrid, that the statue, together with a Veronese painting of *Venus, Cupid and Mars*, would make a perfect gift to celebrate his visit.[20] His hint-dropping efforts bore fruit, in a rare derogation from the maxim that gifts serve the interests of the giver.

Gifting Heroes: The Many Statues of Bolívar

Among the subjects of statues most frequently gifted, in pride of place stands, and sometimes sits, Simón Bolívar, the 'Liberator' who led a raft of countries to independence from the Spanish Empire. There have been suggestions that the statues of no other historical personage have such a global reach as Bolívar.[21] Statues of Bolívar populate the Latin American countries he helped bring to independence. Some are replicated in several different cities, a reflection of the desire in each place to possess an iconic monument to their liberating hero. In 1846, a statue of Bolívar was erected at the heart of Plaza Mayor in Bogotá, replacing John the Baptist. The work of Italian sculptor Pietro Tenerani, who made a good living from sculpting Bolívar, replicas of the bronze sculpture depicting a standing Liberator in military regalia appeared later in other cities, such as Ciudad Bolívar in Venezuela in 1869. Another Italian sculptor, Adamo Tadolini, who learned his trade under Antonio Canova, delivered the first equestrian statue of Bolívar in the continent, installed in Lima in 1859. This in turn was replicated, turning up in 1874 in Plaza Bolívar in Caracas.[22]

While the erection of statues to the hero of independence was part of the nation-building work of Latin American states liberated by Bolívar, the appearance of statues outside the continent owed much to their use as diplomatic gifts, a strategy embraced with particular fervour by Venezuela, since 1999 the Bolivarian Republic of Venezuela, the place of Bolívar's birth, for whom the Liberator serves as a calling card and icon. The placing and portrayal of these statues of Bolívar however embodies different gifting strategies, exploiting different aspects of Bolívar's life and modern meaning. In London's Belgrave Square a standing statue of Bolívar was installed in 1974, the work of Italian-born Venezuela-based sculptor Hugo Daini. Its plinth carries a quotation from the Liberator: 'I am convinced that England alone is capable of protecting the world's rights as she is great, glorious and wise.'

The statue unveiled five years later in the square in Cairo renamed in Bolívar's honour presented a different view of Britain. Its setting was the former Midan Qasr Al Dubara, once an important centre of British rule in Egypt, a place associated with protests by Egyptian nationalists and their dispersal.[23] The statue was flown in from Caracas. A plaque on the plinth described it as a 'symbol of friendship between the Republic of Venezuela and Republic of Egypt'.[24] In choosing to locate the statue in Midan Qasr Al Dubara, the Venezuelan authorities linked Bolívar to the liberation not just of Latin American countries from Spanish rule, but also to the liberation of Egypt from the British one, casting Bolívar as a symbol of universal liberation.

That connection was taken up by Egyptians during the 2011 revolution, when Bolívar would be invoked as a liberating ally by those seeking to overthrow the regime of Hosni Mubarak. The proximity of the statue to Tahrir Square, epicentre of the revolution, facilitated this role, and the statue was draped with an Egyptian flag, and even given bandages over his eyes after security police used tear gas on protestors.[25] Commemoration of the Bolívar statue in Cairo had hitherto largely been confined to gatherings of diplomatic representatives of the Latin American countries liberated by Bolívar every 5 July, Venezuela's independence day. Revolution in Egypt summoned Bolívar's wider appeal as a symbol of liberation of the people in a broader sense.

Portraying the Hero

Where a statue of an icon of the gifting country is used as a diplomatic gift, care will be taken over portrayal of the subject, to ensure that the monument emphasises those characteristics the giver wants to underline. A gift of statues of two American icons to the United Kingdom makes this point. The gift celebrated a century of peace among English-speaking peoples, following ratification in 1815 of the Treaty of Ghent, the treaty ending the 1812 war between the United States and the United Kingdom. An American Peace Centenary Committee had been established in 1909, to work up plans for the commemoration. Various suggestions were considered, amongst them a World Statue of Peace in New York Harbour on an artificial island facing the Statue of Liberty. A 'Fraternity' to accompany Liberty, as it were. Also mooted were four Pillars of Peace, two at each end of the Panama Canal, and, more modestly, a blow-out banquet in Ghent.

Plans actually materialising included a British-American Peace Centenary Ball, held at the Royal Albert Hall on 10 June 1914. This was organised by a committee involving seven Duchesses, eight Marchionesses, thirty-two Countesses, fifteen Viscountesses and Princess Alexandra of Connaught. The hall was bedecked in red, white and blue. A replica of Columbus's ship, the *Santa Maria*, stood in front of the organ. Lady Maud Warrender was dressed as

Britannia. Other ball-goers were attired as Pilgrim Fathers, Quakers, Christopher Columbus and signatories of the Treaty of Ghent.[26] That last one must have prompted puzzled conversations at fancy dress shops throughout London. Two months later Britain declared war on Germany. The commemoration of a century of peace felt somewhat inappropriate.

The American Peace Centenary Committee had however resolved the previous year to mark the peace anniversary by sending London two replica statues of American heroes: Jean-Antoine Houdon's statue of George Washington, and Augustus Saint-Gaudens's statue of Abraham Lincoln. The war delayed the project, but both statues eventually reached London. That a second, different, statue of Abraham Lincoln ended up in Manchester has much to do with controversies over how precisely American heroes should be depicted.

The George Washington statue proved straightforward. The original version, by noted French sculptor Houdon, had been commissioned by the Virginia General Assembly, completed in France around 1792, and delivered to Richmond in 1796. It stands in the rotunda of the Virginia State Capitol. The State of Virginia bore the cost of the replica bound for London. The statue portrays a suitably distinguished Washington, standing amidst a mix of military and civilian artefacts. His left arm rests on a fasces on which sword and cape are slung. He holds a cane in his right hand, and there is a plough behind him. The fact the United Kingdom happily accepted a statue of the man who led the Patriot forces to victory against them in the American Revolutionary War is a sign of the subsequent improvement in relations between the two powers, though the choice of location is interesting. The statue stands in front of the National Gallery in London, in the shadow of the column to Horatio Nelson, victor over the French navy, the very navy that earlier helped Washington against the British. Tour guides will tell you that Virginia soil was placed under the statue, in order not to negate Washington's vow never to set foot on British soil again.[27]

Augustus Saint-Gaudens's statue of Abraham Lincoln was completed in 1887 and placed in Lincoln Park in Chicago. It too portrays a distinguished subject: a contemplative president who has just risen from the chair of state behind him. He has a serious expression, his left hand holding the lapel of his jacket. He appears to be about to start an evidently important speech. Saint-Gaudens researched Lincoln meticulously. He was apparently enticed to Cornish, New Hampshire, to work on the statue there, by a promise from his friend Charles Beaman that the area had 'many Lincoln-shaped men' who might be suitable models.[28]

The problem for the American Peace Centenary Committee was that they hadn't identified a benefactor to bear the cost of the replica of Saint-Gaudens's statue in the way the State of Virginia was financing the Houdon one.[29] A solution appeared. Politician and newspaper editor Charles Taft, older half-brother of US President William Howard Taft, offered a replica of a different statue of Lincoln, by George Grey Barnard, the original of which would be erected in Lytle Park in Cincinnati, Ohio. Barry Schwartz, an expert on Abraham Lincoln's place in the American memory, notes however that the replacement of one statue of Lincoln with another was to prove problematic, since the statues represented different visions of Lincoln's character and role.

Barnard portrayed Lincoln as far from distinguished. His Lincoln is lanky, stooped, his clothes worn. His hands rest awkwardly over his midriff, suggesting to some that he is suffering from a mild stomach-ache. To Barnard and his supporters, this portrayal of Lincoln underlined his identification with the common people. The statue depicted an egalitarian American democracy, a Lincoln of the people and for the people.[30] There was no opposition to such a portrayal of Lincoln in Cincinnati. But objections were raised to the use of its replica as a gift for London. It was felt that a statue of Lincoln as a diplomatic gift had a responsibility to represent the country as an influential power, a leader among Western democracies. Barnard's down-at-heel vision did not work. A more statesmanlike composition, like the distinguished Neoclassical portrayal by Saint-Gaudens, the original choice of the Committee, was indeed called for.

In December 1917, the National Academy of Design surveyed members of the American Peace Centenary Committee, discovering that most respondents favoured the Saint-Gaudens statue over the Barnard as an appropriate gift for London. The Vice-President of the Academy wrote to Sir Alfred Mond, First Commissioner of Works in the British Government, urging him to decline the Barnard statue in favour of Saint-Gaudens's portrayal.[31] The British Committee, not about to look a gift horse in the mouth, declared both Lincoln statues quite acceptable. It was indeed though the Saint-Gaudens statue given the prime location in London's Parliament Square, where it was unveiled in 1920.

The Barnard statue went to Manchester, where it was placed in Platt Fields Park, moving in 1986 to a new central location in the unprepossessing Lincoln Square. The Manchester statue's origins in commemorating a centenary of peace have been entirely forgotten in favour of a celebration of Lincoln's ties with the city. These lie in the cotton industry, the basis of Manchester's wealth. A major source of the raw cotton fuelling the industry was the Confederate south. The blockade of the south ordered by Lincoln in 1861 thus hit Manchester hard. Mills closed. Workers went hungry. The shipping bosses in Liverpool sided with the Confederacy, and many mill owners joined suit. There were calls for the Royal Navy to break the blockade. Yet many cotton workers, despite the impact of the blockade on their pockets and bellies, wanted an end to slavery. At a mass meeting in Manchester's Free Trade Hall in 1862, a motion was passed urging Lincoln to maintain the blockade, win the war and abolish slavery.[32] On 19 January 1863 Lincoln wrote to thank the workers of Manchester for their 'sublime Christian heroism' in accepting the suffering wrought by the blockade. The text of that letter appears on the plinth. A gift of thanks to the United Kingdom has been reworked as a gift of thanks to Manchester.

Diplomatic Gifts Honouring Local Heroes

Standing on a hilltop overlooking the Icelandic capital Reykjavik is a statue of Leif Erikson, the explorer who in reaching the territory of Vinland became the first European to arrive in America, preceding Columbus by 500 years. The statue was conceived as a US gift to the people of Iceland to mark the thousandth anniversary of the establishment of the Icelandic parliament in 930. It follows then a different gifting strategy to the statues of Bolívar and Lincoln: praising not the heroes of the gifting country but those of the recipient one, as a mark of admiration and respect. It was kicked off by a resolution of Congress. The task of selecting a sculptor fell to the US Commission of Fine Arts, who invited a group of US sculptors to submit proposals. Their choice fell on Alexander Stirling Calder, who delivered a completed statue in 1932. The plinth, of Texas red granite, had been manufactured by a company in Vermont, put in place in 1931 to await the statue.

Calder's design plays to stereotypes of Vikings as noble warriors. Erikson is portrayed as clean shaven and resolute, bearing an axe, but also with his sword in its scabbard. The plinth resembles the prow of his ship, with Erikson looking forward to new horizons. Calder envisaged that the statue would stand on a pond, representing the Atlantic, but this was never realised.

The process of agreeing the precise location proved challenging. The Americans wanted their fine gift to have a prominent place, and had identified the hill known as Skólavörduholt, overlooking the city. The Icelandic authorities had their own plans for the hill, earmarked as the site for the future Hallgrimskirkja, a church to honour the memory of Hallgrímur Pétursson, the seventeenth-century author of the fifty Hymns of the Passion, known to every Icelander. Members of the city council proposed that the statue be placed on another hill in a more peripheral location. The US authorities would have none of this, and agreement was finally reached, under which the statue would be placed on Skólavörduholt, but in a slightly less central location on the hill to allow the future Hallgrimskirkja to be built behind it. Although born of compromise, the outcome was to prove successful, and statue and church today form a satisfying ensemble. Most visitors to Reykjavik, or at least those who give the matter any consideration, assume the church was built first, with the statue later placed in front.

Another challenge surrounded the spelling of the subject for the inscription on the plinth. How should the Old Norse be rendered for a modern audience? Different Nordic countries used different spellings, and there are numerous different versions in English. After consultations with an Icelandic law professor in Illinois, the

EXPORTING STATUES

US government settled on Leifr Eiricsson. There was considerable local disquiet too that the statue was being used as a public toilet. The city council resorted to paying for a guard to dissuade micturition. Someone suggested connecting the statue to the electricity grid, to give urinators a shock. The installation of a British army camp on the hill in World War II solved the problem, bringing the statue under de facto British military protection.

Icelanders grew proud of the gift. Particularly welcome was the reference on the inscription to Erikson as a 'son of Iceland.' This offered US endorsement of Icelandic claims in their squabbles with Norway over the ownership of Erikson. The US was not however altogether consistent on that matter. When they decided in 1964 to celebrate Leif Erikson Day, they chose 9 October, a date marking the arrival of a shipload of Norwegians to the New World in 1825.

The Icelandic government was sufficiently pleased by the statue to request permission to use Calder's plaster model for a second casting, for their use at the 1939 New York World's Fair. It was coupled with a casting of the statue we have already encountered of Thorfinn Karlsefni, another Viking explorer of the New World, by Einar Jónsson. After plans for a permanent site for the second Erikson statue in Washington fell through, it has found a home at the Mariners' Museum and Park in Newport News, Virginia. The Calder statue has become an iconic image of Vikinghood. A bas-relief, featuring an image based on the statue, stands at the Leifur Eiriksson Air Terminal at Keflavik, where it was installed at the 1987 opening of the terminal.

The Statue of Liberty

Let us conclude our look at diplomatic gifts of statues with one that embodies neither a hero of gifting nor recipient country, but a value associated with the recipient country that was particularly prized by those who conceived the project. It is The Statue of Liberty, or more properly *Liberty Enlightening the World*. Its origins lay in private initiative, its genesis resting with a Frenchman named Édouard René Lefebvre de Laboulaye, professor of comparative law at the Collège de France. He admired the United States, seeing in that country a model for stable democracy contrasting with the chaotic French experience of autocratic rule punctuated by violent revolution. The practice of slavery and divisions resulting in the American Civil War tarnished the role of the United States as an exemplary republic: the victory of the Union was critically important to Laboulaye, demonstrating that US democratic government could remain true to its principles in the face of such a grave threat.

The transformation of admiration for US democracy into a proposal for a statue is traced by some accounts to a dinner hosted by Laboulaye in 1865, attended by a young sculptor named Frédéric Auguste Bartholdi, enthused by Laboulaye's suggestion that a public monument be constructed through the effort of France and the United States, symbolising the friendship of the two countries at the heart of the American War of Independence.[33] The proposal had a slow gestation, and no action was taken to progress it for a further five or six years.[34] Plans finally developed following the traumatic French defeat in the Franco-Prussian War of 1870.

In 1875, Laboulaye established the Franco-American Union as a vehicle to marshal funding for the project, its members hailing largely from the moderate republican political space. The French side would fund the statue, as a gift from France, while costs of the pedestal would fall to the United States. The processes of fundraising and construction were so protracted that Laboulaye did not live to see the completion of his statue. His role in the Franco-American Union was taken over by Ferdinand de Lesseps, developer of the Suez Canal, who was attempting to repeat the feat in Panama.

The statue was assembled in France and handed over to the minister of the United States to France on 4 July 1884. The French government, wishing to demonstrate that it endorsed the views that had inspired the project, made available a ship to transport the statue to the United States. US fundraising for the pedestal progressed even more slowly, but the statue was finally dedicated on 28 October 1886.

There were perhaps four major motives underpinning the project, each varying in importance during the long period from conception to realisation. The first was to honour the achievement of the United States in providing an enduring model for stable and democratic government. What precisely was being celebrated was not constant. If the statue was indeed conceived over dinner in 1865, the year of Lincoln's assassination, the timing suggests a focus on abolition of slavery. Laboulaye was chair of the French Anti-Slavery Society, and the broken shackles at the statue's feet suggest liberation from slavery. Bartholdi's first design however featured broken shackles more prominently, including in the female figure's left hand. Laboulaye reportedly suggested that these be replaced by a tablet inscribed 'July 4, 1776', arguing that the shackles suggested the process of liberation rather than the permanent concept of liberty.[35] The abolition of slavery became a less prominent part of the statue's messaging with increasing distance from the American Civil War.

A second motive was to encourage the adoption of this form of government in France. The form of liberty celebrated by the statue derives from the views of its promoters as to how this should come about. Bartholdi's Liberty is a world away from that of Eugène Delacroix in his 1830 painting, *Liberty Leading the People*. For Delacroix, Liberty is revolutionary, bare-breasted, leading the call to arms while sporting the Phrygian cap espoused by French revolutionaries. Bartholdi's Liberty is calm and reassuring, the Liberty of Laboulaye's conservative republicanism, which opposed both autocracy and revolutionary anarchy.[36]

The third motive was to stress the vitality of Franco–US relations, and underline France's role in the American War of Independence. The backdrop was fear that France was losing its influence in the United States in relation to both Britain and Germany. The United States had favoured the Prussian cause in 1870, and large-scale German migration to America created a strong lobby. Business interests were an important consideration for members of the Franco-American Union. For de Lesseps, the statue was a means to secure US support for his Panama Canal project.[37]

The fourth motive was that of the sculptor, Bartholdi, long interested in colossal sculpture. Entranced by the Colossi of Memnon, he had resolved to create his own colossus. In 1869, he put before the Khedive of Egypt a proposal for a huge statue at the entrance to the Suez Canal. His design was based on a *fellaha*, a female Egyptian field worker. Holding a torch aloft as a beacon for maritime traffic, the sculpture was to be called *Egypt Bringing Light to the Orient*. With no funding for the project, it was never progressed, and Bartholdi wisely avoided suggestions that the Statue of Liberty was a repurposing of the failed Egyptian project. The design parallels were nonetheless strong.[38]

The meaning of the Statue of Liberty today does not however precisely correspond to any of these motivations. A sonnet written in 1883 by Emma Lazarus to help raise funds for the pedestal reinvented the statue as a symbol of the United States as a land of opportunity for immigrants. Lady Liberty in *The New Colossus* calls out to the old world: 'Give me your tired, your poor, your huddled masses yearning to breathe free.'[39] This interpretation of the statue overtook associations with Franco–US friendship or moderate republicanism, fuelled by its geographical location: a beacon for new arrivals to the country on New York Harbour.[40]

8

STATUES OF WOMEN

On 22 March 2017, seven garishly coloured busts of their sculptor, Irina Tomova-Erka, were installed across the Bulgarian capital, Sofia, in a temporary initiative organised by the Bulgarian Helsinki Committee. The plaque on each read: 'the first monument of a woman in Sofia'. The genesis of the initiative lay in the realisation that, among the statues peppering the city, not one honoured a real female historical figure.[1] Sofia is far from alone in the rarity of statues to real women in its public spaces, as against allegorical female figures, the latter often honouring the achievements of men.

The Immortalisation of Women and Goats in the United Kingdom

British artist collective non zero one embarked in 2018 on an artwork entitled *put her forward*. Getting beyond the affinity of the collective to the e e cummings approach to capital letters, one discovers that this initiative aimed to address the shortage of statues of non-mythical, non-royal women in Britain. Their website reported that, of 925 public statues in the UK, just 158 were of women, of which only 25 were of non-mythical, non-royal women. 'There are more statues of people called John. There are more statues of goats.'[2]

Goats? The suggestion that, having removed queens and mythological women from the equation, there are more statues of goats than women across the United Kingdom elicits two responses. The first is to lament the shortage of statues of women suggested by this statistic. The second is to wonder about all those goats. The first question is more important, and we will return to it. But let us first consider the second: the evident plethora of goat statues dotted across the British Isles. Where are they? And what is so statue-worthy about goats?

London's best-known goat statue stands on a pile of packing cases in Spitalfields, site of a market since the seventeenth century (see fig. 17). *I Goat*, by Scottish sculptor Kenny Hunter, won the 2010 Spitalfields Sculpture Prize, a £45,000 commission chosen by public vote from eight shortlisted designs. The sculptor reportedly explained that the goat should not be understood as a goat, or at least a specific one, but rather a symbol of the migrants who have found sanctuary in, and helped to shape, the Spitalfields area over the centuries. The association of goats with persecution and sacrifice represented the challenges these migrants had overcome.[3]

To the west of the capital, in Kingston upon Thames, a bronze goat with a traffic cone on its back was erected in the town market-place. *Party Animal*, the work of sculptor Alex R. T. Davies, was one of seven temporary sculptures set up in the town as part of a 2021 sculpture trail. The goat statue stormed the ensuing public vote to determine the overall winner, earning its sculptor £10,000 and the statue a permanent site. The goat's heart-shaped nose seems designed for rubbing, and David Mach, chair of the selection committee, gushed that Kingston had found its equivalent of Florence's *Porcellino* statue, whose nose had turned gold from contact with the hands of innumerable tourists. And not just the nose: 'the cone on the back of Alex's goat is going to be just as shiny.'[4]

Wales is richly endowed with statues of goats. There are two, or at least their heads, at the crenelated manor house of Cyfarthfa in Merthyr Tydfil, commissioned in 1824 by William Crawshay II, who appears to have lived for much of his adult life bearing the title 'The Ironmaster', which while suggesting a successful career in professional wrestling, refers to his control of the Cyfarthfa Ironworks, overlooked by the castle. The goat heads guard the entrance, though in a curiously inefficient way, looking inwards towards the building.

Let us head to Llandudno, and the visitor centre below the summit of the Great Orme, a limestone headland north-west of the town. Here in 2002 a sculpture was unveiled, commissioned by

STATUES OF WOMEN

Conwy County Borough Council. The bronze statue depicts a goat with impressive curling antlers, standing on a stylised mountain. The statue celebrates the herd of Kashmiri goats that has long thrived on the headland. Its origins lie in the Royal Windsor Herd, which developed in the early nineteenth century when cashmere became fashionable in Britain. Goats reached North Wales courtesy of Lord Mostyn, who acquired a pair from the Royal Herd later in the century, and released them onto the Great Orme, their home ever since.[5] The goats hit the headlines during the 2020 Coronavirus lockdown when, emboldened by the paucity of traffic and people on the streets, they took over the town, munching their way through whatever flowers they could find.[6]

The Kashmiri goats of the Great Orme have a connection with our next goat statue, in Wrexham, close to the border with England. It honours the animal's connections to the Royal Welsh, an armoured infantry regiment, and its antecedents, the Royal Welch Fusiliers and the Royal Regiment of Wales. The links began during the American War of Independence, when a goat reportedly strayed onto the battlefield at Bunker Hill in 1775 and hooked up with the colour party of the Royal Welch Fusiliers. A tradition was born. All three battalions of the Royal Welsh now maintain a goat as mascot. That of the Third Battalion, formerly the Royal Welsh Regiment, is invariably named Shenkin, from the Welsh pronunciation of Jenkins.[7] The latest goat to hold this coveted position, Shenkin IV, part of the Royal Herd on the Great Orme, was eventually captured after running the army team deployed to secure him quite a chase. The Regimental Goat Major, Sgt Mark Jackson, was determined to get his goat: 'he's got a lovely quiff of hair on top of his horns—he's the one we want', he told journalists.[8]

In March 2023, a life-sized bronze statue of Shenkin leading the Regimental Goat Major was unveiled at the entrance to Hightown Barracks in Wrexham. The project was the initiative of local councillor Graham Rogers, with a fundraising campaign led by Offa Community Council raising some £130,000. Sculptor Nick Elphick had worked from 3D scans of Lance Corporal Shenkin IV, and an army cadet named Matteo Molica-Franco in the role of Regimental Goat Major.[9]

Two points of note here. First, this is the first goat statue we have encountered that features a specific, named, goat. A goat hero, if you will. Second, the statue dates from 2023, so like *Party Animal* is not included in non zero one's claim about goat statues being more numerous than non-mythical, non-royal women.

Other goat statues are encountered in unexpected corners of the British Isles. There is a *Putto with Goat* adorning Leeds Civic Hall, the 1930s work of Joseph Hermon Cawthra, a suitable companion piece for his *Putto with Turkey*. An abstract four-metre-tall statue of a leaping wild goat, given a mystical quality by the freshwater pearl mussels adorning its beard and scattered at its feet, was installed near the source of the River Rede in Northumberland in 2023 as part of a National Lottery Heritage Fund-supported project to revitalise the Redesdale landscape. The mussels apparently reference efforts to improve the water quality of the Rede.[10]

Goats indeed then take a starring role in public statues across the United Kingdom. This is not altogether surprising, given the important role of the goat in art since ancient times, sometimes used to depict ribaldry or lewdness, as with the Greek God Pan, with horns and hindquarters of a goat. Taking lewdness to the next, and darker, degree, the unfortunate goat has also served as a symbol of devilry. More upliftingly, it has been presented as a mark of endurance. International goat statues include the 2015 temporary installation *Capricorn Two*, the work of Austrian art collective Steinbrener/Dempf & Huber, sounding more like a respectable firm of Central European solicitors. They placed an aluminium and plastic ibex on the head of the colossal 1906 statue of 'Iron Chancellor' Bismarck in Hamburg, transforming Bismarck from statesman to mountainscape, apparently making a statement about an emerging nationalistic Bismarck cult.[11]

And yet. Do goats really outnumber statues of non-mythical, non-royal women across the United Kingdom? In 2018, presenter Tim Harford and the team at BBC Radio 4's *More or Less* were urged to investigate by listener Ken Powell, suspicious of the claim. The BBC approached non zero one about its origin, to be told that they had heard it at a conference. The BBC consulted a database set up by the Public Monuments and Sculpture Association, albeit one last updated in 2002, which listed 925 statues in the United Kingdom. This is the list cited by non zero one. Campaigner Caroline Criado Perez established that while more than 500 of these were statues of men standing on their own, only 160 depicted women. Take out allegorical statues and those portraying royalty, the number of female statues goes down to 27. The BBC team could find only three statues of goats on the list, and one of those was an urn.[12]

Addressing the Gender Imbalance

There are then more statues of women than goats in the United Kingdom. But there are many more statues of real men than real women. The campaign of non zero one, one of several seeking to address that imbalance, sought to double the number of statues of non-mythical, non-royal women in England. This was to be achieved by receiving nominations of living women who had 'positively impacted the people around them', and converting twenty-five of these, via 3D scanning and printing, into sandstone figurines. Thus, a statuette was unveiled at the National Theatre in London in September 2018 of Taban Shoresh, founder of The Lotus Flower, an organisation working with female survivors of conflict in Kurdistan. The *put her forward* website proudly proclaimed a goal achieved: 'we aimed to double the statues of non-mythical, non-royal women in England by September 2018. And thanks to you, we did it!' The figures were in: 'we have raised the percentage of statues of non-mythical, non-royal women from 2.8% to 5.5%.'[13]

Except that they hadn't. The sandstone figurines generated by the project honoured some remarkable women but were too small to have qualified for the database set up by the Public Monuments and Sculpture Association. That organisation was wound up in 2020, but out of its ashes emerged a new Public Statues and Sculpture Association, which in 2021 launched a new database of public statues of women. It excludes royal and allegorical figures, identifying 146 statues of named non-royal women and another 27 of 'generic women' (for example, statues representative of specific occupations), suggesting a leap forward from the 27 non-female, non-allegorical statues identified by the organisation's predecessor in 2002. All without the aid of the statuettes produced by non zero one.

This progress is the product of campaigns to highlight the achievements of individual women through immortalisation in bronze or stone. The unveiling in 2018 on the prestigious site of Parliament Square in London of a statue of suffragist leader Millicent Fawcett followed a campaign led by Caroline Criado Perez to bring the first female statue to a square hitherto dominated by monuments to men. The campaign was taken up by the government, with support from its Centenary Fund for artistic works linked to the centenary of World War I. The work of Gillian Wearing, the statue depicts Fawcett holding a banner inscribed with her words 'courage calls to courage everywhere.'[14] Two years earlier, a statue had been erected just over the River Thames, in the grounds of St Thomas' Hospital, honouring nurse and businesswoman Mary Seacole, voted the greatest black Briton in a 2003 survey (see fig. 18). The work of Martin Jennings, the statue depicts its subject stepping forward into the future. Behind her is a vertical bronze disc, etched with a representation of the terrain at the site where she established her British Hotel during the Crimean War, a touch intended to hint at the futility of imperialistic struggles over dusty scraps of earth.[15] The statue followed a twelve-year fundraising campaign by the Mary Seacole Memorial Statue Appeal, and faced opposition from Canadian academic Lynn McDonald and the Nightingale Society, champions of another remarkable nineteenth-century woman, Florence Nightingale. The Society was particularly upset that the Seacole statue was placed at St Thomas' Hospital, to which Seacole had no connection but which had been the site of the school of nursing founded by Nightingale.

One interesting feature of this effort to 'redress balance' by erecting statues to honour distinguished women is that it takes for granted the notion that statues are an appropriate way to honour their subjects. Not everyone agrees. Art critic Jonathan Jones questions 'why is it conservative to want a statue of Keith Park but radical to want an equally uncreative and old-fashioned statue of Mary Seacole? Artistically, both are absurd.' For Jones, 'the dead art of statuary' is a bad way to attempt to keep the radical past alive.[16]

STATUES OF WOMEN

Statues of Women in Ancient Rome

A gender imbalance in public statues is characteristic of many times and places. Consider Ancient Rome. Here, the rarity of public statues of non-divine women stems from a separation drawn between a public masculine world and a domestic female one. Statues granted by a senate decree and erected at public expense were typically rewards for military triumphs, great acts of courage or civic generosity. The rarity of statues of women was not however true of all parts of the empire: such statues had long been a feature of Greek-speaking provinces in the east, following a local tradition of erecting statues to female relatives of rulers.

The late historian Marleen Flory studied the slow emergence of grants of public honorific statues for women in Rome. She argues that these at first treated their female subjects as honorary men. An equestrian statue of Cloelia, a legendary heroine of the early days of Rome, honoured her heroic deeds in rescuing fellow female hostages taken by the Etruscan King Porsenna. Livy's account describes her actions as an example of masculine courage 'new in a woman'.[17] The Temple of Magna Mater on the Palatine Hill honoured the Anatolian mother goddess known as Cybele to the Greeks and the 'Great Mother' to the Romans. A statue of a noblewoman named Quinta Claudia was erected here in 204 BCE, in recognition of a remarkable feat of strength during her efforts to bring the sacred image of the Great Mother from Asia Minor to Rome. The boat holding the image became stuck on a sandbar in the Tiber, but our heroine, after praying to the goddess for help, managed single-handedly to release the boat and bring it to shore.

Flory argues that the grounds for granting statues of women evolved to embrace the subject's role in giving birth to children who went on to carry out exalted deeds. The decision over granting such statues was still made by men, its motivation rooted in the politics of the time. Both Pliny and Plutarch describe a seated statue in Rome's Porticus Metelli of Cornelia, mother of Tiberius and Gaius Gracchus, champions of the *populares*, that political faction who used the popular assemblies in opposition to the senate. Flory believed the decision to erect a statue to Cornelia was linked to the political power battles of the late Roman Republic. In honouring the mother, the statue highlighted the sons, and the triumph of the popular will over the entrenched aristocracy.[18] The statue itself has not survived, though its marble base bearing an inscription to Cornelia was unearthed at the Porticus Octaviae, the renovated and reworked Porticus Metelli.

In 35 BCE, Octavian, one of the rulers of the Second Triumvirate, granted privileges unprecedented for Roman women to his sister Octavia and wife Livia, among them criminalisation of verbally insulting them, immunity from male guardianship, or *tutela*, and the right to have statues displayed in public places. Octavia was the wife of Mark Antony, the other Triumvir, and political rival to Octavian. Mark Antony was enjoying a love affair with Cleopatra of Egypt, which did nothing to endear him further to Octavian. The privileges accorded to Octavia appear to have been part of a wider strategy on her brother's part to use Cleopatra to undercut Mark Antony, in this case by exalting Octavia's virtues to underline the appalling way this noble woman was being treated by her husband. Flory argues that the granting of privileges to Livia was an incidental by-product of this political objective, simply to keep honours accorded to the wives of the two Triumvirs, Antony and Octavian, at an equal level.[19] If, incidentally, you are wondering why the joint rulers were referred to as Triumvirs when there were only two of them, I should clarify that the third co-ruler, Lepidus, had already been out-manoeuvred by Octavian and forced into retirement in 36 BCE.

Academic disagreements are always enlivening, and historian Emily Hemelrijk argues that Flory underestimates the novelty and importance of Octavian's grant of 35 BCE. Hemelrijk notes that the earlier statues of women cited by Flory, such as those of Cloelia and Quinta Claudia, have been lost. Public statues of non-divine women erected in the Greek-speaking east were generally standing figures, wearing a long tunic and elaborate mantle. Yet the statue of Cornelia was seated, a composition usually reserved for portrayal of a goddess or occasionally an empress. An equestrian statue of a woman, such as that mooted for Cloelia, was unheard of.[20] Hemelrijk speculates that these earlier statues may never have existed, forming part of an invented tradition of public statuary to justify Octavian's grant of statues to Octavia and Livia.

But what of the surviving base to the statue of Cornelia? That, surely, constitutes evidence of the statue's existence. Hemelrijk, as you have guessed, has an answer. She notes that the surviving inscription to Cornelia on the statue base has been generally ascribed a relatively late date, to the rule of Augustus, the name by which Octavian became known after the demise of Mark Antony and the commencement of his sole rule as the first Roman emperor. Porticus Metelli where the statue resided was constructed by Metellus Macedonicus, in celebration of his victory over Macedonia. It contained numerous Greek works. Perhaps, therefore, the seated female statue was originally a Greek statue of a goddess. The area was renovated by Octavian and dedicated to his sister as the Porticus Octaviae. Hemelrijk speculates that Octavian repurposed the statue to honour Cornelia, by replacing the Greek inscription with the Latin one seen today. This would account for a curious feature of the statue remarked upon by Pliny: the subject was wearing sandals. These would have been standard wear for a Greek goddess, but not of a Roman matron.[21] A statue of Cornelia served as another 'precedent', masking the novelty of Octavian's actions in granting statues to his wife and sister.

For Hemelrijk, Octavian's actions in 35 BCE were revolutionary, in elevating Octavia and Livia far above the status of other women. The privilege of portrait statues to Octavia and Livia appears at first to have been used sparingly in Rome, a mark of the novelty of such statues for local audiences. The earliest of these statues emphasised the virtuousness of their subjects, choosing simple hairstyles and dress and spurning elaborate adornments. This supported Octavian's propaganda against Mark Antony, contrasting these virtuous ladies with the showier Cleopatra.

Livia was the subject of a further public grant of statues by the senate in 9 BCE. This appears to have been linked to the death of her son Drusus following a fall from his horse. He had been an able commander and was a popular figure. The grant of statues, along with further privileges, was intended as a consolation to Livia. But this is all a little odd. A gesture of consolation for the loss of a loved one would more logically involve statues of the person who had died, a source of solace to be grieved over, not the granting of statues of the grieving relative. Livia indeed commissioned statues of her dead son. So, what is going on here? The award of a statue recognises Livia as a mother—bringing into the world two sons, Drusus and Tiberius, whose great achievements are her merit. For Flory, Livia's children have become the equivalent of the great acts for which statues were typically awarded to successful men. Seen in this light, the award's timing is not solely a matter of Drusus's death in 9 BCE but also reflects the increasingly prominent roles of Tiberius and Drusus, including through their military commands, a matter relevant to the succession to Augustus.[22] They had not always been the leading candidates. Gaius and Lucius Caesar, the sons of Augustus's daughter Julia and his chief lieutenant, Agrippa, once held pole position. But following Agrippa's death in 12 BCE, Livia gradually managed to persuade Augustus to favour her sons (from a former marriage). Tiberius was even forced to divorce his wife and marry Julia, an experience that proved unhappy for both. The grant of statues to Livia underlined her status as the mother of two great men worthy of the succession, one of whom had tragically died, leaving Tiberius as prime candidate for the job.

Flory notes that Augustus seems to have been particularly keen on glorification of childbearing as a central role of women. He ordered a monument to honour a slave from the imperial house following the birth of quintuplets. None of the children long survived the delivery, nor apparently did the mother, but despite the downbeat back-story, the monument seems to have been intended as a spur to motherhood.[23] In a similar vein, the statues to Livia were intended not solely to console Livia for her loss or to underline the achievements of her sons, but also had a more general purpose in encouraging Roman mothers to produce more children.[24]

Granting public statues to Octavia and Livia thus broke new ground, removing the taboo that had largely been maintained in Rome over public statues to living women. During the ensuing Imperial period, public honorific statues other than to the emperor and members of his family became rather rare. The erection of statues in the city, though notionally remaining the prerogative of the senate, was in practice at the discretion of the emperor. Outside the city, across the Latin-speaking west of the empire, many public statues of women appeared, mirroring the longstanding practice in the Greek east. Octavian's decision in 35 BCE to grant public statues to Octavia and Livia thus had profound consequences.[25]

Statues of Women to Glorify Men

They call Knole a calendar house as it supposedly has 365 rooms. Once the palace of the Archbishop of Canterbury, once one of the many royal residences of King Henry VIII, it was acquired in 1604 by Thomas Sackville, Earl of Dorset, and Lord Treasurer to Queen Elizabeth I and King James I. He had the place transformed from draughty medieval mansion into Renaissance palace, putting his family stamp everywhere. Twenty-seven stone leopards hold the Sackville coat of arms on the gables. Knole was a symbol of Thomas's wealth and status, and the Sackville family still lives in the house, although the place has been in the possession of the National Trust since 1946. The family that has stewarded the palace from one generation to another has weathered vicissitudes and scandals. Author Vita Sackville-West, one of their number, called them 'a rotten lot, and nearly all stark staring mad.'[26]

Before ascending the Great Staircase, its walls painted with allegorical scenes of the Virtues and Senses, its newel posts sculpted with more Sackville leopards, visitors encounter under the stairs a sculpture that does not speak to any of the virtues. It is a life-sized plaster figure depicting a woman lying on a mattress, propped up by her elbows resting on cushions, quite naked. Her bare buttocks unselfconsciously greet the viewer. The statue, the work of John Baptist Locatelli, depicts Giovanna Francesca Antonia Guiseppe Zanerini, born in Venice in the mid eighteenth-century, who toured as a ballet dancer in France, where she was known as La Baccelli. During her English debut in 1774 at the King's Theatre, Haymarket, she caught the eye of John Frederick Sackville, the Third Duke of Dorset. The performance was *Le Ballet des Fleurs*. She was the rose. Evidently not an English one. She became the duke's mistress, living with him at Knole.

John Frederick had succeeded to the dukedom in 1769 at the age of 24. He had three passions: art, sports and women. La Baccelli was the longest lasting of a stream of mistresses. As well as the Locatelli statue, she was the subject of portraits by Gainsborough and Reynolds. At Knole, she bore the duke a son, named John Frederick Sackville, like his father. The duke was appointed ambassador in Paris in 1783, attempted to introduce the French to cricket, wrote gossipy trivia-laden reports that exasperated their recipients in the Foreign Office, and seems to have been bored with the country, finding a friend only in the Queen, Marie Antoinette, referring to her in letters home as Mrs Brown. La Baccelli accompanied the duke for part of his posting and danced at the Paris Opéra. Following the French Revolution, the duke returned to England, taking with him a dislike of the French. He wrote in anguish to the Duchess of Devonshire, who had been one of his amours, 'we must *take care* or else democracy will gain ground.'[27]

The duke's lifestyle required large amounts of cash, and having parted ways with La Baccelli in 1789 he married the following year the young Arabella Cope, heiress to a fortune in estates in Staffordshire and Oxfordshire. With the arrival of the twenty-year-old bride to Knole, the presence of a naked statue of the duke's former mistress must have become awkward. The predicament was resolved in two ways. One was a matter of location. The statue was banished to an obscure part of the house, at 'the Top of the Stairs, next the Wardrobe',[28] as a 1799 inventory put it. The second was to change the identity of the subject from a real woman to a mythological one. She was now described simply as 'Naked Venus.' The statue was not the only awkward reminder of La Baccelli's former presence. Her son, John Frederick, joined the army and died of fever in Santo Domingo in 1796. The duke himself died three years later, aged 54, following a period of mental degeneration.[29]

The statue of La Baccelli aimed more to glorify the duke, its commissioner, in making a statement about the beauty of his mistress, than its subject. And female figures as statues are far from rarities in an abstract sense, portraying not actual women but virtues or muses. Here, statues of unreal women are frequently employed to illustrate the achievements or strengths of character of real men. Photographer David Robinson toured the cemeteries of France and Italy, capturing statues of mourning female figures tending nineteenth-century graves. Robinson found that the act of mourning was a gendered one; he found no images of grieving men. The female statues were of abstract, not real, women, and depicted physically beautiful subjects. This beauty was made the more obvious by the fact that, in their grief, their clothes simply tumbled off them. The figures were always barefoot, wearing revealing dresses or in some cases nothing at all, save perhaps a strategically placed drape or bunch of flowers.[30] The female virtues decorating the plinths of eminent men and beautiful stone female mourners at male graves all speak to Simone de Beauvoir's depiction of woman in Western culture as the 'Other': defined in relation to man.[31]

Some sculptors are fighting back. The Beaux-Arts façade of the Metropolitan Museum of Art in New York, completed in 1902, sports four vacant niches, which had been intended to house works by Austian-born sculptor Karl Bitter until the project ran short of funds. In 2019, as the inaugural commission from the museum to populate the vacant niches, Kenyan American artist Wangechi Mutu created a composition entitled *The NewOnes, will free Us*. The niches were occupied by two kneeling and two seated stylised bronze female figures, their bodies sheathed by horizontal coils, their faces adorned by a mirrored disc referencing the traditional ornamentation of high-ranking women in some African cultures. The figures are suggestive both of human and otherworldly forms.[32]

Mutu's work was a rejoinder to the architectural form of the caryatid: the female figure often encountered in architecture whose role is to provide physical support to buildings. Mutu noted that in African sculpture, such load-bearing female figures sometimes supported male elites literally rather than just implicitly, in sculpted forms holding up the throne of a king.[33] The collection of the Metropolitan Museum itself includes a painted wooden veranda post designed for a Yoruba palace in present-day Nigeria in which a female caryatid must bear the considerable burden of supporting a mounted male warrior. Four caryatids, allegorical representations of painting, sculpture, architecture and music, stand higher up on the museum's façade, carrying out their load-bearing role. Mutu's figures have been freed from any such burden: they are no longer required to carry the weight of others.

The Restricted Range of Representations of Women

Holocaust researcher Judith Tydor Baumel has studied the representation of women on Holocaust memorials in Israel. Such memorials are different in style in Israel as against other countries. First, they have been built with a Jewish viewership in mind, requiring less background context given the direct personal connections of their audience to the horrors of the Holocaust. Second, they have a nationalistic flavour, linked to the building of Israel as a Jewish state. Baumel concludes that Israeli memory of the Holocaust from the mid-1940s tended to stress one of two aspects: armed uprisings and active resistance, and the progression from Holocaust to rebirth.[34] Third, religious and cultural constraints have influenced designs. Particularly outside the secular kibbutzim, religious prohibition of graven images has led to reluctance to depict human figures, with abstract designs preferred. Where women are portrayed, they tend to be chaste. The copy of Nathan Rapoport's Warsaw Ghetto Uprising Memorial unveiled at the Yad Vashem Holocaust Memorial in 1975 sanitised the depiction in the original of a bare-breasted mother, arm raised in homage to Delacroix's vision of Liberty, the offending breast concealed by a tunic.[35]

Baumel found that women portrayed in Israeli Holocaust monuments were presented in a specific and small number of contexts. The most common was the depiction of women as mothers, usually portrayed holding or protecting children. Standing at Yad Vashem is Ilana Goor's haunting 1973 statue *Never Again*. A portrayal of an abstract mother, oversized hands and feet and a void where her head should be, holding her dead child, it symbolises the Jewish nation, the child representing a destroyed future.[36] These mother images draw from socialist iconography of the mother seeing off her son to defend the homeland and Christian images of the Madonna, but also from a more Jewish image of the mother, modelled on the matriarch Rachel who both weeps for her children and joins them in exile.[37] Unlike the Christian and socialist imagery, often associated with war memorials involving women mourning sons who will never return from battle, the Jewish woman depicted in the Holocaust memorials is more directly a victim; at the centre of the atrocities.

A second motif is woman as resistance fighter or warrior, a rejoinder to Holocaust images of passivity. A statue at Yad Vashem sculpted by Yosef Salmon, depicting four abstract female figures huddled together, honours the Union Werke Resistance Women. These were four young Jewish women who smuggled small amounts of gunpowder from a munitions factory in the Auschwitz complex to the camp resistance movement. Prisoners working in the crematorium planned to use the gunpowder to destroy the gas chambers and lead a revolt. This sadly came to little, and the four women were identified and executed.

Two other motifs identified by Baumel were young girls portrayed in a virginal style, and elderly or weeping women, though the latter were more common in Holocaust memorials outside Israel than within. Baumel finds though that men are portrayed in a greater variety of ways than women on Israeli Holocaust memorials: whether fighting, being tortured, praying, being transported or being murdered. And men are frequently displayed with symbols of Judaism—whether wearing religious clothing or holding religious artefacts. This is rarely true of depictions of women on Holocaust memorials in Israel. Motherhood, then, is the central cultural motif used to depict women on these monuments. In many ways, that very motherhood was the target of the Nazis, in seeking to destroy the Jewish race by preventing its propagation.[38]

In many times and places then there are far fewer statues of real women than real men. Allegorical statues of women serve frequently to praise the achievements and qualities of men, some statues of real women are more about the glorification of the men who commissioned them than their subjects, and women portrayed on statues perform a more restrictive range of roles than do male subjects. There is thus much work still required in the pursuit of equality, but undertaking this work presupposes that figurative statues remain a relevant and worthwhile way of honouring their subjects.

9

LOCATION

The most prestigious spot in Britain for the erection of statues lies in central London, focused on the Houses of Parliament, Whitehall, home to UK government ministries, and the regal landscape around Buckingham Palace to the west. It is where the powers of parliament, government, the judiciary and royalty meet: the heart of the state. The area falls under the purview of Westminster City Council, which is accordingly blessed with some of the most notable statues in the land. Their fine open-air collection, running to more than three hundred statues and monuments, continues to expand, with memorials to Diana, Princess of Wales and to the Battle of Britain notable recent additions. For the council, however, this is an embarrassment of riches. They lament that 'demand for new statues and monuments continues today at a level unequalled since the Victorian period',[1] while places to put them are increasingly hard to find. Almost seventy per cent of applications for new memorials fall within the busiest site in the council's patch, the area around Whitehall.

In a 2003 article in *The New Republic*, Andrew Butterfield identifies the precinct as one of the four constitutive elements of the monument.[2] Location is not an incidental consideration, but an intrinsic part of the monument. Butterfield argues that one of two kinds of sites tend to be chosen. The first is along major routes, visible to the greatest number of people. In antiquity, monuments crowded the main roads into Rome and Athens. The second is a space that has been specially demarcated, perhaps with a fence or barrier. Set off from humdrum concerns of daily life, it is a place where an individual might reassert their membership of the group, whether family or nation. Examples might include the statue of a leading light of the family in a prominent position in the family chapel, or a national hero in the central square. These spaces may hold a rich and indeed sanctified significance:

> Owing to the sacral and symbolic character of the precinct, the members of the group approach a monument with a high expectation that the monument will provide an epiphany of meaning, and specifically that it will be an expression of the identity, the history and the philosophy of the group.[3]

Not all monuments are placed in one of these two types of sites. Butterfield gives the example of modern statues placed in city parks, places which while pleasant enough never served as the focal point for a community. For Butterfield, such monuments are likely to fail, 'in the sense that individuals whom they seek to commemorate are often forgotten.'[4] Urban design lecturer Quentin Stevens makes the point more brutally, in describing parklands as 'dumping grounds for memorials deemed unimportant to official histories.'[5]

Location then is vital to the impact of a statue. Prestigious sites are important to the success of a monument, but while statues may therefore occupy valuable sites they are not 'productive' in an economic sense. This wastefulness in the use of expensive urban space is a measure of the importance of memorials. The prime locations of many of the world's capitals are essentially void spaces: the small number of monuments allowed to occupy this space have a correspondingly great prominence.[6] With prime city space at a premium, there is heavy competition for the best sites. Not all monuments will secure a good spot. The question of which are successful is often dependent on access to power and resources.

Securing a Spot in Westminster

Westminster City Council has issued guidelines to handle applications for new statues and monuments. Entitled 'Statues and Monuments in Westminster', these do their best to put off anyone thinking about applying to erect a statue in the heart of London.

LOCATION

They first appeal to the Lewis Mumford in us, making the case that monuments and statues are fuddy-duddy installations unsuited to the modern world. The guidelines urge that 'there are many alternatives to three-dimensional sculptural monuments, which may be more appropriate to twenty-first century London than the Victorian concept of memorialisation.'[7] How about, for example, a memorial tree? Or if a monument it must be, perhaps two dimensions rather than three? Much easier to accommodate, and plaques these days can embody relief carving offering impressive figurative detail. The claim that statues are no longer relevant to a modern world is however rather undone by the background to the guidelines as a response to the burgeoning demand for new statues in the overcrowded streets of central London.

The guidelines set out a criterion of site specificity, arguing that 'many proposals for new statues and monuments seek a site in Westminster for reasons of prestige only, while other sites in London or the UK would have greater relevance to the subject matter.'[8] Proposed statues must have a clearly defined link with the central London location. A cautionary tale is offered about the 1959 statue of Sir Walter Raleigh, erected to commemorate the 350th anniversary of the foundation of the Commonwealth of Virginia, with the US ambassador given unveiling honours. According to the Westminster City Council guidelines, the statue was however later removed from its Whitehall location 'where it had little connection either to the site, the surrounding architecture, or to the other statues nearby'.[9]

The statue was moved in 2001 to a new location in Greenwich, close to the former Royal Naval College, full of suitable naval connections. The inference is clear: if we are prepared to boot out Raleigh, don't even think about asking for a Whitehall site for your proposed monument. All of this feels rather tough on Raleigh. He did have connections with the area, albeit not ones he would be keen to remember—he was beheaded at the site of Old Palace Yard, close to the present parliament. If the House of Commons had kept to its original plan to place Raleigh in front of the National Gallery, he would have found himself appropriately next to George Washington—a gift from the Commonwealth of Virginia. But the

Raleigh statue jarred with those of more recent military heroes being erected along that stretch of Whitehall in front of the Ministry of Defence, not least in height, where the relatively shorter Raleigh statue looked awkward.

The guidelines also set out a ten-year principle, in response to public clamouring for a statue or memorial upon the death of a well-loved figure or following a major disaster or terrorist act. The council's concern here is that decisions made while feelings are running high 'can lead to the emotional investment in the subject overriding issues of aesthetic design or good planning.'[10] Statues or memorials should wait ten years following the death of the beloved figure or the tragic event.

A quality principle is also insisted on. 'As befits a world-class city, Westminster requires only the best quality examples of new sculptural work for its streets and spaces.'[11] Competitions involving an expert selection panel are favoured, and direct invitation should be considered only if the artist concerned is of the highest calibre. Experienced architects and landscape architects should be employed to ensure that the setting matches the quality of the monument. The reader is left in no doubt that this will all work out mightily expensive, and that is before we come on to responsibility for maintenance. If the statue will be gifted to the council, note that the latter is indeed one to look a gift horse in the mouth. To mix animal metaphors, the council has no intention of taking on any white elephants and will insist on a one-off payment to cover future maintenance costs, currently calculated as the estimated maintenance cost over thirty-three years at current prices. The champion of even a simple bronze life-sized figure is warned not to expect change from £40,000 for maintenance alone.[12]

A final principle in the guidelines speaks directly to the pressure for space at the most prestigious locations. It establishes a Monument Saturation Zone. Areas within it, broadly corresponding to the Whitehall and St James's areas and the Royal Parks, are deemed to be full—no further statues or monuments will be permitted without 'an exceptionally good reason.'[13] Among proposals to have fallen foul of the Monument Saturation Zone principle, one finds the strange bedfellows of Homeless Jesus and Margaret Thatcher.

LOCATION

Homeless Jesus was a proposed life-sized bronze of a figure shrouded by a blanket and laid out on a bench. The only clue to his identity was the crucifixion marks visible on his naked feet, protruding from the blanket. The statue, by Canadian artist Timothy Schmalz, was reportedly inspired by a homeless man in Toronto, and versions had been put up in the Canadian city, as well as the Vatican, Dublin, Madrid and Washington. But not Westminster. The council considered in 2016 an application to erect the statue in front of the Methodist Central Hall, concluding that it did not meet the 'exceptionally good reason' required of the Monument Saturation Zone.[14]

Two years later, the council examined proposals for a statue of former Prime Minister Margaret Thatcher, who had died in 2013, to stand on the prestigious—and crowded—site of Canning Green, to the side of Parliament Square, between George Canning and Abraham Lincoln. The application came from Ivan Saxton of the Public Memorials Appeal, which would be providing the funding. The statue, by Douglas Jennings, depicted Baroness Thatcher in sumptuous robes of state, eyeing parliament with a stern gaze. The council was having none of it. In addition to location in the Monument Saturation Zone, they noted that the ten-year principle had not been met, and that there was already a statue to Lady Thatcher in parliament over the road. Worries were expressed too over risks around vandalism, given Baroness Thatcher's divisive legacy, and the fact that the backers of the statue had failed to demonstrate the support of the Thatcher family. Saxton is reported to have commented earlier, in reference to Lady Thatcher's daughter, that 'Carol's upset that there's no handbag.'[15]

The travails of Westminster planners are matched by similar stories in cities like Washington and Berlin, also saturated with memorials. Here too new proposals are redirected to more peripheral sites, or less permanent forms of commemoration encouraged.[16]

Locating to Unite

The choice of location may be intended to make a specific point or secure a specific objective. Thus, the monument to Canadian statesman George-Étienne Cartier in Montreal was deliberately placed between majority English- and French-speaking districts of the city (see fig. 19). Cartier, a French Canadian, was a father of the Canadian Confederation of 1867 and supporter of stronger Anglo–French relations. His very name brought together English and French Christian names, hyphenated in unity. Those commissioning the statue chose its location as a bridge between the two groups, promoting the cause of national harmony. The iconography of the monument, the work of sculptor George William Hill, similarly aimed to emphasise Cartier's heroic place in the national narrative[17] through a complex composition topped by a winged Goddess of Liberty. Cartier is depicted standing above four figures, each representing a province that signed the Confederation.

Over time however the function of the Cartier monument changed, as it was used to commemorate different aims. It served as a rallying point for French protests, including those against the Constitutional Agreement signed by Prime Minister Trudeau in 1982, as well as for local disputes, such as campaigning against the planned opening of a McDonald's fast-food restaurant.[18]

Statues and Placemaking

Globalisation has provoked concerns around the anonymisation of urban spaces, as cities increasingly resemble each other. In the United Kingdom, as across much of Europe, local authorities have also become preoccupied with the demise of the high street, as shoppers moved first to suburban malls and later online. Faced with these dual challenges of anonymisation and decline, there has been interest among local authorities in 'placemaking', including through the revitalisation of central spaces through initiatives seeking to bring out their distinctiveness. Public statues can play a role in this process. We looked in an earlier chapter at statues of footballers as a means of highlighting a club's glorious history and placing a stamp of individuality on otherwise identikit stadium designs. Statues of comedians in the United Kingdom provide another example of the placemaking role of the public statue.

Cultural figures such as writers, artists and composers were frequently immortalised in bronze during the 'statuemania' of the nineteenth century, but these were generally of a high culture variety. The commemoration through public statues of more lowbrow figures like comedians is more recent. A statue of Charlie Chaplin was installed in London's Leicester Square in 1979, but the celebration of comedians through statues in the United Kingdom really kicked off with a statue to Eric Morecambe, half of the much-treasured Morecambe and Wise variety act, put up in the town of Morecambe in 1999. Researcher David Wright identified twenty-one statues of comedians across Britain as of 2023.[19] He notes that many have been installed in towns in northern England characterised in recent years by 'the reassertion and revival of an English "nativism" in response to a perceived dominant urban multiculturalism.'[20] Commemoration of these comedians emphasises their personal connections to the town. Unveiling ceremonies, as well as the campaigns to build the statues, focus not just on the achievements and celebrity of the subject but also on their 'ordinariness' and rootedness in the quotidian life of the town. They are 'one of us'.

In 2016, a statue of singer and all-round-entertainer Gracie Fields was erected in her hometown of Rochdale. The initiative emphasises that, despite her national fame, she never lost her roots and pride in Rochdale. Her song *In a Little Lancashire Town* sums up the whole nostalgia-steeped enterprise, with its longing for the ordinary folk of Rochdale past, and her self-deprecating and prophetic complaint that a statue to her has been 'bunged up.'[21] At the 2019 unveiling of a statue to comedian Victoria Wood in her hometown of Bury, the leader of the local council managed to reference the hospital in which she had been born, all the places she had lived in the town and the schools she had attended. These projects make use of national figures for local purposes.

Such projects often involve an alliance between the placemaking goals of the local authority and campaigning by local enthusiasts of the proposed subject of the statue. Some are fully funded by donations from fans, providing a clear sense of community endorsement. There is a demonstration effect. The perceived success of the statue of Eric Morecambe, a winning composition depicting its subject dancing to the duo's signature song *Bring Me Sunshine*, in supporting the regeneration of the town, provided a stimulus for statue-raising projects elsewhere (see fig. 20). The commonality between the projects has extended to the use in several schemes of the same sculptor, Graham Ibbeson, who has professed a commitment to the production of sculptures of more 'popular' subjects.[22]

Statues can have a gentrifying effect on their immediate location. Calvinist Netherlands was not a propitious environment for public statues even during the nineteenth-century heyday of European statuemania, but if there was one thing that could prompt the appearance of a statue here it was the generation of one in Belgium. And so it was that the statue of seventeenth-century painter Peter Paul Rubens, appearing in Antwerp in 1846, determined a group of prominent Dutch painters that they would not be outdone. They raised funds for a fine statue in celebration of home-grown seventeenth-century painter Rembrandt van Rijn. The project was portrayed as the collective patriotic undertaking of every Dutchman, even if it was in the end underwritten by a modest 402 subscribers. The statue, inaugurated in 1852, both reflected Rembrandt's renown and sought to enhance it, identifying him as the symbol of the Dutch 'Golden Age'.

The site chosen for the Rembrandt statue was the Botermarkt, which turns out to be Dutch for 'Butter Market', a busy marketplace. A poem by schoolteacher Jan Schenkman, entitled *Lamentation by Rembrandt van Rhijn*, involves a critique of the statue in which various fictional city dwellers complain about the cost of the thing or its general uselessness. A local trader moans that it takes up valuable commercial space in the market square. But the statue had the last laugh. The presence of such a prestigious statue inspired moves towards gentrification. In the battle between statue and market, it was not Rembrandt that was to be ousted, but the market itself. In 1876, when a statue of the liberal statesman Johan Thorbecke was placed nearby, this was deemed an opportunity for renovation of the whole area. The traditional marketplace was replaced by a more formal space suited to admiration of the statues. The Botermarkt was renamed Rembrandtplein. Art had defeated butter.[23]

Public Statues in Private Places

We have argued that location is vital to a statue's impact, with a prestigious site promoting its intentional commemorative value and its success. But some statues derive their impact and importance from their inaccessibility, in places reserved to a privileged few, or indeed in the extreme case of the Japanese *hibutsu*, to almost nobody at all.

Blenheim Palace in the English county of Oxfordshire was built as a reward to John Churchill, the First Duke of Marlborough, for his military triumphs in the War of the Spanish Succession, culminating in the Battle of Blenheim. Its Long Library contains a marble statue of Queen Anne, the work of John Rysbrack, commissioned by Sarah, Duchess of Marlborough, in 1735. As historian Christopher Dickenson has noted, everything about the statue, from its huge size to its inscribed pedestal, suggests that it should be a public sculpture in a prominent location.[24] Its siting in an interior room is not however to suggest that it was intended for the private enjoyment of the immediate family. Rather, it was designed to perform an important public function: the intended audience however was the influential visitors to the palace.

The 2018 feature film *The Favourite* tells the story of Sarah's complex relationship with Queen Anne, charting the loss of influence of the queen's one time closest confidante, a process which would lead to the loss of court positions, funding for the construction of the palace, and the three-year exile of the Duke of Marlborough and his wife to the continent, from where they returned the day after Anne's death. The inscription on the plinth of Rysbrack's statue dedicates it to Queen Anne, thanking her for the gifting of land and funds for the palace, and praising the Duke of Marlborough's military success. In ignoring the breakdown in the relationship between duchess and queen, the statue is an attempt by Sarah to rewrite history on her terms.

Many Japanese Buddhist temples contain a small shrine, a *zushi*, housing an icon, frequently a Buddha statue, known as *hibutsu* ('Secret Buddhas'). These are typically withheld from public view, though the degree to which they are inaccessible varies. Some *hibutsu* are never displayed. This includes some of the most famous examples of the genre, such as the triad of Amida, also known as Amitābha, portrayed with two assistant bodhisattvas at Zenkōji in Nagano. Brought here in 552 from an ancient kingdom of the Korean

Peninsula, it is believed to be one of the first Buddhist images to reach Japan, and has not been seen since 654, not even by the head priest. Also out of sight is the image of Kannon, bodhisattva of compassion, at the busy temple of Sensō-ji in Tokyo. Other *hibutsu* are displayed perhaps once in a generation, while a third group, treated more liberally, are shown off once or twice each year. In some cases, priests of high status within the temple have access to the *hibutsu*. Some may be viewed if a special offering is made.[25]

Italian academic Fabio Rambelli, in a study of *hibutsu*, argues that they are often unusual or noncanonical images. Some are nude or sexually charged statues. Rambelli recounts a visit to the Shin Yakushiji temple in Nara, where he secured permission to view the *hibutsu*, which proved to be a wooden statue of the naked bodhisattva Jizō, bearing the unusual feature of spherical genitalia.[26] Which must have made for an interesting day out. Other *hibutsu* include statues that have faced trauma, even disfigurement, before being placed out of sight as *hibutsu*. Thus, according to legend, the Amida triad at Zenkōji was rescued from anti-Buddhist persecution, and the Kannon image at Sensō-ji is said to have been dragged from the Sumida River in 628 by two fishermen. For Rambelli, these 'secret Buddhas' are often the outcome of a complex process in which a Buddha image is created, then suffers some form of damage or distress from which it is retrieved, then worshipped as a hidden *hibutsu* image. This dispensability of their physical form, argues Rambelli, serves only to emphasise their power.[27]

The sacredness of these Buddhist statues is intensified by their hidden nature. Many temples housing *hibutsu* are major attractions, notwithstanding that the object of worship cannot be seen. Copies exist of some of the most famous *hibutsu*, though these are often 'copies' in the vaguest of senses, since they do not always resemble each other and, in the case of the most private *hibutsu* like the Zenkōji Amida triad, no one has a clue what the original looks like. The copies themselves are the object of worship, without detracting from the importance of the original. In some cases, including that of the Zenkōji Amida triad, copies are placed in front of the shrine containing the 'secret Buddha'. They form an intermediary role in respect of the relationship between worshipper and unseen statue.[28]

LOCATION

Setting Statues

We have looked at the role of plinths and columns in raising statues, literally and metaphorically, above the viewer. The way a statue is set into the landscape is itself central to the meaning and commemorative value of the statue, and highlights the partnership between sculptor, architect and landscape designer. Some purists would however disagree with the previous sentence. For Daniel Henri-Kahnweiler, theorist of cubism, a statue should exist as 'the object pure and simple, detached from everything surrounding it.'[29] There may be an attempt to establish a self-sufficiency of the sculpture, minimising 'interference' from the surrounding environment. Art historian Alex Potts looks at the custom-built sculpture galleries of eighteenth-century England, displaying works gathered by aristocratic young men during their grand tours, such as that at Newby Hall in Yorkshire completed in 1767 by Robert Adam. Here, the sculptures are set against blank walls; a departure from the Baroque and Rococo taste to integrate sculpture with the surrounding architecture.[30]

Insulating a sculpture from the surrounding environment is not however a luxury easily enjoyed by statues erected in outdoor public locations. Archaeologist Brunilde Ridgway has examined the evolution of attention to the setting of sculpture in ancient Greece. She finds little evidence of landscaping in the Classical period. The prime consideration of donors in siting statues in Classical shrines was that they should be visible, with the main strategies in play those of elevation, including by placing the statue on a column, and prominence, such as a location close to the temple or along the sacred road. The sanctuary does not seem to have been 'landscaped' in a modern sense, and Ridgway suggests that today's viewer would regard it as over-crowded.[31]

In the Hellenistic period that followed there was more evidence of attention to the landscaping of statues, a development Ridgway believes was facilitated by the formation of the Hellenistic kingdoms on the territories conquered by Alexander the Great and the creation of large private estates.[32] Evidence of the setting of bronze figures over a natural rock is provided by the inclusion of a rock in marble replicas. The setting of the famous *Winged Victory of Samothrace* contributed to the power of the statue, as Nike, goddess of Victory, alighted on the prow of a stone warship set on the hillside overlooking the temple complex,[33] battling wind blowing into the ravine. Hellenistic attention to the landscaping of sculptural compositions in turn influenced the Roman focus on spectacular arrangements in natural settings, reaching its zenith in the great Roman villas.[34] The sculptures discovered in 1957 in the grounds of the former villa of Emperor Tiberius at Sperlonga, on the coast between Rome and Naples, are arranged in groups within a natural grotto facing the sea, connecting to a larger pool outside. The ensemble seems to have been a single project, serving as a setting for Tiberius' dining.

Unlike a painting, there is no definitive way of viewing a three-dimensional sculpture.[35] The difficulty of encompassing sculpture in the round in a single view gives it a quality described by Kirk Savage as 'maddeningly unstable.'[36] Sculptors such as Augustus Saint-Gaudens and their architect collaborators used setting[37] to address this challenge of the undirected viewing of the statue from various different angles by embedding it into an architectural landscape that 'transformed the experience into a narrative of beholding.'[38] Saint-Gaudens's bronze standing statue of *Abraham Lincoln: The Man*, installed in Chicago in 1887, which we encountered in Chapter 7, incorporates a carefully choreographed ensemble of steps, pedestal and exedra to give the viewer the sensation of being in the audience at a speech given by the great man. Savage argues that the use of setting here is part of a wider shift from the function of a public statue as an object of reverence to one as a 'space of subjective experience.'[39]

PART TWO

LIFE

10

COMMEMORATION

In 13 BCE the Senate commissioned a grand altar in Rome to honour the victorious return of Emperor Augustus following three years away in Hispania and Gaul. The Ara Pacis Augustae was a celebration of the triumph of Rome, and specifically of Augustus, in establishing an era of peace and prosperity across the empire. The role of the altar was firmly based on the act of commemoration. The date, 4 July, of the commissioning (*constitutio*) of the monument in 13 BCE, and that, 30 January, of its inauguration (*dedicatio*) in 9 BCE were each commemorated in annual sacrifices held at the altar.[1] The marble reliefs decorating the altar include depictions of the legendary past of Rome, and a magnificent decorative frieze of entwined acanthus, vine and laurel among which lurk all manner of small creatures, an allusion to the fertility of Augustus's empire.[2] But they also depict processions.

Two processional friezes on the exterior northern and southern sides of the outer enclosure portray real people, among them Augustus himself and members of the imperial family as well as priests and senators. Art historian Peter Holliday is among those to identify the procession as a portrayal of the *constitutio* of 13 BCE.[3] There are some difficulties in this. At least one of the priesthoods was vacant at the time, and yet the office-bearer is represented on the relief.[4] The frieze thus appears to have been a portrayal of the idealised form of commemoration rather than the actual event as it unfolded historically, a depiction of the *lex arae*, the law governing the ritual taking place at the altar.[5] Not all scholars are even convinced that the friezes depict the *constitutio* at all. As a portrayal of a sacrificial procession there is oddly no sacrifice shown as the natural culmination of proceedings, nor any poor animals being led to the slaughter.[6] However, there is a further processional frieze on the altar itself, which does show animals en route to their demise, accompanied by figures brandishing knives and an axe, as well as six Vestal Virgins. Perhaps the altar reliefs were intended to be read together with those on the exterior walls of the enclosure as representing successive parts of the procession.[7]

The Ara Pacis Augustae is thus embellished with scenes suggesting how commemorations at the monument should take place. It is far from unique in this regard. Another Rome monument, the Arch of Titus, built by Domitian around 81 CE, depicting the victory of his older brother Titus over the Jewish rebellion in Judaea, incorporates a relief showing Titus riding in a triumphal four-horse chariot, referencing the kind of victorious parade the arch was designed for. These depictions make the point that commemoration is an integral part of the monument.

If the aim of a monument is to engender memories of specific events or people, and the acts and virtues associated with them, then its success, at least from the perspective of those responsible for its installation, depends on its ability to continue to engage. A neglected monument is a failure: it has lost, in Riegl's terms, its intentional commemorative value. Without rituals and reminders around the monument, its significance may be forgotten.[8] As Musil would have it, it turns invisible. Commemoration is thus critically important. As Andrew Butterfield puts it, 'the monument can only be understood in terms of its use.'[9]

Commemorative activities help turn monuments into *lieux de mémoire*. Commemoration can be orchestrated by those in power, for example through parades and wreath-layings at the monument. Or it can emerge from popular activity, such as placing votive symbols at statues of saints. Commemorative events and rituals involve a repetition, through which individual interpretations are blurred and a composite framework created. Over time, individual memories tend to fit within this composite picture. The economic and political power of the groups producing and maintaining these remembrances is closely linked with the likelihood that they can be sustained.[10] Monuments can become static, then subject to re-energisation as they are used for new commemorative events. Where different forms of commemoration surround individual monuments, the latter can become a palimpsest.[11]

Inauguration

The inauguration of a monument has been an occasion for celebration since antiquity. As we have seen, statues and monuments frequently display only limited information about their subject: an inauguration ceremony provides an opportunity not just to celebrate the establishment of the monument, but also to provide the backstory, to explain why the statue has been erected and what should be commemorated by it. Inauguration ceremonies amplify the official interpretation of the monument's symbolism through the language used in speeches and additional musical and symbolic events.

During the nineteenth-century 'statuemania', inauguration ceremonies were often grand affairs. They represented, after all, the moment of triumph for benefactors who had toiled for many hours over the project, and marshalled the necessary funding, including their own. The inauguration ceremony was their moment in the spotlight, their opportunity for their endeavours to be recognised. In some cases, almost as much attention went into planning the inauguration as that of the statue itself. The committee responsible for the delivery of a statue to Benjamin Franklin outside City Hall in Boston in 1856 were so determined to ensure that the inauguration ceremony of 17 September was remembered in every detail that they invited Nathaniel Bradstreet Shurtleff, himself a future mayor of the city, to write a book about the day. It runs to more than 400 pages.[12]

Shurtleff spares no detail of an event 'surpassing anything of the kind ever before witnessed in Boston'.[13] The procession ran to nine divisions, each with its own chief marshal. Shurtleff proclaims that the marching figures occupied the entire route, of around five miles. A military escort headed the procession, followed by the fire department, the dignitaries of the city, invited guests and members of the Statue Committee in the first division, while the second, also accorded a prominent place, was made up of representatives of the mechanical trades. Carriages from the Bay State Iron Works of South Boston offered 'fine specimens of iron ore, pig iron and car rails', while their workers held up a banner with the motto 'we handle our tools without mittens',[14] referencing Franklin's homespun injunction to approach life's challenges without hesitation. Shurtleff chronicles the efforts made by the citizens and shopkeepers of Boston along the route to decorate their premises with flags, streamers, portraits and busts of Franklin and banners featuring his best-known sayings. 'Time is money' crops up frequently: advice that clearly resonated with the small business owners of the city. Decorations at the Boston Corn Exchange, appropriately, included another saying from Franklin's *Poor Richard's Almanack*, 'it is hard for an empty sack to stand upright.'[15]

The drive for a statue to Franklin had been launched by Whig politician Robert C. Winthrop at an 1853 lecture to the Massachusetts Charitable Mechanic Association, a venerable organisation promoting the mechanical arts and trades. The Association took up his call, its president, Jonas Chickering, agreeing on 7 December to establish a Statue Committee. On 8 December, Jonas Chickering died. Fortunately for the statue, his successor, Frederic W. Lincoln, supported the project, and agreed also to chair the Statue Committee. Of the three main speeches of an inauguration ceremony lasting well over three hours, the longest was the first, from Winthrop, a detailed account of Franklin as 'the greatest of our native-born sons',[16] chronicling his career as mechanic, philosopher, patriot and ambassador. Then came Lincoln, who presented the statue to the city authorities. The third speech was that of the mayor, receiving it.

The speeches, procession and decoration sought to anchor Franklin to Boston, the city of his birth and youth but from which he had fled his printing apprenticeship at the age of seventeen. The central place of the Massachusetts Charitable Mechanic Association in the statue project is reflected both in the prominent position of the mechanical trades in the procession and the emphasis in the speeches to Franklin's early start as a printer and hence member of those trades. Four reliefs on the plinth illustrate Franklin's life: one is dedicated to Franklin the printer, a relief sponsored by the Massachusetts Charitable Mechanic Association. And there was a goodly dose of civic and national pride: with speakers emphasising both that the sculptor was a local man and that the bronze statue was cast in Massachusetts.

Given the vastness of the crowd that day, one wonders how much of the fine rhetoric could be heard by those at the back. We encountered in our last chapter the statue of Dutch painter Rembrandt van Rijn, erected in Amsterdam in 1852. At the inauguration, the mayor hoped it would provide a stimulus for citizens to support the national arts and uphold the national honour. Not that most of those citizens could hear him. An admission ticket was required for places close to the statue, in the company of the king and other important guests, so non-paying spectators had but a distant view. As historian Anne Petterson notes, it is unlikely that most of the crowd received anything of the intended messaging around the statue beyond the overall buzz of the event.[17] Similarly, looking at late nineteenth-century monuments in Berlin, Paris and London, Helke Rausch notes that access to inauguration ceremonies was often restricted to the upper classes, and often to men. Where there were concerns about potential conflicts, for example in Paris, opposition groups were excluded from the ceremonies or accommodated only at the margins.[18]

Inauguration ceremonies then, while underlining the esteem in which the subject of the statue is held, provide only the most fleeting sustenance of intentional commemorative value for a monument. They provide no clear guidance as to how a monument should be commemorated in the longer term, a point to which we will now turn.

Unclear Commemoration

Given that the success of a monument depends on its continued ability to engage, it is striking how little attention is paid by so many promoters of statue projects to the question of how the project they have so carefully nurtured will engage audiences beyond the day of inauguration. In our example of the installation in 1856 of a statue of Benjamin Franklin in his birthplace of Boston, Mayor Alexander Rice hoped at the inauguration that, we, at every sight of this beautiful memorial, renew our recollection of his life and that of his immortal compeers; so that clinging, ourselves, to the same nobility of purpose, and imbued with admiration of their ineffable virtues, we may vie with each other and with them in patriotic devotion to our beloved city, to her honor, her happiness, her prosperity.[19]

The desire here is that the statue offers a demonstration effect, a spur to all who view it to emulate its illustrious subject. The values embodied in the statue are those its promoters have identified as values needed by society as a whole: the statue offers the example of a figure who embodies them. But the only guidance given as to what the viewer must do to receive the desired message is to look at the statue, which seems decidedly hopeful.

Benedict Anderson argues that many statues emerging as projects of nineteenth- and twentieth-century nationalism suffer a significant risk of descending into the anonymity described by Musil because they offer little guidance as to how the individuals or values honoured by the monuments are supposed to be commemorated.[20] The risk befalls even such well-known monuments as the Lincoln Memorial in Washington, a point made in an episode of American cartoon series *The Simpsons* entitled *Mr Lisa Goes to Washington*. Itself a spoof of the serious-minded 1939 James Stewart movie *Mr Smith Goes to Washington*, the plot involves young Lisa Simpson winning a pro-America patriotic essay competition, the prize for which is a family holiday to Washington. While there, her witnessing of a corrupt deal threatening her beloved national park disillusions her, and she substitutes her essay for a new one about how Washington 'stinks'. At the end, the corrupt deal is unmasked, and Lisa's faith in the system restored. English language scholar Lauren Berlant characterises Lisa's behaviour, and indeed the James Stewart/Mr Smith model on which the story is based, as 'infantile citizenship': a naïve belief in idealised national values that comes up against cynical realities, eventually winning over the cynics through their own nostalgia for an innocent past.[21]

In a central scene of the cartoon, a disillusioned Lisa seeks out the Lincoln Memorial for guidance. But this visit highlights the lack of clear instruction on how Lincoln should be commemorated or addressed. In the absence of this, crowds of Americans simply fire questions at the statue, from 'what can I do to make this a better country?' to 'would I look good with a moustache?'[22] The neighbouring Jefferson Memorial is no help either—all she gets there is moaning from the statue that his accomplishments have been neglected in the face of his showier neighbour.

One answer to the unclear commemorative purpose of statues is to anchor them into a wider commemorative landscape by giving the statues functions in relation to celebrations that would be performed anyway. In ancient Greece, for example, statues played a central role in ritual dramas, such as sacred marriage.[23] In the Soviet Union, war memorials were integrated into all manner of activity, providing the focus of army parades and the presentation of awards, and serving as a site for newlyweds to lay a bouquet. This commemorative exposure facilitated the role of the war memorial in serving as a focal point for the cult of Soviet war dead. For Michael Ignatieff, writing in 1984, 'if Soviet society does worship anything it is the horror of its collective sacrifice.'[24] War memorials served as 'sermons in stone'.[25] Monuments may serve as one element in the production of grand spectacles to convey the messaging of the regime; through choreographed events involving an interplay between the 'fixed' (monuments, flags, lights) and the 'mobile' (marches, pageants, meetings).[26] Nazi Germany, in fusing architecture and monuments with mass rallies and marches, all illuminated by expressive lighting, took this to its extreme.

Offerings to Statues

One of the most basic forms of commemoration at a monument is to leave something behind as a mark of attachment to or respect for its subject.[27] Flowers left at a statue on the birthday, or date of death, of its subject provide a powerful demonstration of remembrance.

Offerings to statues of deities, or to those who it is hoped might intercede with deities, are found across many times and cultures.[28] Archaeologist Folkert van Straten notes that in ancient Greece, there were three principal means of entering into and maintaining a productive personal relationship with the gods: prayer, sacrifice and making a votive offering.[29] These were closely connected. For van Straten, sacrifice relates to objects intended for consumption (by either human or deity) while votive offerings are durable,[30] but lines are blurred and consumables such as cakes baked in the form of body parts would usually be considered votive offerings. Sacrifices and votive offerings are usually focused on a particular object in a temple or sanctuary: while this might be the altar, it is frequently a statue with perceived miracle-working qualities.[31]

Ittai Weinryb, a specialist on votive offerings, describes them as 'physical artifacts imbued with emotion, a spiritual gift secured in an object.'[32] Also sometimes known as an ex-voto, a name deriving from formulaic Latin statements such as *ex voto suscepto* ('from the vow made'),[33] they make tangible the relationship between humans and gods. Votive offerings are given to deities, or others such as saints believed to have an intercessory function with the divine, in one of two broad contexts: either as an offering for favours desired, or to give thanks for favours received through the intercession of the deity. Their use differs in time and place. In ancient Egypt, gifts for deities were usually given in anticipation of blessings or to appease the deity, rather than as thanks for an answered prayer.[34] In ancient Greece, many votive offerings incorporate elements of both gratitude and hope. Thus, where a prayer has been answered and the grateful devotee presents a votive offering in fulfilment of the vow made during their prayer, the offering implicitly includes the hope that the donor will continue to enjoy protection of the deity going forward.[35]

Many objects have been used as votives. Thus, models of body parts point to the ailment from which the god or saint has freed the grateful donor, or a plea to be so delivered. Not all such anatomical votives had a medical meaning. The dedication of model ears to Egyptian deities such as Amun-Ra and Hathor encouraged the deities to listen to the prayers of the donor.[36] In Sagalassos, in modern-day Turkey, in the early second century CE, votives of little bronze feet were placed in twenty-five cavities on the base of a statue of Asclepius in the Nymphaeum. There is continuing debate as to whether the votives have a medical intent, representing feet cured by the intercession of the god, or are intended to suggest the physical proximity of the worshipper to the god.[37]

COMMEMORATION

Votives might be valuable items, crafted of precious metals and stones. The most celebrated offering at the shrine of St Thomas Becket in Canterbury was a ruby given in 1179 by French king Louis VII.[38] But most were of less costly material. The most popular votive gift at Becket's tomb and shrine was the wax candle, though these were sometimes personalised as trindles and rotulas, lengthy candles coiled for ease of transportation, whose length identified them with the donor: matching the length of their body or the circumference of the afflicted body part.[39] Specific materials could be relevant to certain deities or saints. Votives of iron are common in shrines dedicated to the Frankish St Leonard of Noblac, referencing his association with miracles linked to the freeing of prisoners and hence removal from iron shackles.[40] At the shrine of St Thomas Becket, at the other end of the spectrum from the French king's glorious ruby, were numerous discarded crutches and splints. Although of little material value, these objects were useful to the church in providing an arresting visible proof of the saint's power to let the lame walk again. And then there is Agnes's tapeworm. This ailing lady, after taking the precious Canterbury Water, reputed to be tinged with Becket's blood, vomited out a four-foot worm, pronounced herself cured, and gratefully donated the worm as a votive offering.[41]

Ittai Weinryb argues that votive offerings have two distinct phases of life. The first, centred on the act of giving, emphasises the personal relationship between donor and deity. The second begins once the votive has been deposited: it becomes part of a collection of objects embellishing the statue or shrine.[42] With donors wanting their votive as close as possible to the miracle-working statue or altar, the religious authorities at popular sites faced a challenge in keeping the place in order. Eventually, the quantity of votives might all become too much. Votives in precious metal might periodically be melted down, providing income for the church.[43] There is evidence of the burial of terracotta votives at the sanctuary of Diana Nemorensis, southeast of Rome, though the good condition of many figurines suggests that this was done with reverence, respecting the sacred character of the donations.[44]

It was not however in the interest of the religious authorities to tidy the shrines and statues too thoroughly. While they needed to maintain access to the shrines, the impact of an impressively large number of votives was valuable, in serving as a visual demonstration of the power of the deity or saint. The authorities at Hereford Cathedral specifically mentioned the 2,000 wax ex-votos at the tomb of their former bishop Thomas de Cantilupe in a document of 1307 making the case for his canonisation.[45] The presence of votive images at a statue of a deity or saint changed the character of that statue, providing a testament to its power to work miracles. In a similar vein, in a secular context, we have seen the role of personal artefacts left to loved ones at the Vietnam Veterans Memorial in Washington DC in giving that monument commemorative power. The power is not generated through an officially directed programme of commemoration, but through the personal commemorations of thousands of visitors. The aggregate of individual actions becomes the actions of a shared community, bound together by common experience.[46]

How about dressing a statue in grand clothes? The Infant Jesus of Prague is one of the finest attired statues (see fig. 21). This 48-centimetre representation of the Infant Jesus is made of wax-covered wood. The figure holds a golden cross-bearing orb in his left hand, while his right is raised, making a benediction. The statue originated in Spain and was brought to Bohemia in 1556 by Maria Maximiliana Manriquez de Lara y Mendoza upon marriage to a Czech nobleman. One story has it that Maria's mother received the statue from Teresa of Ávila. Maria's daughter donated it to the monastery of the Discalced Carmelites in Prague dedicated to Our Lady of Victory. The monastery was plundered during the Thirty Years' War, and the image was damaged and forgotten until rescued and repaired by one Father Cyril. The little statue became the object of worship, credited with miraculous healings. On 4 April 1655, the Archbishop of Prague placed a crown on the statue's head, and the anniversary of his coronation has henceforth been marked on the first Sunday after Easter.

The statue is adorned not just with a crown, but also fine embroidered clothing, which since around 1713 has been changed according to liturgical principles. Dressing the statue is the responsibility of the Carmelite Sisters of the Infant Jesus. It involves a white

COMMEMORATION

undergown, coloured robes, cloak, ruffs on the arms and around the neck, and the golden orb and crown. The statue's wardrobe has expanded through donations from wealthy benefactors, including Empress Maria Theresa, whose 1754 gift of a costume in velvet and satin is preserved in a museum at the back of the church. Violet robes, a solemn colour of repentance, are used during Lent and Advent, red robes during Pentecost, white at Christmas and Easter, and green on ordinary days, but there are numerous variations. The Infant Jesus now possesses more than three hundred robes, mostly donations of gratitude.

Replication

The replication of statues in the form of smaller figurines and statuettes is a mark of the commemorative value of the original. It suggests that the statue has sufficient meaning to justify the making or purchase of a replica. Replication may also suggest physical challenge in visiting the original on a regular basis, perhaps because of geographical distance. The statue may be a prized symbol of national identity during a period of stress or division. Latvian exiles in western Europe and the United States during the Cold War cherished images and occasionally models of the Freedom Monument in Rīga.[47] There is even a large replica in the village of Vārpa in Brazil, founded by Latvian immigrants in the 1920s. Or the statue may be prized for its miracle-working powers: a means of communication with the deity that can be replicated through a model. Let us return to the Infant Jesus of Prague. With the popularity of the image among Catholic communities far from Prague, numerous copies have been fashioned. Across Ireland the statue, known as the Child of Prague, is said to solicit good weather, and may be placed on the windowsill or buried in the garden.

It is at this point that we must take a short detour, to discuss the process of hypnotising chickens. A trance-like state may apparently be induced by drawing a line along the ground, starting at the chicken's beak and extending straight outwards. The chicken will stare at the line, remaining immobile for up to half an hour. The tale of a hypnotised chicken featured in a 2011 episode of the BBC Radio

Ulster series *On the Air*, when a man named Pat phoned broadcaster Gerry Anderson's show in distress. He had attempted to hypnotise one of his chickens using the method described on an earlier broadcast, but it had remained immobile for twenty-five hours. Pat was concerned that it was a laying hen, and he could feel an egg on the way, but now stuck. Gerry helped Pat revive the chicken from its stupor, by suggesting that he rub out the line with a wet cloth. This went rather too well, and listeners were treated to a colossal squawking and flapping of feathers. It transpired that the awakened bird went berserk, knocked down Pat's Child of Prague statue, and escaped through a window. Pat and Gerry fret about the implications of the damage to the statue. 'Do you know what that means?' asks Gerry. 'Bad luck, is it? It's not good.'[48]

Auto-Commemoration

The erection of a statue to a living subject offers the prospect that the subject may themselves interact with the statue. Attendance at the inauguration is the most obvious example, but Arnold Schwarzenegger took engagement with his statue to another level. A statue was erected to the bodybuilder in Columbus, Ohio, in 2012, reflecting Arnold's long relationship with the city. This dates from 1970, when sports promoter Jim Lorimer staged the 'Mr World' contest in the Franklin County Veterans Memorial Auditorium. Schwarzenegger, representing Austria, took the crown. In 1989, Lorimer set up the annual Arnold Classic competition and expo in the city. The relationship was important for Columbus, helping develop the city's event business. The statue was erected outside the Veterans Memorial Auditorium. It features Arnold in bodybuilder pose, all muscle and sinew. The eight-foot-tall statue stands on a two-level platform, its subject identified by the single word 'Arnold'. A quote from the great man next to the statue urges us to reach for the next goal. Life's joy, we are told, is in the doing. The statue was moved outside the Columbus Convention Center a couple of years later when the Veterans Memorial Auditorium was demolished. Schwarzenegger attended both the unveiling and rededication ceremonies.

COMMEMORATION

In January 2016 Arnold posted a photograph to his Instagram account portraying himself lying at the base of the statue in a sleeping bag, apparently trying to get a nap. The text accompanying the photo was simply: 'how times have changed'. The tendency of social media to take stories in unexpected directions took over, with elaborate posts accompanying Schwarzenegger's photo with a different and convoluted story that the star slept beside the statue outside a hotel he had once opened when Governor of California. The hotel manager promised him at the time that there would always be a free room for him but now, when he had tried to claim that room, the manager had reneged on the promise. He was no longer Governor, and they had cut him adrift. It was suggested that Arnold's Instagram post, 'how times have changed', had highlighted what happens when you fall out of a position of influence.[49]

All total hokum. The building is a convention centre, not a hotel, and Arnold has hardly faded into obscurity.

11

MOVING, TALKING, LIVING STATUES

It was summertime, and there was a fly buzzing around. The sculptor Gian Lorenzo Bernini had completed a portrait bust of Pope Alexander VII, and it was time to present the bust to its illustrious subject. Bernini's friend, the Jesuit cardinal Francesco Sforza Pallavicino, was present, and predictably enough praised Bernini's magnificent likeness of the pope, before more unexpectedly and somewhat bravely going on to comment that notwithstanding Bernini's considerable skill, the statue was much less like the pope than was the buzzing fly. Fortunately for Pallavicino's career, and indeed head, the pope saw the point. There was a fundamental resemblance between all living creatures. No sculpture, the work of human hands, could bridge the gap to living creatures, the work of God.[1] Many have however tried to make that bridge.

The usual assumption about statues is that they do not move. This is, after all, at the root of expressions like 'as still as a statue.' There is apparently an ancient Greek saying, 'to tickle a statue', referring to activities carried out in vain.[2] That stillness is sometimes considered a deficiency. It was mocked in the second century CE by Clement of Alexandria, railing against idolatry, for whom what was being worshipped was 'not gods and daemons, but earth and art, which is all the statues are. For a statue is really lifeless matter shaped by a craftsman's hand.'[3] For Sartre, 'for three thousand years sculptors have been carving only cadavers'.[4] Sculptors expended great effort in attempting to give their creations the impression of movement through appropriate gestures and expressions. But the statues remained still.

VOICES IN STONE

Moving Literary Statues

The perceived limitations around the motionlessness of statues perhaps explain why in literary treatments, where it is easier to lift such restrictions, statues spring to life so frequently, often also developing the faculty of speech. They become a rock that rolls, driving their plot forward as they gyrate, gesticulate, levitate or just nod slightly.

A statue coming to life forms the denouement of Shakespeare's *The Winter's Tale*. The statue of the virtuous though sadly deceased Queen of Sicily, Hermione, reportedly the work of 'that rare Italian master, Julio Romano', provides the only reference to a living artist in Shakespeare's work, albeit one known for painting and architecture rather than sculpture.[5] Recently finished at the country house of Paulina, Hermione's faithful friend, it is visited by Leontes, grieving and repentant King of Sicily, sixteen years after the tragic family quarrels that precipitated Hermione's death. The statue miraculously comes to life, as the play ends happily for (almost) all concerned. But the meaning here is unclear as to whether Hermione has indeed been miraculously reincarnated from her statue, or whether Paulina simply hid her friend away for sixteen years to escape her husband's wrath, and she stood still as a statue on Leontes' arrival.

Pushkin's poem *The Bronze Horseman* (*Mednyy vsadnik*), written in 1833, stars the real-life equestrian statue of Peter the Great in St Petersburg, now commonly referred to as the Bronze Horseman in homage to the poem. It describes the great flood of 1824, which takes the life of lowly clerk Evgenii's love, Parasha. Evgenii roams the streets, deranged with sadness, for a year, until, reminded of the storm, he curses the statue. The curse brings the bronze horseman to life, and it pursues poor Evgenii through the night. His corpse is later found. The statue though only comes to life in the fevered mind of Evgenii.[6]

A recurring literary example of a moving statue, its many versions spanning several centuries, with the statue moving ever more literally rather than figuratively, is the tale of Venus and the Ring. An early appearance comes in William of Malmesbury's twelfth-century *Chronicle of the Kings of England*. It is the wedding day of a young nobleman in Rome. The wedding banquet was evidently substantial, for the man and his friends go out afterwards to play ball to help the food go down. The man puts his wedding ring on the outstretched finger of a bronze statue of Venus for safe keeping. When he returns to the statue after the game, he is unable to remove the ring. Venus's fist has clenched around it. That night, a dense form appears between the nobleman and his bride, preventing intimacy. Venus's voice whispers to him that it was her he wedded that day, and she has no intention of giving the ring back. All eventually ends well. The young man tracks Venus down, and a demon forces her to return the ring. Unlike some later retellings, there is no sense of any initial attraction of the youth towards the statue, which simply provides a convenient place to put the ring during the ball game.[7]

The tale of Venus and the Ring received a further lease of life during the period of European Romanticism, whose authors in turn adapted it from Renaissance sources, including Robert Burton's 1621 *The Anatomy of Melancholy*. For Theodore Ziolkowski, the Romantic fascination with the story stemmed in part from a revival of interest in magic, following the waning of Enlightenment single-mindedness, which had no patience with anything that could not be explained rationally, coupled with a new attention to statuary and fascination with automata.[8]

The tone of some of these retellings darkened considerably. Prosper Mérimée had a professional interest in statuary, serving as inspector-general of historical monuments in France. His 1837 story *The Venus of Ille (La Vénus d'Ille)* is narrated by a visiting archaeologist, whose role and interests match those of the author. The story moves to Ille in southern France, its setting contemporary. There is a menace around the bronze statue of Venus: discovered near an olive tree, it had already caused the broken leg of the village's star sportsman, the result of an accident during excavation. The luckless groom in this story is Alphonse, son of the archaeologist's host. There is no happy ending. Alphonse is killed on his wedding night, his new bride offering a crazed tale about the statue of Venus entering the room, embracing her husband and crushing him to death, before returning to her pedestal. In this retelling, it is the statue itself, not the spirit of Venus, that turns up in the groom's bed, with devastating consequences.[9]

The story continues to be told. The 1943 Broadway musical *One Touch of Venus* stars a barber named Rodney, drawn to a sculpture of Venus when visiting a museum. On a whim he puts the engagement ring he is carrying onto the statue's finger. This brings the statue to life, creating chaos in the relationship between Rodney and his actual fiancée, Gloria. The latter breaks off the engagement, an understandable action given that by this time the statue has transported her to the North Pole, and Rodney ends up falling for a young woman who looks remarkably like the statue. The musical was remade as a film, starring Ava Gardner as Venus. An arc that stretches ten centuries, from William of Malmesbury to Ava Gardner, is testimony to the power of the story of the moving statue of Venus.

This literary foray into moving statues could not but conclude with the cautionary tale of that dreadful philanderer Don Juan/Don Giovanni. The tale first emerges in the 1630 play attributed to Tirso de Molina, *The Trickster of Seville and the Stone Guest* (*El burlador de Sevilla y convidado de piedra*). It tells of serial seducer Don Juan, who has murdered military commander Don Gonzalo while the latter came to the aid of his daughter Ana, whose honour Don Juan had just taken. As Don Juan passes Don Gonzalo's tomb, he jokingly asks the statue on it to come to dinner. Bad idea. That night, Don Gonzalo's ghost does indeed show up for dinner, politely inviting Don Juan to a return meal in the graveyard. The ghost sets out a table on the tomb, and at the end of a delightful repast of snakes and scorpions, grabs Don Juan by the wrist, killing him. Unlike the later Mozart opera, while the statue nods to accept the invitation, the figure arriving at dinner is not the physical statue but the spirit of the late Don Gonzalo. This parallels early versions of the tale of Venus and the Ring, where most of the movement is undertaken by the spirit of the character depicted by the statue, not the statue itself.[10]

As with Venus and the Ring, the statue gets livelier in later versions. In Giacinto Andrea Cicognini's *The Stone Guest* (*Il convitato di pietra*) of 1640, the statue of the slain military commander enters, announcing his arrival in response to Don Giovanni's invitation, and inviting the philanderer to a return dinner. Similarly, in Molière's *Don Juan or the Feast of Stone* (*Dom Juan ou le Festin de Pierre*) of 1665, it is the statue that turns up for dinner. Lorenzo da Ponte wrote the libretto for Mozart's opera *Don Giovanni* in 1787. Again, it is the statue that walks onto the stage, so terrifying Leporello, Don Giovanni's servant. The success of Mozart's opera spawned further versions of the story, but by now, as Theodore Ziolkowski notes, the idea that it was the statue itself that came to dinner was accepted.[11]

Moving Mythological Statues in the Ancient World

Among the wondrous creations of Hephaestus, the lame god of blacksmiths and artisans, were automata, including golden handmaidens able to think and speak. A passage in Homer's *The Odyssey* refers to the arrival of Odysseus at the palace of the Phaeacian king Alcinous. On either side of the entrance, Hephaestus had constructed guard dogs of gold and silver, described by Homer as 'immortal and unaging'.[12] Animated statues crop up in other myths associated with Hephaestus. The great bronze statue of Talos, guardian of Crete, took its guardianship duties seriously, and ran three times daily around the island's coast. Unwanted arrivals would be pelted with rocks. Under one version of the tale, the giant statue was a gift from Hephaestus to Minos.[13]

Classicist Christopher Faraone argues that these tales of the creation by Hephaestus of animated guardian statues, given to a god or mortal king and used to protect palaces and kingdoms, have parallels in the use across the Near East in the eighth and ninth centuries BCE of actual statues as guardian talismans. The entrances of the palace of Assyrian King Ashurnasirpal II in Nimrud were guarded by colossal stone figures representing all manner of fantastic creatures, from scorpion-men to human-headed bulls. Winged human-headed *lamassu* and *shedu* were minor deities, serving as temple servants to more important gods, performing the role of gatekeepers at temples. The Greeks preferred less exotic animal forms, such as stone lions and dogs, to guard the entrances to important places.

Guardian statues were not necessarily of great size. Smaller statuettes were buried beneath portals by priests, serving the same purpose as the larger statues—barring evil-doers and welcoming well-wishers. Babylonian ruler Nebuchadnezzar is reported to have buried dogs fashioned of gold, silver and bronze at the portal of a temple dedicated to the goddess Gula. Magic was important for the effectiveness of guardian statues. Assyrian statues are often inscribed with complex names or phrases suggestive of magical powers. And an account of a bronze lion buried in Lesbos and attributed to Hephaestus reported that its creator imbued the statue with *pharmaka*, a powerful material which might bring the statue to life.[14]

The god Hephaestus was not the only legendary craftsman said to have powers to bring statues to life. According to Propertius, poet of the Augustan age, a sculptor of ancient Rome named Mamurius Veturius created a bronze statue of Vertumnus, god of seasons, change and plant growth, who would chatter away to passers-by.[15] Daedalus, the skilled craftsman father of Icarus, created statues so full of energy that they had to be bound to stop them rushing off. Ancient commentators such as Diodorus as well as modern ones have attempted to rationalise such descriptions as references not to actual movement, but superb realistic representation, making the statues appear to move.[16] But that is just the language of killjoys.

For a really animated ancient statue, satirist Lucian of Samosata, in his *Philopseudes*, tells of one of a bald, pot-bellied Corinthian general named Pellichus, which descended from his pedestal every night, wandering round the house, sometimes singing. The statue was fond of taking a bath and could be heard splashing around through the night. Coins were laid at the pedestal by those grateful to the statue for curing them of their ills. One night, the money was filched by a Libyan servant, taking advantage of the statue's absence on its nightly perambulation to put his evil plan into effect. On return to its pedestal, the statue was not pleased to discover the theft, and showed no mercy with the thief, beating him nightly in his dreams, an ordeal the thief did not long survive.[17]

Not all movement and speech in ancient statues can be dismissed as products of the more fanciful mythological imaginations. We have evidence of talking statues in ancient Egypt, arising from the desire of priests to dupe the faithful. The Louvre holds a painted wooden head of Anubis, jackal god of the dead, which incorporates a secreted speaking tube deployable by priests to issue 'godly' statements.

Automata in Islamic Palaces

Giving the lie to the widespread idea that the Islamic world lacks a tradition of figurative sculpture, from around the seventh to the thirteenth centuries statues that moved, and in some cases emitted sounds, were to be found at many Islamic palaces. These automata represent fine technological as well as artistic achievements. Automata, already known from ancient times, were under Islamic rulers refined to dazzling effect. Almost always found inside palaces, their purpose was to awe visitors such as diplomatic envoys, serving as an expression of the ruler's power. Artist and academic Terrance Duggan argues that the automata drew theological legitimacy from the wise rule of the prophet Sulaymān (Solomon), son of David. At the command of Sulaymān, the *jinn*, the genies of Middle Eastern literature, made statues, amongst other wonders. For Islamic rulers, expert craftsmen took up the role of the *jinn*, fashioning elaborate moving and speaking statues.

While Latin Christians exposed to these automata sometimes concluded that they represented a form of idol worship, this was not the case. They were intended as marvels, not idols. Duggan notes that, under Islamic tradition, Solomon killed the King of Sidon, taking his daughter Jarada as his wife. Jarada so grieved for her father that Solomon ordered the *jinns* to fashion his image. Jarada and her servants came to worship the image: Solomon then ordered that it be destroyed. A portrait statue was evidently deemed acceptable; but if that statue became the object of worship, it was not.[18]

Thus, the Baghdad palace extended by 'Abbāsid Caliph al-Muqtadir in the tenth century contained a Hall of the Tree centred on a tree of silver and gold which swayed and rustled its leaves, housed chirping birds in its branches, and was crowned with precious stones carved in fruit shapes. Flanking the tank in which it was placed were life-sized horsemen automata that moved as if in battle. Envoys of

Eastern Roman emperor Constantine VII, seeking to arrange a prisoner exchange, were kept hanging around for two months while this and other awe-inspiring sights were prepared for them.

The Eastern Roman court of Byzantium similarly employed elaborate moving sculptures to awe visitors. Liudprand of Cremona, counsellor, priest, diplomat and gossipy author, describes a mission to Constantinople in 949 as the envoy of Berengar of Ivrea during the reign of Constantine VII.[19] He was mightily impressed by a gilded tree standing before the emperor's throne, full of singing birds. The throne itself was guarded by huge sculpted roaring lions that shook the ground with their tails.

The Talking Statues of Renaissance Rome

Rome has, from the sixteenth century, hosted several 'talking statues', though the statues here are not active agents in the speaking, but serve as a kind of fancy bulletin board on which anonymous, risky, political opinions can be posted.

The first example of the genre was Pasquino, a battered statue in a Hellenistic style in a small piazza now located at the corner of the Neoclassical Palazzo Braschi (see fig. 22). The subject of the statue was identified in the eighteenth century by antiquarian Ennio Quirino Visconti as Spartan king Menelaus supporting the dying Patroclus, killed by Hector in the bitter fighting of the Trojan War. Among the tales of the acquisition of the nickname Pasquino, the most popular is that a local sixteenth-century tailor of that name ran a shop noted for the free speech that flowed within, criticising pope, cardinals and other local bigwigs with abandon. Following the tailor's death, the cautious but critical citizens of the city decided to continue their rants in an anonymised literary form, on the statue recently set up near the shop.[20] Another account has it that the statue was unearthed and placed upon its pedestal in 1501 through the munificence of Cardinal Oliviero Carafa. On the feast of St Mark on 25 April the statue would be dressed in classical garb, and harmless verses added to the adornment, which over time became more barbed.[21] Whatever the origins of the practice, Pasquino for hundreds of years provided the medium for posting

MOVING, TALKING, LIVING STATUES

anonymous satirical poems, initially generally attacking the church and its mismanagement of the city. Such lampoons acquired the name pasquinades from the nickname of the statue.

Some of the best, and most scurrilous, of these pasquinades, were published. Given their incendiary content this was no straightforward matter and the 1544 *Pasquillorum Tomi Duo* was published in Basel, outside papal control, even then the place of publication being disguised as the fictitious Eleutheropolis.[22] The most famous of all these mini poems is probably '*Quod non fecerunt Barbari fecerunt Barberini*' ('What the Barbarians didn't do the Barberini did'), referring to the stripping out by seventeenth-century Pope Urban VIII of the prominent Italian noble family the Barberinis of bronze roof trusses in the Pantheon, replacing them with wooden struts. He wanted the bronze for new cannons for the Castel Sant'Angelo. With the Catholic church hierarchy understandably upset at all this anonymous criticism, and resultant fears among posters that Pasquino might be under surveillance, the practice spread to other statues around the city. Among the best known is *Il Babuino* (the Baboon), another ancient statue depicting a reclining Silenus, a creature of Greek mythology combining attributes of both man and horse, and evidently considered somewhat baboon-like to some viewers, a drunken companion to wine god Dionysus. The statue was placed in 1581 in the present-day Via del Babuino to decorate a public fountain.

Moving Statues of the Virgin Mary in Ireland

In 1985 across Ireland came reports of statues of the Virgin Mary that moved. In some cases, movement involved a simple gesture, in others the whole statue levitated off the ground. The statues concerned were mostly centrepieces of outdoor grottoes constructed across the country in or around 1954, marking the centenary of the proclamation of the dogma of Immaculate Conception by Pope Pius IX.[23]

The first reports of moving statues came in February and March, but press attention and crowds peaked in August, with thousands of people visiting the most popular site, near the village of Ballinspittle.[24] Here, a lady named Kathy O'Mahony, a caretaker of the local shrine, claimed that the statue of the Virgin Mary had started to breathe, and then look around from side to side.[25] The phenomenon worked wonders for the local tourist industry, with fast-food vans setting up in the village to dole out 'grottoburgers'. Anthropologist Peter Mulholland argues that this August peak of activity had much to do with the summer lull, when political life in Ireland was at its doziest and the press had little else to write about, and when enterprising coach companies organised visits to sites of reported movements as a holiday tourist attraction.

While many visitors agreed that they 'saw' something, there was overall much suspicion about the phenomenon, and the Catholic church in Ireland retained a neutral position regarding its veracity.[26] A group of three Pentecostalist protesters wielding axes and hammers attacked the statue at the end of October, damaging Mary's head and hands in front of onlookers who had been waiting for the statue to move. One of the latter group shouted at the attackers that they must be Satan, getting back the retort that 'you are worse to be adoring false gods.'[27]

A 1997 episode of British satirical television programme *Brass Eye*, examining the state of moral decline, spoofed the affair of moving statues of the Virgin Mary in a report from the sleepy village of Ballakreen, where local girl Patricia O'Dennell, dubbed 'Miracle Girl', reported seeing the local Virgin Mary statue driving round in a car. A garage owner claimed the statue had pulled in, asked for petrol and made a shocked-looking face, an expression then incorporated by the local faithful into their prayers. Patricia's clearly long-suffering mother suggested that the girl might wish to pray in the middle of the road. While statues of Mary continued to move in Ireland into the 1990s, attention and audiences declined.

Peter Mulholland explores the genesis of the phenomenon, albeit from an academic standpoint that denies the possibility that the Marian movement might have been down to genuine miracle. He places it in the context of disquiet in the Ireland of the mid-1980s, with security concerns fuelled by the Cold War, fears of nuclear bombs, and the ongoing 'Troubles' in Northern Ireland, a challenging economic backdrop of high unemployment and emigration, and internal divisions within the Catholic church, with a liberal wing railing against the still-dominant conservative faction. For Mulholland, the visionaries of moving statues were the 'psychologically disempowered', a disempowerment fed by a 'puritanical morality' and the Catholic church's pessimistic view of humans as born of the Original Sin of Adam and Eve.[28] The church tended to support the possibility of miraculous apparitions and there was a backdrop of considerable Irish precedent for apparitions involving the Virgin Mary. Psychologists based at University College Cork concluded that the phenomenon was all an optical illusion created by staring too long at the statue, during which time the onlookers themselves would start to sway, especially during the dim hours of twilight.[29]

The Giant Dolls of Olinda

The Carnival in Olinda in northeastern Brazil is noted for its giant puppets. These involve smiley fibreglass heads, and torsos sporting loudly patterned oversized dresses or colourful shirts paired with glittery tuxedos, arms to the side ending in papier-mâché hands (see fig. 23). They are held aloft by the noble soul with the sweaty task of manoeuvring the thing around the streets of Olinda, swaying the doll to the rhythm of the frevo music providing the soundtrack to the carnival. A foam cushion protects the bearer's head, as they balance the weight of the large puppet above.

Dolls have been part of the Olinda carnival since 1931. They represent different types of people. Many are invented characters, some of whom play a specific role in the choreography of the carnival. Foremost among this group is the Midnight Man, who appears on the streets of Olinda at one minute past midnight on the Sunday of Carnival week, opening proceedings. His costume changes from year to year, but the essentials are always the same: a black hat, broad gold-toothed smile, dinner jacket and colourful waistcoat. A clock and a large key are paraded with the Midnight Man: the key is delivered to a second carnival group as a mark of permission for the carnival to start.[30]

The Midnight Man has gradually acquired an increasingly complex family life. In 1967, a female companion arrived, the Mulher do Dia ('Woman of the Day'). With long dark hair and gold-toothed smile, she is typically dressed in a combination of yellow and blue. The colours reference Yoruba water spirits Oshun and Yemanjá, a reminder of the underpinning of African-originated religious traditions in so much of Brazilian carnival. The couple have been blessed with two children, the Menino da Tarde ('Afternoon Boy') and Menina da Tarde ('Afternoon Girl'). The latter is a somewhat vain character, who insists on a new outfit for every carnival.

Pérola Negra, the 'black pearl', represents a carnival group founded by women, a doll created to highlight the struggles of black women in Brazil. In 2019, she competed in the Miss Giant Doll of Olinda competition. There were more than fifty contestants, but Pérola Negra was happily one of five finalists. Presentations of the dolls in casual and sporting attire proceeded without a hitch, but it appears the competition went downhill during the swimwear segment, where the dolls were paraded wearing something closer to dental floss than beachwear. A commotion ensued. When order was restored, the master of ceremonies announced that judging had taken place, and that the winner was Vaidosa. The Menina da Tarde was second, the Bela do Guadalupe third. The winner's celebrations had just begun, when the master of ceremonies announced he had made an unfortunate error, having read out the winning order in a back to front fashion. The winner should have been the Bela do Guadalupe, with Menina da Tarde second and Vaidosa third. This prompted a further commotion, which only intensified when someone pointed out that while there were ten members of the jury, eleven votes had been cast. There were cries of foul all round, and someone started to shout for no clear reason 'Bolsonaro out!' The vote was annulled, and the result judged a tie.[31]

Other dolls represent local Olinda personalities; often people who have made significant contributions to the carnival. The Vovó da Tapioca ('Granny Tapioca'), a smiling lady in a white dress and hair net, honours the most famous purveyor of the most famous street food of Olinda, the powdery filled pancakes known as tapioca. A further group of dolls depict celebrities of north-eastern Brazil, like musician Luiz Gonzaga, portrayed in traditional rural attire, featuring a half-moon-shaped leather hat with a decorated brim, and playing the accordion. And finally, there are global icons, both real and fictional, resonating with the Pernambuco public: Bob Marley, Charlie Brown, Super Mario. Their presence broadens the horizons of the event. Though rooted in local traditions, it has a global perspective too. The presence of figures of global renown underlines the honour granted to those local people awarded a doll. Granny Tapioca is equated to Bob Marley—at least in fibreglass.

The giant dolls of Olinda serve many of the same functions as statues in bronze or stone. They honour heroes of the community and wider region. And they help construct Olinda's identity. They sit alongside, rather than completely supplanting, more traditional statues, providing another string in the bow of veneration.

Living Statues

We have explored contexts in which statues move, and talk. But can they come to life? Seeking an answer to this question brings us to an examination of statues of deities, and the question as to whether a statue of a god is simply a lifeless representation of a god, whether it is itself a god, or whether it provides a home for a god to reside.

Austrian writer Rainer Maria Rilke's 1908 sonnet *Archaic Torso of Apollo* (*Archaïscher Torso Apollos*) describes the poet's impression of such a torso. The Miletus Torso at the Louvre has been suggested as the inspiration. The poet is dazzled by the 'brilliance' that suffuses the torso, 'like a lamp', offering a gaze from which there is no hiding place, a direct contact that prompts the realisation that, as the final line of the poem puts it, 'you must change your life.' Powerful stuff, though commentators have interpreted both this line, and the relationship between poet and statue that underpins it, in different ways. Perhaps befitting a distinguished scholar of German studies, Theodore Ziolkowski offers a straightforward, literal, reading of this relationship in underlining that this is not the word of the headless statue but of the poet.[32] Angela Voss, a researcher of myth, cosmology and the sacred, takes a leap that allows for a less literal interpretation. The statue has come to life through the attention paid to it by the poet. With rational thought disengaged, a deeper dialogue becomes possible, with life-changing consequences for the poet.[33]

Voss argues that the Enlightenment constrains our answer to the question of whether statues simply imitate the being portrayed, or whether they may embody that being, as a living presence.[34] We cannot conceive of the possibility that a statue might also be a living god, since such a proposition would not stand up to empirical scrutiny. Yet the animation of statues, known as *telestiké*, was an important part of rituals described in the magical texts of Hermeticism, ancient and medieval writings attributed to the legendary Hermes Trismegistus, a figure associated with the Egyptian god Thoth and Greek god Hermes. Priests were able to implant the souls of living cosmic spirits into ritual statues, assisted by a mix of suitable plants, stones and spices. The god would become present in its own image, though the statue was only brought to life through the devotee's perception.

For Proclus the Successor, fifth-century Greek philosopher and practitioner of such rituals, there are four levels through which we can interact with symbolic images. The first is to treat them as just matter—a statue is simply a lump of stone. The second is to treat them as a representation, for example of a god. The third is to treat the image as a reflection of what is represented, revealing a presence. The fourth level represents the identity of the image and what it represents: the god and its form are identical. It is up to the viewer, and the extent to which they are able or willing to extend normal vision, how far they proceed along this spectrum.

In ancient Egypt, realistic funeral effigies of the deceased pharaoh attempted to attract his life force, or *ka*, and give it a new home, assuring the pharaoh's immortality. The pharaoh, although human, was a living god. The creation of colossal statues of the pharaoh could both serve as an advertisement of their power and virtues and provide a further home for the pharaoh's *ka*, a spirit which served to mediate between human and divine realms. The statue gave the spirit a physical body. Animation was accomplished through the ritual of 'opening the mouth', when with special tools, the statue was readied to receive the pharaoh's spirit.[35] It is important to underline here that the statue itself was not considered to be alive, but the spirit making its home in the statue was.

While the pharaoh was alive, the statue represented their divine essence, which was distinct from their physical being. Thus, depictions on the temple of Amenhotep III at Soleb in Nubia portray the pharaoh making offerings to his divine self: a practice which has been described as 'auto-adoration' and was repeated at some temples to Ramesses II. The imagery emphasises the status of the pharaoh's divine persona as worthy of royal adoration.[36] In contemporary Hindu culture, statues similarly have a functional role—that of housing divine life. Images of Hindu deities do not simply represent those deities: they embody them.

Historian Angelos Chaniotis argues that, in ancient Greece, statues of gods were not themselves gods—they were not invested with permanent powers. This was different to the figurative images used in magic we have examined. But they did exercise an important role in communication between worshippers and gods. Herodotus describes a plain young woman of Sparta, brought daily by her nurse to the temple of Helen, where she prayed before the image of the goddess, through whose intercession she grew to be the fairest woman in the land. A key consideration was that Greek gods were not omnipresent. In Epidaurus, a city used to the miraculous healing feats of Asclepius, ancient Greek god of medicine, a surgery was on one occasion performed by his sons because the god himself was out of town. They botched the job, much to the dismay of the patient, who was left without his head, a situation only resolved when Asclepius returned from his trip.[37]

Gods did not live permanently in every statue dedicated to them, for they could only be in one place at a time. They might however decide to pay the statue a visit. Aphrodite is for example said to have rushed to Knidos to look at Praxiteles' statue of her, ending up wondering whether the sculptor had seen her naked, so accurate was the depiction. Elaborate Greek ceremonials were an attempt to attract the god's attention, to persuade the deity to visit the statue. These included washing the statue and ensuring that its environment was ship-shape, the use of attractive fragrance such as incense, offerings of food or wine, appealing acoustic signals like songs and prayers, and visual ones such as dressing the statue in bright clothes. When the god showed up to inhabit the statue they could manifest their power through an epiphany. Requests of the faithful could be accepted, an act sometimes signalled by movement of the statue.

But if the god was angry, the statue might become the instrument through which that anger was manifested. A poem within the *Idylls* of Theocritus tells of a beautiful youth who remained cruelly indifferent to the suicide of a man who had unsuccessfully sought his attentions. A statue of Eros took revenge on the youth by falling on top of him and crushing him to death.

Worshippers fretted that the deity might not turn up, despite their hard work in enticing the god. Thus, the poet Callimachus, in his hymn to Apollo, describes the collective anxiety over the prospective arrival of that god to his statue on Delos. Worshippers are exhorted not to do anything that might put the god off. Thetis, mother of Achilles, in eternal mourning for her son's death, had to take a temporary break from her wailing.[38]

Angela Voss identifies a significant moment in the animation of statues in both ancient Egypt and Greece as the completion of the eyes—often using polished rock crystal in Egypt, painting in Greece. At this point the god could inhabit the image, meeting the gaze of the viewer.[39] In Roman portrait statuary too, the eyes were the subject of particular attention, the work of specialist craftsmen, the 'eye makers.' Into eyeballs of polished white limestone were set irises of green glass paste and pupils of black paste, each set within a copper ring. Lashes involved serrated sheets of bronze or copper.[40] We have already encountered the bronze portrait head of Roman emperor Augustus, whose piercing eyes render it one of the most haunting exhibits of the British Museum. The focus on the eyes made Augustus seem all-seeing and charismatic, adding life to the statue.

Humans as Statues

In the modern-day 'living statues' soliciting money from passers-by in large Western cities, as Angela Voss notes, the paradox has been reversed. Rather than statues that are not alive, but convince the viewer that they are, here the statues really are alive, but seek to convince the viewer that they are not.[41]

There is a long history to attempts by living humans to resemble statues. We have explored the ancient Greek obsession with the idealised human body, an obsession resulting in the crafting of anatomically impossible statues, depicting a bodily form that was such a vision of idealised perfection that it was unachievable. And yet, historian of physical culture Charles Stocking has observed that athletic training literature of the Greco-Roman period sought to recreate in the human body the unachievable ideal portrayed in sculpture. The *Gymnasticus* of Philostratus, written in the third century CE, describes the symmetry and ideal bodily proportions of an athlete in a way that would have been familiar to fifth century BCE sculptor Polykleitos, a conception 'grounded in art rather than anatomy.'[42]

Philostratus judges the bodies of actual athletes not in relation to a physically attainable model but in relation to unrealistic statues. He wants wrestlers to adopt a straight back, on the grounds that this is a 'pleasing' form, while aware that it is not the most suitable posture for the task in hand. For Stocking, 'Philostratus insists on aesthetic form over athletic function.'[43] Philostratus was writing against a backdrop of perceived athletic decline from mythic heroes like Heracles and Theseus, through the legendary exploits of historical athletes like Milo of Croton, to a more modest Roman present. The prioritisation of bodily form based on idealised sculptures was an attempt to return to the glories of an equally idealised past, characterised by a pinnacle of physical perfection. The Baths of Caracalla, built in the third century CE, were a Roman monument to the body. The frigidarium was dominated by two colossal statues of Hercules, a hero who as Heracles embodied the mythic Greek past, serving as a role model for the bathers.[44]

This reverses the traditional assumption that sculpture takes its cue from the body. Here, the body is taking its cue from sculpture. Stocking argues that the same process is evident in the bodybuilding craze emerging in the late nineteenth century. Its populariser, Eugen Sandow, states in his 1894 work *Sandow on Physical Training* that he was inspired towards his future career when gazing upon Greco-Roman sculpture in childhood.[45] Bodybuilding was closer to a Greco-Roman than recent past too in that Sandow's act was less to do with the demonstration of feats of physical strength than the adoption of poses in the manner of ancient sculpture. He posed in mimicry of the Farnese Hercules statue from the Baths of Caracalla, depicting the naked, muscular Hercules leaning on his club, over which is draped the skin of the Nemean lion he has just killed. For Kenneth Dutton, 'Sandow's posing introduced a revolutionary concept: that of the live display of a male body in the public arena, as an object to be admired solely by virtue of its advanced muscular development.'[46]

The attempt to realise the Greek ideal through the muscular development of a real human body, though unattainable, continues in modern times. Joe Weider, coach of celebrated bodybuilder Arnold Schwarzenegger, was entranced by the Farnese Hercules, just as Sandow had been, declaring of that statue: 'what he has is what we want.'[47] We have already discussed the bronze statue of Schwarzenegger unveiled in 2012 in Columbus, Ohio. That statue was both larger than life and based around an exaggerated pose redolent of Arnold's glory days. It was an idealised statue of a man seeking to transform his body in the mould of an idealised statue.

Statues were coming under scrutiny in Latvia in the later years of the Soviet occupation; the period of the National Reawakening of the 1980s, which was starting to look towards restoration of Latvian independence. Human mimicry of the form served to subvert all those statues of heroes of the Communist regime that had served for decades as its ubiquitous symbols. Miervaldis Polis was a young artist known for his work in photorealism.[48] In response to a request from a West German television director, Polis agreed in 1987 to walk around central Rīga painted bronze. He went to town on the outfit: a bronze suit and hat, and all visible skin fully bronzed. An apple juice ordered at a café served as his bronze drink. He briefly stood on a vacant pedestal to become a living bronze statue. Polis's *Bronze Man* was a response to the bronze statues of Lenin and other Soviet icons populating the cities of the USSR.

Art historian Amy Bryzgel argues that the bronze paint covering the artist's body hints at the fake nature of many Soviet statues—with a metallic sheen applied over the plaster in which they had been so cheaply constructed.[49] In the same way that the statues were faked, cheap objects dressed up to resemble something expensive, so too was the Soviet interpretation of Latvia's history, portraying the USSR as Latvia's saviour in World War II and the bestower of prosperity thereafter, largely false.

MOVING, TALKING, LIVING STATUES

Polis replicated his *Bronze Man* persona on several occasions. Its final outing came in 1992, in an independent Latvia, when the *Bronze Man*, whose career seems to have been shaped by the dares of foreign television companies, was persuaded by a Swedish TV crew to stand on the pedestal from which Lenin had been removed the year before. Some alarmed bystanders, surveying the scene too quickly, thought the Communist leader had returned.[50] The *Bronze Man* moved on to Cathedral Square in Rīga, where Polis's associate Vilnis Zābers applied a layer of white paint over the bronze. With Latvia no longer under Soviet rule, the *Bronze Man* was free. As the Soviet statues had been removed, so the *Bronze Man* had been rendered redundant. Polis's own career mirrors this shift towards a new capitalist future. He abandoned performance art, to become a portrait painter to the rich and famous, particularly noted for his official portraits of Latvian presidents.

12

INTERFERING WITH STATUES

Victor Noir was the pen name of French journalist Yvan Salmon, who had a short and tragic life, ending with his losing a duel in 1870 with Pierre Bonaparte, cousin of Napoleon. He has found little peace in death. He was initially the subject of commemoration for political reasons: as a journalist, he had been critical of the imperial regime, and at his funeral, to which 100,000 people turned out, the manner of his death was regarded as symbolic of imperial repression.[1] The focus of commemoration of Victor Noir has however moved from the political realm to the sexual one, a transition down to Aimé-Jules Dalou, sculptor of his recumbent tomb effigy in the Père Lachaise Cemetery in Paris. Dalou's 1891 work, completed two decades after Victor's death, for some reason crafted Noir with unbuttoned trousers and a bulge in his pants. Art historian Caterina Pierre suggests that it brings together the concepts of *eros* and *thanatos*, respectively the sexual instinct driving us and the death instinct reminding us of mortality.[2] This has turned his grave into a pilgrimage site for those in search of love. Rub Victor's groin, kiss him on the lips and, since this is France and we need to be romantic about it, leave a flower in his hat to ensure fertility and/or a great sex life, depending on what you hope for.

Statues are anthropomorphic. They can match in proportion and volume the body they represent. We share space with statues. Unlike a painting, there is no clear boundary separating the viewer from what is being viewed. And as Prussian philosopher Johann Gottfried von Herder explained in 1778, sculpture lacks a single point of view: one's experience of a sculpture depends on where of the many possibilities you happen to be standing in relation to it. Herder claims that the whole sculpture, as against various individual views of it, cannot straightforwardly be understood by vision alone. It is guided by the experience offered by touch. He goes further, arguing that we understand the meaning of a statue by identifying with it: 'transposing' ourselves onto its stance.[3] The experience of figurative statuary then derives from our own experience as human beings with bodies. Statues can sometimes be treated almost as if they were living subjects. But they are not subjects. The exchange with a statue is therefore one-sided, with an object neither able to move nor to speak.

For art historian David Getsy, this builds an unbalanced power relationship under which the subject, the viewer, has power over the object, the statue. He suggests that the stillness of statues may be recast as a performative act; not just inability to move but refusal to do so. For the viewer, responses to this performative act of stillness can take many forms, among them violation, destruction and fantasy, but Getsy argues that a common denominator is the desire to control. The stillness of statues is taken as a taunt, a defiant unresponsiveness, a form of passive resistance that invites a reaction from the viewer, attempting to assert control.[4] It encourages the taking of liberties with statues. For Getsy, engagement with a statue is not simply a matter of aesthetic judgements about the quality of the object, but is about our interpersonal relationship with that object, and the ethical issues that flow from this. The viewer must choose how to act in relation to the statue.[5]

Rubbing Statues

We all know the experience of that walking tour of the historic centre of just about every major city, where the guide brings his captive group to a bronze statue and invites them to rub a particular part of its anatomy, already gold and shiny from rubbing by the tour groups that went before. Good luck, wealth, or a guaranteed return to the city are promised.

Rubbing a statue speaks to the desire to control and exercise power identified by Getsy. Where more sensitive body parts are concerned, it also offers temptations to touch territory usually forbidden. Statues typically occupy public spaces, giving the viewer a licence to touch not true of artworks in museums. The fact that persistent rubbing of bronze statues turns them a pleasing golden hue through the removal of surface oxide acts as a further spur to a good rub.

Physical touching of statues may be an act of religious devotion, or even a necessary part of the communion with the deity inhabiting the statue. In ancient Greece, the swearing of an oath sometimes involved not just verbally invoking the god, whose divine punishment would be requested in case of breach, but also physically touching the statue of that deity. In one Athenian inscription, the expression 'to touch the statue' was used in reference to oath-making.[6] The thirteenth-century seated statue of St Peter in the Vatican, credited to Arnolfo di Cambio, is one of the few surviving monumental bronze statues of the Middle Ages. St Peter is seated, giving a blessing with his right hand while clutching the keys to heaven in his left. His right foot protrudes forwards, offering an inviting target for rubbing. In this context, rubbing is an act of communion with the subject of the statue, offering hope of a blessing from St Peter. Rubbing the large belly of Budai, the laughing Buddha, typically portrayed with a cloth sack representing prosperity and contentment, is a popular tradition within East Asian Buddhism, a means of invoking his help.

Among university students in certain cities, there is something of a fad for touching the feet of great philosophers, evidently in the hope that a little wisdom might rub off. A statue of Scottish philosopher David Hume, the work of sculptor Sandy Stoddart, put up on the Royal Mile in Edinburgh in 1997, employed classical dress linking Hume to the philosophers of ancient Greece, an approach that, significantly for our purposes, left him with bare feet. Philosophy students appear to have initiated the tradition of rubbing the big toe of his right foot to ensure exam success. A superstition that would thoroughly annoy the Enlightenment philosopher Hume, as he didn't believe in them.[7]

In Paris, students at the Sorbonne University focus on a bronze replica of a 1934 statue of sixteenth-century philosopher Michel de

Montaigne. The original was in stone, the work of Paul Landowski. The statue has the philosopher in a relaxed mood, seated on a block, his legs crossed, an action that makes his right shoe more accessible as it dangles invitingly. The routine here to secure that all-important scholarly advantage is apparently to polish the philosopher's right shoe while offering him a friendly greeting of 'Salut Montaigne!' Why Montaigne should feel positively minded towards the students is unclear: the demise of the original statue came during the vandalism of the student protests of the 1960s.

In politics, disciples have sought inspiration from rubbing a statue of their hero. The statue of Winston Churchill unveiled in the Member's Lobby of the House of Commons in London in 1970 features the politician standing, hands on hips, surveying his surroundings. His protruding left foot again provided an enticing target for rubbing, and for years Conservative politicians gave the foot a little rub to facilitate the erudition of their speeches as they headed to the chamber. Labour and Liberal politicians similarly adopted statues of Clement Attlee and David Lloyd George, respectively. In 2013, however, the Advisory Committee on Works of Art, alarmed that repeated touching was damaging the statues, determined that action was needed. The press reported the installation of a 'do not touch' sign. And deputy curator Melanie Unwin revealed that 'new MPs are no longer told of the tradition' of statue rubbing.[8]

Feet and toes are not the only body parts targeted for rubbing. In Hamburg, a lemon seller named Henriette Johanne Marie Müller, better known as Zitronenjette, was immortalised in 1986 by sculptor Hansjörg Wagner, who depicted her holding her lemon basket. Her left hand stretches forward, and Zitronenjette's finger has been rubbed gold by viewers hoping for luck. This makes Zitronenjette one of a band of purported luck-bringing statues of subjects who in life had little luck themselves. Henriette became an alcoholic, ending her days in an asylum. The plaque makes clear that luck is unlikely to be forthcoming here, pointing out that her life was as sour as the lemons she sold, making her a symbol for those for whom luck has no time. And yet she still possesses a gold finger.

In a part of the crypt of Wawel Cathedral in Kraków reserved for tombs of Polish cultural greats, a bronze commemorative plaque was installed in 1993 on the 110th anniversary of the death of Cyprian Norwid, a Polish poet and dramatist who spent much of his life in exile in Paris, where he was buried in the Polish Cimetière des Champeaux de Montmorency. An urn containing soil from his grave was placed in a nearby niche eight years later. The plaque depicts the writer in relief. An outstretched finger of his right hand has been rubbed gold, as has the back of his left hand. A woman passing me rubs his finger. I ask her why she decided to do so. She has no idea—she noticed from the colour of the finger that it seemed the thing to do, so thought she would give it a try. Perhaps it might bring good luck. Which tells us two things about statue rubbing. First, the power of the demonstration effect—people rub because others have rubbed before them. Second, that accessibility is all-important. It is no accident that few statues of nineteenth-century leaders on tall plinths are rubbed. The viewer can't get close to them. Polished body parts must be accessible—many rubbed statues are therefore more modern bronzes, humanised at street level and so rendered vulnerable.

In Brussels, the relief of the body of Everard t'Serclaes, strategically sited on a tourist route near the Grand-Place, is a target for rubbers looking for luck. T'Serclaes was a fourteenth-century citizen of Brussels celebrated for leadership of efforts to drive the Flemings from the city in 1356, only to be murdered on the orders of one Sweder of Abcoude. The relief is the 1898 work of Belgian sculptor Julien Dillens, and the chief body part in question is the patriot's right arm, considered a bringer of luck since at least World War I.[9] Tour guides now mostly tell their flock that rubbing the arm will ensure a return visit. Some embellish the tale with more convoluted instructions necessitating the rubbing of other objects on the relief, principally a shield, the face of an angel and a dog, which all gleam a correspondingly shiny golden hue. Many visitors seem to have concluded that, if rubbing the arm brings a certain amount of luck, rubbing the whole figure must multiply it, as Everard now shines gold in his entirety.

The complex tales of tour guides are also in evidence at the Charles Bridge in Prague. From here in 1393 the Bohemian saint John of Nepomuk is said to have been thrown to his death into the

Vltava River, following torture on the orders of King Wenceslaus IV. According to some accounts, the dispute was down to the king's anger over John's support for the 'wrong' candidate for the post of Abbot of Kladruby. According to others, and the basis of St John's present-day popularity among Catholics, it was for his refusal to break the seal of Confession and reveal to the king details of her extra-marital love life confided to him by the queen. Reliefs at the base of the statue of St John of Nepomuk on the bridge are a target for rubbers. So too is the alleged place of the saint's literal downfall, a little way along the bridge, where a metal grille jutting out over the river is festooned with locks, symbols of eternal love (and cut off every fortnight). A relief here shows St John falling into the river. The instructions given by guides, and pay attention here, require the visitor to place each finger of one hand on one of the stars encircling the saint's head. The fingers of the other hand must simultaneously be placed on the ends of the double cross on the parapet beside the grille, while one foot should rest on a metal patch on the pavement below. Good luck, or possibly a pulled muscle, will follow.

Traditions around rubbing body parts of specific statues are often relatively recent inventions and can be big tourist business. Researchers Thomas Blom and Mats Nilsson call it 'tactile tourism'.[10] In 2023, Croatian travel writer and film maker Boris Veličan decided to invent a statue-rubbing tradition in Zagreb. On Croatian television he adopted the role of tour guide, persuading visitors to rub the breasts of the statue of Maria Jurić Zagorka, a women's rights activist and the first female journalist in Croatia. Good luck, he assured visitors, necessitated closing one's eyes and cupping the hands over both breasts. There was however a backlash against this stunt from those who felt it demonstrated misogynistic disrespect for Maria's career and achievements.[11]

Female breasts remain, however, a frequent target of statue rubbers. Consider the French singer Dalida, who sold more than 140 million records worldwide. She was closely associated with the Montmartre district of Paris, where she lived from 1962 until her death in 1987. In 1997, as part of elaborate commemorations of the tenth anniversary of her death, orchestrated by her brother

Orlando,[12] a Montmartre square was named after the singer, and a bronze bust placed there in her honour (see fig. 24). The inauguration was attended by Orlando alongside Jean Tiberi, the then Mayor of Paris. The breasts of Dalida's statue have been rubbed gold, to bring luck. Luck? In 1967, Dalida found her new lover Luigi Tenco dead in their hotel room of a self-inflicted gunshot wound after they had performed a duet at the San Remo Music Festival. The song they had sung was called *Bye Bye, My Love*. Her former husband killed himself, as did another former lover. Dalida herself committed suicide at the age of 54. And rubbing the breasts of her statue is supposed to bring luck.

Creepily, not least in view of her youth, the most vigorously rubbed breasts of any statue probably belong to Juliet, the female half of Shakespeare's star-crossed lovers, whose statue occupies the courtyard of a house in Verona said to have once belonged to a family who were possibly an inspiration for the fictional Capulets. A suitably romantic balcony is a twentieth-century addition. The first Juliet statue here was put up in 1972, but the belief that caressing Juliet's right breast would improve your love life led to so much damage to the breast that a replacement was called for in 2014. Juliet's fans seem to have become more ardent, for this time it took only a decade of touristic rubbing to create a hole in the right breast.[13]

There has been a backlash against breast rubbers. When a Boston gynaecological surgeon named Jon Einarsson included a photograph of himself rubbing Juliet's breast at a medical conference in 2017, and this makes you wonder about the theme of his presentation, the outcome was a petition to the governing board of his medical group arguing that the photograph was a symptom of a wider problem of the sexual harassment, intimidation and objectification of female surgeons by male colleagues.[14]

Are opponents of the rubbing of statuary breasts in the ascendancy? There are certainly suggestions of a turning tide. Let us consider sweet Molly Malone, the purveyor of cockles and mussels in Dublin's fair city, tragically struck down by fever in a celebrated nineteenth-century song. A bronze statue of Molly, the work of Jeanne Rynhart, was unveiled in 1988 during Dublin's Millennium celebrations. The statue depicts Molly in a low-cut dress struggling to retain her ample breasts, a nod to a later embellishment of her tale, not present in the chaste original song, in which she supplemented her income through prostitution. In the fine Dublin tradition of christening city monuments with distinctive names, this one was dubbed 'the tart with a cart'. Molly's breasts have been rubbed gold by those seeking the luck of the Irish.

Opponents of the practice included graffiti sprayers, who daubed the breasts with 'please don't, TY' and '7 years bad luck', substituting one form of interference with another. In 2024, busker Tilly Cripwell launched a campaign to encourage people to 'leave Molly mAlone'.[15] Dublin City Council announced that stewards would be placed next to the statue for a pilot scheme in May 2025 to discourage people from touching it. The Council also announced plans to re-patinate Molly's breasts so that they would again resemble the rest of the statue.[16]

For Cripwell, rubbing Molly Malone's breasts was 'a misogynistic tradition': as regards, say, the nearby statue of Oscar Wilde, 'you don't see people rubbing his crotch for good luck.'[17] While Oscar Wilde's crotch may indeed have escaped wandering fingers, this is far from true of all male crotches in the world of statuary. A typically corpulent statue of a naked Adam and Eve by Fernando Botero was unveiled in 1981 close to the casino at Monte Carlo. Adam's penis has been rubbed gold by gamblers hoping for the luck they need to secure some real gold. Given the association between statue rubbing and superstitions around luck, it is not surprising that the vicinity of casinos seems to favour rubbed body parts. For years in Las Vegas, the rubbers' focus was on the G-stringed buttocks of the Crazy Girls, a line-up of seven burlesque dancers, backs to the viewer and arms interlocked, the 1997 work of Michael Conine, entitled *No Ifs, Ands, or Butts*. Neither the Crazy Girls themselves nor the sculpture have survived a change in customer tastes.

Prague Castle once sheltered a bronze statue of a naked boy entitled *Youth*, the 1965 work of Miloš Zet, whose member was shined the brightest gold by intense rubbing. The statue has been removed, in part perhaps around concerns that the location of the work, outside the Toy Museum, was not the most appropriate given the uses to which it was being put. Which brings us back to the rubbing of the crotch of recumbent journalist Victor Noir, an act that goes to show, as Croatian journalist Ivan Kralj puts it, 'the penis mightier than the sword'.[18]

Playing Games with Statues

Rubbing is not the only means through which it is hoped statues may bring luck. The Fontanka River scythes through the Russian city of St Petersburg, its banks walled and steep. Several feet below street level, close to the First Engineer Bridge, a small ledge has been fixed to the wall. On this has been placed the diminutive bronze statue of a bird, more precisely a siskin. The 1994 work of Georgian polymath Rezo Gabriadze, it was installed during a city festival of humour. The bird is named Chizhik-Pyzhik, taking its name from a Russian rhyme about a little bird who drinks vodka along the Fontanka until its head spins. The siskin is 'chizh' in Russian. One theory surrounding the rhyme's origin runs that Chizhik-Pyzhik was a nickname of students at the nearby Imperial Law School in Tsarist times, owing to their green and yellow uniforms, resembling the bird's plumage.[19] The students were evidently a drunken lot.

The Chizhik-Pyzhik statue is considered a bestower of fortune by virtue of the small size of the ledge on which the bird stands and its physically inaccessible location down the stone wall. These qualities make the ledge a difficult but not quite impossible target for the lobbing down of coins. Land one on the ledge and good things will follow. Most coins bounce straight off into the Fontanka below. But the opportunity to lose a very small amount of money by tossing a coin in the direction of a bronze siskin has made Chizhik-Pyzhik among the city's favourite monuments. Its small size and challenging location, while bringing good fortune to champion tossers, have however brought ill fortune to the bird itself. It has been a favoured target for theft, the perpetrators perhaps to be found among the new generation of the drunken students of St Petersburg that inspired the statue in the first place. A local museum reportedly retains copies of the statue from Gabriadze's original cast so the siskin may quickly be returned to its perch after each theft.[20]

VOICES IN STONE

Sex With Statues

We have explored the long tradition of attempts of sculptors to create an idealised image of beauty or allure. This has consequences. Sexual attraction to statues has a name: agalmatophilia, sometimes also called Pygmalionism, after the best-known literary example of falling in love with a statue.[21] In Ovid's poem *The Metamorphoses*, Pygmalion was a sculptor of Cyprus, priggish by nature, who was so disgusted with the sinfulness of women that he resolved to remain celibate, devoting himself to his sculpture. It was clear what was really on his mind, as he made an ivory statue of a beautiful girl, so lovely that he fell in love with his creation. He kissed and fondled the statue, and took it to bed, but it remained stubbornly cold to his advances. On the feast day of Venus, the sculptor made offerings at her altar, imploring the goddess to grant him a bride as lovely as the statue. On returning home, as he embraced the statue, it lost its hardness, becoming warm to the touch. It turned into a woman, referred to in later literary treatments as Galatea. Pygmalion married his statue, and they had a child together, Paphos.

Ovid's tale derives from an earlier work of Greek mythology. Later sources suggest he may have drawn on a now lost account of Philostephanus, a Hellenistic writer of the third century BCE. This concerns a Cypriot king called Pygmalion who, in his madness, fell in love with a naked statue of Aphrodite, taking it to bed as if the statue were his wife.[22] Historian György Németh suggests the tale may have been of more ancient, perhaps Phoenician, origin. Ovid reworked it into a story about an artist and his perfect creation.[23]

Philostephanus' story of King Pygmalion and his passion for the naked statue of Aphrodite is not the only ancient account of carnal desire for a statue. The rhetorician Athenaeus of Naucratis tells of the infatuation of Cleisophus of Selymbria for the marble statue of an unnamed female figure, probably a goddess, made by Ctesicles on the island of Samos. Cleisophus attempted to make love to the statue, but found it was too cold and hard. He came back the next day with a piece of raw meat, tied that to the statue, and had an altogether better experience.[24]

The statue of Aphrodite on Knidos by the sculptor Praxiteles had many admirers. It is said that the model was Phyrne, lover of

INTERFERING WITH STATUES

Praxiteles and a noted prostitute. An account in *Loves* (*Amores*), attributed to Lucian, seeks to explain a blemish on one of the thighs of the statue, likened to a stain on clothes. A young man, infatuated with the statue, had remained alone with it when the sanctuary was closed. He tried to make love to the statue, an enterprise that was evidently unsuccessful as he then committed suicide by jumping into the sea. All that remained as evidence of the act was the blemish.[25]

Erotic literature has also addressed the theme of sex between humans and statues. *The School of Venus*, an anonymous work of 1680, translated from the earlier French-language work *L'Escole des Filles*, tells of a king's daughter who, lacking a suitable beau, makes use of a bronze statue painted flesh-coloured and adorned with a swinging member 'composed of a soft substance, hollow, yet stiff enough to do the business', with the bonus features of a 'thwacking pair of stones' and the facility to squirt a lukewarm liquor.[26]

Psychologist Murray White, writing in *The Journal of Sex Research*, a publication presumably found on the top shelf of academic libraries, finds little evidence that agalmatophilia exists as a genuine behavioural perversion, identifying only one modern example, and that based on hearsay, of a gardener attempting sex with a statue of the Venus de Milo.[27] Then again, 'outrage' was reported in Florence when in summer 2024 a female tourist was pictured miming a lewd act on a statue of Bacchus, a replica of a sixteenth-century work by Giambologna.[28] One suspects that Bacchus would probably have approved.

Vandalism

Deliberate damaging of a statue may arise through various motives. A statue may be the innocent target of vicious intent, or the goal may be the theft of part of the statue. Or the damage may express opposition to the values the statue seeks to portray, or to the character and career of the subject. It is helpful to distinguish between acts of vandalism, defacement or simple student pranks where the subject of the statue is not germane to the actions taken, and acts of vandalism directed against the subject, events, ideals or values represented by the statue.

An example of the former crops up in Erich Kästner's 1929 children's novel *Emil and the Detectives*. Our young hero, Emil, living in an archetypal provincial German town named Neustadt, is wracked with fear that the police may find out about his vandalism. For Emil, with a group of schoolfriends, placed an old felt hat on the statue of Grand Duke Charles in the marketplace. To make matters worse, it was Emil who had been hoisted up by his friends to chalk a red nose and black moustache on the statue's face. Emil's consequent apprehension that the police may be on his trail explains why, when robbed on the train by the dastardly man with the bowler hat, he opts not for the straightforward route of going to the police (which would have made for a dull story) but enlists a gang of Berlin child detectives to help catch the thief (which makes for an exciting one).[29]

The Duke of Wellington Acquires a Traffic Cone

Another example of vandalism incidental to the subject centres on the equestrian statue of the Duke of Wellington standing outside the Royal Exchange in Glasgow, now the Gallery of Modern Art. The statue is typical of its kind: one of many statues across Britain honouring the hero of Waterloo. What is not typical is his headwear.

The statue, financed through public subscription, was the work of Italian sculptor Carlo Marochetti. It depicts the duke astride his favoured horse, Copenhagen. Erected in 1844, it led an uneventful life until some point in the 1980s. While the origins of the practice are unclear, it is believed that one night a drunken but inventive soul, perhaps a student, decided that the duke could do with adornment, scaled the statue and placed a traffic cone on his head (see fig. 25).[30]

This act set in motion a forty-year battle of wills. The combatants were on the one hand Glasgow City Council, concerned for the dignity of the statue, who endeavoured to remove offending cones as they appeared. The council fretted about the risks posed by the heavy and frequently intoxicated feet of the cone-placers on their Grade A-listed monument, and the accompanying risk that the vandal, or artist, depending on your point of view, might come a cropper while scaling the thing. Their opponents were those who viewed council efforts to return the duke to his intended state as a challenge, and an enticing one. By 2005 it was reported that the poor duke had lost his spurs and a good part of his sword.[31] Battle lines hardened, with Strathclyde Police warning that anyone caught climbing the statue risked prosecution.

In 2013, the council decided on drastic action. Their frustration with the whole cone business was palpable. They lamented that cone removal was costing £100 a time, an annual cost of some £10,000. According to their report, the cones, 'appearing after the revelries of the weekend', presented 'a depressing image of Glasgow.' They fumed that 'this unfortunate impression of the city has been supported by former Lord Provosts and even adopted occasionally by the city's marketing bureau.'[32] The problem, the council determined, arose from a plinth that was too low, allowing easy access via the rear. They had a solution. They proposed raising the duke by adding an 86-centimetre granite-clad concrete base.

This proposal to lift the good duke out of reach had the effect of demonstrating Glaswegian affection towards the cones. A 'Keep the Cone' Facebook page gathered 72,000 fans, who stylised themselves Coneheids.[33] An online petition was launched, 'Save Wellington's Cone', whose central argument was that placement of the cone on Wellington's head meant more to the people of Glasgow than the duke himself. In any case, raising the plinth would hardly act as a deterrent to the brave and foolhardy drunks of Glasgow—it would simply increase the risk of injury.[34] Glasgow City Council dropped the proposal.

The coned statue has become part of the Glasgow tourist offer—featuring on key rings and coasters.[35] Travel publishers Lonely Planet featured the statue in a 2011 list of the most bizarre monuments on earth. The cones started to appear in different colours, to make commemorative or political statements. In 2012, a gold-painted version evidently honoured the performance of Scottish athletes as part of Team GB in the London Olympics. In March 2022, a cone in the colours of the Ukrainian flag protested the Russian invasion of that country.

Launching his first official solo exhibition for fourteen years at the Gallery of Modern Art in 2023, street artist Banksy described the cone-topped statue as his 'favourite work of art in the UK',[36] suggesting he had chosen to bring the exhibition to the Gallery because of its location behind the statue. The banner advertising his exhibition replaced the 'A' in 'BANKSY' with a traffic cone. At the end of Banksy's ten-week 'Cut and Run' exhibition, it was observed that the statue had acquired a new cone with a propeller top on the duke's head, and another cone under his arm. Copenhagen had gained a horn, giving the appearance of a unicorn, the national animal of Scotland. Journalists wondered whether Banksy had offered his favourite work of art a parting gift.[37]

The cones have kept the statue of the duke alive, ensuring it has not fallen into the invisibility forecast by Robert Musil. Up to a point—the fact the statue depicts the Duke of Wellington is incidental; any former statesman with a head located at a moderately challenging but not unattainable height would have done.

Vandalism Directed Against the Subject of the Statue

Physical attacks on statues may seek to undo their claim to command respect[38] where the vandals oppose the values represented by the statue or the character and actions of the subject. Vandalism in this context may simply be about damaging as much as possible of the hated image or may seek to change the statue's meaning. Alan Rice uses the term 'guerilla memorialisation' to refer to the latter process, where graffiti or other alterations to statues made without permission seek to change what it is they signify.[39]

Targeted vandalism of statues is far from rare. Between 2018 and 2019 Nick Wilson and colleagues at the University of Otago Wellington endeavoured through literature and online searches and site visits to examine all statues of named modern-era people in New Zealand in outdoor public settings for evidence of past defacements. They identified 123 statues falling within their criteria, the first unveiled in 1867. Twenty-eight, some 23% of the total, had been attacked at least once. Graffiti or daubing with paint were the most common forms of attack, but more violent methods were also recorded, including nose removals and several decapitations—a fate befalling a statue of King George V at Matakana no less than five times. They concluded that subjects linked with colonisation or harm to the Māori people were most likely to be physically attacked. A few attacks seemed to have an anti-war motive. Statues of royals, military personnel, explorers and politicians were often subjected to deliberate damage, while they recorded no evidence of attacks on statues of sports personalities.[40]

The statue of Winston Churchill on Parliament Square in London was daubed in graffiti during Black Lives Matter protests in 2020. The vandalism involved scrawled quotations from the former prime minister to highlight his use of racist and imperialist language. The timing of the vandalism, close to the 6 June anniversary of the D-Day landings, accentuated outrage around the act. The statue acquired a protective box and police guard ahead of a further protest scheduled for 12 June, and a counter-protest on the following day with the stated aim of 'protecting' the Churchill statue. The prospect of the latter protest engendered pre-emptive boarding up of statues of Nelson Mandela and Mahatma Gandhi lest the 'protective' counter-protestors themselves turned to thoughts of iconoclasm.[41]

Vandalism of a statue has on occasion not been a matter of concern about the character and values of its subject, but of its sculptor. The façade of Broadcasting House in London, home of the BBC, has been enlivened since 1933 by a limestone relief depicting characters from Shakespeare's *The Tempest*. The robed Prospero surrounds Ariel protectively. The latter is depicted as a naked child, holding a flute. The relief is the work of artist and designer Eric Gill, who died in 1940. In 1989, a biography of Gill was published by Fiona MacCarthy, drawing from Gill's own diary, recounting the sexual abuse inter alia of his daughters and the family dog.

The statue was attacked in 2022, and the BBC came under fire for starting work the following year on restoring the damage. Sexual abuse campaigner Dawn Carrington told journalists that 'the decision to restore this statue by a paedophile is a smack in the face to the BBC's audience and employees, an estimated one in five of whom has experienced at least one form of child abuse.'[42] Restoration work did not start smoothly: a man wearing a Spider Man mask climbed the scaffolding to inflict further damage with a hammer and chisel. Campaigners had no concerns about Shakespeare, or the characters of Prospero and Ariel as portrayed in his play, but the way they were depicted on the relief, a naked boy shielded by an older man, was problematic in the context of what is now known about the artist. The restored sculpture was unveiled in April 2025, now covered by a protective glass case. Explanatory wording, accessed via a QR code, explains that while the BBC 'in no way condones Gill's abusive behaviour', it 'draws a line between his life and his artistic creations.'[43]

Theologian and art historian Robin Jensen explores an early fifth century example in which vandalism of a statue was accepted as a compromise by the authorities to avert destructive removal of the whole monument, potentially precipitating social disorder. Bishop Augustine of Hippo sought to remove the commemorative value associated with pagan idols, insisting that those caught preparing sacrifices to them would be subjected to capital punishment. He also however wanted to keep the peace, dissuading local Christians from acting against pagans and their statues with excessive zeal. Augustine was concerned around the risks of a riot in Carthage, where devotees of the cult of Hercules wanted to regild his statue, an expense that would have required a tax assessment and offended Christians regarding all of this as idolatry. Local Christians then vandalised the statue, removing Hercules's beard. Facing demands for the demolition of Hercules altogether, and indeed all temples and cult images in the town, Augustine took the line with the Christian agitators that the vandalism already perpetrated better suited their purposes than destruction of the statue. Removing the beard had obliterated the symbol of Hercules's strength and demonstrated Christian superiority. Humiliation of Hercules was more effective than removal.[44]

The Daubing of Indro Montanelli

In 2006 a bronze statue was unveiled in Milan to Indro Montanelli, an Italian journalist who had died some five years earlier. The work of sculptor Vito Tongiani, it portrays the journalist prodding away on his typewriter while seated on a pile of newspapers. The low wall surrounding the statue symbolises a longstanding column written by Montanelli for the *Corriere della Sera* newspaper, entitled *Montanelli's Room* (*La stanza di Montanelli*). There was little opposition to a statue to such a celebrated figure of the Italian media on its inauguration, and early criticism focused on the rigid, almost funereal, feel of the sculpture.[45]

INTERFERING WITH STATUES

This would soon change. The first episode of vandalism against the statue was recorded in 2012. In 2018 a sticker proclaiming 'children's rapist' was placed over the reference to 'journalist' on the plinth. In June 2020, a week after the statue of slave trader Edward Colston ended up in Bristol harbour, Montanelli's statue was spray painted in red, and the words 'racist' and 'rapist' sprayed in black on the pedestal. The perpetrators were apparently members of local student organisations, who claimed responsibility via social media to a soundtrack of Gil Scott-Heron's song *The Revolution Will Not be Televised*.[46] Later that month, an activist adorned the statue with a puppet of a young girl.

These actions sought to highlight racist ideas and language used by Montanelli while writing for fascist publications in the 1930s, and his 'marriage' to a reportedly twelve-year-old Eritrean girl during his participation as a volunteer in the Italian invasion of Abyssinia.[47] Montanelli's blasé justifications over his relationship with Desta, the Eritrean girl, added fuel to his critics' fire. In a 1969 Italian television interview, he was challenged by an Eritrean-Italian audience member named Elvira Banotti. Montanelli dismissed her concerns, arguing that it was normal in the context of the place and time for girls of that age to marry, leading Banotti to describe his acts as 'the violent relationship of the colonialist who arrived there and took possession of a twelve-year-old girl.'[48] At the time of writing, the statue remains in place, within a park also bearing Montanelli's name. The authorities have resisted calls to remove it, and prominent journalists have spoken in support of the statue. Its vandalism serves to contest the narratives underpinning it.

13

RELOCATION

A bronze statue of the poet Byron, the work of sculptor Richard Belt, was installed in 1880 in the tranquil setting of Hamilton Gardens, within London's Hyde Park. The charming work depicts the poet accompanied by his dog Bo'sun. The marble pedestal was a gift from the Greek government in recognition of Byron's support for their independence struggle. A happy situation was however disturbed by the traffic planning of later twentieth-century London, and specifically by the enlargement of Park Lane into a three-lane dual carriageway in the 1960s. The eastern boundary of Hyde Park was shifted to the west, and poor Byron found himself marooned amidst fast-moving traffic. The Byron Society has long campaigned for relocation of the statue. The House of Lords debated the proposal in April 2024; an occasion for learned Peers to populate their interventions with Byronic quotes. Lord Kirkhope of Harrogate, noting that 'to have joy, one must share it', opined that Byron was hardly being shared in his present location.[1] It seems that lovers of Byron may soon be able to enjoy the statue in a more peaceful setting, as at the time of writing it had been announced that the statue will be relocated to a seemlier and more accessible spot within the park.[2]

We have described statues that move: an act associated with some remarkable and magical statues. It is now time to turn to statues that *are* moved. As with the statue of Byron, that act is sometimes motivated by the desire to care for and protect the statue, for example when its original location is threatened by urban redevelopment. Relocation is however more often about demotion, violence and disgrace.

VOICES IN STONE

Stealing Statues

Numerous stories from the ancient world involve the theft of prized statues. The city of Aphrodisias, in present-day Anatolia, was known in ancient times for her cult image, the *Aphrodite of Aphrodisias*. Its archaeological site is famed for the inscriptions at its so-called 'Archival Wall', which collates a selection of documents, carefully chosen to put the city in the best possible light, dwelling on the privileges awarded to the place by Rome. One of the documents immortalised on this wall is a letter from Octavian to the Ephesians. The emperor writes that an ambassador sent by Aphrodisias had called on him, reminding him of the loyal service Aphrodisias provided to Rome in combating renegade Roman general Labienus. In recognition of this support, Octavian was minded to take the side of Aphrodisias in relation to a golden statue of Eros dedicated to Aphrodite by Julius Caesar, Octavian's adoptive father, which had evidently ended up at the temple of Artemis in Ephesus. Octavian requested its return to Aphrodisias, appealing to the Ephesian respect for lawful claims. The statue had been given by his father as an offering to Aphrodite, not Artemis, and a representation of Eros was hardly suitable for Artemis, a goddess associated with chastity.[3]

We have encountered Praxiteles' famed statue of Aphrodite at Knidos, responsible for erotic longings in many who gazed upon it. That sculptor's Eros at the ancient Greek city of Thespiae was almost as famous. According to Cicero, the statue was a focus of early art tourism, with people journeying to the city just to set eyes upon it.[4] Eros was depicted as an adolescent winged youth without a bow, importing erotic longing not through arrows but through his gaze. The two statues were linked by the sculptor's passion for the courtesan Phryne, who seems to have been quite a character. When on trial in the Athenian courts she was reportedly acquitted when her lawyer tore open her dress and, in an evidently successful plea for mercy, exposed her breasts to the jurors. While the statue of Aphrodite was by some accounts modelled on her naked form, that of Eros was modelled on the desire Praxiteles felt for her. He gave her the statue as payment for her favours, and she dedicated it in Thespiae, her hometown.[5]

RELOCATION

Such a famous statue attracted the avaricious attentions of greater powers, and the career of the Eros of Thespiae provides a dizzying sequence of theft and return. According to some sources, Roman general Lucius Mummius removed the statue to Athens in 146 BCE, where it was placed with another Praxiteles statue, that of Nike, in the theatre of Dionysus. It was restored to Thespiae by Sulla in gratitude for Thespian support. Only to be taken to Rome, perhaps during the reign of Caligula, returned again to Thespiae by Claudius, and nabbed back by Nero, who installed it in the Porticus of Octavia, where it was destroyed by fire in 80 CE.[6] At Thespiae, an imitation was made by the sculptor Menodorus to replace the lost original, though it doesn't seem to have been entirely successful, attracting criticism around a decision to gild the wings. The geographer Pausanias, who viewed the replacement in the second century, is indignant at the behaviour of the Roman emperors who stole the statue from the Greeks.[7]

Sometimes, removal of statues was not just about the theft of something prized, but also about subjugation and conquest: the transportation of the most valued statues of a defeated power to the land of the victor. This practice seems to have been characteristic of the ancient Near East.[8] Within the Parthian kingdom centred on present-day Iran, the overall ruler, the King of Kings, presided over client kings, who enjoyed considerable autonomy. For the King of Kings, it was important to place on these thrones monarchs who would be loyal, ideally a close member of their family. In 147 CE, Vologases IV seized the throne of the King of Kings in a coup d'etat, establishing a new branch of the Arsacid dynasty. This presented him with a problem. The small client kingdom of Characene, also known as Mesene, at the head of the Persian Gulf, had a significant position on trade routes between Mesopotamia and India, enabling its ruler, Meredates, to accumulate wealth and power. Meredates was however the brother of Vologases III, the man the new King of Kings had ousted. Vologases IV could not allow someone who had displayed such loyalty to the previous regime to keep his throne.

Accordingly, in 151 CE, Vologases IV made his move. Our story is taken up by a statue of Heracles found in central Mesopotamia, on which an inscription had been added in Greek and Parthian (see fig. 26). This tells us that Vologases led a military expedition against Meredates, which had evidently proved a great success. Meredates had been expelled from Mesene, and Vologases had established himself both as ruler of Mesene and of this bronze statue of Heracles, which he had brought back with him, placing it in a sanctuary of the god Apollo, where it guarded the Bronze Door.[9] With Meredates out of the way, Vologases was able to install Orabazes II, probably a relative, as the new king of Mesene.

Heracles had evidently enjoyed an important role as a protective god of Mesene, making the act of removal of the statue a significant one. The statue's powers were clearly considered useful for Vologases IV as well, given the decision to place the statue close to the Bronze Door of the temple of Apollo, exploiting the powers of Heracles as a protector of gates.[10]

In December 1910, an archaeological excavation in Sudan, on the eastern bank of the Nile, led by Professor John Garstang of Liverpool University, unearthed an extraordinary find. It was a bronze portrait bust of Roman emperor Augustus, buried beneath the doorway of a building in the city of Meroë, capital of the ancient kingdom of Kush.

We have already encountered this head, which lives in the British Museum, in discussing the importance placed on the modelling of the eyes of classical sculptures. The site of the head's discovery is relevant to our current examination of plundered statues, as Meroë was not part of Augustus's great empire. The story of the statue of Augustus, or more precisely its severed head, is a story of the feuding between Kush and Roman Egypt. It was in Egypt that Augustus, then known as Octavian, achieved his decisive victory over his major rival, Mark Antony, near Alexandria in 30 BCE, after which Egypt became a Roman province.

When in 25 BCE the Roman governor of Egypt embarked on a military expedition into southern Arabia, the rulers of Meroë saw their opportunity and seized the Roman settlements of Syene, Elephantine and Philae. According to the Greek geographer Strabo, they 'threw down the statues of Caesar.'[11] In the case of this statue of Augustus, they seem not just to have thrown it down but also to have brought back its severed head to their capital. The building in

RELOCATION

whose doorway the head was found featured wall paintings hailing Meroë's military triumph, with depictions of enthroned figures whose footstools were ornamented with representations of bound captives. Thorsten Opper, a curator at the British Museum, concludes that the building appears to have been a victory shrine. The burial of Augustus's head in the doorway was probably a deliberate act, ensuring that those entering the shrine trampled over the face of the enemy.[12]

Meroë's victory was short-lived. The new Roman governor, Gaius Petronius, marched south, forcing the Meroites to retreat into their former territory. The king of Meroë was dead by this point, and Petronius dealt with representatives of his widow and successor Amanirenas, described less than flatteringly by Strabo as 'a masculine woman who had lost an eye.'[13] Preoccupied with their war with the Parthians, the Romans did not press home their advantage, and were happy to make peace with Meroë.

The theft of a statue can increase its profile. At 10.30 in the evening of 19 March 2023, CCTV footage showed a car arriving at the Reynard Nurseries in Lanarkshire in Scotland. The occupants unbolted an eight-foot fibreglass gorilla named Gary from the garden centre. A couple of hours later, a van turned up and removed the gorilla. Nursery owner Andrew Scott was distraught. Gary had been a much-loved feature of the nurseries, welcoming visitors for a decade. He had been dressed up for Christmas and wore a face mask during the Covid pandemic. A few weeks later, a breakthrough was reported. A gorilla of similar appearance had been spotted tied to a trailer on both the M25 and M40 motorways in England. Alas, it transpired that this was a different eight-foot fibreglass gorilla.[14]

Among those listening to radio reports of Gary's snatching was Tom Ogden of indie rock band Blossoms. Tom was moved to pen a song in honour of the missing ape, urging us all to keep an eye out for Gary. The music video featured crooner Rick Astley in the role of Andrew Scott. The song caught on, and the band named its next album *Gary*, touring with yet another eight-foot fibreglass version of the creature. Happily, Gary turned up a year later, albeit the worse for wear, in a layby on the A92 near Dundee.

VOICES IN STONE

A Suitable Destination

Where a statue is not stolen, but deliberately relocated by the authorities, the aim is frequently to demote the statue: to take it down from a prestigious location and put it somewhere less prominent. Out of sight, out of mind. The decision to remove frequently proves more straightforward than the choice of new location, where differences emerge as to the appropriate degree of humiliation for the subject of the statue.

Let us consider the statue of King George V erected in 1936 at the heart of New Delhi, the purpose-built capital of India. George V was the only British monarch to travel to India for his proclamation as emperor, in 1911. The Delhi Durbar had been a colossal event, with 100,000 spectators, and it was at this event that the announcement had been made that the capital of British India would move from Calcutta to Delhi.[15] With funding from the Maharaja of Kapurthala, a statue of the monarch was commissioned by Edwin Lutyens, architect of New Delhi, from Charles Sargeant Jagger. The sculptor, taking inspiration from the Delhi Durbar, alighted on a design featuring the monarch in a howdah on the back of an elephant, which busily collected the fruits of empire in its trunk. That design was rejected for being too focused on the elephant, and the final statue was a more conventional affair, depicting the king standing, in long ermine robes.[16] By the time it was inaugurated in 1936, under a sandstone canopy fashioned by Lutyens, both monarch and sculptor were already dead. British rule in India would end just eleven years later.

As we will discover, while there was no immediate push by the new rulers of India to remove colonial-era statuary, calls to take down reminders of foreign domination became increasingly insistent as years passed, and as statues of viceroys in New Delhi came down in the mid-1960s, it became clear that George V would not survive long in the heart of the ceremonial space of the nation's capital. For the British government, the major concern was that the statue's fate should be suitably dignified.[17] By summer 1964, seven colonial statues had been moved to the Exhibition Grounds, a wasteland on the outskirts of New Delhi, where according to an article in *The Statesman* of the following year, they lay 'dirty and untended'.[18] The sorry fate of colonial statues became a political issue in Britain. In November 1968, John Peyton, Conservative MP for Yeovil, wrote to the Commonwealth Relations Office, criticising the government for allowing British statues in India to be neglected. Rather than permitting statues to languish in dumps, he suggested that India might in the last resort be asked instead to break them up: 'death before dishonour!'[19]

An attack on the statue in August 1965 by supporters of the Samyukta Socialist Party, removing portions of nose, ear and crown and adding a portrait of nationalist politician Subhas Chandra Bose, brought urgency to the task of alighting upon a long-term future for the monument.[20] The Indians suggested that the statue might be rehoused within the grounds of the British High Commission, an idea rejected by the British since these were deemed insufficiently spacious properly to display the monument. The British also refused on cost grounds to entertain the suggestion that it might be repatriated to Britain. The municipal authority rejected relocation to a city park.[21] In 1968, the statue was taken down and placed in storage, joining some sixty other colonial statues for which no permanent home had been found.

The Indian government finally identified a site which appeared to offer a fine compromise. After all, Coronation Park in the suburbs of Old Delhi had been the setting for George V's Delhi Durbar. But it was far from unproblematic. The location was peripheral and prone to flooding, and the Indian government was understandably reluctant to devote much funding to the enterprise. With no better solution, George V, with other homeless colonial statues, was moved to the site in 1982. Since then, and notwithstanding a modest renovation in 2011 for the centenary of the Delhi Durbar, it has been largely forgotten. Four other colonial statues stand in a semicircle around King George V. Other pedestals remain vacant: in some cases, because their intended occupants were stolen, in others because the statues were in the event retained where originally installed. While the relocation of the statues in Coronation Park may have been an attempt to 'museumise rather than memorialise the British era',[22] the general air of neglect is an eloquent comment about the degree of priority accorded to that undertaking.

The city-centre site vacated by the statue long remained a canopy in search of an occupant, following the collapse of an earlier plan to replace George V with a statue of Gandhi. In September 2022 a statue of Subhas Chandra Bose was finally installed beneath Lutyens' canopy, fulfilling the prediction of the Samyukta Socialist Party back in 1965. Bose is depicted in the military uniform of his Indian National Army, a celebration of different qualities than a statue of Gandhi, champion of nonviolent resistance, would have offered.

Relocation to Museums

Statues Also Die (*Les statues meurent aussi*) is a short documentary film made in 1953 by Chris Marker, Alain Resnais and Ghislain Cloquet. It was commissioned by Paris-based publishing house *Présence Africaine*, a collaborative venture of French-based writers and intellectuals of African descent.[23]

The film commences with the assertion, delivered authoritatively by narrator Jean Négroni, that 'when men die, they enter History; when statues die, they become Art.'[24] A dizzying sequence of images of African figurative sculpture is presented, offering little context other than a generic description as '*l'art nègre*', 'Black art'.[25] The statues are then shown behind glass exhibition cases, being viewed attentively. The central message is that statues created to be used, commemorated or worshipped have been taken to Western museums where they have been classified, labelled and conserved, becoming in the process simple objects of art history. They have died, in the way that when men die, they become part of history. They have been transformed into commodities.[26] As Alois Riegl might have put it, they have been stripped of commemorative value and anointed instead with artistic value. Négroni's confident voice laments: 'these statues are mute. They have mouths and don't speak. They have eyes and don't see us.'[27] In another sequence, images of these statues are placed back in a living context, juxtaposed with the African setting from which they were taken,[28] perhaps suggesting the power of film to reconstitute the statues' original functions.[29]

Denuded of their cultural context, African sculptures become just things. Adored as art by Western consumers, they are churned out as objects to be sold at bazaars. A white man is portrayed instructing Africans on how to make their own objects. The filmmakers take this as their starting point for a withering critique of colonialism, with colonial exploitation likened to scientific experimentation on laboratory mice.[30] Small wonder that the film was banned in France for several years.

Socialist Statue Parks

We will look later at the removal of statues of Lenin and other heroes of the Communist world accompanying the break-up of the Soviet Union and removal of its sphere of influence in 1991. One immediate question, both practical and political, for states across a swathe of central and eastern Europe, was what to do with all the statues taken down. In several places, the answer alighted on was to group them together in an open-air statue park, among them Memento Park in Budapest, Grūtas Park near Druskininkai in Lithuania, and the Museum of Socialist Art in Sofia. Off Cape Tarkhankut in Crimea, scuba diver Vladimir Broumensky was the driving force, or perhaps diving force, behind an underwater repository of Soviet sculptures and busts, known as the 'Alley of Leaders', who share their subterranean gallery space with a miscellaneous collection of other statuary, including a replica Eiffel Tower, a laughing Buddha and a pelican.[31]

The question of the function performed by these parks is not straightforward. Art historian Ina Belcheva notes they are commonly colloquially referred to as 'sculptural graveyards'. Yet a graveyard is related both to memory and to burial.[32] Is the intention here to remember or to forget? Taken from their original location, their intentional commemorative value is gone. Their remaining value is a mixture of historical and artistic. But what form does this historical value take?

The example of Grūtas Park in Lithuania suggests there are conflicting motivations at work. On the one hand, the park may be seen as a form of punishment towards the heroes of the past, and a warning about the evils of the regime they served. Descriptions inside the exhibition halls, many the work of historian Vytautas Tininis, mince no words about the brutality and anti-democratic nature of the regime, asserting for example that elections were 'illegal, anti-democratic, forced, fictitious, discriminatory and criminal in their character'.[33] The purpose of the information materials is described on the park's website as no less than to 'disclose the genocide of the Lithuanian nation.'[34]

The presence of the statues within the park is a visual reminder of their banishment from prestigious city centre locations. It is a cautionary tale of reduced circumstances: they are displayed on functional concrete plinths, which sometimes lower them from their original height. A 1984 statue of Lenin, depicting the Communist leader from the waist up, which once stood in the city of Jonava, rests on a low concrete plinth offering the impression that Lenin's legs are stuck in the ground (see fig. 27). The statues are grouped along paved alleys, adding to the impression of a cemetery. While Lenin is the most depicted subject, there are also statues of Lithuanian Communist functionaries, like Vincas Mickevičius-Kapsukas, who headed the short-lived Lithuanian Soviet Socialist Republic in the wake of World War I. A plaque tells us he spent time in Germany as a 'radical bellringer.'[35]

The sense in which inclusion in these parks marks a punishment for the statues is illustrated by the efforts of supporters of Bulgarian poet Nikola Vaptsarov to get his statue extracted from the Museum of Socialist Art in Sofia. The statue, the 1952 work of Nikolay Shmirgela, depicts Vaptsarov taking a break from his laborious work, a spade resting on his leg and pile of stones at his feet, while he jots a poetic thought into his notebook. Vaptsarov was a communist revolutionary, executed in 1942, but his supporters argued that the presence of his statue in a museum dedicated to socialism served to subordinate his poetry to his political activism. They campaigned successfully for the statue to return to its original site in central Sofia.[36]

On the other hand, the tone set by Grūtas Park sometimes veers more towards nostalgia for the Communist past than outright condemnation of it. The café offers retro Soviet-era dishes, bored-looking staff wearing red Pioneer scarves, and witty notices in the toilets recalling Soviet period hardships ('a paper towel is a scarce commodity. It is issued only to CPSU members.').[37] The site incorporates a playground and zoo, which say nothing about the evils of communism. And with its green-painted watchtowers and barbed-wire perimeter, as if to stop the statues from escaping, press coverage of its opening on April Fool's Day in 2001 drew parallels with theme parks, describing the place as 'a Disney-style "Leninland."'[38] Proposals that would have pushed the park even further in this direction were it seems toned down, such as an initial idea to bring visitors into the park on cattle-truck style train carriages, escorted by guards in Soviet uniforms.[39]

These conflicting motivations are for some reconcilable in a strategy of what Paul Williams refers to as 'derisive nostalgia',[40] dealing with the evils of the communist regime by laughing at its absurdities. But others found nothing to laugh about in the Soviet occupation, and regarded the park as too flippant, and implicitly forgiving of past brutalities. The park became the subject of fierce debate. The initiative of mushroom exporter Viliumas Malinauskas, his scheme to establish the park won a competition launched in 1998 by a parliamentary committee, seeking a solution to the problem of what to do with the socialist monuments removed from their plinths. Its success probably had much to do with the fact that, unlike most of the other proposals, it was not seeking public funding.[41] Opponents of the park included Labora, a pressure group comprising former partisans who fought the Red Army in the very forests now occupied by the relocated statues, and local parliamentarian Juozas Galdikas, who argued that 'we need monuments in Lithuania which reflect the reality of how people suffered—not a park that puts these murderers back on their pedestals.'[42]

Not all sculpture parks dedicated to fallen Soviet statuary have taken an explicitly condemnatory approach, even one couched in derisive nostalgia. Benjamin Forest and Juliet Johnson examine the Park of Arts in Moscow, a repository of removed Soviet-era monuments since the early 1990s. They note that the texts of plaques installed in the late 1990s at the most important statues ended with a disclaimer which was an exercise in neutrality: 'It has historical and artistic value. The monument is in the memorialising style of political-ideological designs of the Soviet period. Protected by the state.'[43] Ina Belcheva argues that, in having no specific story to tell, the Park of Arts is rendered 'almost obsolete.'[44]

14

RECONTEXTUALISATION

On 25 May 2020, George Floyd, a 46-year-old unarmed African-American man, was murdered by a white police officer, Derek Chauvin, in the US city of Minneapolis. Chauvin had knelt on his back and neck for over nine minutes as he arrested Floyd, fatally asphyxiating him. Floyd's brutal death triggered protests in Minneapolis and across the United States, soon spreading around the world, under the banner 'Black Lives Matter.' The protests, initially focused on police violence and racial discrimination, also sparked other demands, including calls to demolish public monuments to figures associated with slavery and colonialism. In Australia, targets included the statue of Captain Cook in Sydney's Hyde Park. In July 2020, the Council of the Royal Australian Historical Society considered its position on the matter, concluding that 'as public statues, memorials or plaques embody cultural memory, the RAHS neither condones nor supports their arbitrary defacement, removal or destruction. Instead, the RAHS suggests that alternative interpretations of public statues, memorials or plaques could be displayed and/or communicated.'[1]

As opposition grows to the values expressed by the person or event portrayed by the statue, the question arises as to how the statue can remain in situ, while acknowledging concerns around it? Recontextualisation involves keeping the statue in place but either adding to it or altering the context in which it is presented to effect a change in its meaning.[2] The recontextualisation of a statue can include the addition of a new explanatory plaque, providing a broader context about the individual or events portrayed than the simplistic hagiographic depiction in stone or bronze. Or the statue can be recontextualised by artworks, or even by another statue, creating a dialogue with it.

'Retain and Explain'

The then Conservative government in the United Kingdom, confronted by the destruction of the monument of Edward Colston in Bristol during the political heat of the Black Lives Matter rallies and the ensuing politicised debates between opponents and defenders of specific statues, resolved to establish a clear policy for the management of statues and other heritage assets. Speaking to the House of Commons in January 2021, Secretary of State for Housing, Communities and Local Government, Robert Jenrick, made clear that 'criminal acts and mob rule' would not be tolerated. He continued that: 'the knee-jerk removal of statues does harm rather than good. Our aim should be to use heritage to educate people about all aspects of Britain's past rather than censoring our shared British history.'[3] The government's policy in the face of contestation of statues was that of 'retain and explain.'

The Secretary of State for Digital, Culture, Media and Sport established a seven-member Heritage Advisory Board in May 2021, charged with developing new guidelines on the management of difficult heritage assets. This 'retain and explain' policy guidance was published on 5 October 2023. The guidance, addressed to custodians of heritage assets, including public memorials, sought to answer the question of what should be done when 'a commemorative heritage asset in a public space depicts people or events that we might disapprove of today.' That answer was that 'government policy is that these commemorative heritage assets should remain in situ.' Their removal 'diminishes our understanding of the past', 'suppressing our ability to understand and learn from aspects of our history, including past actions which may not be considered acceptable today.'[4] A case-by-case approach was called for as regards whether the monument required additional 'explanation' to respond to concerns around it.

If the custodian of an asset concluded that something needed to be added, this must be done 'in a balanced way', involving consulta-

RECONTEXTUALISATION

tions with the community and stakeholders. Custodians were urged to be 'mindful of those who cannot be consulted, including past and future generations.' The decision should not be rushed. 'Explanation' might mean the addition of a plaque, providing additional context, but this was not the only option. It might also take the form, inter alia, of a nearby exhibition, material accessed digitally via a QR code placed close to the memorial, the organisation of cultural events, or via 'a complementary statue or other artwork to provide commentary or a counter-perspective.' We will explore the latter approach later. Removal of the monument could be contemplated only in 'exceptional circumstances', such as 'a "heritage benefit" in a move that might involve returning an object that has been moved in the past back to its original position.'[5] The guidance contains dark warnings about the time and cost involved in pursuing the relocation of monuments.

The plight of the Guy's and St Thomas' Foundation in London well illustrates the 'retain and explain' approach. An independent charitable foundation, supporting Guy's and St Thomas' Hospitals, it is the custodian of heritage assets including a statue of Thomas Guy in the forecourt of the hospital that bears his name. Guy was a generous philanthropist, who provided substantial support to St Thomas' Hospital, and later embarked on the provision of a new hospital, for which an endowment in his 1724 will of more than £200,000 constituted the largest individual charitable donation of his generation in Britain. Notable generosity indeed, and the hospital governors decided to reflect this by commissioning a statue in his honour. The statue sought also to address criticism of Guy arising after his death. This was based not around the source of his wealth but concerns that in focusing his philanthropy on the hospital he had neglected his own family. Erected in 1734, the statue was the work of Peter Scheemakers. It focuses on Guy's philanthropy, with reliefs on the plinth anchoring his generosity to the values of Christian giving.

The twenty-first century contestation of Guy's statue focuses on the source of Guy's wealth. He owned a large shareholding in the South Sea Company, wisely selling at a high price just before the company's celebrated collapse in the affair of the South Sea Bubble. The main business of the company was selling slaves to the Spanish colonies, and thus the statue joins a depressingly long list of London memorials whose subjects are linked in some manner to the slave trade.[6]

The focus on such problematic statues engendered by the Black Lives Matter protests of 2020 and the toppling of Edward Colston in Bristol posed a challenge for the Guy's and St Thomas' Foundation, as custodians of Thomas Guy's statue, over how to respond. Their answer was to encase the statue in a wooden box while they came up with a longer-term solution, to be informed both by historical research and 'the views of people and communities'.[7] In November 2023, three interpretation panels were installed around the now unboxed statue. They provide fuller context than the inscription on the statue's plinth, which simply informs us that Guy was the 'sole founder of this hospital in his lifetime.' The panels acknowledge Guy's charitable work, though comment that 'the statue of Guy tells an incomplete story about how Guy's Hospital was founded'. The connections between his wealth and the trade of enslaved African people are clarified, and the panels criticise earlier handling of the statue in ways which failed to illuminate its darker side, such as a 1979 listing of the statue by Historic England in relation to its artistic merit, which 'did not account for Guy's connection to the trade of enslaved people.'[8]

For custodians of statues, the process of agreeing a 'balanced' explanatory text in the face of widely different interpretations of the subject from different stakeholder groups can prove daunting. Claudine van Hensbergen, a lecturer in English literature, worries that while 'retaining a statue or monument takes very little work; explaining it is a mammoth and contested task.'[9] Agreeing the text of 'explanatory' plaques is a political and frequently fraught undertaking. We will be looking in the next chapter at the tearing down of the statue of slave trader Edward Colston in Bristol in June 2020. Two years before that event, Bristol City Council decided to add a plaque to the statue, to contextualise the monument and acknowledge its subject's links to the slave trade. They proposed a version which began: 'As a high official of the Royal African Company from 1680 to 1692, Edward Colston played an active role in the enslavement of over 84,000 Africans (including

17. *I Goat*. The goat as a symbol of the migrants finding sanctuary in Spitalfields, London (see p. 152).

18. Statue of nurse and businesswoman Mary Seacole, voted the greatest black Briton in a 2003 survey, London (see p. 156).

19. George-Étienne Cartier Monument, deliberately placed between majority English- and French-speaking districts of Montreal as a symbol of unity (see p. 172).

20. Bringing us sunshine. Eric Morecambe statue, Morecambe (see p. 173).

21. The Infant Jesus of Prague: among the best dressed of statues, owning more than three hundred robes (see p. 190).

22. Pasquino, one of the 'talking statues' of Renaissance Rome (see p. 202).

23. Giant Dolls of Olinda, celebrating real and invented heroes of the carnival (see p. 205).

24. The strange affair of breast rubbing. Bust of Dalida, Montmartre, Paris (see p. 221).

25. Duke of Wellington with added traffic cone, Glasgow (see p. 226).

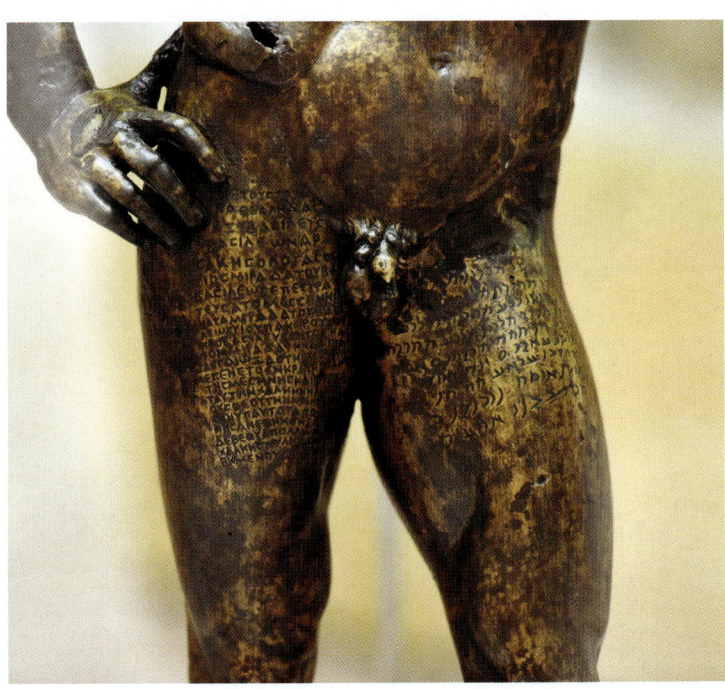

26. Statue of Heracles with an added inscription telling of its seizure as a spoil of war, Seleucia, Mesopotamia (see p. 235).

27. Remembering through 'derisive nostalgia'. Statue of Vladimir Lenin, Grūtas Park, Lithuania (see p. 242).

28. A monument turned memorial to the boy who modelled for it. *Boy with a Dolphin*, London (see p. 250).

29. Great Siege Monument, Valletta, repurposed as a memorial to murdered Maltese journalist Daphne Caruana Galizia (see p. 253).

30. Theodosian Obelisk, Istanbul. Remembering Theodosius' victory over an emperor officially forgotten (see p. 268).

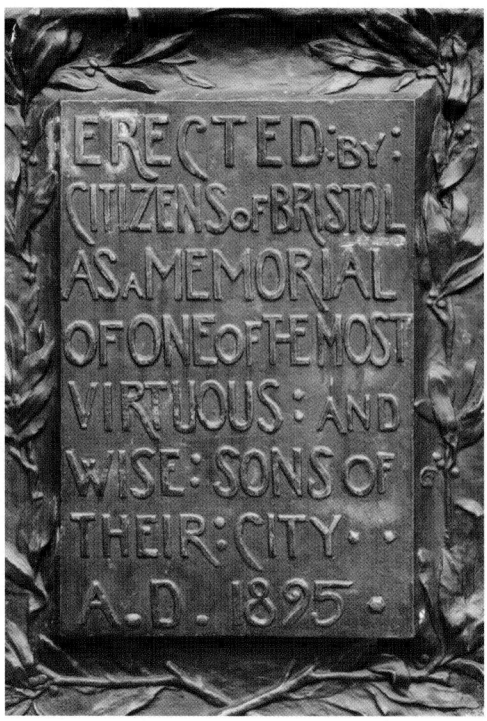

31. Inscription on the plinth of the Edward Colston statue, Bristol, once 'erected' by citizens of Bristol, has now been 'rejected' by them (see p. 281).

32. Statue of Joseph Stalin, Budapest, its bronze secured from the destruction of earlier statues of Hungarian heroes (see p. 291).

12,000 children) of whom over 19,000 died en route to the Caribbean and America.'[10]

The Society of Merchant Venturers was appalled, and proposed a rewritten version, beginning: 'Edward Colston, 1636–1721, MP for Bristol 1710–1713, was one of this city's greatest benefactors.'[11] His role in the slave trade was acknowledged, but at the end of a text that majored on his philanthropy. As author Alex von Tunzelmann has noted, both versions of the plaque are essentially true. But they create entirely different impressions.[12] Facts have evaluative implications. Faced with disagreement over what to say, the idea of an explanatory plaque came to nothing.

The addition of an explanatory plaque has an interesting consequence for the monument: it makes it seem more important. A plaque or QR code next to a statue proclaims: 'there is something of interest here'. Musil's invisible monument has been rendered visible. For those denouncing the subject of the statue as an inappropriate figure for 'heroic' commemoration in bronze or marble, the use of explanatory plaques can then be a double-edged sword. They help put the subject's deeds into context, flagging unsavoury aspects of their actions or character ignored by those who put up the monument in the first place, and support a more informed reassessment. But they do this by enhancing the monument's profile, flagging it more explicitly as a site of interest.

If an explanatory plaque helps recontextualise the monument, allowing its evaluation against modern-day values, this is not the end of the story. Perspectives change, explanation will be challenged, and reexplanation will be called for. A further source of criticism of explanatory plaques is the concern that they don't work very well. A plaque is smaller than the statue onto which it is affixed. Not everyone viewing the statue will read a plaque, and it is difficult for a short text to communicate in such a vivid way as a figurative statue. Moreover, proponents of plaques can on occasion be less interested in coming to terms with the wrongs committed by the subject than in defusing criticism in a way that allows the statue to remain. The underpinning risk is that the 'explained' statue still asserts the power of the subject.[13]

VOICES IN STONE

Adding Meanings to Statues

The use of a 'retain and explain' strategy to acknowledge the contestation of narratives around a statue is but one of many motives behind alteration of the meaning of a monument. Let us consider some of the contexts in which new meanings may be added, whether to run alongside the old or to supplant them entirely.

Monuments Turned Memorials

On Chelsea's Cheyne Walk, opposite the approach to Albert Bridge, stands a charming sculpture of a dolphin, alongside whom a boy swims in an apparently gravity-defying composition secured by a double cantilever (see fig. 28). Installed in 1975, it is the work of David Wynne, a specialist in portrayals of animals, though known also for sculpting the heads of the Beatles, who he is said to have introduced to the Maharishi Mahesh Yogi.[14] An inscription on the base tells us that *Boy with a Dolphin* was erected with the support of Wates Limited. The model for the boy was Wynne's young son Roly, who with his brother Ed would go on to establish psychedelic rock band Ozric Tentacles. Its name, incidentally, reportedly emerged from a conversation regarding possible names of alien breakfast cereals. Tragically, Roly committed suicide in 1999 at the age of 35. Another inscription has been added to the plinth: 'In memoriam, Roland David Amadeus Wynne, 1964–1999, who posed for this sculpture.' A statue representing celebration of carefree youth has been transformed into a memorial to a life cut short.

Multifunctional Monuments

The interplay between later historical developments and the events or subjects depicted on a monument can give it additional functions beyond those for which it was originally intended. We have already encountered the *Freedom Monument* in the Latvian capital of Rīga, which today commemorates both the securing of Latvian independence and its restoration following decades of Soviet occupation. The *Liberty Monument* in Nicosia also possesses a dual function, commemorating both the struggle it was built to depict and a later one. Sitting in the open Podocattaro Bastion of the Venetian walls, the monument features seventeen bronze figures within a pyramidal white marble structure. The work of Greek sculptor Ioannis Notaras, it was conceived in 1959, commissioned by Greek Cypriot leader Archbishop Makarios to commemorate Cypriot liberation from British rule.[15] At the top of the monument, on a plinth, is Liberty in classical garb. With her index finger pointing skywards, she gives the orders to two figures in military outfits below her. They represent fighters of guerilla group EOKA. Each pulls on a chain, lifting a gate to free Greek Cypriots from their prison below. Out stream peasants and priests, young and old, men and women, heading up two lateral staircases towards Liberty.

The 1960s were a troubled time on the island, riven by tensions within and between Greek and Turkish communities that would culminate in the 1974 coup d'etat and Turkish invasion. Progress on the monument was correspondingly slow, and the original design muted. Notaras had planned statues of Makarios and EOKA leader Georgios Grivas, a pool of water symbolising the sea surrounding Cyprus and laurel leaves with the names of EOKA fighters carved inside them. None of these materialised.[16] Political developments during this period, including a rift between Makarios and Grivas, who in 1971 set up the EOKA-B paramilitary organisation to push for union of Cyprus with Greece, would also have encouraged its redesign.

The Turkish invasion stymied plans for the unveiling of the monument. Film director Michael Cacoyannis's 1974 documentary *Attila '74: The Rape of Cyprus* incorporates footage of Makarios concluding that 'the unveiling will take place when freedom is reestablished in the entirety of the Cypriot land.'[17] This identifies the monument not just with independence from the British but also with opposition to the Turkish occupation of the north of the island. The latter identification is made more explicit by Cacoyannis: the monument is portrayed concealed in a white cloth, waiting to be unveiled. Close-ups of Greek Cypriot relatives of some of those missing following the events of 1974 are alternated with shots of bronze figures from the monument. Cypriot academic Chrystalleni Loizidou argues that 'what was intended as a monument of victory came to stand for the continuation of suffering.'[18]

The monument was damaged during the Turkish invasion, caught in the crossfire in fighting close to the nearby Archbishop's Palace. Liberty was shot through the chest, and other figures were shot or damaged by shrapnel. The scars have not been repaired, further anchoring the monument to the events of 1974. In 1987, an attempt was made to remind of its original purpose. Plaques were added, recording that the monument had been recognised in 1987 by the Cypriot House of Representatives as *The Monument of the EOKA Struggle*. This was all part of a 1987 law recognising the liberation struggle of 1955–9 and the role of EOKA within it.[19]

Repurposing a Monument to Mark a Tragic Event

An existing monument may be appropriated by civil society groups or members of the public as a spontaneous memorial to mark a tragic event. The Flamme de la Liberté in Paris is a gold-leaf covered replica of the flame of the Statue of Liberty, a gift to Paris from monies collected by the *International Herald Tribune* to mark, like the Statue of Liberty itself, the friendship between the United States and France. Because of the monument's proximity to the site of the death in 1997 of Diana, Princess of Wales, the flame was transformed into an unofficial memorial to the late princess. We now head to Malta for another example of the appropriation of an existing monument to mark a more recent tragic event.

In a climate of developing nationalist sentiment in twentieth-century Malta, the Great Siege of 1565 served as an important historical moment whose memory could be resurrected in the cause of building Maltese national identity. The Knights of St John, led by Jean Parisot de la Valette, saw off the attempt by the mighty Ottoman Empire to conquer the island in a siege lasting nearly four months.[20] It was a shining example of David versus Goliath heroism. In 1925, Malta's legislative assembly approved a proposal to erect a monument to the siege. The work of sculptor Antonio Sciortino, the Great Siege Monument, a Neoclassical composition with Art Deco touches, involves three bronze figures on a stone base. At the centre stands the crowned bare-chested male figure of Valour, holding a sword. He is flanked by two female beauties: Faith, holding a papal tiara, and Civilisation, holding the mask of Minerva, Roman

RECONTEXTUALISATION

goddess of wisdom. Speakers at the 1927 unveiling addressed the gathering variously in English, Italian and Maltese, a reflection of the complex language politics of the time.[21]

On 16 October 2017, a car bomb claimed the life of Maltese journalist and anti-corruption activist Daphne Caruana Galizia. Following her murder, pupils and staff at the San Anton School, where her three sons had studied, laid flowers and drawings at the Great Siege Monument. It was rapidly repurposed as a monument simultaneously to the murdered journalist, to the campaign for bringing to justice those responsible for her death and to the continuation of her work unearthing high-level corruption (see fig. 29). Commemorations at the repurposed monument were centred on the sixteenth day of each month. The use of the Great Siege Monument as the vehicle for a repurposed memorial to Daphne Caruana Galizia owed less to the iconography and values expressed by the monument than to its physical location on the main street of the capital, opposite the law courts, an important venue for efforts to bring those responsible for her death to justice.

The transformation with flowers, photographs, candles and banners of the Great Siege Monument into a memorial to the murdered journalist was not uncontested. Then Minister of Justice, Culture and Local Government, Owen Bonnici, came under criticism for ordering repeated cleaning of the monument, a process that involved the removal of objects placed upon it, and in September 2018 a hoarding appeared when the minister announced that the monument would be undergoing restoration.[22] This failed to deter supporters of the journalist. On the morning of 15 September 2018, civil society activist and blogger Emanuel Delia and some colleagues placed a banner on the hoardings, together with a Maltese flag on which the word 'justice' was written and a photograph of Daphne Caruana Galizia. They also placed flowers and candles on the site. All this was removed later that day by workers reporting to the Ministry of Justice, Culture and Local Government. Over the next few days, the objects were returned to Delia and his colleagues, reinstalled and removed again, at which point Delia took the matter to the Constitutional Court, claiming that his right to freedom of expression had been breached. The court found in January 2020 substan-

253

tially in favour of Delia, concluding that the systematic destruction of the monument to Daphne Caruana Galizia by government workers violated the freedom of expression of protestors, holding that the routine removal of objects, ostensibly to protect the Great Siege Monument, was arbitrary, and aimed to hinder the protests.[23] The court did though ask supporters of Daphne Caruana Galizia to avoid affixing items to the statue and its pedestal. Items such as candles and flowers could be placed at the foot of the monument.[24]

Reenvisioning the *Discobolus*

Where famous statues are invoked to support a cause or point of view, the manner of their use may have little to do with the intents of their sculptor or commissioners. Let us return to our discus-throwing friend, the *Discobolus*. It is possible that this fifth century BCE work of Greek sculptor Myron commemorated a victorious athlete at one of the great sporting events of the time.[25] The statue's enduring fame owes much to its portrayal of idealised sporting success. But modern-era evocations of the *Discobolus* have drawn on different attributes of that statue to further their purposes. Nazi Germany used its hosting of the 1936 Olympic Games to present the Reich as an embodiment of classical achievement. In 1938, the Munich Glyptothek purchased one of the best-known Roman copies of *Discobolus*, that in the possession of the Lancelotti family. The opening scenes of the 1938 documentary film *Olympia* by Leni Riefenstahl, a chronicle of the 1936 Berlin Olympics, move from classical statuary to images of toned German athletes, featuring the German decathlete Erwin Huber emerging from the *Discobolus*.

The statue also played a role in the next Olympics, held in London in 1948, when it featured in a transport poster by designer Walter Herz, placing it in front of the Houses of Parliament. The *Discobolus* was used to link the democracy of ancient Greece with that of modern Britain; an assertion of a world at peace after a brutal war in which those democratic ideals came under threat.[26]

Recontextualisation through Artworks

Let us return to Bristol, and to Edward Colston. MSMR Architects came up with an interesting response to the question 'who decides

RECONTEXTUALISATION

who and how we remember?', posed by Historic England in a competition launched in 2018. Their proposal involved a shallow excavation around the statue of Edward Colston, forming the outline of a slave ship. Two-dimensional outlines of human figures would be laid within this form, packed together to represent the human cargoes of the ships. Colston, standing on his plinth, was placed in the role of master of the appalling human cargo. The proponents of the scheme argued that *Contextualising Colston* was additive, not subtractive, as simple removal of the statue would be. It allowed the Grade II-listed bronze statue to remain standing, preserving its historical and artistic value, but fundamentally changing the statue's meaning. This would now be about reflecting, not honouring, and Colston would be held accountable for his sins.[27]

The MSMR proposal was overtaken by events, although to mark anti-slavery day in 2018 a temporary installation was added around the statue which similarly depicted the outline of a ship infilled with numerous corpse-like figures, accompanied by the names of professions like 'fruit picker' and 'kitchen worker' at high risk of exploitation in modern day forms of slavery. Another suggestion as to how to recontextualise the Colston statue was made after it had been dumped into Bristol harbour. Graffiti artist Banksy, himself from Bristol, suggested that the dredged-up statue might be returned to its plinth, but at a slanted angle. A new bronze statue of Black Lives Matter protestors would be depicted pulling Colston down. The commemoration would no longer be of Colston at all, but of the act of removal of his statue.

The central point here is that the act of recontextualising a statue through additional artworks changes its meaning.[28] It is not a straightforward undertaking. A statue that is the proposed subject of recontextualisation is almost by definition controversial. Just as agreement on the text of an 'explanatory' plaque is, as we have seen, a politically charged affair which must navigate between different viewpoints, so the creation of symbolic language of recontextualised structures is an intensely political act. The proponents of the MSMR Architects' design were aware, for example, that despite best intentions, it was open to criticism from those of African and Caribbean descent in its passive depiction of the African figures and the continued presence of Colston elevated above them.[29]

VOICES IN STONE

Dialogic Monuments

A monument may be placed in intentional juxtaposition to a pre-existing monument deliberately to subvert the former, generating new meanings. The aggressor monument is sometimes referred to in German as a *Gegendenkmal*. Quentin Stevens, Karen Franck and Ruth Fazakerley note however that this phrase, translated as 'counter-monument', awkwardly confuses such monuments with the counter-monument as proposed by James E. Young. They suggest the use of the term 'dialogic monument' instead.[30]

A *Monument to the Fallen of Infantry Regiment No 76*, the 1936 work of Richard Kuöhl, was long regarded as problematic by the Hamburg authorities. A limestone cubic form inscribed by a relief of soldiers marching into battle, its focus seemed to be more about glorification of war than remembering the fallen. The Hamburg senate launched a competition in 1982 for a new monument in juxtaposition to the old, explicitly using the term *Gegendenkmal* in the competition brief, possibly for the first time. The resultant monument, albeit not the original winning design of the competition, is by Alfred Hrdlicka.[31] It was originally intended to be in four parts, but only two were constructed. *Hamburg Firestorm* features bronze and marble sculptures of burned bodies around a crumbling bronze wall, while the marble *Fleeing the Cap Arcona* commemorates former prisoners of war killed when the ship *Cap Arcona* was mistakenly bombed in 1945. Rather than glorifying war, Hrdlicka's sculptures highlight the suffering of its victims.

In a sense, Maya Lin's *Vietnam Veterans Memorial* is also a dialogic monument, in juxtaposition to the neighbouring commemorative architecture of the Lincoln Memorial and Washington Monument. Frederick Hart's 1984 sculpture *Three Soldiers* is in turn a dialogic monument in relation to Maya Lin's work, a rejoinder on behalf of those who found the original monument too negative.[32] The success of a dialogic monument depends however upon the viewer's ability to interpret the statement and counterstatement made by the two monuments involved.

Hungarian academic Ágnes Erőss has examined the monument dedicated to the victims of the German Occupation of Hungary

RECONTEXTUALISATION

during World War II, installed in Liberty Square in Budapest in 2014 following a government decree the previous year. The monument features columns centred on a statue depicting Hungary as the Archangel Gabriel, under attack from the German eagle. The iconography was controversial, both aesthetically, in its somewhat kitsch character, and substantively, in glossing over the role of Hungarians themselves in the Holocaust in that country.[33]

During the monument's construction, civil society groups set up a dialogic counter-monument, entitled *Eleven Emlékmű* (Living Memorial) on the pavement in front of the occupation monument, whose construction they wanted to thwart. Everyone was invited to bring mementos of their family experiences of the German Occupation of Hungary. The evolving composition comprised photographs, written stories and personal belongings. Two white chairs were an integral feature of the monument: an invitation for discussion about the events. The focus on conversation was itself a critique of the lack of proper discussion around the German Occupation monument. The focus on personal stories similarly challenged their absence in the official monument.

Erőss argues that while the dialogic monument failed in its original purpose of thwarting the construction of the official monument, it proved more successful than the original in commemorating the German Occupation of Hungary. The official monument, squeezed into an awkward position in the southern part of Liberty Square, is difficult to get close to, has not been used for official ceremonies, and essentially 'failed' as a monument. The Living Memorial engaged locals and tourists in its evolving form. Ironically, the Living Memorial served to keep the official monument 'alive'.[34]

Dialogic monuments then are disruptors, a rejoinder to the idea that commemorative landscapes and memorials are orderly and completed.[35]

Recontextualisation and New Narratives

Some commentators, like philosopher Helen Frowe, have no sympathy with the use of recontextualisation to facilitate the retention of problematic statues. As we shall see in the next chapter, she argues that states have a duty to remove public statues of the perpetrators of serious rights violations. The use of plaques and other recontextualisations to facilitate conversations about those wrongs in her view does not justify the retention of the statue since it is perfectly possible to inform ourselves about the context without keeping the statue.[36]

Other equally fervent critics of certain statues are more conflicted as to their proper fate. US novelist Siri Hustvedt, while appalled at monuments to Confederate leaders which in her view represent America's 'shame and the shame of the White people who championed or tolerated its ideology of White supremacy'[37] is less clear as to what should be done with them. She suggests two alternatives: 'It is time to relegate old Confederate statues in the United States to the rubbish heap or to commemorate them as images of a shameful, brutal, White supremacist lie.'[38]

This hesitancy over the relative merits of removal versus recontextualisation of problematic statues reflects the consideration that, while challenging to get right, recontextualisation offers potential advantages over destruction, and not just the matter of preservation of a monument containing historic and artistic value. Where a statue has become toxic through new narratives challenging its very premise, as with the statue of Edward Colston and the highlighting of his slave-trading past, its complete obliteration, though often what is demanded, may not be the most helpful course if what is sought is the generation of a new counter-memory.

As scholar of memory studies Ann Rigney has noted, the toxic monument serves as a potential resource: helping illuminate the concerns being combatted. Thus, a statue of a figure involved in the slave trade can act as a means of calling out past efforts to 'forget' a nation's complicity in such activities, and a focus for the projection of new narratives.[39] Recontextualisation keeps the subject in the public eye, now as a critique in relation to the injustices they have committed. Removing statues may offer a sense that their subjects are escaping punishment.[40] Or rather, that while removal itself represents a moment of punishment, the subjects are then forgotten, to be left in peace. The objective of campaigners is generally not to remove all memory of the subject of the monument but to revise

RECONTEXTUALISATION

the way they are remembered, changing them from hero to villain.[41] Resignification or recontextualisation through new plaques or counterposing artworks can if done well better serve the interests of those promoting new narratives than simply destroying the toxic monument. But that 'if' is far from straightforward, particularly given that the actors in the process of recontextualisation are rarely neutral players in the conflict between different interest groups around the monument's meaning and future.

PART THREE

DEATH

15

TOPPLING STATUES

In 1934, a bronze statue was erected on the campus of the University of Cape Town. The statue was in many ways an unremarkable example of the fashion we have already explored among large institutions for the proprietorial erection on their grounds of a monument to a prominent benefactor, in this case one who had bequeathed the land on which the university was built. But the subject of the statue was remarkable, mostly in a bad way. Cecil Rhodes was a mining magnate who championed British imperial expansion as a means of furthering his business interests. An 1892 cartoon in *Punch* magazine depicted *The Rhodes Colossus* straddling the continent of Africa, referencing his dream of a rail and telegraph line running through British territory from the 'Cape to Cairo'.

On 9 March 2015, a student at the university named Chumani Maxwele threw a bucket of human excrement at the statue. He had collected the contents from a portable lavatory in a poor township.[1] Rhodes was the target because of his imperialism, and more particularly because his statue, seated on a bench gazing paternally across the campus, appeared to symbolise the continued lack of racial equality in post-apartheid South Africa. By attacking Rhodes, Maxwele sought to attack racism and Eurocentricity at the university.[2] A movement was born demanding the statue's removal, acquiring the hashtag #Rhodesmustfall. The university duly took down the statue the following month.

Ann Rigney argues that, when the values the monument seeks to radiate are no longer desired, it can become a 'toxic presence.'[3] A failure to act on calls to recontextualise or relocate statues aggravates the sense of injustice felt by those seeking new narratives, for whom inaction can be taken as a sign that the toxic former order remains extant. This sense of injustice can build towards iconoclasm.

For philosopher Helen Frowe, there are no ifs or buts here: states have a duty to remove statues of anyone responsible for serious rights violations. Nor should exemptions be made in the case of the 'morally ambiguous' wrongdoer, who has both perpetuated rights violations and achieved significant positives. Her argument is that public statues typically express a positive evaluative attitude towards the person commemorated. The subjects of statues now regarded as problematic were by and large not regarded as wrongdoers by the community that erected them. She argues that states have a duty both to repudiate historical wrongdoings in which they themselves have been compliant, and to condemn wrongs committed by others. These duties, she argues, are incompatible with retaining statues of people either involved in wrongdoings in which the state was once complicit, such as slavery, or when it comes to light that the subject of the statue has committed some serious violation independent of the state, such as child abuse.[4]

The challenge is that judgement of the culpability of past historic figures in rights violations is frequently contested. The fate of controversial statues often involves a dispute between different groups, each with very different views of the subject of the statue. Psychologist Peter Hughes considers the destruction of statues as an outcome of the creation of identity groups. Such groups require the creation of an Other, in counterposition to which they can understand themselves. While, as we have seen, statues mostly stand harmlessly in the background of our lives, whenever our identity group feels itself coming under threat, they come starkly into focus. We fight to preserve our statues and symbols, and to destroy those of the Other. The destruction we mete out on statues of the Other is justified as an act of self-defence, or a legitimate bringing down of privileges and powers they have usurped. Hughes, who takes a different view to Frowe as regards the desirability of tearing down statues, sees this as boiling down to a loss of tolerance of difference. The erection, defence and destruction of statues solidifies divisions between groups, and pushes us into a spiral of hate. 'This may begin with the destruction of statues, but it ends in the killing of people.'[5]

TOPPLING STATUES

At times of political turbulence, accompanied by challenges to preexisting conceptions of national identity, the politics of memory becomes acute. Statues and monuments become sites of conflict. Benjamin Forest and Juliet Johnson, analysing the impact of the break-up of the USSR on the monumental landscape of Moscow during the 1990s, identify three fates for the monuments they look at: glorification, disavowal or contestation. The monuments are battlegrounds between rival political elites, each seeking to impose a different vision of Russian national identity[6] as the monuments undergo transformation from symbols of the Soviet Union to symbols of Russia.

The destruction of a statue is an extreme response to it. It can suggest that the statue is viewed as a danger. As art historian Joseph Koerner puts it, destruction is 'the most decisive and final of responses'.[7] The moment of destruction is, at least as regards the spectacle involved, the most significant moment in the statue's history.[8] Some view the destruction of a statue as much an act of immortalisation as the construction of a new one: both proclaim the power of the victor.[9] For British historian David Olusoga, the tearing down of statues does not erase history, it creates it.[10] The destruction of a statue can itself be immortalised through the medium of film, which in the view of philosopher Mikhail Yampolsky can become its own brand of monument.[11] Sergei Eisenstein's 1928 silent film *October*, known in the west as *Ten Days That Shook the World*, incorporates repeated footage of the destruction of the statue of Alexander III. Other commentators are not convinced. Historian Simon Schama is among those warning that destruction of statues tends to shut down debate just as much as the uncritical acceptance of the statue. He believes a better answer is to put contested statues into museums, to properly curated contexts allowing continued debate.[12]

Damnatio Memoriae

We head to Imperial Rome, and the practice of *damnatio memoriae*: a series of Senate decrees whose aim was the reverse of that of deification of deceased emperors. Rather, the emperor retrospectively found wanting was to be removed from history. Their statues were to be destroyed, along with all other symbols and descriptions of the emperor.[13] St Jerome, in his *Commentary on Habbakuk*, gives a flavour of the process, writing: 'when a tyrant is destroyed, his portraits and statues are also deposed. The face is exchanged or the head removed, and the likeness of he who has conquered is superimposed.'[14] Archaeologist Marina Prusac argues that statues of disgraced emperors had to be demolished because the statue was not simply a visual representation of the emperor but also incorporated their presence. The power of the subject remained in the image, which thus had to be destroyed.[15]

This can all suggest that *damnatio memoriae* was an officially sponsored erasing of its target from the history books. Indeed, a law of emperors Arcadius and Honorius, sons of Theodosius the Great, promulgated in 395 and relating to legal decisions made during the rule of the now damned Flavius Eugenius, ends: 'let that time be considered as if it never was.'[16] Historian Adrastos Omissi has shown however that characterising *damnatio memoriae* as a systematic attempt to remove disgraced opponents from the history books is a misreading; if such a thing were even possible. *Damnatio memoriae*, though a satisfyingly ancient-sounding Latin term, is a relatively modern construction, first used in 1689. It describes not a single act, but various processes that could be applied to those convicted as traitors, usually posthumously. Far from systematically erasing all traces of disgraced opponents from the history books, Roman emperors used their memories for their own purposes. Thus, General Stilicho was a military commander who had once been the most powerful man in the Western Roman Empire as guardian to the youthful emperor Honorius. Following his downfall in 408 CE, when Honorius turned against him, an equestrian statue of Stilicho was indeed torn from its base, and the general's medals and honours cut away. But the base was left in situ, complete with disfigured inscription, in a prominent site. The inference is that Honorius wanted to preserve reminders of the general's fall, presumably so that all would remember that the emperor took the upper hand in the process.[17]

We have looked in Chapter 4 at statues to Roman emperors erected in Messene in the Southern Peloponnese during the Imperial period. The fate of statues of disgraced former emperors in this city was not consistent, and in no cases were all traces of the ruler obliterated. As regards the three bronze statues of Nero whose erection was sponsored by members of the local elite it is noteworthy that Nero's name was not removed from the inscriptions. Historian Christopher Dickenson suggests this may have been linked to the continued influence of the local families that paid for the statues.[18] A cluster of Imperial statues of the Flavian dynasty, comprising Vespasian, Titus, Domitian and the latter's wife Domitia Longina, had a different end. Domitian was subject to a particularly brutal *damnatio memoriae*, and such was the fate of his statue in Messene too: torn down, its name obliterated from its inscription. But while Domitian's name has also been removed from the base of his wife's statue, the lettering has been carefully chiselled away, suggesting that the statue itself may have been retained. As with the equestrian statue of general Stilicho, the defaced base of Domitian's statue was found in situ, suggesting a desire to remember the emperor, but in the condition of his downfall and disgrace. As Christopher Dickenson puts it, 'this act of *damnatio memoriae* was then as much a strategy of remembering as of forgetting.'[19]

The preservation of memories of those ostensibly subjected to their erasure was not just a matter of incomplete destruction of monuments. Omissi explores the defeat of Magnus Maximus by emperor Theodosius the Great to discuss how additional commemorative material was generated, highlighting the figures supposedly being forgotten. Magnus Maximus had in 383 CE ousted and executed Gratian, the Western Roman Emperor, at a time when Theodosius ruled in the east. There was a short uneasy peace, with Maximus ruling in Gaul and Britannia, Theodosius in the east, and Valentinian II, young half-brother of Gratian, in Italy. Maximus' move against Valentinian prompted Theodosius to come to the latter's aid, defeating Maximus. The latter was executed in 388 and his memory excised, inter alia through the chiselling of his name from inscriptions and the annulment of his appointments and legal judgements. Yet Omissi identifies several examples drawing attention to Maximus, at least to his defeat, among the impressive new constructions of Theodosius in Constantinople, as he endeavoured to make it a city to rival Rome.

The Theodosian Obelisk, now standing in Istanbul's Sultanahmet Park, was raised in the Hippodrome in 390 (see fig. 30). It had been taken by Constantine from the Temple of Karnak in Luxor and long languished on the ground. Theodosius raised it on a base covered with reliefs depicting himself and members of his family. A Latin inscription recorded that the obelisk commemorated Theodosius' victory over 'the extinct tyrants',[20] a reference to Maximus and his infant son Victor. The Forum of Theodosius was the emperor's greatest contribution to the architecture of the city. At its heart stood a triumphal column, with a statue of Theodosius on top, consciously aping Trajan's Column in Rome. It too was decorated with a spiralling frieze depicting the emperor's victories. The column was dismantled around 1500, and only fragments of the relief have been preserved. One depicts soldiers in Roman dress in the act of surrendering. A Chi Rho design on a shield suggests an imperial bodyguard. The scene thus appears to depict the surrender of Maximus' bodyguard to Theodosius. Finally, Omissi argues that the impressive Golden Gate, forming part of the Theodosian Wall at the edge of the city, was originally constructed as a freestanding triumphal arch. A combination of literary and architectural evidence suggests it originally included the inscription: 'Theodosius decorates this place after the death of a tyrant.'[21]

The subject of *damnatio memoriae* was thus not forgotten, but recalled in new architectural forms, in seeming violation of the purpose of the measures. Significantly, however, Maximus was remembered in an anonymised way, through the term 'tyrant.' Creating memories of Maximus served Theodosius' goals in highlighting his own victories. To have erased Maximus from history would have been counterproductive for Theodosius, who wished to portray himself as a victorious leader. This required the retention of memories of Maximus, but a Maximus dehumanised and anonymised, turned into a caricature 'tyrant', defeated by the glorious ruler Theodosius.[22]

The Demise of Colonial Statues in Independent India

Where colonial rule ended with a peaceful transfer of power to a new regime with which the former colonial power endeavoured to maintain a positive relationship, the consequences for statuary associated with colonial rule were by no means always abrupt and brutal. Historian Paul McGarr has examined the fate of colonial statuary following Indian independence in 1947.[23]

In the first few years, relatively few attempts were made to do away with statues of British monarchs and viceroys. There were scattered defacements, such as that during independence celebrations of an 1863 marble statue of *The Angel of the Resurrection* by Italian sculptor Carlo Marochetti, which stood in Kanpur in Uttar Pradesh at the site of a notorious episode of the Indian Rebellion of 1857, when British women and children, taken hostage by Indian forces led by Nana Saheb, were killed and their dismembered bodies thrown into a well. During the colonial period, Indians had not been allowed into the park where the statue stood. At the independence celebrations, thousands entered, and the statue ended up the worse for wear and with its face painted black.[24] But by and large, statues were left where they stood. Continuing close ties between Britain and India were a disincentive to actions that might disturb harmonious relations. Indian Prime Minister Jawaharlal Nehru opposed removal of British statuary, on the grounds that it was part of India's history,[25] there was disagreement as to the heroes of modern India who might replace colonial statues, and the government was faced with more pressing tasks.

As the years passed, pressures to remove statues associated with the colonial regime started to build. The centenary of the Indian Rebellion of 1857, accompanied by an upsurge in nationalist sentiment, provided a flashpoint. The issue developed a domestic political dimension, with the ruling Congress Party under pressure from both socialist politicians and Hindu nationalist groups over what was depicted as their prevarication over removal of statues representing colonial humiliations. In Uttar Pradesh, a heartland of the 1857 Rebellion, there was a series of attacks on British statues. The nationalist Bharatiya Jana Sangh Party were responsible for events at Gorakhpur involving the covering of a statue of Queen Victoria in a black cloth, with a portrait of the Rani of Jhansi, a leading figure of the 1857 Rebellion, placed on the pedestal. The Congress government running Uttar Pradesh responded to the attacks by determining that statuary 'reminiscent of foreign domination' be removed and put in store.²⁶ The governments of several other states followed suit, though this was not the practice everywhere.

In May 1957, Nehru, attempting to respond to mounting criticism of colonial statues, proposed a systematic approach to the matter. There is an air of Alois Riegl's categorisation of forms of value about it. He determined that British statuary should be divided into four groups. The first, statues of historical importance. The second, those with artistic merit. The third, those with neither artistic nor historical value. The fourth, those offensive to Indian national sentiment.²⁷ The first two groups would ultimately be relocated to museums. The third might be given away if anyone would take them. The fourth would be removed, but not in such a way as to provoke ill-will internationally. Events on the ground however overtook central planning. Mumbai decided to replace its statue of King George V with Chhatrapati Shivaji Maharaj, a seventeenth-century Maratha ruler, revered in Maharashtra as a national hero. In Kolkata it was announced that Queen Victoria and Lord Lawrence would give way to statues of nationalist figures Bal Gangadhar Tilak and Subhas Chandra Bose.

The ill-health and in May 1964 death of Nehru, that opponent of unrestrained iconoclasm, accelerated the removal of colonial statues. It was announced that all British statues would be removed from New Delhi. Monuments to former viceroys Lord Irwin, Lord Chelmsford and Earl Willingdon came down. By 1970, British colonial statuary had largely disappeared from northern India. This was not true of the south, where statues of British monarchs and colonial administrators were still to be found in public spaces. McGarr suggests that this regional variation owed something to the more bitter contestation of British rule in northern India, and something to southern fears of cultural colonisation by the Hindi north.²⁸

Statues linked to British colonial rule in India were, as we have seen, not all devoted to British monarchs and officials. Many depicted Indians who had supported the colonial order. Historian Robin Jeffrey's work in Trivandrum shows that statues of Indian figures associated with the old order might be removed more hastily than those of their British counterparts.²⁹ The main victim here was

TOPPLING STATUES

Sir C. P. Ramaswami Aiyar, dewan of the state from 1936 until 1947. Two busts of him had been installed in prominent locations: the products of attempts by local elites to keep on the right side of the powerful dewan.[30] Aiyar was a focus of ire of the emerging nationalist movement. In part, this was because it was politically safer to attack the dewan, the administrator, than the maharaja directly. But Aiyar had plenty of qualities in his own right to make him a prime target. He was not a native Malayali but a Brahmin Tamil. He was the confidante of the maharani, and his knighthood from the British placed him as a servant of the imperial regime.

Following independence in August 1947, Aiyar left for Madras. The new government elected in March 1948 was dominated by nationalist leaders. Chief Minister Pattom A. Thanu Pillai however rather fancied his new position as heir to the dewans of old, relishing his contacts with the maharaja. He opted not to pursue campaign rhetoric about the removal of Aiyar's busts, much less about extraditing Aiyar from Madras to stand trial for assorted alleged crimes. The statues of Aiyar acquired a political resonance, as the chief minister's opponents sought their removal, and police guards were installed to protect them. It took the ouster of the Pattom Thanu Pillai government to secure the removal of Aiyar's bust in front of the Assembly building in January 1949.

Removing Soviet Monuments in Latvia

For Latvia, as in the other Baltic States of Lithuania and Estonia, the Soviet period is viewed as an occupation: an annexation by the USSR against its will under the secret protocol of the Molotov-Ribbentrop Pact of 1939. Monuments glorifying the Soviet Union and its heroes erected across its territory during that occupation period were thus obvious targets of iconoclasm following the restoration of Latvian independence in 1991, as the country looked to reestablish its own national identity.

The removal of Soviet monuments has been carried out in distinct phases or waves of iconoclasm. Statues of Soviet leaders came down almost immediately. War memorials were initially largely left alone. With their associations with mourning and family sacrifice, theirs was a more complex story. The Russian invasion of Ukraine in 2022 provided the spur for a further wave of iconoclasm, in which most of these memorials also came down, sparing only those linked with physical burials. Since then, there have been further removals of statues, widening the net to include monuments to pre-Communist Russian heroes and Latvian scientific and cultural figures close to the Soviet regime who prospered during that period. Latvia's experience mirrors the wider region. Historian Mischa Gabowitsch similarly describes waves of iconoclasm across the former Soviet Union and its satellites, a first at the start of the 1990s, with a second wave developing since 2015, though noting considerable variation between individual countries.[31]

Among the statues of Soviet leaders targeted on the restoration of Latvian independence, one stood out for sheer ubiquity: Vladimir Ilyich Lenin, the founder and first leader of the Soviet Union. There are many ironies around the Lenin personality cult, not least that he opposed the idea of statues to living Bolshevik leaders, including himself.[32] The cult was the work of his successors, for their own purposes. Propaganda posters featured Vladimir Mayakovsky's slogan: 'Lenin lived, Lenin lives, Lenin will live.' Statues everywhere ensured his immortality. Their proliferation inspired Soviet jokes, such as that of the competition for the best monument to the poet Pushkin. Third place went to a statue of Pushkin reading Lenin, second to a statue of Lenin reading Pushkin, and first prize went to 'just Lenin'.[33] Lenin's ubiquity as a symbol of the Soviet regime meant the dismantling of his statues across Latvia in the turbulent summer of 1991 took on a special significance as a marker of the demise of the regime: a significance reflected in the number of history museums across the country offering video footage of the departure of the local Lenin. The Popular Front Museum in Rīga is typical. There is a mock-up of an upended Lenin statue, his head and upper body lost behind the skirting board. A television screen set into the upturned base broadcasts a two-minute film of the dismantling of the Lenin monument in Rīga on the night of 24 August, in the wake of the failure of the putsch in Moscow. A crane prises the statue from its base as dawn breaks. A choir sings on the soundtrack. Latvia is freed.

TOPPLING STATUES

While as we have seen, in neighbouring Lithuania toppled statues of Lenin were preserved and critiqued in a park set up for the task, there was no clear plan for the fallen Lenins of Latvia, and the newly discovered market forces took over. A 1974 Lenin statue by sculptor Otto Kalējs was an unremarkable example of the genre, on display in the provincial city of Jelgava. With statues of Lenin coming down across the region, a Danish art collector named Aage Damgaard, who had made his money in shirt manufacturing, decided he wanted one. He sent his sons Lars and Søren to the Baltics to purchase a statue. This was not straightforward, and Aage died in 1991 with the quest unfulfilled. Eventually a deal was struck over the Jelgava Lenin. Ten thousand dollars was fixed on. Intriguingly, the purchase agreement included a provision permitting the sellers to buy back the statue within ten years. The Latvians were evidently hedging their bets.

The Damgaard family decided not to install Lenin in the expected, vertical, manner. They commissioned artist Sven Dalsgaard to create two stainless steel supports, onto which Lenin could be placed horizontally.[34] The statue was given a new title. *Lenin is Dead*. The dead Lenin now lies in the village of Lund, outside the Danish town of Herning. A piece of art purchased not to praise it but to subvert it.

Another Lenin statue formerly gracing a Latvian city square is now in the garden of British Conservative Party politician Lord Heseltine. With his wife Anne, he purchased Thenford House on the border between Northamptonshire and Oxfordshire in 1976.[35] With the house came a major undertaking, the transformation of the extensive grounds into an arboretum and sculpture garden. Surprise value within the latter is provided by a large bronze head of Lenin, purchased by Lord Heseltine at an auction of garden statuary in England.[36]

The bust formerly stood on the square in front of the government offices in the eastern Latvian town of Preiļi. The work of sculptor Dzintra Jansone, it was installed in 1987 for celebrations of the 70th anniversary of the October Revolution. This statue in turn replaced a standing statue of Lenin, put up in 1964. According to staff at the local history and art museum, the first statue had been of poor quality, its design unfashionable by the mid-1980s. The authorities apparently simply took the original statue down and buried it, putting it out of mind. Lenin had other ideas, and his hand emerged from the ground. They buried him deeper.

Local activists of the Popular Front took Lenin down in the heady days of summer 1991. The bust lying on the ground was spotted by a British man who enquired whether it might be for sale. This was negotiated for its scrap metal value, and thus it ended up in a garden sale.[37] Museum staff told me that Preiļi had come under criticism from heritage specialists in Rīga for simply disposing of a bust of high artistic value, but the artistic value of Soviet works was not much on the minds of those campaigning for the restoration of Latvian independence.

Russia's invasion of Ukraine on 24 February 2022 precipitated a second wave of Latvian iconoclasm. While this embraced monuments across the country, the political focus was a 79-metre pillar in a Rīga park. With five bundled columns of different heights, each topped with a Soviet star, it was the central composition of an ensemble with the snappy title of the *Monument to the Liberators of Soviet Latvia and Rīga from the German Fascist Invaders*. It was erected in 1985, in the dying years of Soviet power. On one side, a female figure represented Motherland. On the other, three Soviet soldiers depicted the liberators.

Following the restoration of independent Latvia, the monument became a central actor in the contested memory of World War II. For the Latvian-speaking majority, the laying of flowers at the monument on 9 May rang hollow, recalling a Soviet occupation that had provided Latvia with nothing to smile about. Many members of the Russian-speaking minority continued to commemorate Victory Day on 9 May, though the nature of that commemoration changed, its character influenced by the evolution of Victory Day celebrations in Russia. Marches of the 'Immortal Regiment' were added to the commemorations from 2015, with participants carrying the pictures of relatives killed in World War II.

For many Latvians, the monument was not just a reminder of painful decades of Soviet occupation but had been hijacked by a Kremlin-sponsored agenda of Russian imperial aggrandisement. There had long been calls for its demolition. On the night of 5 June

1997, Latvian ultranationalists claiming to be heirs of the far-right interwar Pērkonkrusts movement attempted to blow it up. They failed, two of the group's members losing their lives in the explosion. But there were obstacles to removal. First, destroying the massive concrete pillar with a steel armature was no easy task, as Pērkonkrusts discovered to their cost. The pillar alone weighed 2,000 tonnes. Second, Latvia had in 1994 signed an agreement with Russia on the social protection of military pensioners living in Latvia, Article 13 of which required it to preserve memorial structures. Third, there were concerns about the reaction of both the Russian government and Russian-speaking Latvians to the destruction of the monument. The Latvian authorities would have been mindful of events following the relocation of the Bronze Soldier memorial in Tallinn in 2007, which resulted in two nights of rioting and cyberattacks on Estonian institutions.

For many Latvians, the Russian invasion of Ukraine in 2022 changed the balance of the arguments. The 9 May Victory Day celebrations in Rīga that year provided the trigger for action. That people should again lay flowers at the monument, in an action consonant with Russian commemorations at a time of emerging evidence of Russian atrocities in Ukraine, enraged many Latvians. Those mainly Russian speakers laying flowers were in turn incensed by their removal on the following day, and promptly returned to lay more flowers, the climate now more hostile. The scenes suggested that the unswerving Latvian support for Ukraine since the start of the invasion, and its hostility to the Russian aggressor, were not sentiments held by everyone living in the country. The 'Victory' Monument was identified as part of a dissenting narrative.

Two days later, on 12 May, the Latvian parliament, the Saeima, voted to suspend Article 13 of the 1994 agreement. The Saeima's actions were carried out at deliberate pace: both readings of the bill voted on in a single day.[38] The sense was one of urgency, of seizing the moment. With the obstacle of Article 13 of the 1994 agreement removed, Rīga City Council held an emergency meeting the following day, instructing the Rīga Monuments Agency to prepare to dismantle the monument. Deputy Mayor Vilnis Ķirsis of the New Unity party argued that the monument glorified both the occupation of Latvia and the war crimes of Russia, as heir to the Soviet Union, in Ukraine.[39]

The suspension of the bilateral agreement made possible the dismantling of Soviet monuments across Latvia. The Saeima now worked to make it happen. On 16 June it voted through a Law on the Prohibition of the Display of Objects Glorifying the Soviet and Nazi Regimes and their Dismantling on the Territory of the Republic of Latvia.[40] It was a law to eliminate monuments promoting an unwanted narrative about Latvian history, one which lauded the activity of occupying powers, freeing the way for a narrative emphasising Latvian resistance to occupation. The new law called for offending monuments to be demolished by 15 November. Monuments linked to burial sites of soldiers killed in the war, and memorials to the victims of Soviet or Nazi terror were explicitly excluded from its scope. The experts set to work, and on 30 June Juris Dambis, head of the National Cultural Heritage Board, informed journalists that they had presented the government with a list of sixty-nine monuments glorifying the Soviet Union to be removed. No monument glorifying the Nazi regime had been identified.[41]

In August 2022, Latvian television set up a live stream in front of the 'Victory' Monument in Rīga. Watching it was for the most part not the most exciting experience. The pillar stood there, as pillars tend to do. Until, at 4:42 in the afternoon on 25 August, it came tumbling to the ground. The authorities endeavoured, largely successfully, to ensure that demolition would not provide an occasion for protest. The site was railed off, and anyone standing nearby was quickly moved on by police.

Russia's invasion of Ukraine thus provided the impetus for Latvia to demolish Soviet war memorials. The imperative to do so had much to do with the contested meanings of such memorials beyond commemoration of death and sacrifice. For some, the 'Victory' Monument was about liberation. The monument stood for Soviet and Russian achievement, a symbol for those Russian speakers in Latvia who mourned a loss of position and prestige. For others, the monument was about occupation, a symbol of the oppression of Latvia by foreign rulers. With Russia seeking to subjugate Ukraine, that imagery became too much to bear. The destruction of the

TOPPLING STATUES

'Victory' Monument and other Soviet-era monuments is part of a wider picture, embracing the renaming of streets and parks and the curtailment of Russian-language teaching in schools. When the 'Victory' Monument came down, then Latvian Foreign Minister Edgars Rinkēvičs tweeted: 'closing another painful page of the history and looking for better future.'[42] For many Latvians, Russian atrocities in Ukraine provided the spur to turn a domestic page.

If there were expectations that removal of those monuments glorifying the Soviet regime identified in the 2022 exercise would draw a line under Latvian iconoclasm, it has not turned out that way. The country embarked on a further phase of the removal of statues; one whose targets were more disparate. With no underpinning new national legislation, unlike 2022, the latest wave of iconoclasm has proceeded in a geographically patchy fashion in which the political complexion of local authorities has played an important role. Those in the Latvian capital have been enthusiastic iconoclasts. In March 2023, Rīga City Council Monument Board called for the dismantling of a further group of statues, ranging from nineteenth-century Russian poet Alexander Pushkin to Latvia-born Soviet mathematician and space programme engineer Mstislav Keldysh. One board member commented that 'we are cleaning our home, we make it one that we want to see in the future.'[43]

The Pushkin statue stood in Rīga's Kronvalda Park. It depicted the writer dressed smartly, holding his top hat in his hand, enjoying a stroll. The monument had acquired a commemorative value for some native Russian speakers, and flowers were often seen at its base. That the statue was in the sights of the local authorities was perhaps less though to do with Pushkin the writer than the provenance of the statue, the work of Russian sculptor Alexander Taratynov, as a gift from the city of Moscow. Its removal in May 2023 was justified with the argument that its original installation in 2009 had not followed the required procedures.[44]

The bust of Mstislav Keldysh, in a park opposite the main building of the University of Latvia, was dismantled in autumn 2023. Removal created few waves: Keldysh, though born in Rīga, left the place in early childhood and retained few connections to the city, and prior to removal his bust had been one of Musil's 'invisible monuments', routinely ignored by visitors to the park. A council statement, specifying that the statue would not be destroyed but moved to the Rīga Monument Agency warehouse, identified the importance of preserving the artistic value of the work of sculptor Lev Bukovsky, while affirming that the ideological value of the statue had necessitated removal.[45]

The Demise of Edward Colston

During a Black Lives Matter demonstration in the city of Bristol on 7 June 2020, protestors pulled down the statue of Edward Colston, a figure associated with the slave trade. A demonstrator knelt on the statue's neck in a symbolic reenactment of the action that had killed George Floyd in Minneapolis on 25 May. It was then dragged through the city centre and dumped into Bristol Harbour close to Pero's Bridge, a landmark taking its name from an enslaved man living in eighteenth-century Bristol.

Colston, born in the city in 1636, made his money from the slave trade, including as Deputy Governor of the Royal African Company, responsible for the transportation of more African slaves to the Americas than any other organisation. He developed his career in London, but returned to Bristol from time to time, and was a member of the city's Society of Merchant Venturers, representing its commercial elite. He had no direct heirs, and could be generous with his wealth, founding schools, hospitals and almshouses.[46]

The statue honouring him was not erected until 1895, 174 years after his death. A bronze figure on a stone plinth, it was the work of John Cassidy, and commissioned by James Arrowsmith, a wealthy printer and publisher. Arrowsmith organised a fund-raising campaign for it, a campaign that tellingly and unsurprisingly made no reference to Colston's involvement in the slave trade, casting him as a merchant and philanthropist. Funding proceeded slowly, and a shortfall was met through the contribution of an anonymous donor, widely assumed to be Arrowsmith himself.[47] It was in Colston's philanthropic activities in Bristol that the motivation for the statue lay. Reliefs decorating the plinth depicted Colston doling out money to the poor and patting an unfortunate child on the head.

TOPPLING STATUES

In the late Victorian period, the local authorities needed a figure who could be presented as a notable Christian philanthropist; a civic hero who could be invoked to promote pride and identity and serve as a moral example for the city. The period was economically difficult for Bristol, whose port was losing its importance.[48] Labour relations were challenging, and there had been strikes and demonstrations in a city characterised by relatively high rates of poverty engendered by slow industrialisation. In the face of this unrest, the local elite needed to underline their role as benefactors. Colston fitted their requirements for a suitably philanthropic figure who could encourage the labouring classes to look to them rather than towards the rival attentions of socialism—not just because of his philanthropic activities when alive, but also because charitable societies set up in his name continued to organise devotional religious services and ostentatious celebrations, particularly around the commemoration of his birthday on 13 November, when sweet Colston Buns were consumed, posthumously embellishing his image as a benefactor. For the old guard from the shipping trade, Colston was one of their own, while for those from a non-shipping background aspiring to membership of the elite, like Arrowsmith the printer, embracing Colston might be a stepping stone into it.[49] Erecting a statue to a philanthropic-minded merchant was also a means by which the city's trading and business elite could establish that members of their own group had the right to be immortalised in this way: it was not just an honour for royalty, aristocrats and military heroes.[50]

By 1895, slavery and the slave trade had long been illegal in Britain, which celebrated its achievements as an abolitionist nation. The erection of a statue to Colston involved an act of forgetting the source of his wealth typical of the late Victorian period, when Britain made claims to a global moral leadership.[51] There is an important and wider point here. Building a nation with a shared identity requires the selective forgetting of inconvenient historical facts as well as the remembering of unifying ones. According to French Orientalist Ernest Renan: 'the essence of a nation is that its members have many things in common, but also that they have forgotten many things.'[52] This is about the forgetting of facts whose memory could divide the nation. But as late Victorian 'forgetting' of the origins of so much of Bristol's wealth in the slave trade makes clear, the risk is that unity so generated is both false and unsustainable, since injustices are erased that should be collectively remembered.[53] As Frederick Whitling puts it: '"memory culture" cannot afford to be solely affirmative and celebratory: its negative aspects need to be visible and present.'[54]

The inscription on the plinth read: 'erected by citizens of Bristol as a memorial of one of the most virtuous and wise sons of their city.'[55] The statue itself reeked of kindly patrician qualities. Colston, hand on his cane, looked down benevolently from his plinth. This was then a statue to the city's new elite—Colston was used as a proxy to entrench their ongoing dominance.[56] It did not serve that purpose particularly successfully or for long—by the early twentieth century, the statue already represented Victorian pomposity in a modernising Bristol.[57]

Destruction of the Colston statue was not an idea originating on the day of the Black Lives Matter protest. Bristol is home to a large Caribbean community. It has long been a centre of social justice campaigning in response to race inequalities, exemplified by the Bristol Bus Boycott of 1963, fuelled by the refusal of the local bus company to employ Black or Asian crews.[58] While the Black Lives Matter protest may have been the event triggering the statue's downfall, the origins of its contestation lay in local as much as global factors. It followed years of campaigning to remember the neglected, or 'forgotten', history of Bristol as a city closely connected with the slave trade. The 'Countering Colston' group sought to obliterate all traces of the man. As we have seen, proposals had circulated to recontextualise the monument through the addition of an explanatory plaque or a new artistic installation enveloping the statue. The violent removal of the Colston statue arose after these attempts at contextualisation, or organised removal through an appeal to official procedures, came to nothing. Heritage scholar Laurajane Smith points to an inherently conservative official discourse around heritage as a reason this is often the case.[59] The statue had also been the target of direct action for decades. The first notable defacement came in 1998, when someone suggested in red paint that it was time for Colston to depart, though not in quite such polite terms.[60]

The deposed statue was fished out of the harbour on the order of the authorities—not least because its presence in a working harbour raised safety concerns. It is on display in Bristol's M Shed Museum, complete with spray-paint daubings and protesters' placards. The display focuses on remembering the manner of the statue's downfall.

The statue having been removed, the problem of the vacated plinth remained. On 11 June 2020, four days after the toppling of the statue, someone went to work on the inscription, adding paintwork to suggest that the statue once 'erected' by the citizens of Bristol was now 'rejected' by them (see fig. 31).[61] An unauthorised statue was placed on the plinth on 15 July, a resin-cast depiction of Black Lives Matter protestor Jen Reid, right arm raised in the defiant pose she had adopted while standing on the plinth during the protests. It was the work of artist Marc Quinn, who we have already encountered as the author of *Alison Lapper Pregnant* on Trafalgar Square's fourth plinth. His initiative divided opinion, with critics characterising the installation, *A Surge of Power (Jen Reid)*, as the appropriative act of a London-based white artist.[62] In any event, it was swiftly removed by the local council, on the grounds that the proper application procedures had not been followed in putting it up.

The empty plinth serves itself as a memorial; a reminder of the dismantling of Edward Colston. In a sense, it displays his absence.[63] The violent removal of the Colston statue had a far greater impact than quiet, legal removal at the conclusion of a municipal planning process would have done. Looking at the dismantling of Colston's statue from the perspective suggested by Riegl is helpful. The statue had long lost any intentional commemorative value. It was mostly ignored by the inhabitants of Bristol as they hurried past. Its value was expressed as a matter of historic and perhaps artistic value, exemplified by the Grade II listed status received in 1977.[64] Destruction was accompanied by a new intentional commemorative value, a dramatic commemoration of the Black Lives Matter movement and efforts to acknowledge Bristol's troubled past. The plaques and banners that long (though no longer) decorated the area around the now vacated plinth following the events of 7 June 2020 are testament to that. The long-term future of the plinth remains, however, a matter of debate.

The removal of Edward Colston's statue is different in nature from the destruction of monuments following a change of political regime, such as Lenin's departure on the collapse of the USSR. Here, the toppling of the statue was not a celebration of the overthrow of a regime, but a demand for change. It is an effort to alter the memorial landscape, to draw attention to wrongs deliberately 'forgotten' and secure the representation of hitherto marginalised groups in the memorial narrative.[65] Destruction of monuments may be viewed in this sense as part of a wider process of effecting change, generating 'counter-memory' by challenging the authority of existing dominant narratives and proposing new ones.

The Ups and Downs of the Vendôme Column

What goes down, can come up. The Vendôme Column in Paris is a story of construction, alteration, demolition and reconstruction through the complex course of nineteenth-century French political life. Completed in 1810 in Napoleon's Paris, it is a triumphal column whose spiralling relief frieze was modelled on Trajan's Column, depicting not Trajan's victory over the Dacians but Napoleon's at Austerlitz. Napoleon apparently wanted physically to move Trajan's Column to Paris, as an expression of continuity between his empire and that of Imperial Rome, but was persuaded to abandon that idea on the grounds that the monument was unlikely to survive the journey.[66] The link with ancient Rome was though made in the statue of Napoleon on the column, depicting the French leader in Roman dress, a laurel crown on his head. It is said the bronze reliefs adorning the column were cast from cannons captured at Austerlitz. There is, in short, something of an apotheosis of Napoleon about the column. Unsurprisingly, following the Bourbon Restoration the statue of the defeated leader was pulled down from the column. Napoleon suffered the ignominy of being melted down to recast an equestrian statue of Henri IV on Pont Neuf. A white Bourbon flag flew in his place.

TOPPLING STATUES

Not everyone accepted the repurposing of the column from Napoleonic monument to Bourbon one. In 1827, Victor Hugo penned the poem *À la colonne de la place Vendôme*, presenting a unified vision of French history, where revolutionary and Napoleonic values continued to thrive, reinforcing a developing mythology around the deceased former emperor.[67] This nostalgia intensified following the 1830 revolution, which saw the removal of Charles X in favour of the more liberal Louis Philippe. In May 1831, marking the tenth anniversary of Napoleon's death, gifts and flowers were placed at the base of the Vendôme Column, now treated as a commemorative place for the former emperor. The Chamber of Deputies blocked an attempt that November to return Napoleon's ashes to Paris for reburial beneath the column, which would have given it a funerary role mirroring that of its model, Trajan's Column. Victor Hugo was so incensed that he turned to verse again, railing in the poem *À la Colonne* against petty-minded bureaucrats afraid of a few ashes.[68] A statue of Napoleon was restored to the column in 1833, though he was not allowed to retain his imperial pretensions, and the new version featured Napoleon in military dress, a 'Little Corporal' rather than 'Little Emperor'.[69] Under Napoleon III, in line with that ruler's embracing of the title of Second Emperor of the French, the Little Corporal was swapped back for a statue of Napoleon again dressed in Roman gear in the latest of a dizzying number of costume changes.

The column's fortunes were to change again during the tumultuous events of 1870 and 1871, with the collapse of Napoleon III's empire during the Franco-Prussian War, replaced by the parliamentary rule of the French Third Republic, and the control of Paris from March until May 1871 by the revolutionary government of the Paris Commune. The destruction of the Vendôme Column during the rule of the Commune, for whom it represented a symbol of hated imperialism, only to be rebuilt three years later under the Third Republic, marked not only the most dramatic turn-around of fortunes of a monument that has seen a good number, but also spelled danger for those who had supported the decision to demolish it. The episode destroyed the standing of one of the best-known painters of the time, Gustave Courbet. At the time presiding over the Commission of Artists, Courbet had asked the Government of National Defense in September 1870 to authorise the dismantling of the column, which he argued was devoid of artistic value and glorified war and imperial conquest, ideas repugnant to a republican nation. Courbet died in 1877 in bitter exile in Switzerland, but he was posthumously defended by his younger friend, critic Jules Antoine Castagnary. Castagnary penned in 1882 a tract entitled *A Plea for a Dead Friend*, making the case that the artist was innocent of charges brought against him over the destruction of the column.[70]

Castagnary argues that Courbet's request had been part of a wider debate on the fate of the column, in which more radical voices sought its destruction. This was not, however, Courbet's intent. While he felt the column lacked artistic value, he recognised that it possessed a certain historical value, and thought that 'it is not for the artist, whose mission is essentially creative, to destroy a work of art, however bad it may be'.[71] Courbet was, rather, suggesting that the column be moved to a different location, such as the Invalides, to take its place among other military mementos. Castagnary argues that, far from seeking to destroy the column, Courbet's intention was to save it, against the more radical voices that wanted it demolished and refashioned into cannons. Nothing however came of Courbet's proposal.

When the Paris Commune took power in March 1871 they moved swiftly and dramatically against the column. On 12 April, the Executive Committee of the Commune proclaimed that the Vendôme Column would be demolished. Castagnary quotes a letter of Courbet pointing out that he was only elected to the Commune on 16 April, and had not taken part in the decision to tear it down.[72] Castagnary unearths a letter of 1874 to *The Times* of London by Félix Pyat, a former member of the Executive Commission of the Commune, who writes that he initiated the proposal to destroy the column, that it was made for political reasons, not artistic ones, and that Courbet was not consulted.

Following suppression of the Commune, Courbet was convicted by a military tribunal in relation to the destruction of the column and his membership of the Commune and sentenced to six months in prison and a fine of 500 francs. Perhaps given the relatively light sentence, he did not appeal. He was even allowed an easel and paints in prison, resulting in a series of still-life paintings of fruit and flowers. This guilty verdict was however to prove the genesis of a far graver problem for Courbet. A decision was taken to rebuild the column, and Courbet, having been convicted in relation to its destruction, was ordered to pay for it: the colossal sum of 323,000 francs, in annual instalments of 10,000 francs. It was the prospect of this bill that forced him into exile. Castagnary concludes that Courbet fell victim to 'the Moral Order.'[73] The column was re-erected in 1874, looking remarkably like the original, and offering few outward signs of the journey it has made.

Rejecting Statues

Statues are sometimes removed from their plinths not because their subject is offensive to changed sensibilities or a new regime, or otherwise deemed unworthy of the honour, but because the subject is particularly revered, and the statue is deemed unworthy of them. The commissioners of the statue, the authorities, or wider public opinion give their verdict and find the sculpture wanting: failing to meet the commemorative purposes for which it was intended.

The Gothic Revival tower of the Wallace Monument in Stirling was completed in 1869 to commemorate the 1297 Battle of Stirling Bridge, where William Wallace's Scottish force defeated an English army. Geographer Tim Edensor argues that the meaning of the monument has changed. Its founders saw in Wallace's heroism the building of a Scottish self-respect and independence that served as a necessary precondition for the later union of English and Scottish crowns. That message has been lost today in favour of a simpler one about Scottish nationhood.[74]

Tapping into that newer interpretation of the monument and fuelled by the success of the film *Braveheart* about Wallace's exploits, stonemason Tom Church produced in 1997 a sculptural addition to the National Wallace Monument complex, a four-metre statue entitled *Spirit of Wallace*, fashioned from sandstone. Wallace was depicted at his most warrior-like, holding a ball and chain flail in his right hand and a shield emblazoned with the word 'Braveheart' over his left arm. On the plinth was written 'FREEDOM' in capital letters, and by his feet rested the decapitated head of the Governor of York. Little is known about what Wallace looked like, and sculptural representations have been accordingly varied, embracing both the warrior and statesman. Church depicted Wallace in the manner of the most recent Hollywood portrayal of the hero, giving him the face of Mel Gibson, the star of *Braveheart*. Mel/William roared out defiantly across the visitor centre car park, where the statue was placed.

This portrayal was greeted with less than universal acclaim. Critics fretted that what they considered a kitsch rendition of the hero would detract from the serious and restrained message of the Wallace Monument as a whole. The statue was vandalised so frequently that it had to be fenced in, and in 2008, using the pretext of expansion of the visitor centre, the statue was removed and returned to Church, who placed it in his Brechin studio. The press reported in 2017 that Church was downsizing, and the statue required a new home. Plans were reported for its relocation to Ardrossan in Ayrshire, to whose castle Wallace laid siege in 1296. Legend has it that he threw survivors of the siege into a cellar where they starved to death: the place thereafter bore the name Wallace's Larder.[75]

Ardrossan was not to be. Evidently tiring of waiting for the projected William Wallace Visitor Centre in Ardrossan to materialise, the statue was unveiled in 2021 outside Brechin City football club.[76] Social media comments around the unveiling were little kinder to the statue than its reception at the Wallace Monument had been. Fans suggested that the face of the beheaded Governor of York owed something to Derek Smalls, the moustache-sporting bass player in the spoof rock band Spinal Tap.[77]

Football supporters are indeed vociferous critics where a statue of their hero is felt to be wanting. In 2007, a statue was unveiled outside Southampton Football Club of Ted Bates, who served the club as striker, coach, manager, director and president over an astonishing 66 years. Unfortunately, fans took against the statue, the work of club supporter Ian Brennan. Amidst claims that it bore a closer resemblance to US President George Bush, diminutive entertainer 'Wee'

Jimmy Krankie and, fatally, the former owner of rivals Portsmouth than to its intended subject,[78] the statue was unceremoniously replaced by a new version, the work of Sean Hedges-Quinn.

The most celebrated recent example of a statue of a footballer deemed not up to the mark was to be found at the international airport in Madeira. On 29 March 2017, a distinguished cast attended a ceremony renaming the place in honour of Portuguese footballer Cristiano Ronaldo, born on the island. Ronaldo attended in person, alongside the Portuguese president and prime minister. The renaming of the airport was accompanied by the unveiling of a bust of Ronaldo outside the terminal building, intended as a permanent reminder of the airport's association with the footballer.

The inauguration ceremony was, as such events tend to be, all smiles and applause. Ronaldo expressed his pride in the island of his birth. The bust however caught the attention of the international press. And not in a way that flattered its sculptor, Madeira artist Emanuel Santos. Whether it was the bronze sculpture's fixed grin, scary eyes gazing out in different directions, or the fact that it didn't much resemble Ronaldo at all, social media users went to town. 'Whoever made the new Cristiano Ronaldo statue is clearly a Lionel Messi fan,'[79] someone commented on Twitter. The controversial bust was substituted fifteen months later by another work closer in appearance to its intended subject.[80]

The age-old challenge confronting realistic portrayals of their subject kicked in. Rather like well-performed karaoke, they can appear boring. A petition was launched to bring back the old statue, citing a lack of respect to Emanuel Santos and his family. Sadly, in vain. Writing in *The Guardian* newspaper, Eddy Frankel found something to admire in the original sculpture, 'almost iconoclastic in its flawed depiction.' He concluded that the original, while indeed a bad sculpture, was 'an ecstatic mess, its face a hybrid of Ronaldo and Santos's, two sets of features squidged together. It's the artist seeing something of himself in the rags-to-riches glory of Ronaldo.'[81]

For statues of living people, or those alive in the era of photography, non-acceptability has much to do with perceived failure to capture the likeness of the subject. For statues of historical and heroic figures, like Wallace, whose likeness is a matter of conjecture, the issue is more about failure to capture the subject in a way that demonstrates appropriate respect or reverence.

Take Michael the Brave, the Romanian hero Mihai Viteazul, who in 1600 briefly ruled Wallachia, Moldavia and Transylvania, the three principalities making up modern Romania, thereby making him a symbol of national unity. Upon the erection of a statue of this heroic figure in the town of Slobozia in December 2014, the general conclusion was that Father Christmas had arrived early. The chubby bearded hero held both a sword and an axe, though giving the impression that deploying either would be quite an effort. The statue lasted less than three years.[82]

Queen Nefertiti, the Great Royal Wife of Egyptian pharaoh Akhenaten in the fourteenth century BCE, was a legendary beauty, her name translatable as something like 'the beautiful one has come forth.' Our view of her appearance has been shaped by a painted stucco-coated limestone bust unearthed at Amarna in 1912 by German archaeologist Ludwig Borchardt, now displayed at the Neues Museum in Berlin. The bust reinforces the legend of Nefertiti's beauty, with its high cheekbones, arched eyebrows, long neck and quizzical smile. Pity about the missing left eye, though.

A statue installed next to a highway in 2015 at the entrance to the Egyptian city of Samalut took its cue from the bust in the Neues Museum, but unfortunately little else. Her face was curiously elongated and given a greenish-yellow hue. Egyptian social media users, incensed at the mangling of a figure long serving as a symbol of national pride, likened her to Frankenstein's monster. One suggested: 'I guess this is what she looked like four days after she died.'[83] The bust was removed, amid promises that a dove of peace would be installed in Nefertiti's place.

The notoriety generated by woeful statuary can however prove its salvation. An absence of artistic value exposed by the brutal judgements of social media commentaries can generate an alternative form of value—curiosity value, monetisable as touristic value. A statue of US actress Lucille Ball was installed in the memorial park bearing her name in Celeron, New York State, in 2009. The work of sculptor Dave Poulin, it endeavoured to depict the star in an iconic scene from a 1952 episode of her hit television show *I Love Lucy*. This centred on the filming of a television commercial for a patent medicine named Vitameatavegamin, in which she was presenting the product. The medicine contained alcohol. Many takes were required. The sculpture was thus an attempt to capture a much-loved personality portraying her much-loved character in an inebriated state. This, it transpired, was a high-risk strategy. The resultant statue just looked deranged. It was nicknamed 'Scary Lucy'.

Scary Lucy managed a few quiet years in Celeron, until it hit a flurry of negative social media attention in 2015 focused on a Facebook campaign ('We Love Lucy! Get Rid of this Statue').[84] Poulin, acknowledging it had not been his best work, offered to rework the statue free of charge, a kind gesture rather brutally declined. A new statue was installed the following year in its place. The work of Carolyn Palmer, it played things safe, offering the hagiographic portrayal expected by fans, with Ball standing on her Hollywood star. It was dubbed 'Lovely Lucy'.

But while Scary Lucy was down, she was not out. She had by now become a tourist attraction, and the authorities had no intention of squandering this. She was relocated close to the original site, so visitors could enjoy both Lovely and Scary versions. Poulin died of a pulmonary embolism aged 59, his friends expressing sadness that this prolific sculptor had been best known for the negative publicity around a 'scary' statue of Lucille Ball.[85]

Punishing Statues

We might also note, admittedly rare, instances when a statue is taken down not because of the misdeeds of its subject, but the misdeeds of the statue itself. Second-century Greek geographer Pausanias tells us that Draco, the first legislator of Athens, the harshness of whose constitution gives rise to the adjective 'draconian', was tough not just on people but also on objects, extending capital punishment to them. He relates the tale of a bronze statue of the Olympian Theagenes of Thasos, noted for his boxing triumphs. The statue of the late Theagenes was beaten nightly by a man who had borne a grudge against the boxer in life. One night, during a particularly intense attack, the statue fell upon the man, killing him. The sons of the deceased man charged the statue with murder. Lacking a voice with which to defend itself, the statue was convicted. Its punishment was to be taken down and thrown into the sea.[86] This was not the end of the matter. The crops of Thasos were blighted. An oracle was consulted, advising that exiles should be returned. The health of the land was only restored when the last of the 'exiles', the statue of Theagenes, was caught up in a fishing net and brought back to Thasos.[87] The conclusion was drawn that this was a truly wonder-working statue, and many copies were made.

16

REBIRTH AND REVENGE

In 1951, a colossal bronze statue of Joseph Stalin was erected in Budapest (see fig. 32). It had been promised two years earlier as a seventieth birthday gift to the Soviet leader from the Hungarian people by the fawning Hungarian communist boss Mátyás Rákosi. Standing on a limestone pedestal, supported by a tribune, Stalin's right arm outstretched, it was the work of a talented sculptor named Sándor Mikus, awarded the commission after the results of the original competition were universally judged to have been appalling.[1]

It is said that the source of the prodigious quantities of bronze required to cast the monument was the bronze statues of Hungarian heroes under the care of the Budapest City Memorial Authority: works that had either been damaged in World War II or dismantled thereafter as failing to conform to the politics of the new Communist regime. Among those notable Hungarians recast to form Stalin's considerable figure were the conservative nineteenth-century prime minister Count Gyula Andrássy, early twentieth-century prime minister Count István Tisza, killed by leftist revolutionaries in 1918, and Artúr Görgei, one of the military leaders of the 1848 Hungarian Revolution.[2] Both the large size of the monument and the use of recycled statues representing the old Hungarian nationalist narratives served to make a point about the power of the regime. That said, it was not a durable point: the statue was pulled down five years later in the 1956 uprising.[3]

Dead statues then may be used to make new ones: an act of recycling and rebirth.

VOICES IN STONE

Recycling Statues as a Cost-Cutting Measure

One motivation for the repurposing of monuments which seems to have been particularly pronounced in antiquity was simply as a cost-cutting measure. In ancient Egypt, the cost and effort involved in quarrying, transporting and carving colossal statues was immense, especially for statues destined for areas such as the Nile Delta, where there was a dearth of hard stone quarries. Thus, later kings transported colossal statues of Ramesses II the relatively short distances from Piramesse to Tanis and Bubastis within the Delta, where they were re-erected and rededicated.[4]

Public statues in ancient Rome were treated as public property, likely to be relabelled if their original subject was forgotten or deemed no longer worthy of remembrance.[5] Historian Christopher Dickenson examines a statue of one Theon, erected in the first century CE in the gymnasium complex in Messene in the Peloponnese during the period of Roman imperial rule. The marble statue, now sadly lacking a head, depicts Theon with hand on chest, his robes twisted around his arm like a sling, a pose suggestive of a politically involved figure. The inscription refers to him as a 'hero', hinting at a monument erected after his death. Its base also contains an inscription to a different, earlier figure, a *gymnasiarchus* or gymnasium master, though the base has been turned to place the original inscription out of sight from the viewer. This simply seems to have been about reusing a conveniently shaped stone block: the original subject was irrelevant. One feels for that poor *gymnasiarchus*, who presumably hoped, like Ozymandias, that his statue would allow memory of his deeds to endure through the ages, only to be summarily dismantled a few generations after his death. Dickenson argues that recycling was most likely to be the fate of monuments of subjects whose families had died out or fallen on hard times, losing the financial means and political clout to preserve the monuments of their ancestors.[6]

Destruction and Construction

The destruction of one statue is often followed by the erection of another in the same spot. As the icons of one regime fall, those of its successor are readied. It is perhaps unsurprising that the new statue is often placed on the site of the old. As we have seen, statues are often given prestigious, central or symbolic locations within the urban fabric. Such locations remain prestigious following regime changes, calling for new statuary to fill the vacated spot. There may be practical reasons too to link new statue to old site, such as a ready-made plinth, ripe for occupation.

Twentieth-century Polish aphorist Stanisław Lec advised: 'when smashing monuments, save the pedestals. They always come in handy.'[7] This approach has frequently been adopted during acts of iconoclasm. One suspects that practical considerations have sometimes held sway: toppling a monument is more straightforward than the demolition of the solid pedestal on which it stands. For the iconoclast, it is also a more satisfying one, culminating in the, er, iconic moment of the icon's fall.

On occasion, salvation of the pedestal while removing the statue has been a deliberate act. Such was the case following the defeat of the 1991 August coup in Moscow. The monument to Felix Dzerzhinsky on Lubyanka Square became a focal point of protests. There is no real surprise over this: Dzerzhinsky was a founder of Soviet secret police organisations and an architect of the Red Terror; his name closely identified with oppression. His monument was not demolished by an angry crowd, but carefully taken down on the orders of the city mayor, and reinstalled near the Central House of Artists on Krymsky Val. The pedestal was retained, on the reasoning that the pedestal was itself a legacy of an earlier monument in the same space, one to General Skobelev, hero of the Russo-Turkish war of 1877–8, and thus possessed historical value of its own. For philosopher Mikhail Yampolsky, the preservation of the pedestal further insulted the removed monument, in reversing the usual value relationship between the two.[8]

Yampolsky, drawing examples from the Soviet Union, argues that the link between the destruction of statues and the building of new ones is deeper than simple common occupancy of prestige locations. He observes a desire to replace monuments as quickly as possible, as if the empty space formerly inhabited by a statue represents a dangerous or destructive force.[9] The swift erection of a new monument on the site of an old one links the destruction of the old order and the glorification of the new. This provides both a break with the old order and an expression of continuity.

Yampolsky links the predilection in the USSR and Russia for new monuments on the site of the old to Russian adherence to 'founding figures'. Thus, the statue of Lenin in the Kremlin was erected on the site of a former monument to Alexander II, a juxtaposition 'legitimising' Lenin as successor to earlier rulers.[10] The act of refounding requires both that there is a predecessor and that the predecessor is destroyed. Thus, as Yampolsky puts it, the new Soviet leaders simultaneously settled on the tsar's throne and blew it up. The role of predecessors is particularly important for totalitarian societies because, lacking well-developed civil institutions, they tend to fall back on family-based leadership motifs, depicting the leader as a father figure.[11]

Revenge of the Statues

Statues do not as a rule pose actual danger to those interacting with them but, like all rules, there are exceptions. We have already considered a couple of ancient examples. That from the *Idylls* of Theocritus of an unfeeling youth crushed by a statue of Eros. And Pausanias' tale of the bronze statue of the Olympian Theagenes of Thasos that took revenge upon its assailant by toppling onto him.

England in 1538, at the height of Thomas Cromwell's campaign against Catholic 'idolatry', provides an example of a statue as the instrument of execution. The weapon was a wooden statue of Saint Derfel Gadarn, a sixth-century monk, said to have been one of the seven warriors of King Arthur to have survived the Battle of Camlan, where Arthur himself met his end.[12] It was an equestrian statue, depicting Derfel as a military rather than monastic figure, and stood in St Derfel's Church in the village of Llandderfel in North Wales, where it was a place of pilgrimage. Under Cromwell's orders, the idolatrous wooden statue was removed and taken to London, though the horse was evidently left in Wales, as it was still there beside the communion rails during a decanal visitation of 1730. The dean ordered that the horse be removed from the church and decapitated forthwith, though these orders seem to have been ignored as the horse took part in later Easter festivities, when locals looked forward to the chance to ride on Derfel's horse.[13]

The focus of our tale now switches to John Forest, a senior figure of the Observant Franciscan community at Greenwich, where he was close to the household of Catherine of Aragon, and is sometimes referred to as her confessor, though this is disputed.[14] The refusal of the Observant Franciscans to accept the king as head of the church resulted in imprisonment and suppression of the order. Forest, having been jailed and released, was imprisoned again in 1538 for encouraging sedition in the confessional, and tried on charges of heresy. In refusing to read his recantation, he condemned himself to the only punishment provided for heretics; death by burning. Cromwell orchestrated his execution at Smithfield in May in theatrical fashion, with thousands in attendance. Forest was suspended in chains over the fire, with the wooden statue of Derfel Gadarn used as fuel. It was said that an old Welsh prophecy had it that Derfel Gadarn would one day set a forest on fire, though this seems to have been made up after the event.[15] The linking by Cromwell of the burning of an 'idolatrous' statue and the execution of the 'heretical' friar was thought through carefully, drawing a link between the powers claimed by the Catholic clergy and the superstitious worshipping of statues.[16]

Forest was the only Englishman to be burned for heresy during the English Reformation. Other Catholic martyrs were convicted instead of treason, which involved hanging and dismembering. Neither exactly enticing options for the accused. Historian Peter Marshall argues that the abandonment of recourse to charges of heresy was in part precipitated by an unenthusiastic crowd reaction to the final sermon preached by Bishop Hugh Latimer at Forest's execution, in part to avoid causing gratuitous additional offence to the Catholic powers by casting their religion as 'heretical' and in part not to prompt awkward questions, given that King Henry VIII had once himself defended this very faith.[17]

In 2014, an American exchange student managed to get stuck inside a red marble sculpture of a vagina outside Tübingen University in Germany. His extrication reportedly required the assistance of five emergency service vehicles and twenty-two firemen.[18] Having just made the stupidest decision of his life, he then made the most sensible, by shunning all publicity over the escapade, thereby avoiding having to live out the rest of his days, whatever his subsequent achievements, bearing the nickname 'Vaginaman'. The firefighters' log offered the nicely factual account of the incident as 'a person trapped in a stone vulva'.[19]

The sculpture, named *Chacán-Pi* in reference to a Quechuan word referring to water flowing through a mountain and, more symbolically, to lovemaking, was the work of Peruvian artist Fernando de la Jara. The sculptor took a relaxed attitude to the student's plight, telling reporters that 'it's participatory art, it should be entered'.[20]

The ability to exit a monument also feels important. It can prove a matter of life or death. In 2021, the body of a 39-year-old man was discovered in a papier-mâché stegosaurus in Santa Coloma de Gramenet, a suburb of Barcelona. The alarm was raised by a father and son, who noticed a foul smell emanating from the dinosaur's leg. Police concluded that the man had climbed into the statue to retrieve a lost mobile phone, had fallen into one of the legs and been unable to escape his dinosaur prison.[21]

We cannot end our account on a downbeat note of conflict between humans and statues. For if statues can harm, they can also save. In autumn 2020, in Spijkenisse outside Rotterdam, a metro train crashed through a barrier at the end of the tracks. Disaster loomed. The train was prevented from plunging into the icy waters below by the fortuitously placed plastic sculpture of two whale tails, one of which held the train suspended in the air. No one was injured.[22] The local authority renamed the artwork *Saved by a Whale's Tail*.[23]

CONCLUSION

We have looked at statues from the perspectives of their full lives. Two interrelationships seem crucial: that between statues and time, and that between statues and place.

Let us first consider time. Carved and cast from durable materials like marble and bronze, the expectation of their originators was that statues would project their message of admiration for their subject far into the future. They would speak many generations hence of the greatness of the works of Ozymandias. Mikhail Yampolsky's suggestion that commemoration seeks to negate the passage of time is a useful one. Commemoration anchors a monument to the objectives of its founders: to their time. But assumptions about the durability of regimes and their heroes prove hubristic. Statues lose their intentional commemorative value, to be sustained, or not, by other forms of value, artistic perhaps, or historical. They might gradually fade into the background, becoming the invisible monuments mocked by Robert Musil.

As the values of societies change around them, the unchanging statue becomes out of step. In most cases, this simply has the effect of making the statue seem out of touch, quaint, or just not particularly relevant to modern society. Occasionally, the statue may take on a revelatory quality, providing inspiration to later societies, as did statues of ancient Greece and Rome for Renaissance and Neoclassical viewers. Sometimes its effect is toxic, where the heroes of the past embody actions and values unacceptable to audiences in the present.

Applied ethics lecturer Carl Fox has suggested that it would be altogether better if statues erected in a public place were put up for a time-limited period. This would not compel their removal on the expiration of this period but would necessitate a conscious decision to keep them. The citizens of Florence might for example opt to retain the copy of Michelangelo's *David* in the Piazza della Signoria. But it would give rise to the expectation that, all else equal, the statue was temporary. Fox believes such an arrangement would have three major benefits. First, he argues that the opportunity cost of existing statues is too high. They have grabbed the best sites, crowding out newcomers. Second, the presumption that statues are there for ever raises the stakes between advocates of different views over who is and who is not worthy of commemoration. Where statues are expected to stay indefinitely, removal becomes a notable and controversial act: perhaps even a violent one. Where those opposing the continued presence of a statue are continually thwarted in their calls for removal through official channels, there may be temptations to act outside the system, through vandalism or iconoclasm. If the presumption is that statues are temporary, these pressures are relieved. Finally, he argues that adding a time limit to statues enhances democratic control over public spaces. With every generation, the civic landscape becomes more cluttered with existing statues, reducing scope for new generations to shape the environment in accordance with their values and priorities.[1]

Like so many thoughtful proposals around the future of statues, it is easy to formulate challenges to it. Is it not possible, for example, that the requirement to consider at the end of a statue's planned life whether it should be retained for a further term or removed will provoke conflict between different constituencies rather than dampening it down?

Time also heals at least some wounds. While there are emotive campaigns for the removal of the statues of slave-owners, nineteenth-century imperialists and Confederate generals, monuments to despotic rulers of the ancient world are allowed a distinguished retirement, cherished for their artistic and historical value. However bad their deeds, they were atrocities committed so far back in time that they cause no personal pain to modern generations.[2]

The second important interrelationship in the lives of statues is that between statues and place. Moving a statue makes a statement about its importance and indeed function. The transfer of a statue from an open public site into a museum suggests that all effort at

CONCLUSION

imbuing the monument with commemorative value has now gone. For the rest of its life the statue is set now to be treated simply as an object of art, or a work illuminating a moment of history.

While the commemorative value of a statue tends in the main to wane with passing time and with removal from a prestigious site, this should not be taken to imply that all statues were successful to begin with. We have seen that statues are intended to serve the purpose of their initiators, and that the latter have typically enjoyed access to political and economic power, facilitating project delivery. But some statues have been poor in communicating their intended messages. Successful statues require compelling memoranda, a good location and vibrant commemoration. Many statues are not successful, even from the outset. Audiences may understand the statue in a different way from that intended. Or just like the fine speeches at the inauguration of the statue whose words fail to reach all but the privileged few standing closest to the speaker, its message may not be heard at all.

Aside from the fantastical creations of Hephaestus and the magical works of practitioners of Hermetic rituals, statues are themselves passive and emotionless participants in their own biographies. The lives of statues are really the lives of the humans who interact with them. Their birth may be accompanied by hard work, nervousness and excitement, as sponsors and sculptors overcome challenges financial, political and technical to realise their project: a statue honouring the achievements of an individual or event, honouring the values and behaviours they embody and honouring the nation or community they represent. The emotions surrounding a successful statue in its youth, while still the focus of commemoration, may range from the joy of the faithful to the desperation of the sick to the dutiful boredom of the official who has been told to turn up. In middle-age, statues may generate few emotions at all, but then the middle-aged rarely do.

Where a statue suddenly jars with members of the community, its subject embodying views or actions now deemed offensive, hostility and hatred may flare. Our survey has suggested that much *can* be done in such an eventuality: whether recontextualisation, or relocation, or removal. In seeking to answer the question as to what *should* be done, if one message emerges above all others from our story of the lives of statues it is the importance of humility. Those who erected the statue in the first place failed to predict the future, and in similar vein today's consensus, if consensus can even be found in the contested business of statues, will not be that of tomorrow. A willingness to listen to and understand the views of all those impacted by the statue becomes crucial.

Some would write the obituary of the public statue. For art historian Kirk Savage, 'old-fashioned sculpture of the human figure, the kind that traced its genealogy to the wonders of the ancient Greeks, has been obsolete for a long time'.[3] Historian Alex von Tunzelmann concludes her account of the demolition of twelve notable statues across time and place with the verdict that 'statuary itself is the problem. It's didactic, haughty and uninvolving.'[4] We have explored strategies adopted to respond to critiques of traditional figurative statues—that of the counter-monuments movement, for example, which endeavoured to ensure that its works were the reverse of 'didactic, haughty and uninvolving.' Yet, while not favoured in every culture and context, the public statue remains obstinately popular in many, from campaigners for new likenesses of their favourite footballer or comedian, to authorities seeking to build the identities of young nation states, to groups protesting the statuary underrepresentation of certain sectors of society. Even Kirk Savage concedes that the statue 'continues to play an odd and ambivalent role in public space.'[5] We continue to erect new figurative sculptures, initiating new statuary biographies whose subjects will entrance, confound, be worshipped, loved, assaulted and ignored by the generations to come, their voices in stone projecting forward to appreciative, hostile and indifferent audiences.

ACKNOWLEDGEMENTS

I would like to thank Michael Dwyer, Publisher and Managing Director at Hurst, for his unstinting support for this project. Alice Clarke, Commissioning Editor at Hurst, for her wise counsel throughout. Tom Feltham, the book's great copyeditor. All those at Hurst who have been, and will be, involved in the emergence of the book into the light, among them Senior Editor Lara Weisweiller-Wu and Sales and Marketing Director Kathleen May along with Daisy Leitch, Jess Winstanley, Alex Bell, and Letty Allen. Charles Clarke and Donatas Kupčiūnas of the Cambridge University Centre for Geopolitics for encouraging me to look at contemporary iconoclasm in the Baltic States. Dzmitry Suslau at University College London School of Slavonic and East European Studies, Dmitrijs Andrejevs at the University of Manchester and Jevgeņijs Gombergs in Jūrmalā for fascinating discussions. The staff of the Preiļi History and Applied Arts Museum for their insights into local Lenin statues. Above all to Adriana and George, for support in so many ways and for their understanding over the amount of time spent looking at statues during family holidays.

·

LIST OF ILLUSTRATIONS

1. The National Windrush Monument, London. Photo by Paul Brummell.
2. Marc Bolan's Rock Shrine, Barnes Common, London. Photo by Paul Brummell.
3. Variant of Alice Nordin's *Andante Patetico*, Nationalmuseum Stockholm. Photo by Linn Ahlgren / Nationalmuseum, CC BY-SA.
4. *The Angry Boy*, Vigeland Park, Oslo. Photo by Paul Brummell.
5. Sardar Vallabhbhai Patel, Gujarat. Photo by Snehrashmi via Wikimedia Commons, CC BY-SA 4.0.
6. The Leshan Giant Buddha, Sichuan. Photo by fannyss via Wikimedia Commons, CC0 1.0.
7. *Järnpojke*, the Iron Boy of Stockholm. Photo by Paul Brummell.
8. Trajan's Column, Rome. Photo by Livioandronico2013 via Wikimedia Commons, CC BY-SA 3.0.
9. The heated statue of Margaretha Krook, Stockholm. Photo by Paul Brummell.
10. *Partners*, Walt Disney World, Florida. Photo by JeffChristiansen via flickr, CC BY-SA 2.0.
11. The Voortrekker Monument, Pretoria. Photo by John Walker via Wikimedia Commons, public domain.
12. The *Monument to the Heroes of Laguna and Dourados*, Rio de Janeiro. Photo by Mike Peel via Wikimedia Commons, CC BY-SA 4.0.

LIST OF ILLUSTRATIONS

13. *Revolt of the Prisoners*, Buchenwald. Photo by Bourgeon via Wikimedia Commons, CC BY-SA 3.0.
14. The Memorial to the 1941 Massacre of Jews at Rumbula. Photo by Dr. Avishai Teicher via Wikimedia Commons, CC BY-SA 3.0.
15. Bust of Ronald Reagan, Skulte, Latvia. Photo by Paul Brummell.
16. Statue of Robert Burns, Sydney. Photo by Pelagic via Wikimedia Commons, CC BY-SA 4.0.
17. *I Goat*, Spitalfields, London. Photo by Eluveitie via Wikimedia Commons, CC BY-SA 3.0.
18. Statue of Mary Seacole, London. Photo by OwenBlacker via Wikimedia Commons, CC0 1.0.
19. George-Étienne Cartier Monument, Montreal. Photo by Kenneth C. Zirkel via Wikimedia Commons, CC BY-SA 4.0.
20. Eric Morecambe statue, Morecambe. Photo by Brian Deegan via Wikimedia Commons, CC BY-SA 2.0.
21. The Infant Jesus of Prague. Photo by VitVit via Wikimedia Commons, CC BY-SA 4.0.
22. Pasquino, one of the 'talking statues' of Renaissance Rome. Photo by Architas via Wikimedia Commons, CC BY-SA 4.0.
23. Giant Dolls of Olinda, Brazil. Photo by the Prefeitura de Olinda via flickr, CC BY 2.0.
24. Bust of Dalida, Montmartre, Paris. Photo by Dudva via Wikimedia Commons, CC BY-SA 4.0.
25. Duke of Wellington with added traffic cone, Glasgow. Photo by Germanlphoto via Wikimedia Commons, CC BY-SA 4.0.
26. Statue of Heracles, Seleucia, Mesopotamia. Photo by Osama Shukir Muhammed Amin FRCP(Glasg) via Wikimedia Commons, CC BY-SA 4.0.
27. Statue of Vladimir Lenin, Grūtas Park, Lithuania. Photo by Paul Brummell.
28. *Boy with a Dolphin*, London. Photo by Lonpicman via Wikimedia Commons, CC BY-SA 3.0.

LIST OF ILLUSTRATIONS

29. Great Siege Monument, Valletta. Photo by Nenea hartia via Wikimedia Commons, CC BY-SA 4.0.
30. Theodosian Obelisk, Istanbul. Photo by Apaleutos25 via Wikimedia Commons, CC BY-SA 4.0.
31. Inscription on the plinth of the Edward Colston statue, Bristol. Photo by Paul Brummell.
32. Statue of Joseph Stalin, Budapest. Photo donated by Nagy Gyula to Fortepan, public domain.

NOTES

INTRODUCTION

1. Chesterton 1946, p. 29.
2. Rossi 2021.
3. Dickenson 2021, p. 3.
4. Frowe 2019, p. 1.
5. Hobbs 2021.
6. Martin 1996, p. 57.
7. Butterfield 2003.
8. Quoted in Preda 2019, p. 44.
9. Exodus 20: 25, Holy Bible, King James Version.
10. Genesis 31: 45–46, Holy Bible, King James Version.
11. Ziolkowski 2015, p. 949.
12. Butterfield 2003, p. 30.
13. Ladd 1997, p. 11.
14. Getsy 2014, p. 6.
15. Schama, 2020.
16. Ibid.
17. Rigney 2022, p. 17.
18. Butterfield 2003, p. 31.
19. Dickenson 2021, pp. 22–3.
20. Pliny the Elder, *The Natural History*, Book 34, Chapter 17.
21. Wilson et al. 2021, p. 10.
22. Savage 2020; von Tunzelmann 2021, pp. 24–5.
23. Quoted in Savage 2020.
24. Mumford 1971, p. 264.
25. Sert, Léger and Giedion 1943.
26. Ibid.
27. Moravánsky 2011, p. 6.
28. Dickenson 2021, p. 24.
29. Savage 2010, p. 10.
30. Ibid., p. 13.

31. Quoted in Richmond 1962, p. 66.
32. Freedman 1986, p. 65, calls this a 'many-lensed gaze'.
33. Ibid., pp. 68–70.
34. Musil 1987.
35. Ibid.
36. Ibid.
37. Ibid.
38. Edensor 2019.
39. Rigney 2022, p. 21, uses the term 'mnemonic fossil'.
40. Billig 1995.
41. Branscome 2021, p. 1.
42. Edensor 2019, p. 61.
43. Ahmer 2020, p. 150.
44. See Arrhenius 2003, Ahmer 2020 and Widrich 2013 for a more detailed analysis of Riegl's essay.
45. Yampolsky 1995, p. 95.
46. Ibid., p. 96.
47. Yampolsky 1995, p. 107, describes this process as 'temporalisation'.
48. Ibid., pp. 107, 110.
49. Chaniotis 2017.

1. PATRONS AND PROMOTERS

1. Schama 2020.
2. Savage 1999, p. 5.
3. Ibid., p. 7.
4. van Hensbergen 2023.
5. Quoted in 'Journey of the National Windrush Monument'.
6. Ibid.
7. Quoted in 'Windrush: "Home Office Ignored Warnings"'.
8. Quoted in Nicholson 2022.
9. Quoted by Nadine White on X: @Nadine_Writes, 22 June 2022.
10. Ibid.
11. Torrington n.d.
12. Ibid.
13. Quoted in Jackson 2024.
14. Mezulanik 2024.
15. marc-bolan.net (accessed 26 November 2024).
16. The TAG website, marc-bolan.net, is a mine of information about the history of the Marc Bolan Rock Shrine.
17. Murphy 2004.

18. Ochser 2001.
19. Vilnis Ķirsis on X: @VilnisKirsis, 31 October 2024.
20. Burk 2003, p. 327.
21. Dwyer 2002, p. 48.
22. Ibid., p. 32.

2. SCULPTORS

1. 'Nationalmuseum Acquires a Sculpture by Alice Nordin'.
2. Miss 2016, p. 21.
3. Dąbrowska 2022, p. 153.
4. Ibid., p. 155.
5. Miss 2016, p. 68.
6. Henderson 2004, p. 84.
7. Kofoed n.d., p. 42.
8. Quoted on a display panel, Thorvaldsen Museum, Copenhagen, visited 2 February 2025.
9. Henderson 2004, p. 90.
10. Ibid., p. 94.
11. Miss 2016, p. 74.
12. Gottskálksdóttir 2011, p. 205.
13. Ibid., p. 207.
14. Ibid., pp. 210–11.
15. Ibid., p. 217.
16. Theodórsdóttir n.d.
17. Ibid.
18. Sagewitz 2020, p. 71.
19. Ibid., p. 72.
20. Ibid., p. 72.
21. Hagen 2022.
22. Skaftun 2018.
23. Yampolsky 1995, p. 94, describes the resultant experience as one of 'traumatic proximity.'
24. Palmer 2009.
25. Ibid., p. 391.
26. See Palmer 2009.

3. PHYSICAL CHARACTERISTICS

1. Garnett 2015, p. 29.
2. Price 2011, p. 411.
3. Derrida 1978.

4. Yampolsky 1995, p. 95.
5. Kruk 2019, p. 98.
6. Wong 2019, pp. 4–5.
7. Ibid., p. 15.
8. Ibid., p. 20.
9. Ibid., pp. 20–21.
10. Yampolsky 1995, pp. 93–4.
11. Farquhar 2004.
12. Quoted in Danner 2023, p. 79.
13. Adshead 1911, p. 97.
14. Kondratieff 2004, p. 9.
15. Jacobson 2011, p. 76.
16. Ibid., p. 86.
17. Ibid., p. 76.
18. Quoted in Davies 1997, p. 60.
19. Ibid.
20. Ibid., p. 62.
21. Ibid., pp. 46, 54–56.
22. Ibid., p. 48.
23. Danner 2023, p. 79.
24. Ibid., p. 89.
25. Jenkins 2012, p. 13.
26. Gunther and Bagna-Dulyachinda 2019, p. 163.
27. Jenkins 2012, p. 15.
28. Tobin 1975, p. 307.
29. Paz 2023.
30. Stocking 2014, p. 53.
31. Spivey 2005, episode 1.
32. Ibid.
33. Ramachandran and Hirstein 1999, p. 19.
34. Spivey 2005.
35. Ramachandran and Hirstein 1999, p. 18.
36. Spivey 2005.
37. Quoted in Dombrowski 2011, p. 183.
38. Ibid., pp. 169–71.
39. Ibid., p. 179.
40. Jones 2015.
41. Ibid.
42. Savage 2010, p. 12.
43. Ibid., p. 13.

44. Kruk 2019.
45. Ibid., p. 109.
46. Quoted in Hollinshead 2002, p. 126.
47. Hollinshead 2002, p. 127.
48. Ibid., p. 122.
49. Ibid., pp. 142–4, 152.
50. Ridgway 1966, p. 32.
51. Hollinshead 2002, p. 125.
52. Ibid., p. 138.
53. Layton 1860, p. 141.
54. Opper 2014, p. 38.
55. Ridgway 1966, p. 32.
56. Hollinshead 2002, p. 146.
57. Ridgway 1966, p. 42.
58. Garnett 2015, pp. 22–3.
59. Stevens et al 2012, p. 12.
60. Ridgway 1966, pp. 38–41.
61. Panzanelli 2008, p. 8.
62. Bradley 2009, p. 446.
63. Hodne 2020, p. 194.
64. Quoted in Panzanelli 2008, p. 10.
65. Ibid.
66. Bradley 2009, p. 428, Brinkmann 2008, p. 22.
67. Kiilerich 2016, pp. 2–3.
68. Bradley 2009, p. 448.
69. Liverani 2005, p. 194.
70. Bradley 2009, p. 449.
71. Ibid., p. 448.
72. Liverani 2005, p. 193.
73. Bradley 2009, p. 438.
74. Quoted in Panzanelli 2008, p. 2.
75. Kiilerich 2016, p. 15.
76. Bradley 2009, p. 437.
77. Ibid., p. 446.
78. Ibid., p. 442.
79. Ibid., p. 445.
80. Panzanelli 2008, p. 13.
81. Bradley 2009, p. 430.
82. Garnett 2015, p. 26.
83. Bradley 2009, p. 429.

84. Quoted in Liu and Huang 2023, p. 4.
85. Ibid., p. 4.
86. Ibid., pp. 13–14.
87. Stewart 2003.
88. van Tilbury 2021.
89. Opper 2014, p. 38.
90. Dąbrowska 2022, p. 150.
91. Sirén 1914, pp. 458–60.
92. Lanzi and Lanzi 2004, p. 23.
93. Ibid., p. 22.

4. PROPRIETARY STATUES

1. Opper 2014, p. 39.
2. Quoted in Opper 2014, p. 45.
3. Opper 2014, p. 41.
4. Rigney 2022, p. 10, uses the term 'memorial colonisation' to refer to the erecting of statues related to the history and memories of the occupying power in colonial territories.
5. Dickenson 2017, p. 136.
6. Ibid., p. 137.
7. Jeffrey 1980, p. 485.
8. Ibid., p. 487.
9. Luik 2015.
10. Korkis (2011) offers a good account of the story behind the *Partners* statue.
11. Stride, Wilson and Thomas 2013.
12. Ibid.
13. Stride, Wilson and Thomas 2013A, p. 1.
14. Stride, Wilson and Thomas 2013.
15. Stride, Wilson and Thomas 2013A, p. 15.
16. Ibid., pp. 1–2.
17. Ibid., p. 11.
18. See Thomas and Stride 2013.
19. Cialdini et al. 1976, p. 366.
20. Stride, Wilson and Thomas 2013A, p. 9.
21. Ibid., pp. 9–10.
22. Quoted in Boucher, 2018.

5. STATUES AND NATIONAL IDENTITY

1. Kruger and van Heerden 2005, p. 246.

NOTES

2. Ibid.
3. Anderson 2003, p. 7.
4. Centeno 1999, p. 79.
5. Crampton 2001.
6. Halbwachs 1992.
7. Nora 1989, p. 14.
8. Ibid., p. 7.
9. Ibid., p. 19.
10. Hartog 1995, p. 1231; English-language translation from Montaño 2008, p. 3.
11. See Montaño 2008, p. 11.
12. Nasar 2020, p. 1224.
13. Rigney 2022, p. 17.
14. Montaño 2008, pp. 14–15.
15. Ignatieff 1984, p. 158.
16. Ibid.
17. Mitchell 2003, p. 456.
18. 'Moscow reinstates Lenin statue in Ukraine's Melitopol years after Kyiv took it down'.
19. Centeno 1999, p. 80.
20. Söderlind 2008, p. 15.
21. Widén 2008, p. 90.
22. Söderlind 2008, p. 16.
23. Rausch 2007.
24. Ibid., p. 83.
25. Ibid., p. 91.
26. Centeno 1999, p. 88.
27. Mock 2012.
28. Mock 2012, p. 95.
29. Pastana 2020, p. 42.
30. Ibid., pp. 41–2.
31. Ibid., p. 47.
32. Rausch 2007, pp. 77–78.
33. Ibid., p. 79.
34. Ibid., pp. 80–81.
35. Ibid., p. 86.
36. Ibid., p. 86.
37. Ibid., pp. 87–88.
38. McGarr 2015, p. 797.
39. See von Tunzelmann 2021, p. 79, McGarr 2015, pp. 827–8.

40. Jeffrey 1980.
41. Ķeniņš 2012, pp. 25–6.
42. Ibid.
43. Younge 2021.
44. Sumartojo 2013, p. 71.
45. Quoted in Sumartojo 2013, p. 72.
46. Ibid., p. 73.
47. Boris Johnson, 'The Mayor's Speech at the Royal Academy Dinner', 3 March 2008, quoted in Sumartojo 2013, p. 75.
48. Quoted in Sumartojo 2013, p. 75.
49. Sumartojo 2013, p. 77.

6. MEMORIALISING LOSS, TRAGEDY AND EVIL

1. Quoted in Kovel 1999, p. 242.
2. Young 1997, p. 858.
3. Stevens et al. 2012, p. 7.
4. Rigney 2022, pp. 16–17.
5. Marcuse 2010, p. 89.
6. Brummell 2024, p. 133.
7. Krūmiņa-Koņkova 2021, pp. 18–19.
8. Ibid., p. 29.
9. Marcuse 2010, p. 89.
10. Young 1989, p. 72.
11. Ibid., p. 75.
12. Quoted in Young 1989, p. 82.
13. Ibid., p. 90.
14. Ibid., pp. 82–3.
15. Ibid., p. 91.
16. Ibid., p. 92.
17. Ibid., p. 93.
18. Ibid., p. 98.
19. Young 1992.
20. Stevens et al 2012, p. 19.
21. Stevens 2013, p. 185.
22. Lupu 2003, pp. 135–6, Young 1992, pp. 274–6.
23. Stubblefield 2011, p. 8.
24. Lupu 2003, p. 141.
25. Golańska 2017; Young 1997, pp. 859–65.
26. Young 1997, p. 865.
27. Stevens 2013, p. 182.
28. Young 1997, pp. 853–4.

29. Young 2002, pp. 66–7.
30. Ibid., p. 67.
31. Young 1997, p. 855.
32. Young 2002, p. 70.
33. Huyssen 1996, p. 184.
34. Young 2002, pp. 72–73.
35. Baptist 2012, pp. 78–80.
36. Stevens et al. 2012.
37. Young 2002, p. 75.
38. Stevens 2013, p. 184, quoting Huyssen 2003.
39. Young 2002, p. 77.
40. Partridge 2010, p. 829.
41. Ibid., p. 842.
42. See Bareither 2021.
43. Stevens 2013, p. 192.
44. 'Vietnam Veterans Memorial'.
45. Quoted in Marling and Silberman 1987, p. 9.
46. Ibid., p. 10.
47. Sturken 1991, pp. 119–20.
48. Marling and Silberman 1987, p. 12.
49. Tom Carhart, quoted in Marling and Silberman 1987, p. 13.
50. Quoted in Sturken 1991, p. 123.
51. Ibid., p. 125.
52. Marling and Silberman 1987, p. 16.
53. Sturken 1991, p. 135.
54. Ibid., p. 131.
55. Ibid., p. 129.
56. 'May 4 Memorial (Kent State University)'.
57. Post 2016.
58. Centuori 1999.
59. Post 2016.
60. Post 2016.
61. Stevens 2013, p. 188.
62. Ibid., pp. 189–91.
63. Young 1989, p. 101.
64. Ibid.
65. Ibid.

7. EXPORTING STATUES

1. 'Apkārtējos izbrīna māja Skultē ar pieminekli kādreizējam ASV prezidentam Reiganam'.

2. Whatley 2016.
3. Ibid.
4. Whatley 2011, p. 657.
5. Millar 2012, p. 137.
6. Millar 2012, p. 137.
7. Whatley 2011, p. 640.
8. Ibid., p. 645.
9. Pittock 2011, p. 16.
10. Ibid., p. 18.
11. Malgrati 2023.
12. Pittock 2011, p. 19.
13. Mawdsley 2012, p. 258.
14. Mauss 1966, p. 10.
15. Brummell 2022, p. 5.
16. Brummell 2021, pp. 146–7.
17. Behrens-Abouseif 2016, p. 17.
18. Mauss 1966, p. 20. Brummell 2022 offers a full account of the history of and strategies underpinning diplomatic gifting.
19. Redworth 2003, p. 1.
20. Brotton 2016, p. 24; Brummell 2022, pp. 125–30.
21. Naguip and Strønen 2014.
22. Paredes 2013, p. 455.
23. Yehia 2016, p. 30.
24. Quoted in Yehia 2016, p. 34.
25. Naguip and Strønen 2014.
26. Keyte 2014.
27. Stilwell 2020.
28. Quoted in 'Abraham Lincoln in Cornish'.
29. Schwartz 1991, p. 303.
30. Ibid., p. 314.
31. Ibid., p. 311.
32. Mason 2013.
33. Khan 2010, pp. 14–15.
34. Joseph, Rosenblatt and Kinebrew 2000, pp. 25–7.
35. Ibid., pp. 55–9.
36. Boime 1986, p. 12.
37. Ibid., p. 13.
38. Viano 2018, p. 8.
39. Quoted in Khan 2010, p. 6.
40. A more detailed analysis of The Statue of Liberty as a diplomatic gift is provided in Brummell 2022, pp. 215–21.

8. STATUES OF WOMEN

1. Nikolov 2017.
2. Quoted in 'put her forward'.
3. Peng 2011.
4. Quoted in Brown 2021.
5. 'Llandudno and the Great Orme Kashmiri Goats'.
6. 'Coronavirus: Goats Take over Empty Streets of Seaside Town'.
7. The story of the mascots is told in 'Mascots of the Royal Welsh'.
8. Quoted in 'Royal Welsh: New Regimental Goat Evades Army Capture'.
9. 'Life-Sized Statue of Royal Welch Fusilier and Regimental Goat Unveiled in Wrexham'.
10. Mitchell 2023.
11. 'Capricorn Two'.
12. 'Are There More Statues of Goats than Women in the UK?'
13. putherforward.com.
14. Topping 2018.
15. 'Mary Seacole Statue'.
16. Jones 2016.
17. Quoted in Flory 1993, p. 289.
18. Flory 1993. See also Daveloose 2023.
19. Flory 1993, p. 294.
20. Hemelrijk 2005, pp. 311–2.
21. Ibid., p. 314.
22. Flory 1993, p. 300–1.
23. Dasen 2005.
24. Flory 1993, p. 306.
25. Hemelrijk 2005, p. 316–7.
26. Quoted in Sackville-West 2010, p. xviii.
27. Ibid., p. 137.
28. Ibid., p. 139.
29. See Sackville-West 2020, pp. 127–42 for an account of the dissolute life of the Third Duke of Dorset.
30. Robinson 1995.
31. de Beauvoir 1971.
32. Roy-Omoni, Onibere and Osakwe 2024, p. 120.
33. Quoted in Cascone 2019.
34. Baumel 1996, pp. 114–5.
35. Ibid., p. 112.
36. Ibid., pp. 117–8.

NOTES

37. Ibid., p. 116.
38. Ibid., p. 122.

9. LOCATION

1. 'Statues and Monuments in Westminster'.
2. Butterfield 2003, p. 30.
3. Ibid., p. 31.
4. Ibid., p. 31.
5. Stevens 2013, p. 184.
6. Ibid., p. 182.
7. 'Statues and Monuments in Westminster'.
8. Ibid., p. 20.
9. Ibid., p. 20.
10. Ibid., p. 22.
11. Ibid., p. 24.
12. Ibid., p. 25.
13. Ibid., p. 21.
14. Sherwood 2016.
15. Quoted in Hartley-Parkinson 2018.
16. Stevens 2013, p. 183.
17. Osborne 1998, p. 440.
18. Ibid., pp. 450–51.
19. Wright 2023, p. 557.
20. Ibid., p. 555.
21. Quoted in Wright 2023, p. 565.
22. Wright 2023, p. 563.
23. Petterson 2019.
24. Dickenson 2021, p. 4.
25. Rambelli 2002, pp. 272–74.
26. Ibid., p. 272.
27. Ibid., pp. 296–300.
28. Ibid., pp. 292–3.
29. Quoted in Potts 2001, p. 7.
30. Potts 2001, p. 11.
31. Ridgway 1971, pp. 341–2.
32. Ibid., p. 337.
33. Wasley 2017.
34. Ridgway 1971, p. 356.
35. Potts 2001, p. 8; Zuckert 2009, p. 287; Hopkins 2004.
36. Savage 2010, p. 10.

NOTES pp. [178–188]

37. Potts 2001, p. 10, refers to 'the staging of sculpture'.
38. Savage 2010, p. 12.
39. Ibid.

10. COMMEMORATION

1. Holliday 1990, p. 544.
2. Kellum 1994, p. 32.
3. Holliday 1990, p. 547. See also Ryberg 1949, p. 84; Kellum 1994, p. 26.
4. Ryberg 1949, p. 85.
5. Holliday 1990, p. 554.
6. Billows 1993, p. 80.
7. Ryberg 1949, p. 89.
8. Centeno 1999, p. 80.
9. Butterfield 2003, p. 31.
10. Mitchell 2003, p. 443.
11. Ibid., p. 446.
12. Shurtleff 1857.
13. Ibid., p. 11.
14. Ibid., pp. 151–2.
15. Ibid., pp. 93–4.
16. Ibid., p. 223.
17. Petterson 2019.
18. Rausch 2007, pp. 74–5.
19. Quoted in Shurtleff 1857, p. 295.
20. Anderson 1993, pp. 3–4.
21. Berlant 1993, p. 399.
22. Quoted in Berlant 1993, p. 405.
23. Chaniotis 2017.
24. Ignatieff 1984, p. 159.
25. Ibid., p. 161.
26. Mitchell 2003, p. 444.
27. Butterfield 2003, p. 31.
28. Weinryb 2016, p. 4.
29. van Straten 1981, p. 65.
30. Ibid., p. 66.
31. Weinryb 2016, p. 12.
32. Weinryb 2018, p. 34.
33. Weinryb 2016, p. 1.
34. Pinch and Waraska 2009, p. 2.
35. van Straten 1981, p. 72.

36. Pinch and Waraska 2009, pp. 3–4.
37. Chaniotis 2017.
38. Blick 2011, p. 50.
39. Ibid., p. 32–4.
40. Weinryb 2018, p. 42.
41. Blick 2011, p. 44.
42. Weinryb 2016, pp. 11–12.
43. Weinryb 2018, p. 46.
44. Hughes 2016, p. 35.
45. Blick 2011, p. 31.
46. Ibid., p. 32.
47. Ķeniņš 2012, p. 41.
48. Link to the recording in Wilson 2022.
49. For example, @taironaguilera on Instagram (accessed 8 September 2025).

11. MOVING, TALKING, LIVING STATUES

1. Anecdote in Pallavicino's treatise on ethics *L'arte della perfezion cristiana* (The Art of Christian Perfection), described in Delbeke 2000, p. 182.
2. Chaniotis 2017.
3. Quoted in Getsy 2014, p. 4.
4. Sartre 1965, p. 390.
5. Ziegler 1985, p. 204.
6. Ziolkowski 2015, p. 952.
7. Németh 1997, p. 121.
8. Ziolkowski 2015, pp. 959–60.
9. Németh 1997, pp. 116–18.
10. Ziolkowski 2015, pp. 962–3.
11. Ibid., p. 964.
12. Quoted in Faraone 1987, p. 257.
13. Ibid., pp. 260–61.
14. Ibid.
15. Ziolkowski 2015, p. 910.
16. See Németh 1997, p. 123, Faraone 1987, p. 280.
17. Németh 1997, p. 124.
18. Duggan 2009, p. 236.
19. Brummell 2022, pp. 59–60.
20. Spaeth 1939, pp. 242–3.
21. Ibid., pp. 243–4.
22. Ibid., pp. 245.

23. Mulholland 2008, p. 159.
24. Ibid.
25. Egan 2015.
26. Ibid.
27. Quoted in 'Operation Zero: Smashing the Moving Statues'.
28. Mulholland 2008, p. 176.
29. Ryan and Kirakowski 1985.
30. da Silva 2018, p. 47.
31. Nascimento 2019.
32. Ziolkowski 2015, p. 952.
33. Voss 2006.
34. Ibid.
35. Garnett 2015, p. 29.
36. Price 2011, pp. 404–5.
37. Chaniotis 2017.
38. Ibid.
39. Voss 2006.
40. Opper 2014, p. 50.
41. Voss 2006.
42. Stocking 2014, p. 53.
43. Ibid., p. 55.
44. Ibid., p. 58.
45. Ibid., p. 59.
46. Dutton 1995, p. 122.
47. Quoted in Stocking 2014, p. 64.
48. Bryzgel 2010, pp. 134–5.
49. Ibid., p. 137.
50. Ibid., p. 141.

12. INTERFERING WITH STATUES

1. Emelyanova-Griva 2010.
2. Pierre 2010, p. 173.
3. Zuckert 2009, p. 289.
4. Getsy 2014, p. 8.
5. Ibid., p. 17.
6. Chaniotis 2017.
7. Kralj 2023.
8. Quoted in 'Do Not Touch Thatcher or Churchill Statue Feet, MPs Told'.
9. Blom and Nilsson 2023, p. 560.
10. Ibid.

11. Kralj 2023.
12. Sniter 2008, p. 168.
13. Giuffrida 2024.
14. Montgomery 2018.
15. Donohoe 2024.
16. 'Dublin's Molly Malone Statue to Get Stewards to Stop "Groping"'.
17. Quoted in Donohoe 2024.
18. Kralj 2023.
19. Peters 2014.
20. Ibid.
21. Getsy 2014, p. 7.
22. Németh 1997, p. 126.
23. Ibid., p. 128.
24. Ibid., p. 131.
25. Bottenberg 2020, pp. 129–30. See also Németh 1997 p. 130; Chaniotis 2017.
26. *The School of Venus, or the Ladies Delight, Reduced into Rules of Practice* 1680, pp. 112–13.
27. White 1978, pp. 247–9.
28. Gozzi 2024.
29. Kästner 2012, pp. 11–12.
30. McDonald 2017.
31. Todd 2005.
32. 'Plans to End Cone Tradition on Glasgow's Wellington Statue'.
33. McDonald 2017.
34. 'Plan Dropped to End Cone Tradition on Glasgow's Wellington Statue'.
35. Scott 2023.
36. Quoted in Scott 2023.
37. 'Duke of Wellington: Is the Statue's New Hat a Parting Gift from Banksy?'
38. Rigney 2022, p. 21.
39. Rice 2010.
40. Wilson et al. 2021.
41. Branscome 2021, pp. 5–7.
42. Quoted in Hajjaji 2023.
43. Quoted in Harris 2025.
44. Jensen 2019, pp. 216–7.
45. 'Indro Montanelli Statue in Milan, Italy'.
46. Pesarini and Panico 2021, p. 103.
47. Ibid., pp. 99–103; Contested Histories Case Study #86.
48. Quoted in Berhane and Malara 2020.

13. RELOCATION

1. 'Park Lane Byron Statue Move Planned 66 Years After Go-Ahead'.
2. 'Rescuing the Byron Memorial Statue'.
3. Chaniotis 2017.
4. Corso 1997–8, p. 76.
5. Gutzwiller 2004, p. 385–6.
6. See Gutzwiller 2004, pp. 386–7, Chaniotis 2017, Corso 1997–8, p. 76.
7. Corso 1997–8, p. 76.
8. Gregoratti 2013, p. 281.
9. Ibid.
10. Chaniotis 2017.
11. Quoted in Opper 2014, p. 24.
12. Opper 2014, p. 27.
13. Quoted in Opper 2014, p. 25.
14. 'Stolen Gary the Gorilla Statue Discovered in Layby'.
15. von Tunzelmann 2021, pp. 72–3.
16. Ibid., p. 75.
17. McGarr 2015, p. 820.
18. Quoted in McGarr 2015, p. 821.
19. Ibid., p. 825.
20. von Tunzelmann 2021, p. 81.
21. McGarr 2015, pp. 824–5.
22. Arnold 2019.
23. Dixon 2014.
24. Quoted in Aparício 2015.
25. Devriendt 2014.
26. de Groof 2010, p. 31 suggests that 'African artefacts are degraded from the cultual to the cultural.'
27. Quoted in de Groof 2010, p. 37.
28. Vilensky 2012.
29. Aparício 2015,
30. Dixon 2014.
31. McGuire 2016.
32. Belcheva 2017, p. 105.
33. Grūtas Park signage, visited in August 2024.
34. Grutoparkas.lt.
35. Grūtas Park signage, visited in August 2024.
36. Belcheva 2017, pp. 115–6.
37. Grūtas Park signage, visited in August 2024.
38. Connolly 1999.

39. Ibid.
40. Williams 2008, p. 186.
41. 'Grūtas Sculpture Park', Contested Histories Case Study #96, pp. 3–5.
42. Quoted in Connolly 1999.
43. Forest and Johnson 2002, p. 537.
44. Belcheva 2017, p. 111.

14. RECONTEXTUALISATION

1. Quoted in Yeats 2021, p. 3.
2. Burch-Brown 2022, p. 815.
3. Jenrick, 18 January 2021.
4. 'Guidance for Custodians on How to Deal with Commemorative Heritage Assets that have Become Contested'.
5. Ibid.
6. Dresser 2007, p. 173.
7. 'The Statue Interpretation Panels'.
8. Ibid.
9. van Hensbergen 2023.
10. Quoted in von Tunzelmann 2021, p. 184.
11. Ibid., p. 185.
12. Ibid.
13. Burch-Brown 2022, p. 816.
14. Masters 2014.
15. Loizidou 2010, p. 93.
16. Ibid., p. 94.
17. Quoted in Loizidou 2010, p. 96.
18. Loizidou 2010, p. 98.
19. Ibid., p. 93.
20. Brummell 2022, p. 162.
21. Meilak 2019.
22. 'Activists Undeterred by Government's Latest Attempt to "Kill Daphne's Memory"'.
23. 'Delia v. Minister for Justice of Malta Owen Bonnici'.
24. Brincat and Carabott 2020.
25. Jenkins 2012, p. 11.
26. Ibid., pp. 53–55.
27. Crellin and Kirkpatrick 2022, pp. 188–9.
28. Ibid., p. 190.
29. Ibid., p. 191.
30. Stevens et al. 2012, p. 14.

31. Ibid., pp. 14–16.
32. Ibid., pp. 16–17.
33. Erőss 2018, p. 25.
34. Ibid., pp. 25–31.
35. Stevens 2013, p. 187.
36. Frowe 2019, p. 25.
37. Hustvedt 2021, p. 42.
38. Ibid., p. 37.
39. Rigney 2022, p. 20.
40. Burch-Brown 2022, p. 820.
41. Jensen 2019, p. 211.

15. TOPPLING STATUES

1. von Tunzelmann 2021, p. 146.
2. Teulié 2024.
3. Rigney 2022, p. 18.
4. Frowe 2019.
5. Hughes 2021, pp. 3–10, quotation p. 10.
6. Forest and Johnson 2002, p. 525.
7. Koerner 2016/17, p. 5.
8. Yampolsky 1995, p. 101.
9. Ibid., p. 100.
10. Olusoga 2020.
11. Yampolsky 1995, p. 100.
12. Schama 2020.
13. Whitling 2010, p. 88.
14. Quoted in Omissi 2016, p. 171.
15. Prusac 2022.
16. Omissi 2016, p. 174.
17. Ibid., pp. 170–75.
18. Dickenson 2017, p. 137.
19. Ibid., p. 139.
20. Quoted in Omissi 2016, p. 179.
21. Ibid., p. 192.
22. Omissi 2016.
23. McGarr 2015.
24. Ibid., p. 797.
25. Ibid., p. 800.
26. Quoted in McGarr 2015, p. 812.
27. Pati 2012, p. 234.

28. McGarr 2015, pp. 826–7.
29. Jeffrey 1980.
30. Ibid., p. 489.
31. Gabowitsch 2021.
32. von Tunzelmann 2021, p. 106.
33. Young 2024; von Tunzelmann 2021, pp. 110–111, quotes the same joke but with a different order of prizewinning statues.
34. Jensen 2020.
35. Fraser 2022.
36. Edwardes 2016.
37. Ibid.
38. 'Saeima decides to legally allow Soviet monument demolition'.
39. 'Rīga City Council orders demolition of "Victory" Monument'.
40. 'Latvian Saeima passes law that allows demolition of Victory Monument in Pārdaugava'.
41. 'Experts present Latvian government list of 69 Soviet monuments to tear down'.
42. @edgarsrinkevics 25 August 2022.
43. Quoted in 'More monuments might be hidden from public space in Rīga'.
44. 'Pushkin monument gone from Rīga park'.
45. 'Soviet scientist Keldysh's monument in Rīga to be dismantled'.
46. von Tunzelmann 2021, p. 179.
47. Branscome 2021, p. 15.
48. Ibid., p. 19.
49. Ibid., p. 19.
50. Rigney 2022, p. 24.
51. Nasar 2020, p. 1220.
52. Quoted in Rigney 2022, p. 13.
53. Rigney 2022, p. 13.
54. Whitling 2010, p. 91.
55. Quoted in von Tunzelmann 2021, p. 182.
56. Branscome 2021, p. 19.
57. von Tunzelmann 2021, p. 183.
58. Nasar 2020, p. 1222.
59. Smith 2006.
60. Branscome 2021, p. 16.
61. Rigney 2022, pp. 29–30.
62. Bakare 2020.
63. Branscome 2021, p. 27.
64. Nasar 2020, p. 1219.

65. Rigney 2022, pp. 10–12.
66. Kowalska 2020, p. 111.
67. Smith 1996, pp. 152–6.
68. Ibid., p. 157.
69. King 2006, p. 304.
70. See Cannon and Trapp, eds., 1971.
71. Quoted in Cannon and Trapp, eds., 1971, p. 502.
72. Ibid., p. 504.
73. Ibid., p. 507.
74. Edensor 2019, pp. 65–66.
75. 'William Wallace Statue to Move to Site Where English Killed'.
76. Jones 2021.
77. Sommerlad 2021.
78. Walter 2007.
79. Quoted in Valentine 2017.
80. 'Cristiano Ronaldo: Mocked Statue at Madeira Airport is Replaced'.
81. Frankel 2018.
82. 'Statuia lui Mihai Viteazul care aducea cu Moş Crăciun, demolată după 3 ani'.
83. 'Egyptians Lambast "Ugly" New Nefertiti Statue'.
84. 'New Lucille Ball Statue Replaces "Scary Lucy" in Actor's Hometown'.
85. Hurst 2020.
86. Németh 1997, p. 124.
87. Chaniotis 2017.

16. REBIRTH AND REVENGE

1. James 2005, pp. 41–2.
2. Ibid., pp. 45–6.
3. Rigney 2022, p. 18.
4. Garnett 2015, p. 32.
5. Stewart 2003.
6. Dickenson 2017, pp. 132–3.
7. Quoted in Vladislavić 2020.
8. Yampolsky 1995, pp. 105–7.
9. Ibid., p. 100.
10. Ibid., p. 102.
11. Ibid., p. 103.
12. Hughes 2021, p. 1.
13. Suggett 1996, p. 97.
14. Marshall 1998, p. 354.

15. Ibid., p. 356.
16. Ibid.
17. Ibid., pp. 372–3.
18. Butterly 2014.
19. Quoted in Hartey-Parkinson 2014.
20. Quoted in Kirby 2014.
21. Sullivan 2021, Beachum 2021.
22. 'Whale sculpture catches crashed Dutch metro train'.
23. Boffey 2020.

CONCLUSION

1. Fox 2023.
2. Hobbs 2021.
3. Savage 2010, p. 9.
4. von Tunzelmann 2021, p. 213.
5. Savage 2010, p. 9.

BIBLIOGRAPHY

Author unknown, 'Abraham Lincoln in Cornish', National Park Service, 4 July 2016, nps.gov.

———, 'Activists Undeterred by Government's Latest Attempt to "Kill Daphne's Memory"', *The Shift*, 8 September 2018, theshiftnews.com (accessed 9 December 2024).

———, 'Apkārtējos izbrīna māja Skultē ar pieminekli kādreizējam ASV prezidentam Reiganam', Latvijas Sabiedriskais medijs, 27 May 2022, lsm.lv (accessed 12 July 2025).

———, 'Are There More Statues of Goats than Women in the UK?', BBC Sounds, bbc.com (accessed 11 May 2025).

———, 'Capricorn Two', steinbrener-dempf.com (accessed 5 October 2024).

———, 'Coronavirus: Goats Take over Empty Streets of Seaside Town', BBC News, 31 March 2020, bbc.com (accessed 28 September 2024).

———, 'Cristiano Ronaldo: Mocked Statue at Madeira Airport is Replaced', BBC Sport, 18 June 2018, bbc.com (accessed 30 May 2025).

———, 'Delia v. Minister for Justice of Malta Owen Bonnici', Global Freedom of Expression, Columbia University, 30 January 2020, globalfreedomofexpression.columbia.edu (accessed 9 December 2024).

———, 'Do Not Touch Thatcher or Churchill Statue Feet, MPs Told', BBC News, 2 August 2013, bbc.com (accessed 24 April 2025).

———, 'Dublin's Molly Malone Statue to Get Stewards to Stop "Groping"', BBC News, 2 April 2025, bbc.com (accessed 15 April 2025).

———, 'Duke of Wellington: Is the Statue's New Hat a Parting Gift from Banksy?', BBC News, 29 August 2023.

———, 'Egyptians Lambast "Ugly" New Nefertiti Statue', BBC News, 7 July 2015, bbc.com (accessed 31 May 2025).

BIBLIOGRAPHY

———, 'Experts present Latvian government list of 69 Soviet monuments to tear down', LETA, 30 June 2022.

———, 'Grūtas Sculpture Park', Contested Histories Case Study #96, July 2021, pp. 3–5, contestedhistories.org.

———, Grūto parkas, grutoparkas.lt (accessed 18 May 2025).

———, 'Guidance for Custodians on How to Deal with Commemorative Heritage Assets that have Become Contested', gov.uk, 5 October 2023 (accessed 4 May 2025).

———, 'Indro Montanelli Statue in Milan, Italy', Contested Histories Case Study #86, May 2024, contestedhistories.org (accessed 23 February 2025).

———, 'Latvian Saeima passes law that allows demolition of Victory Monument in Pārdaugava', Baltic News Network, 16 June 2022.

———, 'Life-Sized Statue of Royal Welch Fusilier and Regimental Goat Unveiled in Wrexham', The British Army, 23 March 2023, army.mod.uk (accessed 28 September 2024).

———, 'Llandudno and the Great Orme Kashmiri Goats', 21 April 2020, gonorthwales.co.uk (accessed 28 September 2024).

———, 'Mary Seacole Statue', maryseacoletrust.org.uk, n.d. (accessed 11 May 2025).

———, 'Mascots of the Royal Welsh', Southwest Medals & Collectables, southwestmedalsandcollectables.co.uk (accessed 28 September 2024).

———, 'May 4 Memorial (Kent State University)', n.d., https://www.library.kent.edu/special-collections-and-archives/may-4-memorial-kent-state-university (accessed 17 July 2024).

———, 'More monuments might be hidden from public space in Rīga', Latvijas Sabiedriskais medijs, 4 March 2023, ENG.LSM.lv (accessed 6 April 2025).

———, 'Moscow reinstates Lenin statue in Ukraine's Melitopol years after Kyiv took it down', AFP, 5 November 2022.

———, 'Nationalmuseum Acquires a Sculpture by Alice Nordin', Nationalmuseum Stockholm, 13 January 2021, nationalmuseum.se (accessed 20 April 2025).

———, 'New Lucille Ball Statue Replaces "Scary Lucy" in Actor's Hometown', *The Guardian*, 6 August 2016 (accessed 31 May 2025).

———, 'Operation Zero: Smashing the Moving Statues', Come Here to Me! Dublin Life & Culture, 16 February 2015, comeheretome.com (accessed 3 January 2025).

BIBLIOGRAPHY

———, 'Park Lane Byron Statue Move Planned 66 Years After Go-Ahead', BBC News, 19 April 2024, bbc.com (accessed 15 September 2025).

———, 'Plan Dropped to End Cone Tradition on Glasgow's Wellington Statue', BBC News, 12 November 2013.

———, 'Plans to End Cone Tradition on Glasgow's Wellington Statue', BBC News, 11 November 2013.

———, 'Pushkin monument gone from Rīga park', Latvijas Sabiedriskais medijs, 30 May 2023, ENG.LSM.lv (accessed 6 April 2025).

———, 'put her forward', nonzeroone.com, 2018 (accessed 27 September 2024).

———, 'Rescuing the Byron Memorial Statue', The Byron Society, n.d., thebyronsociety.com (accessed 29 June 2025).

———, 'Rīga City Council orders demolition of "Victory" Monument', Latvijas Sabiedriskais medijs, 13 May 2022, ENG.LSM.lv.

———, 'Royal Welsh: New Regimental Goat Evades Army Capture', BBC News, 2 February 2018, bbc.com (accessed 28 September 2024)

———, 'Saeima decides to legally allow Soviet monument demolition', Latvijas Sabiedriskais medijs, 12 May 2022, ENG.LSM.lv.

———, 'Soviet scientist Keldysh's monument in Rīga to be dismantled', Latvijas Sabiedriskais medijs, 19 October 2023, ENG.LSM.lv (accessed 6 April 2025).

———, 'Statues and Monuments in Westminster', westminster.gov.uk, n.d., p. 10 (accessed 5 October 2024).

———, 'Statuia lui Mihai Viteazul care aducea cu Moş Crăciun, demolată după 3 ani', Stirile Pro TV, 16 October 2017, stirileprotv.ro (accessed 31 May 2025).

———, 'Stolen Gary the Gorilla Statue Discovered in Layby', BBC News, 25 March 2024, bbc.co.uk (accessed 18 November 2024).

———, 'The Statue Interpretation Panels', Guy's & St Thomas' Foundation, gsttfoundation.org.uk, accessed 10 May 2025.

———, 'Vietnam Veterans Memorial', US Department of War, n.d., defense.gov (accessed 21 July 2024).

———, 'Whale sculpture catches crashed Dutch metro train', BBC News, 2 November 2020, bbc.com (accessed 12 January 2025).

———, 'William Wallace Statue to Move to Site Where English Killed', *The Scotsman*, 6 October 2017.

BIBLIOGRAPHY

———, 'Windrush: "Home Office Ignored Warnings"', BBC News, 5 December 2018.

Adshead, S. D., 'Monumental Columns: The Decoration and Furnishing of the City—No 2', *The Town Planning Review*, Vol 2, No 2, July 1911, pp. 95–8.

Ahmer, Carolyn, 'Riegl's "Modern Cult of Monuments" as a Theory Underpinning Practical Conservation and Restoration Work', *Journal of Architectural Conservation*, Vol 26, No 2, March 2020, pp. 150–65.

Anderson, Benedict, 'Replica, Aura, and Late Nationalist Imaginings', *Qui Parle*, Vol 7, No 1, Fall/Winter 1993, pp. 1–21.

———, *Imagined Communities: Reflections on the Origin and Spread of Nationality* (London: Verso, rev. ed. 2003).

Aparício, Maria Irene, 'Film and Memory: Where do Pictures Come From, in Statues Also Die?', in *Photography and Cinema, 50 Years of Chris Marker's La Jetée*, eds. Margarida Medeiros, Teresa Mendes Flores and Joana Cunha Leal (Cambridge: Cambridge Scholars, 2015), pp. 244–68.

Arnold, Katherine, 'Coronation Park and the Forgotten Statues of the British Raj', LSE blog, 20 June 2019, blogs.lse.ac.uk (accessed 19 January 2025).

Arrhenius, Thordis, 'The Fragile Monument: On Alois Riegl's Modern Cult of Monuments', *Nordisk Arkitekturforskning*, Vol 4, 2003, pp. 51–5.

Bakare, Lanre, 'Allyship or Stunt? Marc Quinn's BLM Statue Divides Art World', *The Guardian*, 15 July 2020 (accessed 20 February 2025).

Baptist, Karen Wilson, 'Shades of Grey: The Role of the Sublime in the Memorial to the Murdered Jews of Europe', *Landscape Review*, Vol 14, Issue 2, 2012, pp. 75–85.

Bareither, Christoph, 'Difficult Heritage and Digital Media: "Selfie Culture" and Emotional Practices at the Memorial to the Murdered Jews of Europe', *International Journal of Heritage Studies*, Vol 27, Issue 1, 2021, pp. 57–72.

Baumel, Judith Tydor, 'Rachel Laments Her Children: Representation of Women in Israeli Holocaust Memorials', *Israel Studies*, Vol 1, No 1, Spring 1996, pp. 100–126.

Beachum, Lateshia, 'A Father and Son Noticed a Stench near a Stegosaurus Statue. They Found a Corpse in One of its Legs', *The Washington Post*, 25 May 2021.

BIBLIOGRAPHY

Beauvoir, Simone de, *The Second Sex*, trans. H. M. Parshley (New York: Alfred A. Knopf, 1971).

Behrens-Abouseif, Doris, *Practising Diplomacy in the Mamluk Sultanate: Gifts and Material Culture in the Medieval Islamic World* (London: I.B. Tauris, 2016).

Belcheva, Ina, '"Sculptural Graveyards": Park-Museums of Socialist Monuments as a Search for Consensus', in *Discussing Heritage and Museums: Crossing Paths of France and Serbia*, eds. Dominique Poulot and Isidora Stanković (Paris: Université Paris 1 Panthéon-Sorbonne Centre de Recherche HiCSA, 2017), pp. 100–118.

Bennett, Jane, *Vibrant Matter: A Political Ecology of Things* (Durham, North Carolina: Duke University Press, 2010).

Berhane, Fiori, and Diego Maria Malara, 'The Montanelli Case: Sexuality, Race, and Colonial Forgetting in BLM Italy', Allegra Lab, October 2020, allegralaboratory.net (accessed 23 February 2025).

Berlant, Lauren, 'The Theory of Infantile Citizenship', *Public Culture*, Vol 5, 1993, pp. 395–410.

Billig, Michael, *Banal Nationalism* (London: Sage, 1995).

Billows, Richard, 'The Religious Procession of the Ara Pacis Augustae: Augustus' Supplicatio in 13 B.C.', *Journal of Roman Archaeology*, Vol 6, 1993, pp. 80–92.

Blick, Sarah, 'Votives, Images, Interaction and Pilgrimage to the Tomb and Shrine of St Thomas Becket, Canterbury Cathedral', in *Push Me Pull You, Vol 2: Physical and Spatial Interaction in Late Medieval and Renaissance Art* (Leiden: Brill, 2011), pp. 21–58.

Blom, Thomas, and Mats Nilsson, 'Tactile Tourism: Tourist Attractions to Touch', *Tourism*, Vol 71, No 3, 2023, pp. 553–67.

Boffey, Daniel, 'Whale Sculpture Stops Dutch Train Crashing into Water', *The Guardian*, 2 November 2020 (accessed 12 January 2025).

Boime, Albert, 'Liberty: Inside Story of a Hollow Symbol', *In These Times*, Vol 10, No 27, 11–24 June 1986, pp. 12–13.

Bottenberg, Laura, 'Pseudo-Lucian's Cnidian Aphrodite: A Statue of Flesh, Stone, and Words', *Millennium*, Vol 17, No 1, 2020, pp. 115–138.

Bradley, Mark, 'The Importance of Colour on Ancient Marble Sculpture', *Art History*, Vol 32, No 3, June 2009, pp. 427–57.

Branscome, Eva, 'Colston's Travels, or Should We Talk about Statues?', *ARENA Journal of Architectural Research*, Vol 6, No 1, 2021, pp. 1–29.

BIBLIOGRAPHY

Brincat, Edwina, and Sarah Carabott, 'Manuel Delia Wins Case Against Government Over Caruana Galizia Memorial', *Times of Malta*, 30 January 2020 (accessed 9 December 2024).

Brinkmann, Vinzenz, 'The Polychromy of Ancient Greek Sculpture', in *The Colour of Life: Polychromy in Sculpture from Antiquity to the Present*, ed. Roberta Panzanelli with Eike D. Schmidt and Kenneth Lapatin (Los Angeles: Getty Publications, 2008), pp. 18–39.

Brotton, Jerry, 'Buying the Renaissance: Prince Charles's Art Purchases in Madrid, 1623', in *The Spanish Match: Prince Charles's Journey to Madrid, 1623*, ed. Alexander Samson (Abingdon: Routledge, 2016), pp. 9–26.

Brown, Ellie, 'Quirky Goat Statue Named Landslide Winner of Kingston Sculpture Trail', Kingston.nub.news, 11 November 2021 (accessed 29 September 2024).

Brummell, Paul, 'A Gift for a President', *The Hague Journal of Diplomacy*, Vol 16, Issue 1, 2021, pp. 145–54.

———, *Diplomatic Gifts: A History in Fifty Presents* (London: Hurst, 2022).

———, *Latvia* (Chesham: Bradt Travel Guides, 2024).

Bryzgel, Amy, 'The Bronze Man and the Homeless Man: Performance Art in Latvia from Perestroika to Post-Soviet', in *From Recognition to Restoration: Latvia's History as a Nation-State*, eds. David Smith, David Galbreath and Geoffrey Swain (Amsterdam: Rodopi, 2010), pp. 133–157.

Burch-Brown, Joanna, 'Should Slavery's Statues be Preserved? On Transitional Justice and Contested Heritage', *Journal of Applied Philosophy*, Vol 39, No 5, 2022, pp. 807–24.

Burk, A. L., 'Private Griefs, Public Places', *Political Geography*, Vol 22, No 3, 2003, pp. 317–33.

Butterfield, Andrew, 'Monuments and Memories', *The New Republic*, 3 February 2003, pp. 27–32.

Butterly, Amelia, 'Man gets Stuck inside Statue of Vagina in Germany', BBC News, 23 June 2014.

Cannon, Alda, and Frank Anderson Trapp, eds. and trans., 'Castagnary's "A Plea for a Dead Friend" (1882): Gustave Courbet and the Destruction of the Vendôme Column', *The Massachusetts Review*, Vol 12, No 3, Summer 1971, pp. 498–512.

Cascone, Sarah, '"I Didn't Want Her to Carry the Weight": How Wangechi Mutu's African-Inspired Caryatids on the Met's Façade

BIBLIOGRAPHY

Break Free of Tradition', news.artnet.com, 30 September 2019 (accessed 7 September 2025).

Centeno, Miguel Angel, 'War and Memories: Symbols of State Nationalism in Latin America', *European Review of Latin American and Caribbean Studies*, Vol 66, June 1999, pp. 75–105.

Centuori, Jeanine, 'The Residual Landscape of Kent State, May 4th, 1970', *Landscape Journal*, Vol 18, Issue 1, March 1999, pp. 1–10.

Chaniotis, Angelos, 'The Life of Statues of Gods in the Greek World', *Kernos: Revue Internationale et Pluridisciplinaire de Religion Grecque Antique*, Vol 30, 2017, pp. 91–112.

Chesterton, G. K., *The Thing* (London: Sheed and Ward, 1946).

Cialdini, Robert B., et al., 'Basking in Reflected Glory: Three (Football) Field Studies', *Journal of Personality and Social Psychology*, Vol 34, No 3, 1976, pp. 366–75.

Connolly, Kate, 'Soviet Theme Park to House Fallen Idols', *The Guardian*, 6 December 1999 (accessed 18 May 2025).

Corso, Antonio, 'Love as Suffering: The Eros of Thespiae of Praxiteles', *Bulletin of the Institute of Classical Studies*, Vol 42, 1997–98, pp. 63–91.

Crampton, Andrew, 'The Voortrekker Monument, the Birth of Apartheid, and Beyond', *Political Geography*, Vol 20, Issue 2, February 2001, pp. 221–46.

Crellin, Amy, and Melissa Kirkpatrick, 'Contextualising Colston: A Case Study for the Reconfiguration of Contested Heritage through the Composite Medium of Historic and Contemporary Values', *field*, Vol 8, Issue 1, 2022, pp. 187–94.

Dąbrowska, Dagmara, 'Equestrian Statue of Marcus Aurelius as a Starting Point for the Creation of the Monument of Prince Józef Poniatowski', in *Novensia 31*, ed. Piotra Dyczka (Warsaw: Uniwersytet Warszawski, 2022), pp. 149–62.

Danner, Marcel, 'The Man Who Outstrips All Others: Trajan's Column and Senatorial Remembrance Culture', *Babesch*, Vol 98, 2023, pp. 75–99.

Dasen, Véronique, 'Blessing or Portent? Multiple Births in Ancient Rome', in *Hoping for Continuity. Childhood, Education and Death in Antiquity and the Middle Ages*, eds. K Mustakallio, J Hanska, H-L Sainio and V Vuolanto (Rome: Acta Instituti Romani Finlandiae XXXIII, 2005), pp. 72–83.

BIBLIOGRAPHY

Daveloose, Alexis, 'A Roman Matron as Figure of Memory: Social Memory and Cornelia, Mother of the Gracchi', *Historia—Zeitschrift für alte Geshichte*, Vol 72, Issue 4, 2023, pp. 444–468.

Davies, Penelope J. E., 'The Politics of Perpetuation: Trajan's Column and the Art of Commemoration', *American Journal of Archaeology*, Vol 101, No 1, January 1997, pp. 41–65.

Delbeke, 'The Pope, the Bust, the Sculptor, and the Fly', *Bulletin de l'Institut Historique Belge de Rome*, Vol 70, 2000, pp. 179–223.

Derrida, Jacques, *La Vérité en Peinture* (Paris: Flammarion, 1978).

Devriendt, Tom, 'Cinema of Disquiet', africasacountry.com, 3 March 2014 (accessed 27 November 2024).

Dickenson, Christopher, 'Public Statues as a Strategy of Remembering in Early Imperial Messene', in *Strategies of Remembering in Greece Under Rome (100 BC–100 AD)*, ed. Tamara M. Dijkstra, Inger N. I. Kuin, Muriel Moser and David Weidgenannt (Leiden: Sidestone Press, 2017), pp. 125–42.

———, 'Statues and Public Space: An Introduction', in *Public Statues Across Time and Cultures*, ed. Christopher P. Dickenson (New York: Routledge, 2021), pp. 1–31.

Dixon, Carol Ann, 'Reflections on the Legacies of "Statues Also Die" (Présence Africaine, 1953) re. the Museums Sector in France Today', museumgeographies.com, 27 August 2014 (accessed 26 November 2024).

Dombrowski, Damian, 'Apotheosis and Mediality in Bernini's Later Portrait Busts', *Artibus et Historiae*, Vol 32, No 63, 2011, pp. 165–99.

Donohoe, Amy, 'Busker Launches "Leave Molly mAlone" Campaign to End Groping "Tradition"', *Irish Independent*, 28 February 2024 (accessed 15 April 2025).

Dresser, Madge, 'Set in Stone? Statues and Slavery in London', *History Workshop Journal*, No 64, Autumn 2007, pp. 162–99.

Duggan, T. M. P., 'Diplomatic Shock and Awe: Moving, Sometimes Speaking, Islamic Sculptures', *Al-Masaq*, Vol 21, No 3, 2009, pp. 229–267.

Dutton, Kenneth, *The Perfectible Body: The Western Ideal of Male Physical Development* (New York: Continuum, 1995).

Dwyer, Owen J., 'Location, Politics and the Production of Civil Rights Memorial Landscapes', *Urban Geography*, Vol 23, Issue 1, 2002, pp. 31–56.

BIBLIOGRAPHY

Edensor, Tim, 'The Haunting Presence of Commemorative Statues', *Ephemera*, Vol 19, No 1, 2019, pp. 53–76.

Edwardes, Charlotte, 'Lord Heseltine Talks Gardens, Politics and his Mother's Dog Kim', *Tatler*, 1 November 2016.

Egan, Casey, 'Crowds Still Flock to "Moving" Virgin Mary Statue at Ballinspittle, Three Decades On', IrishCentral, 23 July 2015 (accessed 3 January 2025).

Emelyanova-Griva, Maria, 'La Tombe de Victor Noir au Cimetière du Père-Lachaise', *Archives de Sciences Sociales des Religions*, Vol 149, Issue 1, 2010, pp. 89–108.

Erőss, Ágnes, 'Living Memorial and Frozen Monuments: The Role of Social Practice in Memorial Sites', *Urban Development Issues*, Vol 55, 2018, pp. 19–32.

Faraone, Christopher A., 'Hephaestus the Magician and Near Eastern Parallels for Alcinous' Watchdogs', *Greek, Roman and Byzantine Studies*, Vol 28, No 3, 1987, pp. 257–80.

Farquhar, Stephen, 'And Bardot Created Búzios', *The Guardian*, 25 September 2004 (accessed 12 May 2025).

Flory, Marleen B, 'Livia and the History of Public Honorific Statues for Women in Rome', *Transactions of the American Philological Association*, Vol 123, 1993, pp. 287–308.

Forest, Benjamin, and Juliet Johnson, 'Unraveling the Threads of History: Soviet-Era Monuments and Post-Soviet National Identity in Moscow', *Annals of the Association of American Geographers*, Vol 92, Issue 3, 2002, pp. 524–47.

Fox, Carl, 'Down with This Sort of Thing: Why No Public Statue Should Stand Forever', *Critical Review of International Social and Political Philosophy*, Vol 26, Issue 4, Hune 2023, pp. 1–22.

Frankel, Eddy, 'Now Even Worse: Ridiculed Bust of Cristiano Ronaldo Gets a Dreadful Do-Over', *The Guardian*, 3 April 2018 (accessed 30 May 2025).

Fraser, Virginia, 'A Splendid Country Garden Built from Scratch by Michael and Anne Heseltine', *House and Garden*, 3 January 2022.

Freedman, William, 'Postponement and Perspectives in Shelley's "Ozymandias"', *Studies in Romanticism*, Vol 25, No 1, Spring 1986, pp. 63–73.

Frowe, Helen, 'The Duty to Remove Statues of Wrongdoers', *Journal of Practical Ethics*, Vol 7, Issue 3, 2019, pp. 1–31.

BIBLIOGRAPHY

Gabowitsch, Mischa, 'What Has Happened to Soviet War Memorials Since 1989/91', politika.io, 1 September 2021 (accessed 5 April 2025).

Garnett, Anna, *The Colossal Statue of Ramesses II* (London: The British Museum Press, 2015).

Getsy, David J., 'Acts of Stillness: Statues, Performativity and Passive Resistance', *Criticism*, Vol 56, No 1, Winter 2014, pp. 1–20.

Giuffrida, Angela, 'Unlucky in Love: Statue of Shakespeare's Juliet in Verona Damaged by Tourists', *The Guardian*, 7 March 2024.

Golańska, Dorota, 'The Invisible and the "Matter" of Memory: A New Materialist Approach to Countermonumental Aesthetics', *The Polish Journal of Aesthetics*, Vol 47, Issue 4, 2017, pp. 93–107.

Gottskálksdóttir, Júlíana, 'Monuments to Settlers of the North: A Means to Strengthen National Identity', in *Iceland and Images of the North*, ed. Sumarliði R. Ísleifsson (Presses de l'Université du Québec, 2011), pp. 205–227.

Gozzi, Laura, 'Lewd Tourist Antics on Florence Statue Lead to Outrage', bbc.com, 17 July 2024 (accessed 7 January 2025).

Gregoratti, Leonardo, 'Epigraphy of Later Parthia', *Voprosy Epigrafiki: Sbornik Statei*, Vol 7, 2013, pp. 276–84.

Groof, Matthias de, 'Statues Also Die—But Their Death is not the Final Word', *Image and Narrative*, Vol 11, No 1, 2010, pp. 29–46.

Gunther, York H., and Sumetanee Bagna-Dulyachinda, 'From Realism to Idealism: Ancient Greek Sculpture in the Classical Period', *Literature and Aesthetics*, Vol 29, No 2, 2019, pp. 159–83.

Gutzwiller, Kathryn, 'Gender and Inscribed Epigram: Herennia Procula and the Thespian Eros', *Transactions of the American Philological Association (1974–2014)*, Vol 134, No 2, Autumn 2004, pp. 383–418.

Hagen, Maren Kvamme, 'The Hidden Stonemasons', nrk.no, 19 July 2022 (accessed 8 February 2025).

Hajjaji, Danya, 'Man Arrested After Hammer Attack on Eric Gill's Statue at BBC's Broadcasting House', *The Guardian*, 20 May 2023 (accessed 13 July 2025).

Halbwachs, Maurice, *On Collective Memory*, trans. Lewis A. Coser (Chicago: The University of Chicago Press, 1992).

Harris, Gareth, 'BBC Unveils Restored Sculpture by Artist and Sexual Abuser Eric Gill', *The Art Newspaper*, 9 April 2025 (accessed 13 July 2025).

Harrison, Carol E., 'Edouard Laboulaye, Liberal and Romantic Catholic',

BIBLIOGRAPHY

in *French History and Civilisation, Vol. 4: Papers from the George Rudé Seminar*, eds. Briony Neilson and Robert Aldrich (Charleston: H-France, 2011), pp. 149–58.

Hartley-Parkinson, Richard, 'Man Gets Stuck in a Vagina: Student Brings New Meaning to the Phrase "Born Again"', *Irish Mirror*, 23 June 2014.

———, 'Plans for Margaret Thatcher Statue to be Rejected Because of "Monument Saturation"', metro.co.uk, 19 January 2018 (accessed 5 October 2024).

Hartog, François, 'Temps et histoire. Comment écrire l'histoire de France?', *Annales-Histoire Sciences Sociales*, No 6, 1995, pp. 1219–1236

Hemelrijk, Emily, 'Octavian and the Introduction of Public Statues for Women in Rome', *Athenaeum*, Vol 93, Issue 1, 2005, pp. 309–17.

Henderson, John, 'Myth Embedded in Culture: The Murals of Thorvaldsen's Museum, Copenhagen', in *Myth and Symbol II: Symbolic Phenomena in Ancient Greek Culture*, ed. Synnøve des Bouvrie (Athens: The Norwegian Institute at Athens, 2004), pp. 81–110.

Hensbergen, Claudine van, 'Plan to "Retain and Explain" Controversial Statues is Flawed—Why we Should Always Question our Monuments', theconversation.com, 19 October 2023 (accessed 4 May 2025).

Hobbs, Angela H., 'In Memoriam: The Who, How, Where and When of Statues', *Journal of Philosophy of Education*, Vol 55, No 3, June 2021, pp. 430–38.

Hodne, Lasse, 'Winckelmann's Depreciation of Colour in Light of the Querelle du coloris and Recent Critique', *Konsthistorisk Tidskrift*, Vol 89, No 3, 2020, pp. 191–210.

Holliday, Peter J., 'Time, History, and Ritual on the Ara Pacis Augustae', *The Art Bulletin*, Vol 72, No 4, December 1990, pp. 542–57.

Hollinshead, Mary B., 'Extending the Reach of Marble: Struts in Greek and Roman Sculpture', *Memoirs of the American Academy in Rome. Supplementary Volumes*, Vol 1, 2002, pp. 117–52.

Hopkins, Robert, 'Painting, Sculpture, Sight and Touch', *British Journal of Aesthetics*, Vol 44, 2004, pp. 149–66.

Hughes, Jessica, 'Fractured Narratives: Writing the Biography of a Votive Offering' in *Ex Voto: Votive Giving Across Cultures*, ed. Ittai Weinryb (New York: Bard Graduate Center, 2016), pp. 23–48.

Hughes, Peter, *A History of Love and Hate in 21 Statues* (London: Aurum, 2021).

BIBLIOGRAPHY

Hurst, Cameron, 'Sculptor, Best Known for "Scary Lucy" Statue, Remembered by Community as More Than Artist Following Death at 59', *Adirondack Daily Enterprise*, 25 June 2020 (accessed 31 May 2025).

Hustvedt, Siri, 'Tear Them Down: Old Statues, Bad Science and Ideas That Just Won't Die', *Amerikastudien/American Studies*, Vol 66, Issue 1, 2021, pp. 37–45.

Huyssen, Andreas, 'Monumental Seduction', *New German Critique*, No 69, Richard Wagner, Autumn 1996, pp. 181–200.

———, *Present Pasts: Urban Palimpsests and the Politics of Memory* (Stanford: Stanford University Press, 2003).

Ignatieff, Michael, 'Soviet War Memorials', *History Workshop Journal*, Vol 17, Issue 1, Spring 1984, pp. 157–63.

Jackson, Liz, 'Windrush: Charity Loses Trademark Dispute with Government', BBC News, 4 February 2024.

Jacobson, Stephen, 'Interpreting Municipal Celebrations of Nation and Empire: The Barcelona Universal Exhibition of 1888', in *Nationalism and the Reshaping of Urban Communities in Europe, 1848–1914*, eds. William Whyte and Oliver Zimmer (London: Palgrave Macmillan, 2011), pp. 74–109.

James, Beverly A., *Imagining Postcommunism: Visual Narratives of Hungary's 1956 Revolution* (College Station: Texas A&M University Press, 2005).

Jeffrey, Robin, 'What the Statues Tell: The Politics of Choosing Symbols in Trivandrum', *Pacific Affairs*, Vol 53, No 3, Autumn 1980, pp. 484–502.

Jenkins, Ian, *The Discobolus* (London: The British Museum Press, 2012).

Jenrick, Robert, 18 January 2021, questions-statements.parliament.uk (accessed 4 May 2025).

Jensen, Robin M., 'Spitting on Statues and Shaving Hercules's Beard: The Conflict Over Images (and Idols) in Early Christianity', in *Memories of Utopia: The Revision of Histories and Landscapes in Late Antiquity*, eds. Bronwen Neil and Kosta Simic (London: Routledge, 2019).

Jensen, Uwe Max, 'Liggende Lenin og den aktuelle statue-storm', *Herning Folkeblad*, 8 July 2020.

Jones, Jennifer, 'Brechin a Promise as Ardrossan Snubbed Over Wallace Freedom Statue', *Ardrossan and Saltcoats Herald*, 6 September 2021.

Jones, Jonathan, 'Why We're Still Up in Arms about the Mystery of the Venus de Milo', *The Guardian*, 11 May 2015 (accessed 26 May 2025).

BIBLIOGRAPHY

———, 'So Many Causes, So Many Heroes—Why Defame Them with a Statue?', *The Guardian*, 11 May 2016 (accessed 11 May 2025).

Joseph, Rebecca M., with Brooke Rosenblatt and Carolyn Kinebrew, *The Black Statue of Liberty Rumor: An Inquiry into the History and Meaning of Bartholdi's Liberté éclairant le Monde* (Boston: National Park Service, 2000).

Kästner, Erich, *Emil and the Detectives* (London: Vintage Books, 2012 edition).

Kellum, Barbara A., 'What We See and What We Don't See. Narrative Structure and the Ara Pacis Augustae', *Art History*, Vol 17, No 1, March 1994, pp. 26–45.

Ķeniņš, Laura, 'For Fatherland, Freedom and Mother Russia: The Rīga Freedom Monument as Site and Symbol of Resistance in Soviet Latvia' (Unpublished MA Thesis: Central European University, Budapest, 2012).

Keyte, Suzanne, 'The British-American Peace Centenary Ball—10 June 1914', royalalberthall.com, 10 June 2014.

Khan, Yasmin Sabina, *Enlightening the World: The Creation of the Statue of Liberty* (Ithaca, NY: Cornell University Press, 2010).

Kiilerich, Bente, 'Towards a "Polychrome History" of Greek and Roman Sculpture', *Journal of Art Historiography*, No 15, December 2016, pp. 1–18.

King, Ross, *The Judgement of Paris* (New York: Walker and Co., 2006).

Kirby, Jen, 'Artist Has a Pretty Good sense of Humour about Student Getting Caught in Vagina Sculpture', nymag.com, 24 June 2014.

Koerner, Joseph Leo, 'On Monuments', in *Res: Anthropology and Aesthetics*, Vol 67–8, Issue 1, 2016/17, pp. 5–20.

Kofoed, Kira, *Thorvaldsen: Bertel Thorvaldsen (1770–1844)* (Copenhagen: Thorvaldsen's Museum, n.d.).

Kondratieff, Eric, 'The Column and Coinage of C. Duilius: Innovations in Iconography in Large and Small Media in the Middle Republic', *Scripta Classica Israelica*, Vol 23, 2004, pp. 1–39.

Korkis, Jim, 'The History of the Partners Statue', mouseplanet.com, 26 October 2011 and 2 November 2011.

Kovel, Joel, 'Poetry after the Holocaust', *Dialectical Anthropology*, Vol 24, No 3/4, December 1999, pp. 239–53.

Kowalska, Magdalena, 'The Column in Place Vendôme and the Fleeting

BIBLIOGRAPHY

Form of Ancient Rome in the Writings of Cyprian Norwid', *Studia Norwidiana*, Vol 38, 2020, pp. 107–31.

Kralj, Ivan, 'Statue Rubbing: Good Luck or Bad Taste?', pipeaway.com, 13 March 2023 (accessed 27 March 2025).

Kruger, Cecilia, and Marié van Heerden, 'The Voortrekker Monument Heritage Site: A New Statement of Significance', *Historia*, Vol 50, No 2, November 2005, pp. 237–60.

Kruk, Sergei, 'The Mass: A Neglected Plastic Sign of Sculpture', *Punctum*, Vol 5, No 2, 2019, pp. 91–118.

Krūmiņa-Koņkova, Solveiga, 'Places of Memory: Holocaust Memorials in Vidzeme and their Symbolic Language', *Yearbook of Balkan and Baltic Studies*, Vol 4, December 2021, pp. 13–36.

Ladd, Brian, *The Ghosts of Berlin: Confronting German History in the Urban Landscape* (Chicago: University of Chicago Press, 1997).

Lanzi, Fernando and Gioia, *Saints and Their Symbols: Recognizing Saints in Art and in Popular Images*, trans. Matthew J. O'Connell (Collegeville, Minnesota: Order of Saint Benedict, 2004).

Layton, Julia H., 'Marble and Bronze', *Cosmopolitan Art Journal*, Vol 4, No 4, December 1860, p. 141.

Liu, Xiangyu and Xinyi Huang, 'Gold, Skin, and Body: Chinese Buddha Statues are Constantly Being Shaped and Stripped', *Religions*, Vol 14, 155, 2023, pp. 1–19.

Liverani, Paolo, 'La Polychromie de la Statue d'Auguste de Prima Porta', *Revue Archéologique*, Nouvelle Série, Fasc. 1, 2005, pp. 193–7.

Loizidou, Chrystalleni, 'On the Liberty Monument of Nicosia', in *Reenvisioning Cyprus*, eds. Peter Loizos, Nicos Philippou and Theopisti Stylianou-Lambert (Nicosia: University of Nicosia Press, 2010), pp. 89–102.

Luik, Riina, 'Why President Meri Held Press Conference in Airport Toilet', *Postimees*, 30 October 2015.

Lupu, Noam, 'Memory Vanished, Absent, and Confined: The Counter-memorial Project in 1980s and 1990s Germany', *History and Memory*, Vol 15, No 2, Fall/Winter 2003, pp. 130–64.

Malgrati, Paul, 'Into the Cold War: Checkpoint Rabbie (1948–1959)' in *Robert Burns and Scottish Cultural Politics: The Bard of Contention (1914–2014)*, ed. Paul Malgrati (Edinburgh: Edinburgh University Press, 2023), pp. 131–50.

BIBLIOGRAPHY

Marcuse, Harold, 'Holocaust Memorials: The Emergence of a Genre', *American Historical Review*, Vol 115, No 1, February 2010, pp. 53–89.

Marling, Karal Ann, and Robert Silberman, 'The Statue Near the Wall: The Vietnam Veterans Memorial and the Art of Remembering', *Smithsonian Studies in American Art*, Vol 1, No 1, Spring 1987, pp. 4–29.

Marshall, Peter, 'Papist as Heretic: The Burning of John Forest, 1538', *The Historical Journal*, Vol 41, Issue 2, June 1998, pp. 351–74.

Martin, Freya, 'The Importance of Honorific Statues: A Case-Study', *Bulletin of the Institute of Classical Studies*, Vol 41, 1996, pp. 53–70.

Mason, Paul, 'Abe Lincoln and the 'Sublime Heroism' of British Workers', bbc.com, 17 Jan 2013.

Masters, Christopher, 'David Wynne Obituary', *The Guardian*, 23 September 2014 (accessed 2 February 2023).

Mauss, Marcel, *The Gift: Forms and Functions of Exchange in Archaic Societies*, trans. Ian Cunnison (London: Cohen and West, 1966).

Mawdsley, Emma, 'The Changing Geographies of Foreign Aid and Development Cooperation: Contributions from Gift Theory', *Transactions of the Institute of British Geographers*, New Series, Vol 37, No 12, 2012, pp. 256–72.

McDonald, Gillian, 'Why Glasgow's Duke of Wellington Statue was Allowed to Keep his Cone', inews.co.uk, 16 March 2017.

McGarr, Paul M., '"The Viceroys are Disappearing from the Roundabouts in Delhi": British Symbols of Power in Post-Colonial India', *Modern Asian Studies*, Vol 49, No 3, May 2015, pp. 787–831.

McGuire, Caroline, 'For Art Lovers with a Sense of Adventure! The Sculpture Museum off the Coast of Crimea that's UNDERWATER', dailymail.co.uk, 22 January 2016 (accessed 18 May 2025).

Meilak, Daniel, 'David Versus Goliath and the Apotheosis of Malta: Romanticising the Siege of Malta During the Rise of Nationalism (1860–1939)', *Melita Historica*, Vol 17, No 1, 2019, pp. 140–72.

Mezulanik, Eleni, 'UK Government Prevails in Trademark Dispute Against Windrush Foundation', *The Trademark Lawyer*, 15 February 2024.

Millar, Paul, 'Poems to Statues: Robert Burns, Henry Lawson, James K. Baxter, and the Matter of Memorials', *Journal of New Zealand Literature*, No 30, 2012, pp. 132–149.

Miss, Stig, *Director's Choice: Thorvaldsens Museum* (London: Scala, 2016).

BIBLIOGRAPHY

Mitchell, Andrew, 'A Wild Goat Crowns the Source of the River Rede, northumberlandnationalpark.org.uk, 17 March 2023 (accessed 27 September 2024).

Mitchell, Katharyne, 'Monuments, Memorials, and the Politics of Memory', *Urban Geography*, Vol 24, No 5, 2003, pp. 442–59.

Mock, Steven J., *Symbols of Defeat in the Construction of National Identity* (Cambridge: Cambridge University Press, 2012).

Montaño, Eugenia Allier, trans. Christine Walsh, 'Places of Memory. Is the Concept Applicable to the Analysis of Memorial Struggles? The Case of Uruguay and its Recent Past', *Cuadernos del CLAEH*, Vol 4, 2008, pp. 1–26.

Montgomery, Nancy, 'Tradition of Touching Juliet Statue's Breast for Luck Now Cause for Rebuke', stripes.com, 22 February 2018 (accessed 17 April 2025).

Moravánsky, Ákos, 'Peter Meyer and the Swiss Discourse on Monumentality', *Future Anterior: Journal of Historic Preservation, History, Theory and Criticism*, Vol 8, No 1, Summer 2011, pp. 1–20.

Mulholland, Peter, 'Moving Statues and Concrete Thinking', *Quaderns de l'Institut Català d'Antropologia*, sèrie monogràfics 23, 2008, pp. 159–79.

Mumford, Lewis, 'The Death of the Monument', in *CIRCLE*, eds. J. L. Martin, B. Nicholson and N. Gabo (1937, reprint New York: Praeger, 1971), pp. 263–70.

Murphy, Kim, 'His Former Kingdom for a Parking Spot', *Los Angeles Times*, 13 July 2004 (accessed 22 June 2025).

Musil, Robert, trans. Peter Wortsman, 'Monuments', in *Posthumous Papers of a Living Author* (Hygiene, Colorado: Eridanos Press, 1987).

Naguip, Nefissa, and Iselin Åsedotter Strønen, 'Simón Bolívar—A Man of War and a Symbol of Freedom', Chr. Michelsen Institute, cmi.no, 27 March 2014 (accessed 31 May 2025).

Nasar, Saima, 'Remembering Edward Colston: Histories of Slavery, Memory and Black Globality', *Women's History Review*, Vol 29, No 7, 2020, pp. 1218–25.

Nascimento, Edmilson, 'Concurso Miss Boneca Gigante de Olinda', avaidosa.com.br, 7 July 2019 (accessed 15 June 2025).

Németh, György, 'Love of Statues', in *Történeti Tanulmányok VI—Hungarian Polis Studies 2, Studia in Honorem Johannis Sarkady Septuagenarii* (Debrecen: KLTE, 1997), pp. 115–40.

BIBLIOGRAPHY

Nicholson, Kate, 'People Think the New Windrush Monument Still Misses the Mark', huffingtonpost.co.uk, 22 June 2022.

Nikolov, Nikolay, 'This City Has No Monuments to Women so an Artist Did a Colourful Shake-Up', mashable.com, 24 March 2017 (accessed 11 May 2025).

Nora, Pierre, 'Between Memory and History: Les Lieux de Mémoire', *Representations*, No 26, Special Issue: Memory and Counter-Memory, Spring 1989, pp. 7–24.

Ochser, Tim, 'Controversial Monument Millionaire Reveals Future Plans', baltictimes.com, 27 September 2001 (accessed 22 June 2025).

Olusoga, David, 'The Toppling of Edward Colston's Statue is not an Attack on History. It is History', *The Guardian*, 8 June 2020 (accessed 23 December 2024).

Omissi, Adrastos, 'Damnatio Memoriae or Creatio Memoriae? Memory Sanctions as Creative Processes in the Fourth Century AD', *The Cambridge Classical Journal*, Vol 62, 2016, pp. 170–99.

Opper, Thorsten, *The Meroë Head of Augustus* (London: The British Museum Press, 2014).

Osborne, Brian S., 'Constructing Landscapes of Power: the George Etienne Cartier Monument, Montreal', *Journal of Historical Geography*, Vol 24, Issue 4, 1998, pp. 431–58.

Palmer, Scott W., 'How Memory Was Made: The Construction of the Memorial to the Heroes of the Battle of Stalingrad', *The Russian Review*, Vol 68, No 3, July 2009, pp. 373–407.

Panzanelli, Roberta, 'Introduction: Beyond the Pale: Polychromy and Western Art', in *The Colour of Life: Polychromy in Sculpture from Antiquity to the Present*, ed. Roberta Panzanelli with Eike D. Schmidt and Kenneth Lapatin (Los Angeles: Getty Publications, 2008), pp. 2–17.

Paredes, Claudia Cendales, 'The Role of Memorial Monuments in the Formation of Cultural Identity in Latin American Countries', in *The Challenge of the Object/Die Herausforderung des Objeks/CIHA Congress Proceedings—Part 2*, eds. G. Ulrich Großmann and Petra Krutisch (Nürnberg: Verlag des Germanischen Nationalmuseums, 2013), pp. 454–57.

Partridge, Damani J., 'Holocaust Mahnmal (Memorial): Monumental Memory Amidst Contemporary Race', *Contemporary Studies in Society and History*, Vol 52, Issue 4, 2010, pp. 820–50.

BIBLIOGRAPHY

Pastana, Mariana, 'A Epopeia Eternizada em Bronze: O Monumento aos Heróis de Laguna e Dourados', *Temporalidades—Revista de História*, Edição 32, Vol 12, No 1, Jan/Apr 2020, pp. 28–50.

Paz, Carolina Rodriguez, 'Myron's Discobolus—the Tension Between Artistic Idealism and Athletic Pragmatism', medium.com, 8 September 2023 (accessed 26 May 2025).

Peng, Shiliu, 'Spitalfields Gets its Goat After Public Vote', eastlondonlines.co.uk, 21 January 2011 (accessed 27 September 2024).

Pesarini, Angelica, and Carla Panico, 'From Colston to Montanelli: Public Memory and Counter-Monuments in the Era of Black Lives Matter', *From the European South*, Vol 9, 2021, pp. 99–113.

Peters, Gus, 'St Pete's Lucky Bird Statue: Chizhik-Pyzhik', The Moscow Times, 24 August 2014 (accessed 18 November 2024).

Petterson, Anne, 'The Monumental Landscape from Below: Public Statues, Popular Interaction and Nationalism in Late Nineteenth-Century Amsterdam', *Urban History*, Vol 46, Issue 4, 2019, pp. 722–746.

Pierre, Caterina Y., 'The Pleasure and Piety of Touch in Aimé-Jules Dalou's Tomb of Victor Noir', *Sculpture Journal*, Vol 19, No 2, 2010, pp. 173–85.

Pinch, Geraldine, and Elizabeth A. Waraska, 'Votive Practices', in *UCLA Encyclopedia of Egyptology*, eds. Willeke Wendrich, Jacco Dieleman, Elizabeth Frood and John Baines (Los Angeles: UCLA, 2009), pp. 1–9.

Pittock, Murray, 'Introduction: Global Burns', in *Robert Burns in Global Culture*, ed. Murray Pittock (Plymouth: Bucknell University Press, 2011), pp. 13–24.

Pliny the Elder, *The Natural History*, Book 34, Chapter 17, trans. John Bostock, Perseus Digital Library, perseus.tufts.edu (accessed 12 May 2025).

Post, Chris W., 'Beyond Kent State? May 4 and Commemorating Violence in Public Space', *Geoforum*, Vol 76, Nov 2016, pp. 142–52.

Potts, Alex, 'Installation and Sculpture', Oxford Art Journal, Vol 24, No 2, 2001, pp. 5–23.

Preda, Daniela, 'Men and Stones: A Landmark in Mircea Eliade's Literary and Religious Work', *European Journal of Science and Theology*, Vol 15, No 6, December 2019, pp. 39–48.

Price, Campbell, 'Ramesses, "King of Kings": On the Context and

BIBLIOGRAPHY

Interpretation of Royal Colossi', in *Ramesside Studies in Honour of K. A. Kitchen*, eds. S. Snape and M. Collier (Bolton: Rutherford Press, 2011), pp. 403–11.

Prusac, Marina, 'Mimesis and the Necessity of Destruction: Animism and Evil in Damnatio Memoriae Portraits', in *Image et Droit: Du ius imaginis au droit à l'image*, ed. Naïma Ghermani and Caroline Michel D'Annoville (Rome: Publications de l'École française de Rome, 2022), pp. 253–70.

Ramachandran, V. S., and William Hirstein, 'The Science of Art: A Neurological Theory of Aesthetic Experience', *Journal of Consciousness Studies*, Vol 6, No 6–7, January 1999, pp. 15–51.

Rambelli, Fabio, 'Secret Buddhas: The Limits of Buddhist Representation', *Monumenta Nipponica*, Vol 57, No 3, Autumn 2002, pp. 271–307.

Rausch, Helke, 'The Nation as a Community Born of War? Symbolic Strategies and Popular Reception of Public Statues in Late Nineteenth-Century Western European Capitals', *European Review of History: Revue européenne d'histoire*, Vol 14, No 1, 2007, pp. 73–101.

Redworth, Glyn, *The Prince and the Infanta: The Cultural Politics of the Spanish Match* (New Haven, CT: Yale University Press, 2003).

Rice, Alan, *Creating Memorials, Building Identities: The Politics of Memory in the Black Atlantic* (Liverpool: Liverpool University Press, 2010).

Richmond, H. M., 'Ozymandias and the Travelers', *Keats-Shelley Journal*, Vol 11, Winter 1962, pp. 65–71.

Ridgway, Brunilde Sismondo, 'Stone and Metal in Greek Sculpture', *Archaeology*, Vol 19, No 1, January 1966, pp. 31–42.

———, 'The Setting of Greek Sculpture', *Hesperia*, Vol 40, 1971, pp. 336–56.

Rigney, Ann, 'Toxic Monuments and Mnemonic Regime Change', *Studies on National Movements*, Vol 9, 2022, pp. 7–41.

Robinson, David, *Saving Graces: Images of Women in European Cemeteries* (New York: W. W. Norton, 1995).

Rossi, Benjamin, 'Should We Tear Down the Monuments?', publicethics.org, 13 May 2021 (accessed 12 June 2025).

Roy-Omoni, Sylvester, Victor Onibere and Stephen Osakwe, 'Visualizing Diversity: Analyzing the Evolution of Religious Iconography and Graphic Design in Modern African Art', *Abraka Journal of Religion and Philosophy*, Vol 4, No 2, 2024, pp. 115–26.

BIBLIOGRAPHY

Ryan, Tim, and Jurek Kirakowski, *Ballinspittle: Moving Statues and Faith* (Cork: Mercier Press, 1985).

Ryberg, Inez Scott, 'The Procession of the Ara Pacis', *Memoirs of the American Academy in Rome*, Vol 19, 1949, pp. 79–101.

Sackville-West, Robert, *Inheritance: The Story of Knole and the Sackvilles* (London: Bloomsbury, 2010).

Sagewitz, Marthje, 'Rodin, Vigeland and the Middle Ages: An Antimodern Path Towards Modernity?', *Kunst og Kultur*, Vol 103, Issue 2, 2020, pp. 63–76.

Sartre, Jean-Paul, 'The Quest for the Absolute', in *Jean-Paul Sartre: Essays in Existentialism*, ed. Wade Baskin (New York: Citadel Press, 1965), pp. 388–401.

Savage, Kirk, *Standing Soldiers, Kneeling Slaves: Race, War, and Monument in Nineteenth-Century America* (Princeton: Princeton University Press, 1999).

———, 'The Obsolescence of Sculpture', *American Art*, Vol 24, No 1, Spring 2010, pp. 9–14.

———, 'The Question of Monuments', *Lapham's Quarterly*, laphamsquarterly.org, 13 July 2020 (accessed 1 July 2025).

Schama, Simon, 'History is Better Served by Putting the Men in Stone in Museums', *Financial Times*, 12 June 2020.

Schwartz, Barry, 'Iconography and Collective Memory: Lincoln's Image in the American Mind', *The Sociological Quarterly*, Vol 32, No 3, Autumn 1991, pp. 301–19.

Scott, Katy, 'Duke of Wellington: the Traffic-Coned Glasgow Statue that Inspired Banksy', bbc.com, 15 June 2023.

Sert, Josep Lluís, Fernand Léger and Sigfried Giedion, *Nine Points on Monumentality*, 1943.

Sherwood, Harriet, 'Westminster Council Turns Away Homeless Jesus', *The Guardian*, 25 April 2016.

Shurtleff, Nathaniel Bradstreet, *Memorial of the Inauguration of the Statue of Franklin* (Boston: Boston City Council, 1857).

Silva, Felipe Gustavo Soares da, 'O Misticismo do Bloco Carnavalesco Homem da Meia Noite', *Revista Missioneira, Santo Ângelo*, Vol 20, No 1, January/June 2018, pp. 43–56.

Sirén, Osvald, 'The Importance of the Antique to Donatello', *American Journal of Archaeology*, Vol 18, No 4, 1914, pp. 438–61.

BIBLIOGRAPHY

Skaftun, Emily C., 'A Tale of Two Vigelands', norwegianamerican.com, 22 January 2018 (accessed 9 February 2025).

Smith, Kevin C., 'Victor Hugo and the Vendôme Column: "Ce Fut de Début de la Rupture…"', *French Forum*, Vol 21, No 2, May 1996, pp. 149–64.

Smith, Laurajane, *Uses of Heritage* (London: Routledge, 2006).

Sniter, Christel, 'La Gloire des Femmes Célèbres. Métamorphoses et Disparités de la Statuaire Publique Parisienne de 1870 à nos Jours', *Sociétés et Représentations*, No 26, November 2008, pp. 153–70.

Söderlind, Solfrid, 'Introduction: Bernadotte Reconsidered', in *Scripts of Kingship: Essays on Bernadotte and Dynastic Formation in an Age of Revolution*, eds. Mikael Alm and Britt-Inger Johansson (Uppsala: Swedish Science Press, 2008), pp. 7–22.

Sommerlad, Joe, 'Braveheart Statue Unveiled in Scotland Branded "Worst Since Ronaldo"', *Independent*, 6 September 2021.

Spaeth Jr., John W., 'Martial and the Pasquinade', *Transactions and Proceedings of the American Philological Association*, Vol 70, 1939, pp. 242–55.

Spivey, Nigel, *How Art Made the World*, episode 1, 'More Human than Human', BBC One, broadcast 26 June 2005.

Stevens, Quentin, 'Vague Recollections: Obscurity and Uncertainty in Contemporary Public Memorials', in *Terrain Vague: Interstices at the Edge of the Pale*, eds. Patrick Barron and Manuela Mariani (London: Routledge, 2013), pp. 182–95.

Stevens, Quentin, Karen A. Franck and Ruth Fazakerley, 'Counter-Monuments: The Anti-Monumental and the Dialogic', *The Journal of Architecture*, Vol 17, No 6, 2012, pp. 951–72.

Stewart, Peter, *Statues in Roman Society* (Oxford: Oxford University Press, 2003).

Stilwell, Blake, 'Why George Washington's Statue in London Doesn't Touch British Soil', military.com, 10 November 2020.

Stocking, Charles Heiko, 'Greek Ideal as Hyperreal: Greco-Roman Sculpture and the Athletic Male Body', *Arion: A Journal of Humanities and the Classics*, Vol 21, No 3, Winter 2014, pp. 45–74.

Straten, F. T. van, 'Gifts for the Gods', in *Faith, Hope and Worship: Aspects of Religious Mentality in the Ancient World*, ed. Henk Versnel (Leiden: Brill, 1981), pp. 65–151.

BIBLIOGRAPHY

Stride, Chris, John P. Wilson and Ffion Thomas, 'Honouring Heroes by Branding in Bronze: Theorizing the UK's Football Statuary', *Sport in Society*, 2013, pp. 1–23.

———, 'From Pitch to Plinth: Documenting the UK's Football Statuary', *Sculptural Journal*, Vol 22, No 1, August 2013A, pp. 146–61.

Stubblefield, Thomas, 'Do Disappearing Monuments Simply Disappear? The Counter-Monument in Revision', *Future Anterior*, Vol 8, No 2, Winter 2011, pp. 1–11.

Sturken, Marita, 'The Wall, the Screen, and the Image: The Vietnam Veterans Memorial', *Representations*, No 35, Special Issue: Monumental Histories, pp. 118–42.

Suggett, Richard, 'Festivals and Social Structure in Early Modern Wales', *Past and Present*, No 152, August 1996, pp. 79–112.

Sullivan, Rory, 'Man Dies Inside Dinosaur Statue after Trying to Retrieve Mobile Phone', *Independent*, 24 May 2021.

Sumartojo, Shanti, 'The Fourth Plinth: Creating and Contesting National Identity in Trafalgar Square, 2005–2010', *Cultural Geographies*, Vol 20, No 1, January 2013, pp. 67–81.

Teulié, Gilles, '"When Cecil Rhodes' Colossal Statue Has a Foot in Cape Town and the Other in Oxford": Post-Truth Political Reactions to Contested British Imperial Monuments', *Représentations dans le Monde Anglophone: The Unbearable Precariousness of Place and Truth*, Vol 28, 2024.

Theodórsdóttir, Emma, 'Entangled Duality of a Viking Statue: Thórfinnur Karlsefni', theaftermonument.com, n.d. (accessed 13 October 2024).

Thomas, Ffion, and Chris Stride, 'The Thierry Henry Statue: A Hollow Icon', *Leisure Studies*, 2013, pp. 1–20.

Tilburg, Kees van, 'Equestrian Statues, an Inventory', equestrianstatue.org, May 2021 (accessed 1 May 2025).

Tobin, Richard, 'The Canon of Polykleitos', *American Journal of Archaeology*, Vol 79, No 4, October 1975, pp. 307–21.

Todd, Stephanie, 'Council in Road Cone Statue Plea', BBC News, 16 February 2005.

Topping, Alexandra, 'First Statue of a Woman in Parliament Square Unveiled', *The Guardian*, 24 April 2018 (accessed 11 May 2025).

Torrington, Arthur, 'Say No to the Government's Windrush Monument at Waterloo Station', windrushfoundation.com, n.d.

BIBLIOGRAPHY

Tunzelmann, Alex von, *Fallen Idols: Twelve Statues That Made History* (London: Headline, 2021).

Valentine, Claire, 'Twitter Reacts to Horrifying Statue of Cristiano Ronaldo', papermag.com, 29 March 2017 (accessed 10 April 2025).

Viano, Francesca Lidia, *Sentinel: The Unlikely Origins of the Statue of Liberty* (Cambridge, MA: Harvard University Press, 2018).

Vilensky, Daniel, 'Statues Also Die, or Schroedinger's Black Cat', *Senses of Cinema*, Issue 64, September 2012, sensesofcinema.com (accessed 27 November 2024).

Vladislavić, Ivan, 'Save the Pedestals', *The Yale Review*, 1 January 2020, yalereview.org (accessed 18 February 2025).

Voss, Angela, 'The Secret Life of Statues', in *Sky and Psyche: The Relationship Between Cosmos and Consciousness*, eds. Nicholas Campion and Patrick M. Curry (Edinburgh: Floris Books, 2006), pp. 201–228.

Walter, Simon, 'Crisis Talks Pledge Over Ted Bates Statue', *Southern Daily Echo*, 19 March 2007 (accessed 13 May 2025).

Wasley, Paula, 'Searching for the True Origins of the Louvre's Winged Victory', *Humanities*, neh.gov, Vol 38, No 3, Summer 2017 (accessed 5 June 2025).

Weinryb, Ittai, 'Introduction: Ex-Voto as Material Culture', in *Ex Voto: Votive Giving Across Cultures*, ed. Ittai Weinryb (New York: Bard Graduate Center, 2016), pp. 1–22.

———, 'Votive Materials: Bodies and Beyond', in *Agents of Faith: Votive Objects in Time and Place*, ed. Ittai Weinryb (New York: Bard Graduate Center Gallery, 2018), pp. 33–59.

Whatley, Christopher A., '"It is Said that Burns was a Radical": Contest, Concession, and the Political Legacy of Robert Burns, ca. 1796–1859', *Journal of British Studies*, Vol 50, No 3, July 2011, pp. 639–666.

———, *Immortal Memory: Burns and the Scottish People* (Edinburgh: John Donald, 2016).

White, Murray J., 'The Statue Syndrome: Perversion? Fantasy? Anecdote?', *The Journal of Sex Research*, Vol 14, No 4, November 1978, pp. 246–9.

Whitling, Frederick, 'Damnatio Memoriae and the Power of Remembrance: Reflections on Memory and History' in *A European Memory? Contested Histories and Politics of Remembrance*, eds. Malgorzata Pakier and Bo Stråth (New York/Oxford: Berghahn Books, 2010), pp. 87–97.

Widén, Per, 'Dynastic Histories: Art Museums in the Service of Charles

BIBLIOGRAPHY

XIV', in *Scripts of Kingship: Essays on Bernadotte and Dynastic Formation in an Age of Revolution*, eds. Mikael Alm and Britt-Inger Johansson (Uppsala: Swedish Science Press, 2008), pp. 79–96.

Widrich, Mechtild, 'The Willed and the Unwilled Monument: Judenplatz Vienna and Riegl's Denkmalpflege', *Journal of the Society of Architectural Historians*, Vol 72, No 3, September 2013, pp. 382–98.

Williams, Paul, 'The Afterlife of Communist Statuary: Hungary's Szoborpark and Lithuania's Grutas Park', *Forum for Modern Language Studies*, Vol 44, No 2, 2008, pp. 185–98.

Wilson, David, 'Gerry Anderson and the Tale of the Hypnotised Hen', BBC News Northern Ireland, bbc.com, 28 September 2022 (accessed 27 March 2025).

Wilson, Nick, Amanda C. Jones, Andrea Teng and George Thomson, 'The Epidemiology of Attacks on Statues: New Zealand as a Case Study', *PLoS ONE*, Vol 16, No 6, 2021, pp. 1–13.

Wong, Dorothy C., 'Colossal Buddha Statues along the Silk Road', *Acta Via Serica*, Vol 4, No 2, December 2019, pp. 1–27.

Wright, David, '"One of Our Own": Statues of Comedians, Popular Culture, and Nostalgia in English Towns', *European Journal of Cultural Studies*, Vol 26, Issue 4, August 2023, pp. 554–71.

Yampolsky, Mikhail, 'In the Shadow of Monuments: Notes on Iconoclasm and Time', trans. John Kachur, in *Soviet Hieroglyphics: Visual Culture in Late Twentieth-Century Russia*, ed. Nancy Condee (Bloomington: Indiana University Press, 1995), pp. 93–112.

Yeats, Christine, 'Should They Stay or Should They Go?: Contested Statues', *Public History Review*, Vol 28, 2021, pp. 1–3.

Yehia, Enas Fares, 'Was "Qasr Al Dubara" Square Suitable for the Statue of the Venezuelan Hero Simon Bolivar?', *Journal of the Association of Arab Universities for Tourism and Hospitality*, Vol 13, Issue 2, December 2016, pp. 23–36.

Young, Cathy, 'Lenin is Still Dead—Or is He?', thebulwark.com, 23 January 2024 (accessed 6 April 2025).

Young, James E., 'The Biography of a Memorial Icon: Nathan Rapoport's Warsaw Ghetto Monument', *Representations*, No 26, Special Issue: Memory and Counter-Memory, Spring 1989, pp. 69–106.

———, 'The Counter-Monument: Memory against Itself in Germany Today', *Critical Inquiry*, Vol 18, No 2, Winter 1992, pp. 267–96.

BIBLIOGRAPHY

———, 'Germany's Memorial Question: Memory, Counter-Memory, and the End of the Monument', *The South Atlantic Quarterly*, Vol 96, No 4, Fall 1997, pp. 853–80.

———, 'Germany's Holocaust Memorial Problem—And Mine', *The Public Historian*, Vol 24, No 4, Fall 2002, pp. 65–80.

Younge, Gary, 'Why Every Single Statue Should Come Down', *The Guardian*, 1 June 2021 (accessed 12 June 2025).

Ziegler, Georgianna, 'Parents, Daughters, and "That Rare Italian Master": A New Source for The Winter's Tale', *Shakespeare Quarterly*, Vol 36, No 2, Summer 1985, pp. 204–12.

Ziolkowski, Theodore, 'Talking Statues?', *The Modern Language Review*, Vol 110, No 4, October 2015, pp. 946–68.

Zuckert, Rachel, 'Sculpture and Touch: Herder's Aesthetics of Sculpture', *The Journal of Aesthetics and Art Criticism*, Vol 67, No 3, Summer 2009, pp. 285–99.

INDEX

Abbāsid Caliphate (750–1258), 201–2
Abel, Niels Henrik, 42
Abraham Lincoln: The Man (Saint-Gaudens), 143–5, 178
accoutrements, 66, 74–9
Achilles, 59
acid rain, 67
Acropolis, Athens, 59
Adam and Eve (Botero), 222
Adam, Robert, 177
Adams, Tony, 89
Adorno, Theodor, 113
Adshead, Stanley, 55
Aegina, Greece, 30
agalmatophilia, 224–5
Agatha, Saint, 77–9
Agrippa, Marcus Vipsanius, 160
Aiyar, C. P. Ramaswami, 271
Akhenaten, Pharaoh of Egypt, 138, 288
Albert, Prince consort, 11
Albert Square, Manchester, 11
Alexander I, Emperor of Russia, 31
Alexander II, Emperor of Russia, 294
Alexander III, Emperor of Russia, 265
Alexander III, King of Macedon, 68, 177

Alexander VII, Pope, 195
Alexandra, 2nd Duchess of Fife, 142
Alfvén, Hugo, 29
Alison Lapper Pregnant (Quinn), 110, 281
Allies (Holofcener), 54–5
Alloway, Scotland, 136
Amarna Letters, 138
Ambedkar, Bhimrao Ramji, 105
Ambrose, Saint, 77
Amenhotep III, Pharaoh of Egypt, 209
American Civil War (1861–5), 1, 145, 148, 149
American Peace Centenary Committee, 142–5
American Revolution (1775–83), 6–7, 137, 148, 149, 153
Amida, 175–6
Amitābha, 175
amnesia, 95
Amsterdam, Netherlands, 174, 185
An Lushan Rebellion (755–63), 74
Anatomy of Melancholy, The (Burton), 197
Anavysos Kouros, 59
ancestor worship, 6

INDEX

Andante Patetico (Nordin), 29
Andersen, Hans Christian, 34
Anderson, Benedict, 93, 186
Anderson, Gerry, 192
Andrássy, Gyula, 291
Angel of the Resurrection (Marochetti), 269
Angry Boy, The (Vigeland), 44
Anielewicz, Mordechai, 116
Anne, Queen of the United Kingdom, 175
Antinis, Robertas, 131–2
Antony, Mark, 82, 158, 159
Aphrodisias, Anatolia, 234
Aphrodite, 67, 209, 224–5, 234
Aphrodite of Aphrodisias, 234
Aphrodite of Knidos (Praxiteles), 67, 209, 224–5, 234
Apollo Belvedere, 63, 70, 92
Apollo's belt, 60–61
Apoxyomenos (Lysippos), 68
Ara Pacis Augustae, Rome, 181–2
Arcadius, Western Roman Emperor, 266
Arch of Titus, Rome, 182
Archaic Greece (c. 800–480 BCE), 59, 69
Archaic Torso of Apollo (Rilke), 207
Ardrossan, Ayrshire, 286
Argentina, 100–102
Armação dos Búzios, Brazil, 55
Arminius, Cherusci chieftain, 96–7
Arnarhóll, Reykjavik, 38
Arnarson, Ingólfur, 37–9
Arnolfo di Cambio, 217

Arrowsmith, James, 278
Arsacid Empire, *see* Parthian Empire
Arsenal FC, 89–90
Art Deco, 252
Arthurian legend, 294
Asclepius, 209
Ashurnasirpal II, King of Assyria, 199
Assyria (2025–609 BCE), 199
Ast, Bruno, 129–30
Astley, Rick, 237
Athena, 74
Athenaeus of Naucratis, 224
Athens, Greece, 59
Attila '74 (1974 documentary), 251
Attlee, Clement, 218
Atyeo, John, 89
Augustine of Hippo, 230
Augustus of Prima Porta, 71
Augustus, Roman Emperor, 65, 71, 81, 158–61, 181, 210, 234, 236–7
Auld Lang Syne (Burns), 138
Auschwitz concentration camp, 45, 113, 165
Australia, 137, 138, 245
Austro-Hungarian Empire (1867–1918), 11–12
Austurvöllur, Reykjavik, 37
auto-commemoration, 192–3
automata, 201–2
Avalokiteśvara, 52
Ayilyam Thirunal, Maharaja of Travancore, 83

Babuino, Il, 203

INDEX

Babylonian Empire (626–539 BCE), 200
Baccelli, La, 161–2
Bacchus, 225
Baghdad, Iraq, 201–2
Balder, 98
Ball, Lucille, 288–9
Ballinspittle, County Cork, 203
Baltic Germans, 27, 108
Balvi, Latvia, 64
von Bandel, Ernst, 96–7
Bank of England, 90
Banksy, 227–8, 255
Banotti, Elvira, 231
Barberini, Francesco, 62
Barberini family, 203
Barcelona, Spain, 56, 296
Barclay de Tolly, Michael Andreas, 27
Bardot, Brigitte, 55
Barnard, George Grey, 144–5
Barnes Common, London, 23–5
Baroque, 177
Bartholdi, Frédéric Auguste, 148–50
Bates, Ted, 286
Baths of Agrippa, Rome, 68
Baths of Caracalla, Rome, 211
Battle of Actium (31 BCE), 82
Battle of Austerlitz (1805), 97, 282
Battle of Britain (1940), 110–11, 167
Battle of Bunker Hill (1775), 153
Battle of Culloden (1746), 49
Battle of Leipzig (1813), 30–31
Battle of Stalingrad (1942–3), 45–8
Battle of Stirling Bridge (1297), 285
Battle of the Teutoburg Forest (9 CE), 96–7
Baumel, Judith Tydor, 165
Bavaria, 32
Beaman, Charles, 144
Beatles, The, 250
de Beauvoir, Simone, 163
Beaux-Arts, 163
Becket, Thomas, 189
Beckham, David, 109
Belcheva, Ina, 241
Belgium, 174, 219
Belgrave Square, London, 141
Belopolsky, Yakov, 46
Belt, Richard, 233
Benjamin, Floella, Baroness, 17, 20, 21
Benson, William, 19
Berengar of Ivrea, 202
Berlant, Lauren, 186
Berlin, Germany, 69, 99, 121–5, 185, 288
Bermondt-Avalov, Pavel, 107
Bernadotte, Jean-Baptiste Jules, *see* Karl XIV
Bernini, Gian Lorenzo, 62–3, 195
Bharatiya Jana Sangh Party, 269
Billig, Michael, 11
Bindesbøll, Michael Gottlieb, 33
von Bismarck, Otto, 154
Bissen, Herman Wilhelm, 34
Bitter, Karl, 163
Black Lives Matter, 1, 229, 245, 246, 248, 254–5, 278, 280–82
Blaise, Saint, 77

INDEX

Blenheim Palace, Oxfordshire, 175
Blom, Thomas, 220
Blossoms, 237
Bluetooth, 49
Bobbie's Statue (Lawson), 138
bodhisattvas, 175–6
bodybuilding, 192, 211–12
Boethus of Chalcedon, 69
Bogdanas, Konstantinas, 135
Bogotá, Colombia, 141
Bolan, June, 25
Bolan, Marc, 23–5
Bolívar, Simón, 140–42
Bolt, Usain, 20
Bonaparte, Pierre, 215
Bond Street, London, 54–5
Bonnici, Owen, 253
Bonzo Dog Doo-Dah Band, 75
Book of Genesis, 4
Borchardt, Ludwig, 288
Borodai, Vasyl, 95
Bose, Subhas Chandra, 105, 239, 240, 270
Boston, Massachusetts, 183–5
Botermarkt, Amsterdam, 174, 185
Botero, Fernando, 222
Bourbon dynasty, 282–3
Bourdelle, Antoine, 43
Boy Scout Commemorative Tribute (De Lue), 64
Boy with a Dolphin (Wynne), 250
Boyer, Charles, 86
Bradley, Mark, 71
Brady, Sheila, 127
Brandenburg Gate, Berlin, 121, 122, 123
Brass Eye, 204
Braveheart (1995 film), 285–6
Brazil, 55, 100–102, 191, 205–7
Brechin City FC, 286
Brennan, Ian, 286
Brezhnev, Leonid, 64, 95
Bristol City FC, 89
Bristol, England, 1, 231, 246, 248–9, 254–5, 258, 278–82
British Broadcasting Corporation (BBC), 154–5, 229
British Empire, 103–4
    American colonies, 6–7, 137, 148, 149, 153
    Egyptian colonies, 141–2
    Indian colonies, 83, 105, 238, 268–71
    slave trade, 1, 231, 246, 247–9, 254–5, 278–82
    South African colonies, 93, 104
British Museum, London, 73, 210
British Nationality Act (1948), 19
Brixton, London, 22
bronze, 2, 8, 65, 67–9, 212
Bronze Horseman, The (Pushkin), 196
Bronze Man (Polis), 212–13
Bronze Soldier memorial, Tallinn, 275
Broumensky, Vladimir, 241
Brussels, Belgium, 219
Bryzgel, Amy, 212
Bubastis, Egypt, 292
Buchenwald concentration camp, 114
Buckingham, George Villiers, 1st Duke, 140

INDEX

Buckingham Palace, London, 167
Budapest, Hungary, 257, 291
Buddhism, 6, 51–2, 73–4, 105, 175–6, 217
Bukovsky, Lev, 278
Bulgaria, 151, 241, 242
Burghers of Calais (Rodin), 41
Burk, Adrienne, 28
Burlington, Richard Boyle, 3rd Earl, 92
Burns, Robert, 136–8
Burton, Robert, 197
Bury, Manchester, 173
Bush, George, 286
busts, 62, 92
Butterfield, Andrew, 3–5, 167, 182
Byron, George Gordon, 6th Baron, 233
Byström, Niklas, 98
Byzantine Empire (330–1453), 202, 266–8

Cacoyannis, Michael, 251
Caesar, Gaius, 160
Caesar, Julius, 234
Caesar, Lucius, 160
Cairo, Egypt, 141
Calder, Alexander Stirling, 146
Caligula, Roman Emperor, 235
Callimachus, 210
Camisão, Carlos de Morais, 101
Canada, 28, 171–2
Canon of Polykleitos, 59
Canova, Antonio, 7, 141
Canterbury, Kent, 189
cantilever technology, 64–5

de Cantilupe, Thomas, 189
Cape Colony (1806–1910), 93
Cape Tarkhankut, Crimea, 241
Capitoline Hill, Rome, 31
Capricorn Two, 154
Caracas, Venezuela, 141
Carafa, Oliviero, 202
Carmelite Order, 190
Carthage (c. 814–146 BCE), 56
Cartier, George-Étienne, 172
Caruana Galizia, Daphne, 253–4
caryatids, 163
Cassidy, John, 278
Castagnary, Jules Antoine, 284
Castel Sant'Angelo, Rome, 203
Catania, Sicily, 77–9
Catherine of Aragon, 295
Catholicism, 34, 76, 191, 203–5, 220, 294–5
Cato the Elder, 65
Cavendish Square, London, 49
Cawthra, Joseph Hermon, 154
Celeron, New York State, 288–9
Central House of Artists, Moscow, 293
Chacán-Pi, 295–6
Chaniotis, Angelos, 13, 209
Chantrey, Francis, 91
Chaplin, Charlie, 173
Chapman, Herbert, 89
Characene (141 BCE–CE 222), 235–6
Charles I, King of England, Scotland and Ireland, 139–40
Charles X, King of France, 283
Charles Bridge, Prague, 219–20
Chauvin, Derek, 245

INDEX

Chelmsford, Frederic Thesiger, 1st Viscount, 270
Cherusci people, 96
Chervonohorod, Ukraine, 32
Chesterton, Gilbert Keith, 1
Chicago, Illinois, 143, 178
chicken hypnotism, 191–2
Chickering, Jonas, 184
child abuse, 229–30, 264
China, 52, 72, 74, 138
Chizhik-Pyzhik, 53, 223
Chongqing, China, 74
Christian IV, King of Denmark, 33
Christian VIII, King of Denmark, 33
Christianity, 6, 33
    iconoclasm, 6, 294–5
    rubbing traditions, 217, 219–20
    saints, 6, 76–9, 217, 219–20
    Virgin Mary, 203–5
    votive offerings, 189–91
Christiansborg Palace, Copenhagen, 33
Chronicle of the Kings of England, 197
Chuikov, Vasily, 47–8
Church, Tom, 285–6
Churchill, Winston, 54–5, 218, 229
Cialdini, Robert, 89
Cicero, 234
Cicognini, Giacinto Andrea, 198–9
Cincinnati, Ohio, 144
city parks, 168, 239, 241

Ciudad Bolívar, Venezuela, 141
civil rights movement (1954–68), 28
Clapham South Deep Shelter, Brixton, 22
Clary, Désirée, 97
Claudia, Quinta, 157, 158
Claudius, Roman Emperor, 235
Cleisophus of Selymbria, 224
Clement of Alexandria, 195
Cleopatra, Queen of Egypt, 158, 159
Cloelia, 157, 158
Cloquet, Ghislain, 240
Collett, Camilla, 42
Colombia, 141
colonialism, 83, 103–4, 228–9, 238–41, 245
    decolonisation, 6, 105, 238–40, 268–71
Colossi of Memnon, Luxor, 149
colour, 69–74
Colston, Edward, 1, 231, 246, 248–9, 254–5, 258, 278–82
Columbus, Christopher, 56, 143, 145
Columbus, Ohio, 192, 212
comedians, 172–4
commemoration, 1–2, 4–5, 10–14, 94, 120, 122–3, 168, 181–93, 298–9
    auto-commemoration, 192–3
    defeat and, 100–103
    destruction and, 13
    inaugurations, 183–5, 192
    intentional vs unintentional, 12–13

INDEX

lieux de mémoire, 94–5, 110, 182
markers 4–5, 50
memoranda, 4–5, 50
ritual and, 13–14, 58, 181–3, 187–91
unclear, 185–7
Commentary on Habbakuk (Jerome), 266
communism, 7, 13, 51, 64, 105–6, 114, 135, 241–3, 271–8
Confederate States of America (1861–5), 1, 145, 149, 258, 298
Conine, Michael, 222
Constantine I, Roman Emperor, 75, 268
Constantine VII, Byzantine Emperor, 202
Constantinople, Byzantine Empire, 268
contrapposto, 59, 61, 63
Cook, James, 245
Cope, Arabella, 162
Copenhagen, Denmark, 30–31, 33–5
Cornelia Africana, 157–8
Cornish, New Hampshire, 144
Coronation Park, Delhi, 239
Cotter's Saturday Night, The (Burns), 137
counter-monuments, 118–33, 256
Courbet, Gustave, 283–5
Courbevoie, Paris, 102
Crampton, Andrew, 94
Crawshay, William II, 152
Crazy Girls, 222

Cremer, Fritz, 114
Crete, 199
Criado Perez, Caroline, 155
Crimea, 241
Cripwell, Tilly, 222
Croatia, 220
Cromwell, Thomas, 294–5
Crosby, Stills, Nash and Young, 129, 131
Ctesicles, 224
cubism, 177
Cultural Revolution (1966–76), 138
Cumberland, William Augustus, Duke, 49
cummings, e e, 151
Currie, Steve, 25
Cybele 157
Cyfarthfa, Merthyr Tydfil, 152
Cyprus, 250–52
Czechia, 190–91, 219–20, 222–3

Da Ponte, Lorenzo, 199
Dacian Wars (101–6 CE), 57–8
Daedalus, 200
Daini, Hugo, 141
Dalida, 220–21
Dallas, Texas, 119
Dalou, Aimé-Jules, 215
Dalsgaard, Sven, 273
Dambis, Juris, 276
Damgaard, Aage, 273
damnatio memoriae, 265–8
Danner, Marcel, 58
David (Michelangelo), 298
Davies, Alex R. T., 152, 154
Davies, Penelope, 57

361

INDEX

De Lue, Donald, 64
Decius, Roman Emperor, 77
decolonisation, 6, 105, 238–40, 268–71
defeat, 100–103
Delacroix, Eugène, 116, 149, 164
Delhi, India, 238–40, 270
Delhi Durbar (1911), 238–40
Delia, Emanuel, 253–4
Delos, Greece, 210
Denmark, 30–31, 33–5, 37, 97, 273
Derfel Gadarn, Saint, 294–5
derisive nostalgia, 243
Derrida, Jacques, 51
dialogic monuments, 28, 246, 256–7
Diana, Princess of Wales, 118, 167, 252
Diana Nemorensis, 189
Dickenson, Christopher, 2, 82, 175, 267, 292
Dillens, Julien, 219
Diodorus Siculus, 9, 200
Dionysus, 67, 203, 235
diplomatic gifts, 138–50
Dirgha Agama, 73
Discobolus (Myron), 60, 254
Disney, Roy, 87
Disney, Walt, 85–8
Does Haughty Gaul Invasion Threat? (Burns), 137
dolmen, 4
Dombrowski, Damian, 62
Domitia Longina, 267
Domitian, Roman Emperor, 58, 182, 267

Don Giovanni (Mozart), 198, 199
Don Juan or the Feast of Stone (Molière), 199
Donatello, 70, 75–6
Dorset, John Sackville, 3rd Duke, 161–2
Dorset, Thomas Sackville, 1st Earl, 161
Doryphoros (Polykleitos), 59
Dourados, Brazil, 100–102
Draco, 289
Drumm, Don, 131
Druskininkai, Lithuania, 241, 242–3
Drusus the Elder, 159, 160
Dublin, Ireland, 221–2
Duggan, Terrance, 201
Duilius, Gaius, 56, 58
Dumfries, Scotland, 136
Dundee, Scotland, 237
Dürer, Albrecht, 4
Dutra, Eurico Gaspar, 102
Dutton, Kenneth, 212
Dwyer, Owen, 28
dynamic sculptures, 64
Dzerzhinsky, Felix, 293

Edensor, Tim, 10–11, 285
Edinburgh, Scotland, 217
Egypt, 6, 9, 92, 208–9
    Amarna Letters, 138
    Bolívar statue, 141–2
    British period (1882–1956), 141–2
    Colossi of Memnon, 149
    eyes in, 210
    form in, 6

INDEX

ka, 50, 208–9
   materials in, 69
   offerings in, 188
   Ramesses II statues, 9, 50, 73, 292
   recycling in, 292
   Roman period (30 BCE–CE 642), 158, 236–7
   size in, 50
   Suez Canal, 149–50
   talking statues in, 201
Eidsvoll Square, Oslo, 43
Einarsson, Jon, 221
Eisenman, Peter, 123, 125
Eisenstein, Sergei, 265
Eisner, Michael, 86
elevation, 53–8
Eleven Emlékmű, 257
Eliade, Mircea, 4
Elizabeth I, Queen of England, 161
Elphick, Nick, 153
Emil and the Detectives (Kästner), 226
Empire Windrush, 17, 19–23
Enlightenment (c. 1637–1789), 197, 208
EOKA, 251
Ephesus, Anatolia, 234
Epidaurus, Greece, 209
equestrian statues, 75–6
Erasmo da Narni, 75–6
Erikson, Leif, 39, 145–7
Eriksson, Liss, 53
Eritrea, 231
Eros of Thespiae (Praxiteles), 234–5

Eros, 210, 234, 294
Erőss, Ágnes, 256–7
Estonia, 26, 79, 84–5, 271, 275
Eugenius, Western Roman Emperor, 266
Exhibition Grounds, Delhi, 238–9
eye level statues, 54, 113

Fairmount Park Art Association, 39–40
Fallen Man (Lehmbruck), 132
Fantasia (1940 film), 86
Faraone, Christopher, 199
fascism, 44–5, 119
Favourite, The (2018 film), 175
Fawcett, Millicent, 156
Fazakerley, Ruth, 256
Felipe IV, King of Spain, 139
Feltria, Italy, 3
Field of Sacrifice (Antinis), 131–2
Fields, Gracie, 173
figurative statues, 5–6, 8, 58, 63, 88, 113
   elevation and, 53
   memorials and, 114, 132–3
   size and, 50, 51
Finn, Mickey, 25
Flamme de la Liberté, Paris, 252
Flavian dynasty, 267
Flaxman, John, 92
Fleeing the Cap Arcona (Hrdlicka), 256
Fleming, Harold, 88
Florence, Italy, 152
Flory, Marleen, 157–8, 160
Floyd, George, 245, 278

INDEX

Fogelberg, Bernt, 98
football, 88–90, 109, 172, 286–7
Forest, Benjamin, 243, 265
Forest, John, 295
forgetting, 10, 12, 14, 94, 95, 120, 122–3, 168, 181–3
form, 58–65
Fountain, The (Vigeland), 41, 43, 44
Fourth Plinth, Trafalgar Square, 109–11, 281
Fox, Carl, 297
France, 98–9
    Flamme de la Liberté, 252
    Napoleonic Wars (1803–1815), 27, 30–31, 97, 282–3
    Paris Commune (1871), 283–4
    Prussian War (1870–71), 97, 99, 102–3, 148, 283
    Revolution (1789–99), 137, 148, 162
    Revolution (1830), 283
    rubbing traditions in, 215, 217–18, 220–21
    Statue of Liberty gifting (1886), 147–50, 252
    Vendôme Column, 282–5
Franck, Karen, 256
Franco-American Union, 148
Frankel, Eddy, 287
Franklin, Benjamin, 183–6
Fraser, James, 11
Fréart de Chantelou, Paul, 62
Frederik VI, King of Denmark, 33
Free Trade Hall, Manchester, 145

Freedom Monument, Rīga, 106–9, 191, 250
frequency hopping, 49
Frere, Bartle, 104
Frogner Fields, Oslo, 43
From Pitch to Plinth, 88
Frowe, Helen, 257–8, 264

Gabowitsch, Mischa, 272
Gabriadze, Rezo, 223
Gagarin, Yuri, 65
Gainsborough, Thomas, 162
Galdikas, Juozas, 243
Gallery of Modern Art, Glasgow, 226–8
Gandhara, 73
Gandhi, Mahatma, 229, 240
ganosis, 71–2
Garnett, Anna, 73
Garnier, Francis, 103
Garstang, John, 236
Gattemelata, 76
Gegendenkmal, 256
George III, King of the United Kingdom, 6–7
George IV, King of the United Kingdom, 109
George V, King of the United Kingdom, 228, 238–40, 270
Germany, 7, 96–7, 99–100, 118–25
    Gegendenkmal, 256
    Holocaust memorials, 69, 114, 115, 118–25
    national identity, 96–7, 99–100
    Nazi Germany (1933–45), *see* Nazi Germany

INDEX

Gerz, Jochen, 119–21
Geschichte der Kunst des Alterthums (Winckelmann), 70
Getsy, David, 216
Giambologna, 139–40, 225
Gibson, Blaine, 85–8
Gibson, Mel, 286
Giedion, Sigfried, 7
gifts, 138–50
Gill, Eric, 229–30
gimmicks, 79
Gladstone, William, 11
Glasgow, Scotland, 136, 226–8
global financial crisis (2008), 38
globalisation, 172
goats, 151–5
von Goethe, Johann Wolfgang, 10
gold, 73–4
Gombergs, Jevgeņijs, 25–7
Gonzaga, Luiz, 206–7
Goodacre, Glenna, 128
Goor, Ilana, 164
Gorakhpur, Uttar Pradesh, 269
Gorbachev, Mikhail, 108
Gordon, Charles, 104
Görgei, Artúr, 291
Gormley, Antony, 110
Gorpenko, Anatoly, 46
Gould, Thomas Ridgeway, 66
Gove, Michael, 21
Gracchus, Gaius, 157
graffiti, 222, 228–9
Gratian, Western Roman Emperor, 267
Great Orme, Llandudno, 152–3
Great Siege Monument, Valletta, 252–4

Greece, 6, 13–14, 30, 98–9, 297
   accoutrements in, 74
   colour in, 70
   damnatio memoriae in, 266–7
   form in, 6, 58–61, 62, 63, 210–11
   interaction in, 217
   living statues, 199, 200, 209–10
   material in, 65–9
   offerings in, 187–8
   Olympic Games, 254, 289
   Pygmalion myth, 224
   recycling in, 292
   rituals in, 13–14, 187
   setting in, 177
   Trojan War, 59, 139
   women in, 157
Greenwich, London, 169
Gripsholm Castle, Sweden, 97
Grūtas Park, Druskininkai, 241, 242–3
Guanyin of Nanshan, Hainan, 52
guardian statues, 199–200
Gujarat, India, 49
Gustafson, Kathryn, 118
Guy, Thomas, 247–8
Guy's and St Thomas' Foundation, 247–8
Guzman, Jen, 25
Gylfe, 98
gymnasiarchus, 292
Gymnasticus (Philostratus), 211

Hainan, China, 52
Halbwachs, Maurice, 94
Hallgrimskirkja, Reykjavik, 146

INDEX

Hallgrimsson, Jónas, 36, 37
Hamburg, Germany, 119–20, 154, 218, 256
Hamburg Firestorm (Hrdlicka), 256
Hamilton, Thomas, 136
Hamilton Gardens, Hyde Park, 233
Hansen, Christian Frederik, 33
Harburg Monument (Gerz and Shalev-Gerz), 119–20
Harford, Tim, 154
Hart, Frederick, 127–8, 256
Hartog, François, 94–5
Havelock, Henry, 109
Hector, 202
Hedges-Quinn, Sean, 287
Hegel, Georg, 70
Helsinki-86, 108
Hemelrijk, Emily, 158–9
Hench, John, 86
Henri IV, King of France, 282
Henri-Kahnweiler, Daniel, 177
Henry VIII, King of England, 161, 295
Henry, Thierry, 89–90
van Hensbergen, Claudine, 248
Hephaestus, 199, 200, 299
Heracles, 211–12, 235–6
Herculaneum, Italy, 70
Hercules, 98, 211, 230
von Herder, Johann Gottfried, 215
Heritage Advisory Board, 246–8
Hermann, Cherusci chieftain, 96–7
Hermannsdenkmal (Bandel), 96–7
Hermeticism, 208, 299

Herodotus, 209
heroic defeat, 100–103
Hershey, Milton, 87
Herz, Walter, 254
Heseltine, Michael, Baron, 273
hibutsu, 175–6
Hill, Benny, 109
Hill, George William, 172
Hinduism, 106, 209, 269
Hirstein, William, 61, 62
Historic England, 248, 255
Hitler, Adolf, 117
Hljómskálagardur Park, Reykjavik, 36, 37
Hnitbjörg, Reykjavik, 35
Hoheisel, Horst, 121, 122
Holliday, Peter, 181
Hollinshead, Mary, 66
Holocaust (1941–5), 69, 113, 114–25, 164–5, 257
Holofcener, Lawrence, 54–5
Homeless Jesus (Schmalz), 171
Homer, 199
Honorius, Byzantine Emperor, 266
Hope, Thomas, 30, 32
hostile environment policy, 21
Houdon, Jean-Antoine, 143
House of Commons, 218
How Art Made the World, 61
Hrdlicka, Alfred, 256
Huang, Xinyi, 73
Huber, Erwin, 254
Hudiksvall, Sweden, 79
Hughes, Peter, 264
Hugo, Victor, 283
Hume, David, 217

INDEX

Hungary, 256–7, 291
Hunter, Kenny, 152
Hustvedt, Siri, 258
Huyssen, Andreas, 122
Hyde Park, London, 118, 233
Hyde Park, Sydney, 245
hypnotising chickens, 191–2

I Goat (Hunter), 152
I Love Lucy, 289
I Storm (Vigeland), 42
Ibbeson, Graham, 174
Ibsen, Henrik, 41
Icarus, 200
Iceland, 35–40, 145–7
iconoclasm, 6, 263–90, 291, 292–4
   Christianity, 6, 294–5
   Colston statue (2020), 1, 231, 246, 248–9, 254–5, 258, 278–82
   damnatio memoriae, 265–8
   Indian decolonisation, 268–71
   Latvian de-Russification, 271–8
   Vendôme Column, 282–5
idealism, 58–64, 210–11
identity, 264–5
Idylls (Theocritus), 210, 294
Ignatieff, Michael, 95, 187
imagined communities, 94
imperialism, 6, 103–4, 229, 268–71
inaugurations, 183–5, 192
India, 49, 83, 104–6, 238–40, 268–71
Infant Jesus of Prague, 190–91

infantile citizenship, 186
interaction, 54, 55, 215–31
   coin tossing, 223
   rubbing, 43, 53, 54, 79, 152, 216–23
   sex, 224–5
   vandalism 222, 225–31
invisibility, 10–11, 84, 182, 249, 277–8
Ireland, 191, 203–5, 221–2
Irwin, Edward Lindley Wood, 1st Baron, 270
Islam, 6, 201
Israel, 115, 116, 117, 164–5
Istanbul, Turkey, 268
Italy, 30–32, 33–4, 57–8, 71–3, 152, 157
   Milan, 230–31
   Naples, 67, 68
   Rome, *see* Rome, city of
   Vatican City, 34, 63, 68, 71, 92, 217
   Verona, 221

Jäckel, Eberhard, 122
Jackob-Marks, Christine, 122
Jackson, Mark, 153
Jacob, 4
Jacobitism, 49, 138
Jacobson, Stephen, 56
Jagger, Charles Sargeant, 238
Jamaica, 20
James I and VI, King of England, Scotland and Ireland, 139, 161
Jansone, Dzintra, 273
Japan, 105, 175–6
de la Jara, Fernando, 296

INDEX

Jarada, 201
Järnpoike (Eriksson), 53
Jason with the Golden Fleece (Thorvaldsen), 30, 38
Jefferson Memorial, Washington, 187
Jeffrey, Robin, 84, 105, 270
Jelgava, Latvia, 273
Jenrick, Robert, 246
Jensen, Robin, 230
Jerome, Saint, 266
Jerusalem, 116, 117, 164–5
Jesus Christ, 33
Jewish–Roman War (66–73 CE), 182
Jews, 114–25
jinn, 201
Jizō, 176
John of Nepomuk, Saint, 219–20
John, Gus, 21
Johnson, Boris, 111
Johnson, Juliet, 243, 265
Jolson, Leon, 117
Jonava, Lithuania, 242
Jones, Gloria, 23
Jones, Jonathan, 63
Jónsson, Einar, 35–40, 147
Journal of Sex Research, The, 225
Julia the Elder, 160
Jūrmala, Latvia, 25–7

ka, 50, 208–9
Kalanta, Romas, 131–2
Kalējs, Otto, 273
Kannon, 176
Kanpur, Uttar Pradesh, 269
Karl X, King of Sweden, 98

Karl XI, King of Sweden, 98
Karl XII, King of Sweden, 98
Karl XIII, King of Sweden, 97, 98
Karl XIV, King of Sweden, 97–9
Karlsefni, Thorfinn, 39–40, 147
Kästner, Erich, 226
Kaunas, Lithuania, 131–2
Keflavik, Iceland, 147
Keldysh, Mstislav, 277
Ķeniņš, Laura, 107–8
Kent State Shootings (1970), 129–31
Keystone State Skinheads, 40
Khrushchev, Nikita, 46, 47
King, Martin Luther, 20
Kingdom of Kush (c. 780 BCE–CE c. 350), 81, 236
Kingston upon Thames, London, 152
Kirkhope, Timothy, Baron, 233
Ķirsis, Vilnis, 27, 275
Kitchenware Revolution (2009–11), 38
Knidos, Greece, 67, 209, 224–5, 234
Knights of St John, 252
Knole, Kent, 161–2
Kohl, Helmut, 122
Kolkata, Bengal, 270
korai, 59, 69
kouroi, 59
Kraków, Poland, 218
Kralj, Ivan, 223
Krankies, The, 287
Krause, Allison, 129
Kristallnacht (1938), 120

INDEX

Kritian Boy, 59, 61
Kronvalda Park, Rīga, 277
Krook, Margaretha, 79
Kruk, Sergei, 64
Krymsky Val, Moscow, 293
Kuöhl, Richard, 256
Kurzeme, Latvia, 106
Kush (c. 780 BCE–CE c. 350), 81, 236–7
Kyiv, Ukraine, 95–6

Laban, 4
Labienus, 234
Labora, 243
de Laboulaye, Édouard René, 147–50
Lāčplēsis (Pumpurs), 107, 108
Ladd, Brian, 5
Lafontaine, Oskar, 121
Laguna, Brazil, 100–102
Lakshmibai, Rani of Jhansi, 269
Lamarr, Hedy, 49
Lamentation by Rembrandt van Rhijn (Schenkman), 174
Lanarkshire, Scotland, 237
Lancelotti family, 254
Landowski, Paul, 218
Lantau, Hong Kong, 52
Lantéri, Édouard, 84
Laocoön and His Sons, 70
Lapper, Alison, 110, 281
Lara y Mendoza, Maria, 190
Las Vegas, Nevada, 222
Latgale, Latvia, 106
Latimer, Hugh, 295
Latvia, 25–7, 64, 106–9, 114, 136, 191, 212, 250, 271–8

Laube, Eižens, 106
Laussel, Dordogne, 4
Lawson, Henry, 138
Layton, Julia, 67
Lazarus, Emma, 150
Lec, Stanisław, 293
Lectures on Aesthetics (Hegel), 70
Leeds, West Yorkshire, 154
Léger, Fernand, 7
Lego, 65
Lehmbruck, Wilhelm, 132
Leicester Square, London, 173
Lenin is Dead, 273
Lenin, Vladimir, 13, 51, 64, 96, 135, 213, 241–2, 272–4, 294
Lennart Meri airport, Tallinn, 84–5
Leochares, 63
Leonard of Noblac, Saint, 189
Lepidus, 158
Lesbos, 200
Leshan, Sichuan, 52
de Lesseps, Ferdinand, 148, 149
Liberty Leading the People (Delacroix), 116, 149, 164
Liberty Monument, Nicosia, 250–52
Liberty Square, Budapest, 257
Liepāja, Latvia, 114–15
lieux de mémoire, 94–5, 110, 182
Lima, Peru, 141
Lin, Maya Ying, 126–9, 132, 256
Lincoln, Abraham, 143–5, 149, 178
Lincoln, Frederic, 184
Lincoln Memorial, Washington, 126, 186–7, 256

INDEX

Lithuania, 131–2, 135, 241–3, 271, 273
Liu, Xiangyu, 73
Liudprand of Cremona, 202
Liverani, Paolo, 71
Livia, 71, 158–61
living statues, 210–13
Livingstone, Ken, 109
Livy, 65, 157
Llandderfel, Gwynedd, 294
Llandudno, Conwy, 152–3
Lloyd George, David, 218
Locatelli, John Baptist, 161
Loizidou, Chrystalleni, 251
London, England, 167–71
   Allies statue, 54–5
   Bolívar statue, 141
   Boy with a Dolphin, 250
   British Museum, 73, 210
   Cavendish Square, 49
   Chaplin statue, 173
   Diana Memorial Fountain, 118
   Frere statue, 104
   goats, statues of, 152
   Gordon statue, 104
   Guy's and St Thomas' Foundation, 247–8
   inaugurations in, 185
   Lincoln statue, 144–5
   Marc Bolan's Rock Shrine, 23–5
   Monument Saturation Zone, 170–71
   National Windrush Monument, 17, 19–23
   Nelson's Column, 56, 103, 109, 111
   Olympic Games (2012), 227
   Parliament Square, 145, 156
   Raleigh statue, 169
   Royal Parks, 170
   Sir John Soane's Museum, 90–92
   Trafalgar Square, 56, 103, 109–11, 281
   Washington statue, 143, 168
   Westminster Abbey, 18–19
   Westminster, 167–71
   Whitehall, 169–70
   women, statues of, 155–6
Lonely Planet, 227
Lopes, José Francisco, 101
Lord Kitchener, 19
Lord Lawrence, John, 1st Baron, 270
Lorimer, Jim, 192
Lotus Flower, The, 155
Louis VII, King of France, 189
Louis XIV, King of France, 62
Louis Philippe, King of the French, 283
Louvre, Paris, 207
Lubyanka Square, Moscow, 293
Lucian of Samosata, 200, 225
Ludwig I, King of Bavaria, 30
Lushan County, Henan, 52
Lutyens, Edwin, 238, 240
Luxor, Egypt, 149, 268
Lysippos, 68
Lytle Park, Cincinnati, 144

M Shed Museum, Bristol, 281
MacCarthy, Fiona, 229
Mach, David, 152

INDEX

Macon, Nathaniel, 7
Madeira, 287
Madras, India, 271
Madrid, Spain, 140
Magnus Maximus, Western Roman Emperor, 267
Maharashtra, India, 270
Maharishi Mahesh Yogi, 250
Mahdist War (1881–99), 104
Maier, Ruth, 45
Maillol, Aristide, 43
Maitreya, 51, 52
Makarios III, Archbishop, 251
Malinauskas, Viliumas, 243
Malone, Molly, 221–2
Malta, 252–4
Mamaev Kurgan, Volgograd, 45
Mamluk Sultanate (1250–1517), 139
Mamuda, Ana, 101
Man's a Man for A'That, A (Burns), 137
Manchester, England, 11, 145
Mandal, Norway, 41
Mandela, Nelson, 229
Māori, 6, 228–9
marble, 2, 8, 65–7
Marc Bolan's Rock Shrine, London, 23–5
Marcus Aurelius, Roman Emperor, 31, 75
Marcuse, Harold, 114, 115
Maria Anna, Infanta of Spain, 139
Maria Theresa, Holy Roman Empress, 191
Marie Antoinette, Queen consort of France, 162

Marker, Chris, 240
Marker for Change, Vancouver, 28
markers, 3–4, 50
Marlborough, John Churchill, 1st Duke, 175
Marlborough, Sarah Churchill, Duchess, 175
Marley, Bob, 207
Marochetti, Carlo, 226, 269
Marshak, Samuil, 138
Martin, Freya, 3
martyrdom, 33, 76–7, 100, 102, 116, 118
Marx, Karl, 105
Massachusetts Charitable Mechanic Association, 184–5
Matakana, New Zealand, 228
material, 65–9
Mathias, Charles, 126
Matthews, Stanley, 88
Mauriņš, Juris, 64
Mauss, Marcel, 139
Maximilian I, Elector of Bavaria, 32
Maxwele, Chumani, 263
May, Theresa, 17
Mayakovsky, Vladimir, 272
McDonald, Lynn, 156
McGarr, Paul, 269, 270
Medici family, 140
Medieval period (c. 500–1500), 6, 69
megaliths, 4
Melanesia, 139
Melencolia I (Dürer), 4
Memento Park, Budapest, 241
memoranda, 4–5, 50

INDEX

Memorial to the Murdered Jews of Europe, Berlin, 69, 121–5
memorials, 113–33, 250
memory places, 94, 110
Memory, A (Nordin), 29
Menelaus, King of Sparta, 202
menhir, 4
Menodorus, 235
Meredates, King of Characene, 235–6
Meri, Lennart, 84–5
Mérimée, Prosper, 197
Meroë, Kingdom of Kush, 81, 236–7
Merthyr Tydfil, Glamorgan, 152
Mesene, *see* Characene
Mesopotamia, ancient, 6
Messene, Greece, 82, 267–8, 292
Metamorphoses, The (Ovid), 224
Metellus Macedonicus, 159
Methodist Central Hall, London, 171
Metropolitan Museum of Art, New York, 163
Meyer, Peter, 8
Michael the Brave, 288
Michelangelo, 70, 298
Mickevičius-Kapsukas, Vincas, 242
Midan Qasr Al Dubara, Egypt, 141
Midnight Man, 205
Mihai Viteazul, 288
Mikus, Sándor, 291
Milan, Italy, 230
Miletus Torso, 207
Millar, Paul, 137, 138
Miller, Jeffrey, 129
Milo of Croton, 211
Milton, John, 18
minimalism, 113, 118
Mirador de Colón, Barcelona, 56
Mithridates, King of Pontus, 69
Mock, Steven, 100
Modern Cult of Monuments, The (Riegl), 11–12
modernism, 7–8, 88, 113
Moerdijk, Gerard, 93
Mokronowski, Stanisław, 31
Molica-Franco, Matteo, 153
Molière, 199
de Molina, Tirso, 198
Molotov-Ribbentrop Pact (1939), 271
Mond, Alfred, 145
Monolith, The (Vigeland), 41, 44
de Montaigne, Michel, 217–18
Montanelli, Indro, 230–31
Montaño, Eugenia Allier, 95
Montevideo, Uruguay, 95
Montreal, Quebec, 28
Monument Saturation Zone, 170–71
Monument to the Fallen of Infantry Regiment No 76, 256
Monument to the Heroes of Laguna and Dourados, 100
Monument to the Liberators of Soviet Latvia, 274–7
monuments
    commemoration, *see* commemoration
    counter-monuments, 118–33, 256

INDEX

definition of, 2, 3–5
dialogic, 28, 246, 256–7
durability, 3–4
fashion and, 6–8
iconoclasm, 6, 263–90, 292–4
inaugurations, 183–5, 192
intentional, 12–13
invisibility of, 10–11, 84, 182, 249
markers 4–5, 50, 81
memoranda, 4–5, 50, 81
memorials, 113–33
motivations for, 18
national identity and, 6, 18, 37, 93–111
patrons/promoters, 17–28
precinct, 5, 167
recontextualisation, 245–59
replication of, 191–2
ritual and, 13–14, 58, 181–3, 187–91
self-promotion and, 18
timelessness, myth of, 8–10
unclear commemoration, 185–7
unintentional, 12–13
value of, 11–13
war memorials, 99–103, 113, 125–9
More or Less, 154
Morecambe, Eric, 173
Mörner, Carl Otto, 97
Moscow, Russia, 13, 243, 265, 293
Moses, 4
Mostyn, Edward Lloyd-Mostyn, 2nd Baron, 153

Mother Motherland (Vuchetich/Borodai), 95–6
Motherland Calls, The (Vuchetich), 45–8
Mozart, Wolfgang Amadeus, 198, 199
Mr Smith Goes to Washington (1939 film), 186
MSMR Architects, 254–5
Mubarak, Hosni, 142
Mucianus, 6
Mudd, Roger, 126
Mukhina, Vera, 108
Mulher do Dia, 205
Mulholland, Peter, 204–5
Müller, Henriette Johanne Marie, 218
Mumford, Lewis, 7, 169
Mummius, Lucius, 235
Munich, Bavaria, 32, 254
al-Muqtadir, Abbāsid Caliph, 201–2
Museo Nazionale della Magna Grecia, Reggio Calabria, 61
Museum of Socialist Art, Sofia, 241, 242
Musil, Robert, 10, 75, 84, 109, 182, 186, 249, 277, 297
Mutu, Wangechi, 163
Myron, 60, 254

Nagano, Japan, 175–6
Nana Saheb, 269
Napier, Charles, 109
Naples, Italy, 67, 68
Napoleon I, Emperor of the French, 283

373

INDEX

Napoleon III, Emperor of the French, 283
Napoleonic Wars (1803–1815), 27, 30–31, 97, 282
Nara, Japan, 176
National Gallery, London, 143, 169
national identity, 6, 18, 37, 56, 93–111, 186
    colonialism and, 103–4
    heroes, 104–6
    iconoclasm and, 264–5, 268–78, 291
    war and, 99–103
National Theatre, London, 155
National Wallace Monument complex, 285
National Windrush Monument, London, 17, 19–23
Natural History (Pliny the Elder), 6, 72
Nazi Germany (1933–45), 7, 69, 105, 114–25, 187
    Holocaust (1941–5), 69, 113, 114–25, 164–5, 257
    Hungary occupation (1944–5), 256–7
    Latvia occupation (1941–4), 276
    Norway occupation (1940–45), 44–5
    Olympic Games (1936), 254
Nebuchadnezzar, King of Babylon, 200
Nefertiti, Queen consort of Egypt, 288
Négroni, Jean, 240

Nehru, Jawaharlal, 105, 269, 270
Nelson's Column, London, 56, 103, 109, 111
neoclassicism, 30–35, 63, 70, 144, 252, 297
Nero, Roman Emperor, 82, 235, 267
Netherlands, 174, 185, 296
Neues Museum, Berlin, 288
New Colossus, The (Lazarus), 150
New Delhi, India, 238–40, 270
New Republic, The, 167
New York, United States, 118, 119, 142, 147–50, 163, 252, 288
New Zealand, 6, 137, 138, 228–9
Newby Hall, North Yorkshire, 177
NewOnes, will free Us, The (Mutu), 163
Newport News, Virginia, 147
Nicholas II, Emperor of Russia, 26
Nick Wilson, 228
Nicosia, Cyprus, 250–52
Nidaros Cathedral, Trondheim, 41, 43
Nigeria, 163
Nightingale, Florence, 156
Nike, 178, 235
Nilsson, Mats, 220
Nimrud, Assyria, 199
Nine Points on Monumentality (Sert, Léger and Giedion), 7
Niyazov, Saparmurat, 18
No Ifs, Ands, or Butts (Conine), 222
Noir, Victor, 215, 223

INDEX

non zero one, 151, 154–5
Nora, Pierre, 94
Nordin, Alice, 29
Nordraak, Rikard, 42
Norse mythology, 35, 38, 98–9
North Carolina, United States, 7
Northern Ireland, 204–5
Northumberland, England, 154
Norway, 40–45, 97, 99
Norwid, Cyprian, 219
Notaras, Ioannis, 251
Novorossiysk, Russia, 95–6
Nymphaeum of Claudius, Punta Epitaffio, 67

O'Mahony, Kathy, 203
Octavia the Younger, 158–61
Octavian, *see* Augustus
October (1928 film), 265
October Square, Moscow, 13
Odin, 38, 98
Odyssey, The (Homer), 199
offerings, 187–91
Ogden, Tom, 237
Ohio (Crosby, Stills, Nash and Young), 129, 131
Olinda, Brazil, 205–7
Olusoga, David, 265
Olympia (1938 documentary), 254
Olympic Games, 254, 289
  1936 Berlin, 254
  1948 London, 254
  2012 London, 227
Omissi, Adrastos, 266, 268
One and Other (Gormley), 110
One Touch of Venus (Nash and Perelman), 198

Orabazes II, King of Characene, 236
Orlando, Florida, 85
Oshun, 206
Oslo, Norway, 40–45
Östlin, Bosse, 79
Otricoli, Italy, 98
Ottawa, Ontario, 119
Ottey, Merlene, 20
Ottoman Empire (1299–1922), 252
Ovid, 224
owls, 74
Ozric Tentacles, 250
Ozymandias (Shelley), 9–10, 292, 297

Padua, Italy, 76
Paine, Thomas, 137
Palaeolithic period, 4, 61–2
Palatine Hill, Rome, 157
Palazzo Braschi, Rome, 202
palimpsests, 183
Pallavicino, Francesco Sforza, 195
Palmer, Carolyn, 289
Palmer, Scott, 45–6
Panama, 142, 148, 149
Pantheon, Rome, 203
Paraguay, 100–102
Paris Commune (1871), 283–4
Paris, France, 41, 102, 185, 215, 217, 219, 252
Park, Keith, 110–11, 156
Park of Arts, Moscow, 243
parks, 168, 239, 241
Parliament Square, London, 145, 156

375

INDEX

Pärnu, Estonia, 79
Paros, Greece, 59, 71
Parthian Empire (247 BCE–CE 224), 57, 235, 237
Partners (Gibson), 85–8
Partridge, Damani, 124
Party Animal (Davies), 152, 154
Pasquino statue, Rome, 202
Patel, Sardar Vallabhbhai, 49
Patroclus, 202
patrons/promoters, 17–28
Paukštys, Saulius, 135
Pausanias, 235, 289, 294
Peacekeeping Monument, Ottawa, 119
Père Lachaise Cemetery, Paris, 215
Performing Right Society, 24
Pērkonkrusts, 275
Pernambuco, Brazil, 205–7
Pérola Negra, 206
Perspektive Berlin, 122
Peru, 141
Peter, Saint, 77, 217
Peter I, Emperor of Russia, 25–7, 106, 196
Petronius, Gaius, 237
Pétursson, Hallgrímur, 146
Peyton, John, 239
Philadelphia, Pennsylvania, 39
Philopseudes (Lucian of Samosata), 200
Philostephanus, 224
Philostratus, 211
Phyrne, 224–5
physical characteristics, 49–79
  accoutrements, 66, 74–9

colour, 69–74
form, 58–65
gimmicks, 79
material, 65–9
plinths/elevation, 53–8
size, 50–53
Piazza del Santo, Padua, 76
Pierre, Caterina, 215
Pillai, K. Ramakrishna, 105
Pillai, Pattom Thanu, 105–6, 271
Pingdingshan, Henan, 52
Piramesse, Egypt, 292
Pittock, Murray, 138
Pius IX, Pope, 203
Pius VII, Pope, 34
placemaking, 172–4
Plato, 59
Platt Fields Park, Manchester, 145
Platz des Unsichtbaren Mahnmals, Saarbrücken, 121
Plaza Bolívar, Caracas, 141
Plaza Mayor, Bogotá, 141
plinths, 53–8, 242
Pliny the Elder, 6, 55, 67, 68, 72, 157, 159
Plutarch, 157
Poets' Corner, Westminster Abbey, 18–19
Poland, 30–32, 115–18, 164, 218–19
Polis, Miervaldis, 212–13
Polykleitos, 59, 211
Pompeii, Italy, 33, 68
Pompeius, Sextus, 82
Poniatowski, Józef, 30–32, 34
Poninska, Helena, 32
Poor Richard's Almanack (Franklin), 184

INDEX

Popular Front Museum, Rīga, 272
Porcellino statue, Florence, 152
Porsenna, Etruscan King, 157
Porter, Neil, 118
Porticus Metelli, Rome, 157
Porticus Octaviae, Rome, 158, 159, 235
Potts, Alex, 177
Poulin, Dave, 288–9
Powell, Ken, 154
Prague, Czechia, 190–91, 219–20, 222–3
Praxiteles, 67, 209, 224–5, 234–5
precinct, 5, 167
Preiļi, Latvia, 273–4
Présence Africaine, 240
Pretoria, South Africa, 93–4
Price, Campbell, 50
Prima Porta, Rome, 71
Proclus the Successor, 208
proprietary statues, 81–92
Protestantism, 33, 294–5
Prusac, Marina, 266
Prussia (1525–1947), 97, 99, 102–3, 148, 283
Public Monuments and Sculpture Association, 154–5
Punch, 263
Punta Carretas mall, Montevideo, 95
Punta Epitaffio, Campania, 67
Pushkin, Alexander, 196, 272, 277
Putto with Goat (Cawthra), 154
Pyat, Félix, 284
Pygmalionism, 224

Qin Empire (221–206 BCE), 72
QR codes, 135, 230, 247, 249
Quechua, 296
Queens Ride, London, 23
Quinn, Marc, 110, 281

Raffet, Denis-Auguste, 103
Rákosi, Mátyás, 291
Raleigh, Walter, 169
Ramachandran, Vilayanur Subramanian, 61, 62, 63
Rambelli, Fabio, 176
Ramesses II, Pharaoh of Egypt, 9, 50, 73, 209, 292
Rani of Jhansi, 269
Rao, Tanjore Madhava, 83–4
Rapoport, Nathan, 115–18, 164
Rausch, Helke, 99, 102, 103, 185
Rawson, Harry, 138
Razumovsky, Stanislav, 26
Reagan, Ronald, 136
realism, 58–64, 72, 73–4
recontextualisation, 245–59
recycling, 292
Redesdale, Northumberland, 154
Reflecting Absence memorial, New York, 119
Reid, Jen, 281
relocations, 233–43
Rembrandt van Rijn, 174, 185
Renaissance (c. 1300–1600), 6, 12, 70, 75–6, 297
Renan, Ernest, 279
replication, 191–2
Resnais, Alain, 240
retain and explain, 246, 247, 250
Revolt of the Prisoners (Cremer), 114

INDEX

Revolution Will Not be Televised, The (Scott-Heron), 231
Reykjavik, Iceland, 35–40, 145–7
Reynard Nurseries, Lanarkshire, 237
Reynolds, Joshua, 162
Rhodes, Cecil, 1, 263
Rhodes Colossus, The (Sambourne), 263
Riace bronzes, 61
Ribeiro, Antônio João, 100–101
Rice, Alexander, 185–6
Richmond, Virginia, 143
Ridgway, Brunilde, 69
Riefenstahl, Leni, 254
Riegl, Alois, 11–12, 131, 182, 240, 270
Rīga, Latvia, 26, 106–9, 115, 191, 212–13, 250, 272, 274–8
Rights of Man (Paine), 137
Rigney, Ann, 258, 263–4
Rilke, Rainer Maria, 207
Rinkēvičs, Edgars, 277
Rio de Janeiro, Brazil, 100–102
ritual, 13–14, 58, 181–3, 187–91
Rizh, Sergey, 115
Roberts, Aldwyn, 19
Roberts, Eric, 125–6
Robillard, Jean, 24
Robinson, David, 163
Rochdale, Manchester, 173
Rococo, 177
Rodin, Auguste, 4, 41
Rogers, Graham, 153
Romania, 288
Romanticism, 197
Rome, ancient, 3, 6, 31, 33, 81–2, 98–9, 297
  Ara Pacis Augustae, 181–2
  Baths of Caracalla, 211
  Battle of the Teutoburg Forest (9 CE), 96–7
  colour in, 70, 71–3
  Dacian Wars (101–6 CE), 57–8, 282
  damnatio memoriae, 265–8
  form in, 63
  Kush War (c. 27–22 BCE), 236–7
  living statues myths, 200
  material in, 65–9
  Porticus Octaviae, 158, 159, 235
  recycling in, 292
  setting in, 178
  symbolic accoutrements in, 75
  thefts in, 234–5
  triumphal columns in, 55, 57–8
  women in, 157–61
Rome, city of, 30–32, 33–4
  Ara Pacis Augustae, 181–2
  Arch of Titus, 182
  Baths of Caracalla, 211
  Castel Sant'Angelo, 203
  coloured statues, 71–3
  Pantheon, 203
  talking statues, 202–3
  Trajan's Column, 57–8, 72, 282
  women, statues of, 157
Romeo and Juliet (Shakespeare), 221
Ronaldo, Cristiano, 287
Roosevelt, Franklin, 54–5

INDEX

Rosendal, Stockholm, 97–8
Rosh, Lea, 122
Roskilde, Denmark, 33
Rossi, Benjamin, 2
Rotterdam, Netherlands, 296
Royal African Company, 248, 278
Royal Albert Hall, London, 142
Royal Australian Historical Society, 245
Royal College of Arts, 84
Royal Dramatic Theatre, Stockholm, 79
Royal Exchange, Glasgow, 226–8
Royal Naval College, Greenwich, 169
Royal Parks, London, 170
Royal Society of Arts, 109
rubbing, 43, 53, 54, 79, 152, 216–23
Rubens, Peter Paul, 174
ruins, 13
Rumbula, Rīga, 115
Russia
    Russian Empire (1721–1917), 25–7, 30–32, 106–8, 196, 293
    Russian Federation (1991–), 26, 96, 223, 272, 274–8, 293
    Soviet Russia (1917–91), *see* Soviet Union
Rynhart, Jeanne, 221–2
Rysbrack, John Michael, 18, 175

Saarbrücken, Germany, 120–21
Sackville-West, Vita, 161
Sagalassos, Anatolia, 188
Sagewitz, Marthje, 41–2
Saint-Gaudens, Augustus, 143, 144–5, 178
saints, 6, 76–9
Salaspils concentration camp, 114
Salisbury, Robert Gascoyne-Cecil, 3rd Marquess, 104
Salmon, Yosef, 165
Salmon, Yvan, 215
Samalut, Egypt, 288
Samos, Greece, 224
Samson Slaying a Philistine (Giambologna), 139–40
Samuel, Joseph Bunford, 39–40
Samyukta Socialist Party, 239, 240
San Anton School, Malta, 253–4
San Remo Music Festival, 221
Sandow, Eugen, 211
Santa Coloma de Gramenet, Barcelona, 296
Santander, Spain, 140
Santo Spirito Crucifix (Michelangelo), 70
Santos, Emanuel, 287
Sartre, Jean-Paul, 195
Savage, Kirk, 7, 8–9, 18, 63, 178, 300
Saved by a Whale's Tail, 296
Schama, Simon, 5, 17, 265
Scheemakers, Peter, 247
Schenkman, Jan, 174
Scheuer, Sandra, 129
Schmalz, Timothy, 171
School of Venus, The, 225
Schopenhauer, Arthur, 70
Schroeder, William, 129

INDEX

Schwartz, Barry, 144
Schwarzenegger, Arnold, 192, 212
Scotland
    Burns statues, 136–8
    Wallace monument, 285–6
    Wellington statue, 226–8
Scots Wha Hae, 137
Scott, Andrew, 237
Scott-Heron, Gil, 231
Scottish National Party, 137
Scruggs, Jan, 126, 128
sculpture, 5–6, 29–48
    realism vs idealism, 58–64, 210–11
    static vs dynamic, 64
    struts, use of, 66–7
Seacole, Mary, 156
Seated Youth (Lehmbruck), 132
selfies, 124–5
Senso o-ji, Tokyo, 176
September 11 attacks (2001), 119
Serra, Richard, 123
Serrant, Laura, 20
Sert, Josep Lluís, 7
setting, 177
sex, 224–5
Shakespeare, William, 196, 221, 229
Shalev-Gerz, Esther, 119
Shapira, Shahak, 124–5
Sharing the Magic (Gibson), 87
Shelley, Percy Bysshe, 9–10
Shin, Meekyoung, 49
Shin Yakushiji temple, Nara, 176
Shivaji, Chhatrapati of the Marathas, 270

Shmirgela, Nikolay, 242
Shoresh, Taban, 155
Shrine of St Thomas Becket, Canterbury, 189
Shumilov, Mikhail, 47
Shurtleff, Nathaniel Bradstreet, 183
Sicily, 77–9
Siegessäule, Berlin, 99
Sigurðsson, Jón, 37, 39
Silenus, 203
Simpsons, The, 186
Sir John Soane's Museum, London, 90–92
size, 49, 50–53
Skalbe, Kārlis, 107
Šķēde Dunes, Latvia, 114–15
Sklar, Marty, 86
Skobelev, Mikhail, 293
Skólavörduholt, Reykjavik, 35, 146
Skulte, Latvia, 136
slavery, 245, 258, 264, 298
    in British Empire 1, 231, 246, 247–9, 254–5, 258, 278–82
    in United States, 145, 149
Slobozia, Romania, 288
Smith, Horace, 9
Smith, Laurajane, 280
Soane, John, 90–92
socialist realism, 114
Sofia, Bulgaria, 151, 241, 242
Solar Totem #1 (Drumm), 131
Soleb, Nubia, 209
Solomon, King of Israel, 201
Song Empire (960–1279), 74
Sonne, Jørgen, 34

INDEX

Sorbonne University, 217–18
South Africa, 1, 93–4, 104, 263
South Sea Company, 247–8
Southampton FC, 286
Soviet Union (1922–91), 7, 12–13, 29, 51, 187, 241–3, 265
  Burns' poetry in, 138
  collapse (1989–91), 12–13, 135, 241
  Estonia occupation, 84, 271, 275
  Holocaust memorials, 114–15
  iconoclasm, 292–4
  Latvia occupation, 27, 64–5, 108, 114–15, 212, 271–8
  Lithuania occupation, 131–2, 135, 271, 273
  Mother Motherland, 95–6
  Motherland Calls, The, 45–8
  Red Terror (1917–22), 293
Spain, 56, 139–40, 296
Sparta, 202, 209
Sperlonga, Italy, 178
Spijkenisse, Netherlands, 296
Spirit of Wallace (Church), 285–6
Spitalfields, London, 152
Spivey, Nigel, 61–2
St James's, London, 170
St Peter's Basilica, Vatican City, 34
St Petersburg, Russia, 26, 53, 196, 223
St Thomas' Hospital, London, 156
Stalin, Joseph, 46, 291
Stalingrad, Russia, 45
Stand to the Death (Vuchetich), 47

static sculptures, 64
Statue of Liberty, New York, 142, 147–50, 252
statuemania, 6, 53, 65, 88, 93, 136, 172–3, 183
statues
  accoutrements, 66, 74–9
  colour, 69–74
  commemoration and, *see* commemoration
  definition of, 2
  dialogic, 28, 246, 256–7
  eye level, 54, 113
  fashion and, 6–8
  figurative, *see* figurative statues
  form, 58–65, 210–11
  gimmicks, 79
  humans as, 210–13
  iconoclasm, 6, 263–90, 292–4
  inaugurations, 183–5, 192
  interaction with, 43, 53, 54, 55, 79, 152, 215–31
  invisibility of, 10–11, 84, 182, 249, 277–8
  material, 65–9
  motivations for, 18
  moving, 195–213
  national identity and, 6, 18, 93–111
  patrons/promoters, 17–28
  plinths/elevation, 53–8
  private spaces, 174–6
  proprietary, 81–92
  punishment of, 289–90
  recontextualisation, 245–59
  rejection of, 285–9
  relocations, 233–43

381

INDEX

replication of, 191–2
ritual and, 13–14, 58, 181–3, 187–91
self-promotion and, 18
setting, 177
size, 50–53
static vs dynamic, 64
talking, 200–201
timelessness, myth of, 8–10
toppling of, *see* iconoclasm
unclear commemoration, 185–7

Statues Also Die (1953 documentary), 240
Steinbrener/Dempf & Huber, 154
Stevens, Quentin, 132, 168, 256
Stewart, James, 186
Stewart, Peter, 75
Stilicho, 266
Stockholm, Sweden, 29, 53, 79, 97–9
Stocking, Charles, 60, 211
Stoddart, Sandy, 217
Stokowski, Leopold, 86
Stone Guest, The (Cicognini), 198–9
Stonehenge, 4
Strabo, 236
van Straten, Folkert, 187–8
Strathnairn, Hugh Henry Rose, 1st Baron, 104
Stride, Christopher, 88, 89–90
struts, 66–7
Sturken, Marita, 127
Sudan, 81, 236
Suez Canal, 148, 149–50
suffragism, 156

Sugar Loaf, Rio de Janeiro, 100
Sulaymān, Prophet, 201
Sulla, 69, 235
Sultanahmet Park, Istanbul, 268
Sumartojo, Shanti, 110, 111
supernormal stimulus, 61
Surge of Power, A (Quinn), 281
Surprised (Vigeland), 45
Sweden, 29, 53, 79, 97–9
Swindon Town FC, 88
Sydney, New South Wales, 245
symmetry, 59–61

T. Rex Action Group (TAG), 23, 24, 25
t'Serclaes, Everard, 219
Taberner, Ian, 130
Tadolini, Adamo, 141
Taft, Charles, 144
Taft, William Howard, 144
talking statues, 135, 200–201
Tallinn, Estonia, 84–5, 275
Talos, 199
Tang Empire (618–907), 74
Tanis, Egypt, 292
Taratynov, Alexander, 277
telestiké, 208
Tempest, The (Shakespeare), 229–30
Temple of Aphaia, Aegina, 30
Temple of Karnak, Luxor, 268
Temple of Magna Mater, Rome, 157
Ten Commandments, 4
Ten Days That Shook the World (1928 film), 265
Tenco, Luigi, 221

INDEX

Tenerani, Pietro, 141
Teresa of Ávila, 190
Teutoburger Wald, Germany, 96–7
Thampi, Velu, 106
Thatcher, Margaret, 170
Theagenes of Thasos, 289–90, 294
theft, 234
Thenford House, 273
Theocritus, 210, 294
Theodosian Obelisk, 268
Theodosius, Roman Emperor, 266, 267–8
Theon, 292
Theseus, 211
Thespiae, Greece, 234–5
Thetis, 210
Thinker, The (Rodin), 4
Thirty Years' War (1618–48), 190
Thiruvananthapuram, Kerala, 83, 105, 270
This is Spinal Tap (1984 film), 286
Thomas, Christian, 49
Thomas, Ffion, 88
Thorbecke, Johan, 174
Thornycroft, Hamo, 104
Thorvaldsen, Bertel, 30–35, 37–8
Thorvaldsen Museum, Copenhagen, 30–31, 33–5
Three Soldiers (Hart), 127, 256
Tiberi, Jean, 221
Tiberius, Roman Emperor, 68, 157, 160, 178
Tilak, Bal Gangadhar, 270

van Tilburg, Kees, 75
Tinbergen, Nikolaas, 61
Tininis, Vytautas, 241–2
Tisza, István, 291
Titus, Roman Emperor, 182, 267
To Heal a Nation (1988 film), 125–9
Tobin, Richard, 60
Tokyo, Japan, 176
Tomova-Erka, Irina, 151
Tongiani, Vito, 230
Tongnan Buddha, Chongqing, 74
Took, Steve Peregrin, 25
toppling, *see* iconoclasm
Torrington, Arthur, 22
Tottenham Hotspur FC, 90
tourism, 28, 52–3
Trafalgar Square, London, 56, 103, 109–11, 281
Trajan's Column, Rome, 57–8, 72, 282
Travancore (c. 1729–1949), 83, 105, 270
Treaty of Ghent (1815), 142
tree stumps, 66, 74
Trickster of Seville and the Stone Guest, The, 198
Tridentum, Italy, 3
triumphal columns, 55–8
Trivandrum, Travancore, 83, 105, 270
Trojan War, 59, 139
trompe l'oeil, 73
Trudeau, Pierre, 172
Tübingen University, 295
tuhaf, 140
Tunisia, 69

INDEX

von Tunzelmann, Alex, 300
Turkey, 188, 234, 251–2
Turkmenistan, 18
Turnerelli, Peter, 136
Tyrrell, Brinsley, 130

Ukraine, 27, 32, 95–6, 272, 274–8
unclear commemoration, 185–7
Union Werke Resistance Women, 165
United Kingdom
    Albert Square, 11
    Allies statue, 54–5
    Bolívar statue, 141
    British Museum, 73
    Burns monuments, 136
    Chaplin statue, 173
    Churchill statues, 54–5, 218, 229
    colonialism, *see* British Empire
    Colston statue, 1, 231, 246, 248–9, 254–5, 258, 278–82
    comedians, statues of, 172–4
    Cumberland statue, 49
    Diana Memorial Fountain, 118
    footballers, statues of, 88–90, 172, 286–7
    Frere statue, 104
    goat statues, 151–5
    Guy's and St Thomas' Foundation, 247–8
    Heritage Advisory Board, 246–8
    House of Commons, 218
    Iceland occupation (1940–41), 147
    Marc Bolan's Rock Shrine, 23–5
    National Windrush Monument, 17, 19–23
    Nelson's Column, 56, 103, 109, 111
    Northern Ireland, 204–5
    Sir John Soane's Museum, 90–92
    slave trade, 1, 231, 246, 247–9, 254–5, 258
    Trafalgar Square, 56, 103, 109–11, 281
    Wallace Monument, 285–6
    War of 1812, 142–5
    Wellington statues, 103, 226
    Westminster, 167–71
    Westminster Abbey, 18–19
    women, statues of, 151–6
United States
    Black Lives Matter protests (2020), 245, 278
    Boy Scout Commemorative Tribute, 64
    Burns statues, 137, 138
    civil rights movement (1954–68), 28
    Civil War (1861–5), 1, 145, 148, 149
    Confederacy (1861–5), 1, 145, 149, 258, 298
    Disney theme parks, 85–8
    Erikson statue gifting (1932), 145–7
    Franklin statue, 183–6
    Holocaust memorials, 115, 117–18

INDEX

Karlsefni statue, 39–40
Kent State Shootings (1970), 129–31
Lincoln Memorial, 126, 186–7
Reflecting Absence memorial, 119
Revolution (1775–83), 6–7, 137, 148, 149, 153
rubbing traditions in, 222
Statue of Liberty, 142, 147–50, 252
Vietnam War (1955–75), 119, 125–31, 132, 190, 256
War of 1812, 142–5
Universal Exhibition (1888), 56
University of Cape Town, 1, 263
University of Otago, Wellington, 228
Unwin, Melanie, 218
Urban VIII, Pope, 203
Uruguay, 95, 100–102
Uttar Pradesh, India, 269

Vairocana, 51, 52
Valentinian II, Western Roman Emperor, 267
de la Valette, Jean Parisot, 252
Valgre, Raimond, 79
Valladolid, Spain, 140
Valletta, Malta, 252–4
Valmiera, Latvia, 64–5
Vancouver, British Columbia, 28
vandalism 222, 225–31
Vaptsarov, Nikola, 242
Vargas, Getúlio, 101
Varma, Raja Ravi, 84
Vārpa, Brazil, 191

Vatican City, 34, 63, 68, 71, 92, 217
Veličan, Boris, 220
Vendôme Column, Paris, 282–5
Venezuela, 141
Ventspils, Latvia, 65
Venus and the Ring, 196–9
Venus de Milo, 63, 225
Venus of Ille, The (Mérimée), 197
Venus of Laussel, 4
Venus of Willendorf, 4, 61–2
Verona, Italy, 221
Vertumnus, 200
Vespasian, Roman Emperor, 267
Vestal Virgins, 182
Veturius, Mamurius, 200
Victoria, Queen of the United Kingdom, 269, 270
Victoria Embankment Gardens, London, 104
Vidzeme, Latvia, 106
Vienna, Austria, 49
Vietnam Veterans Memorial, Washington, 119, 125–9, 132, 190, 256
Vietnam War (1955–75), 119, 125–31, 190, 256
Vietnam Women's Memorial, Washington, 128
Vigeland Park, Oslo, 41, 43–4
Vigeland, Gustav, 40–45
Vikings, 37–40, 145–7
Villa of Livia, Rome, 71
Vilnius, Lithuania, 135
Vinland, 39, 145
violence against women, 28
Virgin Mary, 203–5

INDEX

Virginia, United States, 143, 169
Visconti, Ennio Quirino, 202
Vision, The (Burns), 136
Volgograd, Russia, 45
Vologases IV, Parthian Emperor, 235
Voortrekker Monument, Pretoria, 93–4
Voss, Angela, 207–8, 210
Vostok, 65
Vuchetich, Yevgeny, 45–8, 95

Wagner, Hansjörg, 218
Wales, 152–3
Wallace Monument, Stirling, 285
Wallace, William, 285–6
Walt Disney World, Orlando, 85
war, 99–103
    heroic defeat, 100–103
War of 1812, 142–5
War of the Triple Alliance (1864–70), 100–102
Warner, Fee, 23, 24
Warner, John, 126
Warrender, Maud, 142–3
Warsaw, Poland, 30, 31
Warsaw Ghetto Monument, 115–18, 164
Washington, DC, United States, 64, 119, 125–9, 132, 186, 256
Washington, George, 143, 169
Waterloo station, London, 17, 19–23
Watson, Basil, 20–22
Wawel Cathedral, Kraków, 218
Wearing, Gillian, 156
Weinryb, Ittai, 188, 189

Wellington, Arthur Wellesley, 1st Duke, 103, 226–8
Wenceslaus IV, King of Bohemia, 220
West Wind, The (Gould), 66
Western Roman Empire (c. 364–476 CE), 266
Western Wall, Jerusalem, 116
Westminster, London, 167–71
Westminster Abbey, London, 18–19
Whatley, Christopher, 137
Wheel of Life (Vigeland), 44
White, John, 92
White, Murray, 225
Whitehall, London, 169–70
Whitling, Frederick, 280
Wilde, Oscar, 222
Wilhelm I, German Emperor, 97
Willendorf, Austria, 4, 61–2
William IV, King of the United Kingdom, 109
William of Malmesbury, 196–7
Williams, Paul, 243
Willingdon, Freeman Freeman-Thomas, 1st Marquess, 270
Wilson, John, 88
Winckelmann, Johann Joachim, 63, 70
Windrush Generation, 17, 19–23
Winged Victory of Samothrace, 178
Winter's Tale, The (Shakespeare), 196
Winthrop, Robert, 184
Wittelsbacherplatz, Munich, 32
women; women's rights, 28, 151–65
Wong, Dorothy, 51–2

INDEX

Wood, Victoria, 173
Worker, A (Vigeland), 41
World Trade Centre, New York, 119
World War I (1914–18), 27, 99–100, 106, 132, 156
World War II (1939–45), 20, 45–8, 49, 64, 110–11, 147
    Holocaust (1941–5), 69, 113, 114–25, 164–5
von Wrangel, Friedrich, 99
Wren, Christopher, 19
Wrexham, Clwyd, 153
Wright, David, 173
Wu Zetian, Zhou Empress, 52
Wujin paper, 74
Wynne, David, 250
Wynne, Roly, 250

Yad Vashem memorial, Jerusalem, 117, 164–5
Yampolsky, Mikhail, 12–13, 51, 265, 293, 297
Yemanjá, 206
Yeryomenko, Andrey, 47
Yoruba people, 163, 206
You Called… And We Came (Serrant), 20
Young, James, 116–18, 121, 122–3, 256
Younge, Gary, 109
Youth (Zet), 222

Zābers, Vilnis, 213
Zagorka, Maria Jurić, 220
Zagreb, Croatia, 220
Zagury, Bob, 55
Zāle, Kārlis, 106, 108
Zanerini, Giovanna, 161–2
Zappa, Frank, 135
Zenkōji, Nagano, 175–6
Zet, Miloš, 222
Ziolkowski, Theodore, 4, 197, 199, 207
Zitronenjette, Hamburg, 218